# Western Sahara

*Syracuse Studies on Peace and Conflict Resolution*
Robert A. Rubinstein, *Series Editor*

# Western Sahara

WAR, NATIONALISM,
AND CONFLICT IRRESOLUTION

**Stephen Zunes** *&* **Jacob Mundy**

SYRACUSE UNIVERSITY PRESS

Copyright © 2010 by Syracuse University Press

Syracuse, New York 13244-5290

*All Rights Reserved*

First Edition 2010

10  11  12  13  14  15        6  5  4  3  2  1

∞ The paper used in this publication meets the minimum requirements of the American National Standard for Information Sciences—Permanence of Paper for Printed Library Materials, ANSI Z39.48-1992.

For a listing of books published and distributed by Syracuse University Press, visit our Web site at SyracuseUniversityPress.syr.edu.

ISBN-13: 978-0-8156-3219-1

**Library of Congress Cataloging-in-Publication Data**

Zunes, Stephen.

Western Sahara : war, nationalism, and conflict irresolution /

Stephen Zunes and Jacob Mundy. — 1st ed.

p. cm. — (Syracuse studies on peace and conflict resolution)

Includes bibliographical references and index.

ISBN 978-0-8156-3219-1 (cloth : alk. paper)

1. Western Sahara—History—1975–    2. Western Sahara—Politics and government—1975–

3. Western Sahara—Ethnic relations.    4. Western Sahara—International status.

5. Nationalism—Western Sahara.    6. Peace-building—Western Sahara.    7. Sahrawi

(African people)    I. Mundy, Jacob.    II. Title.

DT346.S7Z96 2010

964.8'03—dc22                    2010016239

*Manufactured in the United States of America*

≈

*To my beloved partner Nanlouise,*
*for her loving support, patience, and strength—S. Z.*

*To Molly: for making the world a place worth the fighting for—J. M.*

**Stephen Zunes** is a professor of politics and international studies at the University of San Francisco, where he chairs the Middle Eastern Studies Program. He is the author of scores of articles for scholarly and general readership on Middle Eastern politics, U.S. foreign policy, international terrorism, nuclear nonproliferation, strategic nonviolent action, and human rights. He is the principal editor of *Nonviolent Social Movements* (1999) and the author of the highly acclaimed *Tinderbox: U.S. Middle East Policy and the Roots of Terrorism* (2003). He serves as an advisory committee member and Middle East editor for the Foreign Policy in Focus project of the Institute for Policy Studies, an associate editor of *Peace Review,* and chair of the board of academic advisors for the International Center on Nonviolent Conflict. In 2002, he won recognition from the Peace and Justice Studies Association as Peace Scholar of the Year.

**Jacob Mundy** is a Ph.D. candidate specializing in politics and international relations at the University of Exeter's Institute of Arab and Islamic Studies. He is the author of several academic articles and chapters on the Western Sahara issue. In late 2005, he worked as a consulting external analyst with the International Crisis Group, conducting field research on the Western Sahara conflict. During the 2007–2008 academic year, he was a long-term research fellow with the Centre d'études maghrébines en Algérie.

# Contents

LIST OF ILLUSTRATIONS &bull; *IX*

LIST OF TABLES &bull; *xi*

FOREWORD, *George McGovern* &bull; *xiii*

ACKNOWLEDGMENTS &bull; *xvii*

ABBREVIATIONS &bull; *xix*

INTRODUCTION &bull; *xxi*


PART ONE: **War**

**1.** The War for Western Sahara &bull; *3*

**2.** Arab Maghrib Disunity: *Algeria and Morocco* &bull; *30*

**3.** The Franco–American Consensus &bull; *59*


PART TWO: **Nationalism**

**4.** The Historical Formation of Western Saharan Nationalism &bull; *91*

**5.** Expressions of Nationalism: *The Polisario Front, the Sahrawi Arab Democratic Republic, and the Sahrawi Refugee Camps* &bull; *112*

**6.** The Sahrawi Intifada: *Western Saharan Nationalism under Moroccan Occupation* • *140*


PART THREE: **Irresolution**


**7.** Searching for a Solution: *The United Nations and the Organization of African Unity* • *169*

**8.** The Abandoned Referendum • *191*

**9.** The Baker Plan and the End of the Peace Process • *219*


Conclusion • *254*


GLOSSARY • *269*

NOTES • *273*

REFERENCES • *283*

INDEX • *303*

# Illustrations

MAPS

1. Approximate location and development of Moroccan barriers (berms) in Western Sahara and Morocco, 1980–1988 • 7

2. Moroccan invasion of the Spanish Sahara, Oct.–Nov. 1975 • 8

3. Western Sahara, 2009 • 22

4. Greater Morocco • 37

5. Approximate geographical distribution of major Western Saharan social groups before 1975 • 97

6. Spanish Sahara and Spanish-administered Morocco • 101

7. Western Saharan refugee camps • 127

FIGURES

1. Value of arms imports to Morocco by supplier, 1974–1999 • 18

2. U.S. military aid to Morocco, 1950–1983 • 44

3. U.S. military aid to Morocco, 1950–1992 • 45

4. Moroccan military imports and expenditures, 1975–1999 • 46

5. Organization of the Polisario Front and the Sahrawi Arab Democratic Republic, c. 1982 • 117

# Tables

1. Leadership of the Polisario Front, 1971–1989 • *119*

2. Distribution of voter applicants, eligible voters, and appeals filed for the referendum in Western Sahara as of February 2000 • *214*

# Foreword

G E O R G E   M c G O V E R N

Most people have never heard of the country called Western Sahara. I had some famil-
iarity with that desert territory, then known as Spanish Sahara, when I sat on the Senate
Foreign Relations Committee, and the Ford administration was engaging in what we later
found out was a backdoor deal that effectively sold out the fundamental right of the people
of that nation to determine their own destiny. Yet nearly thirty-five years after that crisis
briefly appeared on the evening news, Western Sahara has largely been forgotten.

This should not be the case. The right of self-determination, which Woodrow Wilson so forcefully articulated nearly a century ago and enshrined in the United Nations
Charter, is one of the most fundamental rights of all. I volunteered as a bomber pilot in
World War II fighting the Nazi war machine because I believed in the cause that united
our country with most of the rest of the world's people: that no government should get
away with denying that right by invading, occupying, and annexing another nation and
oppressing its people.

This issue is and has been fundamentally what is at stake in Western Sahara, colonized by the Spaniards in the nineteenth century and occupied by Morocco since 1975. I
have long had great respect for the Moroccan people and have greatly enjoyed my visits to
that beautiful country, with its impressive history, beautiful architecture, wonderful cui-
sine, and rich culture. I respect that Morocco was the first country to recognize the newly
independent United States back in 1777 and has been an important ally for so many years.
Yet just as I respect the state of Israel while opposing its occupation of the West Bank, I can
respect the kingdom of Morocco while opposing its occupation of Western Sahara.

Jacob Mundy and Stephen Zunes have done a great service in putting together this
book, the most comprehensive coverage of the Western Sahara conflict in the English
language in a quarter-century. With scholarly rigor but an accessible style, they have
written this study in a manner appropriate for those of us with little background on this
issue, but they have also included the detail and original analysis from which experts on
the region can learn much as well. I greatly appreciate their emphasis on international

accountability, in particular their well-documented history of the U.S. failure under both Republican and Democratic administrations to uphold the fundamental principles of international law being challenged in this remote region of northwestern Africa.

What is at stake here is more than just the fate of a few hundred thousand Sahrawis living under Moroccan military occupation in Western Sahara and in refugee camps in neighboring Algeria. As the authors observe, what ultimately is at stake is the post–World War II international legal system. If the people of Western Sahara are not granted the right to choose their own future, including the option of independence, and Morocco's control of the territory is allowed to stand, it will be the first time since the founding of the United Nations that the international community has allowed a recognized non-self-governing territory to be forcibly annexed without the population's consent and the first time a country has been allowed to expand its territory by military force against the wishes of a subjected population.

Only the Arab territories still occupied by Israel since 1967 remain under such belligerent foreign control. And although the resolution of that conflict is also long overdue, at least it has gotten the international community's attention, whereas the comparable situation in the Maghrib has remained in relative obscurity.

Zunes and Mundy are uniquely qualified to provide readers with such an important and timely book. I have known Stephen Zunes, who chairs the Middle Eastern Studies Program at the University of San Francisco, for more than twenty years. He is one of the nation's top scholars on the international relations of the Middle East and North Africa. He and I have collaborated in both teaching and writing, and I have great respect for his insight and analysis. Jacob Mundy is an exceptionally bright young scholar who has conducted extensive research in the region. He is widely recognized as one of the up-and-coming authorities on the Maghrib.

The authors' principled support for the right of self-determination and the primacy of international law is clear, but this book is no polemic. They are not uncritical of the Polisario Front (the nationalist movement of Western Sahara), nor are they apologists for the government of Algeria, which has supported the Polisario's struggle for independence from Morocco. Their study is a solid, empirical, balanced, and well-researched study that will be well received by scholars, policymakers, and the general public. As my friend and former colleague Senator Edward Kennedy observed, "In this thoughtful and impressive analysis, Stephen Zunes and Jacob Mundy provide valuable insights on the importance of enabling the people of the Western Sahara to determine their own future." I could not agree more.

As Zunes and Mundy point out, the best hope for the just resolution of this conflict may rest in global civil society. The occupied island nation of East Timor was not long ago at least as obscure in the minds of North Americans and Europeans as Western Sahara is today. Yet through persistent effort, scholars, human rights organizations, church groups, and other people of conscience would not let the issue die. They kept pressing the moral and legal imperative of ending the oppression and granting the East Timorese their right of self-determination, effectively shaming the governments of Australia, Canada, Great Britain, and the United States to end their support for the Indonesian occupation.

To wage such a successful international campaign, one needs scholars who can provide the information and analysis to better understand the conflict's history and dynamics, the different parties' positions, and the issues at stake. During the struggle against the Vietnam War, my understanding of the war was greatly enriched by the work of George Kahin (Zunes's late mentor at Cornell), Frances Fitzgerald, and others. In a similar vein, Professors Benedict Anderson and Noam Chomsky helped raise critical awareness of East Timor in subsequent years.

This book is destined to have a similar impact if we give it the attention it so much deserves.

Mitchell, South Dakota
May 2009

# Acknowledgments

How does one properly thank dozens of individuals at the same time? Over the years, we have incurred numerous debts to those who provided us with much valued information, criticism, and support: Abdelkader Abderrahmane, Adekeye Adebajo, Laurence Ammour, Vladimir Bessarabov, Jean Yves Bouchardy, Donna Lehman, Bob Burrowes, Maria Carrión, Jarat Chopra, Simon Chesterman, Timothy Cleaveland, Roger Clark, Joshua Cochran, Stacy Davis, Charles Dunbar, John Entelis, Salim Fakirani, Elena Fiddian, Shannon Fleming, Marius de Gaay Fortman, Julie Gagne, Ricky Goldstein, Carlos Gonzalez, Erik Hagen, Hurst Hannum, Helen Hardin, Silvia Hidalgo, Michael Hussey, Konstantina Isidoros, Galen Jackson, Jan Janssen, Abel Al Jende, Carmen Johns, Jeremy Keenan, Amine Khelif, Richard Knight, Karen Lange, Bill Lawrence, Donna Lehman, André Lewin, Aidan Lewis, Cate Lewis, Phil Luther, Azzedine Layachi, Enrico Maganani, Patrick Meier, Philip Naylor, Ronald Ofteringer, Arzoo Osanloo, Madeline Otis-Campbell, Richard Parker, Robert Parks, Anthony Pazzanita, Marty Rosenbluth, Frank Ruddy, Carlos Ruiz Miguel, Pablo San Martin, Suzanne Scholte, Toby Shelley, Teresa Smith, Anna Theofilopoulou, John Thorne, Luis de Vega, Alice Wilson, Carlos Wilson, and Yahia Zoubir.

Specific thanks go to Maryellen Bieder and Kalila Zunes-Wolfe, who provided translation assistance, and the two reviewers, whose criticisms ultimately enriched this work. Many thanks to our great team at Syracuse University Press for their support, encouragement, and patience over the past decade (Mary Selden Evans, Annelise Finegan, Mona Hamlin, Marcia Hough, Kay Steinmetz, Fred Wellner, and Glen Wright) and to Annie Barva for her superb editing skills. Stephen Zunes wishes to acknowledge the United States Institute for Peace for providing him with a solicited research grant in 1989–90. As this book was being finalized for publication, we sadly learned about the passing of Thomas Franck in May 2009 and of John Damis the following month. In many ways, the dedication of these two men to the issue of Western Sahara made this work possible.

A special debt of gratitude is owed to Anne Lippert and Daniel Volman for introducing Stephen Zunes to Western Sahara through their early research and dedication to this forgotten conflict. And thanks to Stephen from Jacob for entrusting a young graduate student with his manuscript.

Given that this book has been more than ten years in the making, it is likely that we have forgotten to mention some of the people who helped us along the way. To them, our deepest apologies.

To the Sahrawis who have guided us through the years, we are most grateful. Respecting confidences, we can name only a handful here: Majid Abdullah, Saleh B., Salka B., Nadjem Baidella, Khatry Beirouk, Mohammed Beissat, Yahia Bouhobeini, Bachir L., Malainin Lakhal, Sidi Omar, Salek R. (and his family in the camps, including his late father, a true shaykh, Mohammed R.), Mouloud Said, and—certainly not least!—Zorgan and his delightful family in Smara camp. We especially thank Brahim A. for being our window and sometimes bridge into the occupied Western Sahara.

Our families have been the most vital of support networks, and we are truly grateful to them for that.

Needless to say, all of these people—and then some—have made this work possible. Any mistakes, of course, are ours alone.

# Abbreviations

| | |
|---|---|
| AMDH | Association marocaine des droits humains (Moroccan Association for Human Rights), Morocco |
| AOSARIO | Association des originaires du Sahara anciennement sous domination espagnole (Association of Natives of the Sahara Formerly under Spanish Domination), Morocco |
| CCDH | Conseil consultatif des droits de l'homme (Human Rights Advisory Council), Morocco |
| CDT | Confédération démocratique des travailleurs (Democratic Confederation of Workers), Morocco |
| CIA | U.S. Central Intelligence Agency |
| CMR | Consejo del Mando de la Revolución (Council for the Command of the Revolution), Polisario |
| CORCAS | Conseil royal consultatif pour les affaires sahariennes (Royal Consultative Council for Saharan Affairs), Morocco |
| ELPS | Ejército de Liberación Popular Saharaui (Saharan People's Liberation Army), Polisario |
| EU | European Union |
| FAR | Forces armées royales (Royal Armed Forces), Morocco |
| FLN | Front de libération nationale (National Liberation Front), Algeria |
| FLU | Frente de Liberación y de la Unidad or Front de libération et de l'unité (Front for Liberation and Unity), Morocco |
| Frente POLISARIO | Frente Popular para la Liberación de Saguia el-Hamra y Río de Oro (Popular Front for the Liberation of the Saguia el Hamra and the Río de Oro) |
| GDP | gross domestic product |
| ICJ | International Court of Justice, United Nations |

| | |
|---|---|
| IMF | International Monetary Fund |
| MINURSO | Mission des Nations Unies pour l'organisation d'un référendum au Sahara Occidental (United Nations Mission for the Referendum in Western Sahara) |
| NATO | North Atlantic Treaty Organization |
| NGO | nongovernmental organization |
| OAU | Organization of African Unity |
| PJD | Parti de la justice et du développement (Justice and Development Party), Morocco |
| PLO | Palestine Liberation Organization |
| POW | prisoner of war |
| PPS | Parti du progrès et du socialisme (Party of Progress and Socialism), Morocco |
| PSOE | Partido Socialista Obrero Español (Spanish Socialist Workers' Party), Spain |
| PUNS | Partido de la Unión Nacional Saharaui (Party of Sahrawi National Unity), Spanish Sahara |
| RASD | República Árabe Saharaui Democrática (Sahrawi Arab Democratic Republic), Polisario |
| SNL | Syndicat national des lycéens (National Union of Students), Morocco |
| UMA | Union du Maghreb arabe (Arab Maghrib Union) |
| UN | United Nations |
| UNEM | Union nationale des étudiants marocains (National Union of Moroccan Students), Morocco |
| UNFP | Union nationale des forces populaires (National Union of Popular Forces), Morocco |
| UNHCR | United Nations High Commission for Refugees |
| UNMS | Uniòn Nacional de Mujeres Saharauis (National Union of Sahrawi Women), Polisario |
| USFP | Union socialiste des forces populaires (Socialist Union of Popular Forces), Morocco |
| WSA | Western Sahara Authority, Morocco |

# Introduction

Western Sahara, Africa's last colony, is the site of one of the continent's longest-running conflicts. At first glance, it might not seem like a place worth killing and dying for or a land worth occupying at great human and financial cost. It is a vast desert territory of 266,000 square kilometers, only slightly larger than Great Britain. The dominant image of Western Sahara—an endless rock-strewn plain crashing into the Atlantic—is only partially true. Although the land is bereft of the sand seas found in the Mauritanian, Malian, and Algerian Sahara, the terrain is surprisingly diverse, often hilly, almost mountainous, and replete with normally dry gullies of varying depths. There are few oases, though, and all of the permanent population centers are of relatively recent invention, mostly stemming from European colonialism. It should come as little surprise that, under these conditions, Western Sahara is one of the least-populated countries in the world. In 2000, the United Nations (UN) concluded that there are approximately eighty-six thousand native Western Saharans of voting age. From this statistic, one might extrapolate a total population approaching two hundred thousand. Yet even if this estimate were only half the actual total, doubling the known population would still give Western Sahara one of the lowest population densities in the world.

Thirty years of war, exodus, and colonial occupation have greatly disturbed the demographic situation in Western Sahara. Nearly half the native population has lived as refugees in Algeria since 1976; the other half lives as a minority population under foreign rule. Moroccan soldiers and settlers now outnumber the indigenous population. Also complicating the demographic balance is that among the Moroccan settlers, a sizeable number is ethnic Sahrawis from southern Morocco, who share the same language and social systems as Sahrawis from Western Sahara, but whose overall political allegiance is disputed. Likewise, the term *Sahrawi,* as a synonym for "Western Saharan," is highly contested (see chapter 4). The independence movement of the Frente Popular para la Liberación de Saguia el Hamra y Río de Oro (Frente POLISARIO or just Polisario; Popular Front for the Liberation of the Saguia el Hamra and the Río de Oro)[1] in Western Sahara, founded in 1973, is now the UN-recognized representative of the Sahrawi people. Yet most definitions of *Sahrawi* are forced to concede that the precolonial social groups ("tribes" and "confederations") of the former Spanish Sahara (established in 1884–85) inhabited an area much greater than today's Western Sahara. As an ethnic category coined in the past hundred years, the term *Sahrawi,* which is simply the Arabic for "Saharan," is broader than the political-geographic designation *Western Saharan.* There are ethnic Sahrawis native to southern Morocco, western Algeria, and northern Mauritania. Although all Western Saharans are Sahrawi, not all Sahrawis are Western Saharan natives. For these reasons, we distinguish between ethnic Sahrawis generally (i.e., Moroccan, Algerian, Mauritanian, and Western Saharan) and native Western Saharans specifically. This distinction, however, is still problematic. Few Western Saharan nationalists actually make this distinction explicitly, whereas the position of the Moroccan government tends to dismiss the idea that the Sahrawis constitute an ethnonationalist group. Instead, the Moroccan government has tended to treat the Sahrawis as just another Moroccan ethnic minority group, on par with Morocco's Berber-speaking populations.

Explanations of the conflict's trigger and intractability often cite the country's real and potential wealth in natural resources as a motivational factor. Since independence in 1956, Morocco has been a moderately weak state, heavily dependent on income derived from foreign-export revenue ("rents"). Instead of being used to pursue aggressive development strategies, these funds have gone into sustaining the hierarchical clientelist authoritarian network—the "Makhzan"—that governs the country at the behest of Morocco's 'Alawi monarchy. Morocco's acquisition of Western Sahara in 1975 added significant sources of revenue to state coffers. Foremost are the phosphate deposits at Bukra' in central Western Sahara, first developed by Spain in the 1960s and now exploited by Morocco. Even without Western Sahara, Morocco is the world's leading exporter of this fast-dwindling resource, which is key to modern industrial agriculture. The reserves in Western Sahara are of an extremely high quality and are close to the surface, although they still count for only a small percentage of Moroccan phosphate exports. Perhaps of more value to Morocco has been the rich fishing found off the coast of Western Sahara, which has brought in millions, perhaps billions, of dollars both directly and indirectly through contracts with other countries and, more recently, with the European Union (EU). Furthermore, numerous other sources of revenue remain to be explored or exploited, whether minerals or hydrocarbons. With global oil and gas prices at record levels, the possible presence of hydrocarbons has provoked a flurry of interest from foreign companies, some siding with Morocco and some with Polisario. Yet fish, phosphates, and hydrocarbons are not what is at stake. If they were all that mattered, a negotiated end to the conflict would have been achieved long ago. Furthermore, we have to distinguish between the immediate or trigger causes of a conflict and the sources of its intractability (Crocker, Hampson, and Aall 2005, 4–5), which are often very different. The former in the case of Western Sahara was Morocco's October–November 1975 invasion of Western Sahara; the latter are much more difficult to pin down.

The conflict is imaginary at its most fundamental level—not imaginary in the sense that it is fiction, but in the sense that it is largely based on ideas. In the material world, both sides agree that the dispute is over a piece of land. Yet abstractly, at the level of the "metaconflict," the dispute stems from mutually exclusive differences in the self-perceptions that ground Moroccan and Western Saharan nationalism. It pits Moroccan irredentism against an indigenous desire for independence, both contentiously spacialized over the same piece of land. Among the conflict's numerous asymmetries, we first note that the Moroccan claim seeks the annihilation of Western Sahara as a people and a country, whereas Western Saharan nationalism only threatens serious harm to Moroccan territory and nationalism. Nevertheless, these mutual insults, threats, and injuries to each side's core values constitute a necessary and underlying, albeit "imaginary," condition that makes this specific conflict possible and thus far irresolvable.

Within Moroccan political discourse, we see that it is an article of faith, a cornerstone of the nationalist canon, that Western Sahara is a part of the "real" (i.e., precolonial) territory. Shortly before Morocco gained independence from France and Spain in 1956, the idea of "Greater Morocco" (al-Maghrib al-Kabir) gained currency among the nationalist elite and was quickly introduced into the postcolonial pedagogy. It was asserted, first of all, that Morocco should seek to "reincorporate" the remaining Spanish colonial enclaves within what was generally recognized by the international community as Morocco itself. Second, this claim was radically expansionist, including Mauritania and Spanish Sahara as well as parts of western Algeria and northern Mali. In the eyes of Moroccan nationalists, all these territories had been "severed" from Morocco by European territorial manipulation. Morocco regained northern Morocco—save the two Spanish presidios of Ceuta and Melilla—soon after independence; southern Spanish Morocco, also known as the Tarfaya or "Tekna" zone, strip, or region, followed in 1958, and, last, the southern enclave of (Sidi) Ifni in 1969.

The idea of Greater Morocco provided the internal justification for the invasion of Western Sahara in 1975, the long war to annex it, and the continued national campaign to hold on to it. From the Moroccan national point of view, the Western Sahara conflict presents a double affront: it seeks not only to undo Morocco (again), but also to do so through the validation of boundaries imposed through the original sin of colonialism. Moroccan nationalism strongly asserts that colonialism, adding insult to injury, invented Spanish Sahara and to a lesser extent Algeria—both largely at the expense of the precolonial Moroccan state's alleged territory. Western Saharan nationalism, as the product of Hispano–French territorial machinations, is therefore an artificial construct supported by an even larger artificiality, Algeria.

Indigenous nationalism in Western Sahara has presented a direct challenge to these ideas and thus to the Moroccan nationalist worldview. For Sahrawi nationalists, the conflict is just as much a matter of identity, a democratic claim to their exclusive right to the territory. Their conviction is as much the assertion that they are, first and foremost, Sahrawis—ethnically and nationally. At the same time, however, it is an implicit counterassertion that they are not and never will be Moroccans (or, as we will see, Mauritanians). They will not be subject to a foreign power. Claiming centuries, if not millennia, of continuous habitation, Western Saharan nationalists have constructed themselves as the natives, whereas Moroccans are the settlers, a reflection of the same volatile identity dynamic found in other colonial situations. In such colonist–settler situations, the outcome has historically tended to follow one of three trajectories: total independence for the native population (e.g., Algeria's liberation from France); total subjugation, if not near annihilation, of the indigenes (e.g., the Native Americans in the United States); or an independent, hybridized polity (e.g., postapartheid South Africa). Although Western Sahara has taken on the appearance of the second trajectory, its final status has yet to resolve into focus and so may still take the form of the other two outcomes.

The Western Sahara conflict is likewise juridically colonial in the eyes of the international community. Western Saharan nationalists have continued to seek the right of self-determination afforded all other former European dependencies. Because the *jus cogens* of decolonization must afford the chance to vote for independence, Western Saharan nationalists often describe their struggle as one for self-determination. Yet self-determination is simply code for a democratic expression of the desire for independence. This means that, from the reductionist perspective of so-called political realism, the conflict is essentially a territorial dispute pitting Western Saharan nationalism against Moroccan irredentism.

Yet the apparently irreconcilable nature of these two ideas—Moroccan nationalism and Western Saharan nationalism—only partially explains the endurance of the conflict. As noted earlier, other interests are at play. Most observers are quick to implicate Algeria because of its unparalleled moral and material support of Western Saharan nationalism and a preexisting (i.e., before 1975) regional rivalry between Algiers and Rabat. Although it is important to understand Algeria's role in the conflict, we are strongly opposed to any attempt to simplify the conflict as an effect of Moroccan–Algerian tensions. As we demonstrate over the course of this book and especially in chapter 2, Algeria is neither a causal factor in the initiation of the Morocco–Polisario war nor a necessary ingredient for its resolution. It would be naive to discount Algeria altogether, but too many observers of the conflict have overemphasized Algeria's role and, in so doing, have vastly underrepresented the far more profound and disastrous effects of French and U.S. support for the Moroccan occupation of Western Sahara.

In word and deed, France and the United States have shared a profound and long-standing desire to protect, help, and bolster the Moroccan regime. Holding a key geostrategic point at the mouth of the Mediterranean, the postcolonial Moroccan state has become, by virtue of historical and geographical contingency, pivotal to global stability (i.e., Western hegemony). This reality has translated into alternating modes of implicit and explicit support for the Moroccan annexation and occupation of Western Sahara, whether through direct material support during the war or through indirect support on the UN Security Council during the peace process. We have called this support the "Franco–American consensus": a shared dedication to the stability of the Moroccan monarchy that trumps all else, including the interests of peace and international law in Western Sahara.

Even with so much apparently at stake, more than twenty years have passed since the publication of a comprehensive political history of the Western Sahara conflict in English. Our main goal in writing this book is exactly that: to provide a thorough background and a wide-ranging analysis of the Morocco–Polisario dispute. The conflict is now a generation old. Enough time has passed that it is now possible to assess the war in Western Sahara, which ended in 1991, and the failed peace process that followed. It is also clear that a new generation of Western Saharan nationalists is beginning to influence the independence movement, both within the exiled Polisario Front and in the cities of their occupied land. Likewise, the Moroccan state since 1999 has been under the command of a new monarch, who initially attempted to distance himself from his father's legacy. On the international front, the Cold War has long since ended, but a succession of paradigms—New World Order, the age of globalization, the global war on terror—have supplanted it. For these reasons, we have decided to offer this study of war, nationalism, and conflict irresolution in Western Sahara.

Beyond political history, this work is also situated within a number of academic and policy discourses. Readers of this work will soon become aware of the fact that the Western Sahara conflict not only affects the lives of the Sahrawis, but has come to define Moroccan–Algerian relations, has manifested at the regional and African continental level, and has shaped Western relations with the Maghrib. Experts on regional North Africa and general students of Middle East and Africa in area studies and international relations will thus find our narrative worth the effort. Within Middle East and African studies, our examination of Western Saharan nationalism—a unique hybrid of Arab and African nationalisms—in part two is an original attempt to understand it both in relation to the conflict and on its own. Even in the age of globalization and the so-called clash of civilizations, the ongoing and intense scholarly interest in nationalism provides our study with warrant and traction in an array of ongoing academic conversations.

As our title suggests, scholars, professionals, and officials working in the field of conflict mediation will find a detailed case study of an intractable conflict, a study that contributes both directly and indirectly to the relevant theoretical and practical literatures (e.g., Crocker, Hampson, and Aall 2004, 2005; Fisher et al. 1997; Kriesberg, Northrup, and Thorson 1989; Putnam and Wollondolleck 2002; Ramsbotham, Woodhouse, and Miall 2005; Zartman 1989). Over the past thirty years, the Western Sahara conflict has become protracted and destructive, and efforts by partisans and intermediaries have not been successful in resolving it. It has gone through all the standard phases of such conflicts: initial disruption, escalation, failed peacemaking efforts, and institutionalization (see Kriesberg

2005). In addition to covering the war in Western Sahara, chapter 1 provides background to the current stalemate in Western Sahara and offers a brief case study in asymmetric conflict, guerrilla warfare, and counterinsurgency. Part three devotes significant attention to the UN-mediated peace process in Western Sahara since 1988, which means that this volume also serves as a detailed examination and critique of the UN's capacities to manage conflict.

Last, this study is also an examination of nontraditional forms of conflict and mediation. In chapter 6, we examine the largely nonviolent Sahrawi demonstration movement launched against the Moroccan occupation in 2005. In recent years, there has been growing interest in actors' ability to escalate conflict nonviolently for just social ends (Ackerman and DuVall 2001; Ackerman and Kruegler 1994; Crow, Grant, and Ibrahim 1990; Kriesberg 1998, 2009; Schock 2005; Sharp 2005; Wehr, Burgess, and Burgess 1994; Zunes, Asher, and Kurtz 1999). Western Sahara is not only a site where these political methodologies are currently being practiced, but also a place where international encouragement for such action will be requisite for its success. With that in mind, we argue in chapters 2 and 6 and in our conclusion that the only international interest group that can affect the situation in Western Sahara, bringing it to a lasting and peaceful resolution consistent with international norms, is transnational civil society. In making this argument, we are simultaneously gesturing to a growing literature (e.g., Keck and Sikkink 1998; Moser-Puangsuwan and Weber 2000; Smith, Chatfield, and Pagnucco 1997; Stephan 2009) and submitting a plea for such actors to intervene to help Western Sahara.

OVERVIEW

By organizing this study around the themes of war, nationalism, and conflict (ir)resolution, we have had to forgo a chronological narrative from the first to the last chapter. Each part and each chapter tend to unfold chronologically, but the reader will find significant overlap across the book. Although part one, "War," begins with a chapter on Polisario's insurgency and Morocco's counterinsurgency in Western Sahara, its scope is actually the entire three decades of military and political-diplomatic conflict for Western Sahara. As this part's epigraph suggests, we explore how the war for Western Sahara was politics by other means, just as the peace process after the 1991 cease-fire has become war by other means. The chapters in this part provide an historical analysis, through the present day, of the positions, actions, and motivations of the two key regional state actors in the conflict, Morocco and Algeria (chapter 2), as well as the role of extraregional actors, especially France and the United States (chapter 3). This examination explains the origins of the Western Sahara conflict and describes the conditions that have allowed it to persist. It also sets the stage for the third and final part. However, before we can understand the irresolution of the Western Sahara conflict, we must first look at the most important factor in the dispute: Western Saharan nationalism, the subject of part two.

The second part is the broadest in scope, especially chapter 4, which spans hundreds of years of identity formation in the westernmost Sahara. Chapter 5 is focused on the side of Western Saharan nationalism in exile—the Western Saharan refugees, the Polisario liberation movement, and their government in exile—during the war period (1975–91) and the referendum process (1991–2000). Chapter 6 discusses Western Saharan nationalism under Moroccan occupation. It starts from the 1975 Moroccan invasion and chronicles the repression that Western Saharan nationalism suffered through the war. However, this chapter is most concerned with the ways in which Sahrawi civil society has challenged the Moroccan occupation since the dissolution of the referendum process in 2000.

Part three, "Irresolution," deals with the now intertwined decolonization and peace processes in Western Sahara. This analysis takes us back, in chapter 7, to the early 1960s, when the UN first declared Spanish Sahara a colony. This chapter then looks at the peace efforts of the Organization of African Unity (OAU) after the Spanish withdrawal (1976–84) and the UN's subsequent efforts (1985–91). Chapter 8 deals exclusively with the establishment of the UN mission in Western Sahara after the 1991 Morocco–Polisario cease-fire, its efforts to organize a referendum on independence, and the reasons the vote was postponed in 2000 and then never happened. Chapter 9 deals with the subsequent peacemaking efforts of the lead UN negotiator, former U.S. secretary of state James Baker, up to his resignation in 2004 and then brings the reader to the end of 2006.

To help readers less familiar with the story of Western Sahara, we present a brief chronological sketch here.

1. *Spanish Colonial Period, 1884–1976.* In chapter 4, we explore—painting with very broad strokes—the precolonial history of Northwest Africa generally and Western Sahara specifically. The purpose of this overview is to give readers a feel for where the Western Saharans are coming from, the grounds upon which they are claiming and making their identities as a national people. However, for the purposes of this introduction, the nine decades of Spanish administration (1884–1976) serve as the first period in Western Sahara's contemporary history. Indeed, it was Spanish (and French) colonialism that drew the arbitrary lines in the desert that we now know as Western Sahara.

Spain's initial claim on what would later be called Río de Oro was made in 1884–85 after a commercial presence was established, Villa Cisneros (Dakhla). In 1912, France and Spain set the final borders of their respective areas of rule in Northwest Africa. France controlled Mauritania and Algeria, and both Spain and France had protectorates in Morocco, where they claimed to administer on behalf of the Moroccan sultan. Río de Oro, in contrast, was a colony of Spain because no central authority—Moroccan or otherwise—governed it. Although Madrid relinquished its Moroccan protectorates in the years following independence in 1956, the Spanish attitude toward Río de Oro was radically different. Indeed, Spanish Sahara was redesignated a province of Spain in 1958.

By the mid-1960s, Spanish Sahara was the subject of several UN General Assembly resolutions calling for its decolonization. It was also claimed by Morocco and Mauritania. Madrid, however, continued to invest in the development of the territory's sizeable phosphate reserves and in the Sahrawi population itself. Although Spain had always faced sporadic—sometimes intense—indigenous resistance in the Sahara, an explicitly nationalist-independence movement first coalesced in the late 1960s, but it was quickly suppressed when it went public in 1970. Another movement, the Polisario Front, emerged three years later to continue the struggle for independence.

In 1974, Madrid announced plans to decolonize Spanish Sahara through a referendum to be held within a year. Fearing that the Western Saharans would opt for independence, the Moroccan government demanded an opinion from the International Court of Justice (ICJ) on Morocco's historical claim to the territory. The court's opinion was announced on October 16, 1975, one day after a visiting UN observation team in Western Sahara reported that it had found overwhelming support within the territory for independence under the leadership of the Polisario. The court's opinion, clearly stated, was that even if Morocco had a significant historical title—which the court found it did not—the native Western Saharans' right of self-determination was still paramount over all such claims. Morocco's King Hassan II announced hours later that 350,000 Moroccan civilians would walk, in what became known as the Green March, into Spanish Sahara to claim the territory as part of the kingdom. Meanwhile, in Spain, the final illness of longtime dictator Generalissimo Francisco Franco plunged the Spanish cabinet into factional disarray. With no prospect of tangible support from the UN Security Council, where the veto-wielding United States supported Morocco's forced annexation, Spain was obliged to negotiate with King Hassan or face the prospect of a war. On November 14 in Madrid, representatives of Spain, Morocco, and Mauritania (whose territorial claims were also dismissed by the court) announced an agreement whereby Morocco and Mauritania would gain administrative control over Western Sahara as of February 1976. The UN, however, continued to treat Western Sahara as a colony.

2. *The War for Western Sahara, 1975–91.* When Spain handed Western Sahara over to Morocco and Mauritania in February 1976, Polisario was already a tested guerilla force with two years experience and unrivaled indigenous knowledge of the land. The liberation front also benefited from Algerian material and territorial sanctuary, which increased

following the exclusion of Algeria from the tripartite agreement of November 14, 1975. Polisario spent late 1975 and early 1976 resettling many Sahrawis in Algeria because the armed Moroccan–Mauritanian invasion immediately following the signing of the Madrid Agreement had prompted nearly half the population to seek refuge. The Polisario Front, acting as a government-in-exile from its base in camps outside of the border town of Tindouf, Algeria, proclaimed the establishment of the República Árabe Saharaui Democrática (RASD, Sahrawi Arab Democratic Republic). The refugees began to build a society in exile, but Western Saharan nationalists living under Moroccan–Mauritanian occupation faced repression.

From the start, Polisario's liberation war focused on Mauritania, whose army was far weaker than Morocco's forces. By 1978, Polisario attacks—reaching as far as the capital, Nouakchott, and disabling the economy—precipitated a coup in Mauritania. A Mauritanian–Polisario peace agreement was finally struck in 1979, yet Morocco quickly moved to seize the southern third of Western Sahara that had been Mauritania's domain.

With continued backing from Algeria, Polisario's attacks in the late 1970s became more and more daring, often reaching hundreds of miles into Morocco proper. By 1981, Morocco's grip on the territory was limited to two enclaves: one included a triangular-shaped region in the far northwest corner of the territory around the capital al-'Ayun, the phosphate mines of Bukra', and the city of Smara; the other surrounded the coastal town of Dakhla in the south. At the same time, though, Morocco's tenuous hold on Western Sahara was beginning to affect the stability of King Hassan's regime.

The tide soon began to turn against Polisario, however. With financial assistance from Saudi Arabia and strong backing from the Mitterrand presidency in France and the Reagan administration in the United States, Morocco began to expand its control over Western Sahara through a series of concentrically constructed defensive barriers reaching out from the original enclaves. This strategy allowed Morocco to deny Polisario access to southern Morocco and, more important, to limit the freedom of movement in Western Sahara that had made Polisario's hit-and-run raids so effective. By 1987, with the completion of barriers extending to the South, Polisario had difficulty launching major attacks against anything besides Moroccan positions along the defensive wall itself.

The war in Western Sahara ended in a stalemate. Although on the one hand Morocco controlled most of the territory, it could never destroy Polisario, not without first invading the heavily fortified border regions of Algeria, where the Polisario was based. The Polisario, on the other hand, could neither gain and hold territory nor reasonably hope to win a war of attrition. Each side knew by the late 1980s that if it wanted to win Western Sahara, it would have to win by another means. It just so happened that this solution is exactly what the UN secretary-general was dangling before them in 1988: another means to win Western Sahara—a referendum on self-determination. The spirit of the 1991 cease-fire was thus not one of compromise. It was one of war by other means.

≈

3. *The Proposed Referendum in Western Sahara, 1991–2000.* Building on the work done by the OAU, the UN Security Council took on the Western Sahara issue in 1988. Through secretive shuttle diplomacy, the secretary-general negotiated an agreement for a cease-fire, repatriation of the refugees in Algeria, and then a vote in Western Sahara between independence (under the leadership of the Polisario) or integration (with Morocco). The UN created the Mission des Nations Unies pour l'organisation d'un référendum au Sahara Occidental (MINURSO, United Nations Mission for the Referendum in Western Sahara) in April 1991, and a cease-fire took hold five months later, with peacekeepers arriving shortly thereafter. Yet on almost every other substantive issue of the 1991 Settlement Plan, Morocco and Polisario were at odds. The UN mission was thus only partially deployed while negotiations continued.

The most contentious issue was the question of who had a right to vote in the final-status referendum. Both sides agreed that only ethnic Sahrawis native to Western Sahara should vote, but the criteria for determining relations of blood and land were hotly contested. Polisario wanted to use a 1974 Spanish census as the only touchstone. Rabat, however, argued that the Spanish census was woefully incomplete. The 1974 census counted some seventy-four thousand Sahrawis in Western Sahara, yet Morocco planned to present more than double that number in the vote. Polisario saw this doubling of voters as Morocco's thinly veiled effort to stack the vote in its favor—presenting prointegration Moroccans as native Western Saharans. Indeed, Morocco began moving large numbers of its citizens into Western Sahara, which, like Israel's settlement drive in the West Bank and Golan Heights, constitutes a violation of the Fourth Geneva Convention prohibition against any country's transferring its civilian population into a militarily occupied territory. Morocco also assisted other Moroccan citizens in getting to MINURSO's identification centers to be registered as voters. The process of sorting through the tens of thousands of applicants to the referendum began in 1994 but broke down by 1996.

In 1997, the new UN secretary-general, Kofi Annan, brought in former U.S. secretary of state James Baker to find an alternative to the referendum. Instead, Baker found Morocco and Polisario still committed to holding the vote. The voter-identification process resumed later that year and was completed two years later. By early 2000, it was clear that the vast majority of Morocco's "Sahrawis" had failed to convince MINURSO that they had a right to vote. Meanwhile, however, King Hassan, who wanted to proceed with a referendum, died in mid-1999 and was replaced by his son, Mohammed VI, who was less enthusiastic about holding the plebiscite. Furthermore, the 1999 referendum on the future of Indonesian-occupied East Timor, which resulted in an unexpectedly large majority in support for independence, revealed to Morocco the dangers of a winner-take-all vote. Indeed, late 1999 saw large proindependence demonstrations in the Moroccan-occupied

Western Sahara, further evidence that Rabat might not win the referendum. Rather than hold the vote promised to the Western Saharans since 1991, the Security Council decided to scuttle it in February 2000.

4. *The "Third Way" and the Sahrawi Intifada, 2000 Onward.* From 2000 to 2004, Baker presented two new proposals to settle the Western Sahara conflict. After several rounds of antagonistic negotiations in 2000, Baker unveiled his Framework Agreement in early 2001 once Morocco signaled its willingness to consider a settlement between independence and integration—a "third way." The Framework Agreement gave Western Sahara significant autonomous self-governance under Moroccan sovereignty for a period of up to five years, to be followed by a final-status referendum that did not explicitly offer independence. Although Morocco was willing to consider the plan, Polisario and Algeria would not discuss it. In 2002, the Security Council told Baker that it would accept any proposal that provided for self-determination.

With this in mind, a revised proposal, known as the Peace Plan, appeared in mid-2003 after the parties had time to consider it in private. This plan proposed an even broader degree of autonomous self-governance for Western Sahara under Moroccan sovereignty during a four-year trial period. Then there would be a final-status referendum on independence, integration, or continued autonomy. Just as the Security Council was set to consider the plan, Polisario formally accepted it, followed by Algeria. Morocco, though, clearly uncomfortable with the Peace Plan, requested more time to examine it. Baker demanded a strong response from the Security Council that would impose the framework for peace. He instead received only tepid support once France watered down the resolution to a non-enforceable statement of support. Baker worked with Morocco on a counterproposal but found Rabat's position becoming more and more obstinate. Baker, claiming that he had done all he could, resigned in June 2004.

The peace process, now without its center of gravity, effectively disintegrated from late 2004 to 2006. It was further undermined by growing antagonism between Morocco and Algeria, unconditional French support for King Mohammed, and an increasingly pro-Moroccan tilt by the United States following the September 11, 2001, terrorist attacks. Both Polisario and Algeria continued to demand Morocco's acceptance of the Baker Peace Plan as a necessary condition for any talks. Rabat, however, refused to discuss any proposal that included a referendum on independence. In 2005, Morocco began drafting its own "autonomy" proposal, and in 2006 it began working toward unilateral implementation of this draft plan. A formal proposal was submitted to the Security Council in April 2007, which precipitated the first Morocco–Polisario talks since 2000. However, these talks essentially proceeded under bad faith because Morocco had no intention of respecting the Security Council's calls for self-determination.

The most surprising development following Baker's departure was the May 2005 eruption of the most intense and massive proindependence demonstrations yet witnessed in Western Sahara. Spreading from al-ʿAyun to other Sahrawi areas and including large numbers of ethnic Sahrawis from southern Morocco, the May protests were quickly repressed. Known as the Intifadah al-Istiqlal (Struggle/Uprising of Independence), this generalized movement quickly evolved into smaller, less-centralized acts of disobedience, all united in a blunt antipathy toward the Moroccan administration. From nightly skirmishes between Sahrawi youth and Moroccan police to protests in secondary-level schoolyards to spontaneous and localized manifestations of discontent, the intifada represented a transformation in Western Saharan nationalism. However, it also served to unite visibly the exiled and occupied halves of the Western Saharan population in a way that had only been assumed beforehand. The Polisario-developed national flag, almost never seen publicly in the Moroccan-occupied Western Sahara, has since become ubiquitous in protests as *the* symbol of defiance. By late 2005, Polisario's exiled leadership hailed the nonviolent protest movement as a new front in the fight for a Western Saharan nation. Morocco's firm and steady suppression, coupled with the international community's overwhelming indifference, however, tempered many nationalists' enthusiasm and provoked a dangerous despair in the camps and the streets of al-ʿAyun.

METHODOLOGY, OBJECTIVES, FRAMES,
AND BIASES

In this work, we have attempted to make innovative contributions to the field of Western Saharan studies through the use of new primary sources and a critical reinterpretation of previous accounts. The first part of this study utilizes many previously classified U.S. government documents obtained through the Freedom of Information Act. Not only do these documents help to explain U.S. motivations, but they also often shed light on other states' behavior. We have likewise attempted to return to the original sources that formed the bases of the major secondary works on Western Sahara. With the gift of significant hindsight, we felt it was time to take a fresh look at the wire reports, news dispatches, and magazine analyses from the early years of the conflict. In addition, this book is heavily informed by numerous interviews and conversations with policymakers and officials from the United States, France, Spain, the UN, the EU, the OAU, Morocco, Polisario, and Algeria.

Both of us have traveled independently to the Western Saharan refugee camps near Tindouf, Algeria, and have been escorted into the Polisario-controlled section of the territory, all the way to Morocco's defensive wall that now bisects the country. One of these trips took place in the middle of the night while both sides were still engaged in combat in Western Sahara. The second trip took place more recently, when the only sounds were the occasional overflight of UN peacekeepers. In the refugee camps, we were able to witness the ways in which Western Saharan nationalists democratically self-manage their lives and imagine themselves as a country in exile.

Both of us have also made short trips into the Moroccan-occupied Western Sahara. Officially sanctioned empirical research of a serious and objective manner is still impossible there. If one is not willing to endure close Moroccan scrutiny and control, one must gather information on life under the occupation circumspectly and clandestinely. Independent researchers there also do well to make use of "naturally occurring data," as we did. In recent years, though, the Internet has improved communication between the outside world and the Sahrawis living under Moroccan administration.

In this study, we seek to develop three larger analyses that interconnect the topical themes and narrative. There is significant overlap and interarticulation among these analyses, to the point that they function holistically across this study. To break them apart is to diminish their power, yet for the sake of this introduction we assess them individually and schematically.

The first objective in this study is to examine the *origins* of the Western Sahara conflict. The historical background to the Moroccan–Polisario dispute (i.e., before the war) is explicated primarily in chapters 4 and 7. Chapter 2 also deals extensively with the pre-1975 period in terms of Morocco's territorial claim on Western Sahara and the postcolonial antagonism between Algiers and Rabat. Chapter 4 describes the broad patterns in identity formation in Western Sahara and the makings of the Spanish colony, tracing a history that ultimately leads to the "birth" of Western Saharan nationalism and the end of Spanish rule. The first half of chapter 7 covers the international juridical context: the UN's designation of Spanish Sahara as a non-self-governing territory in the 1960s and the growing international pressure on Spain to decolonize before 1975.

The second objective in this study is to analyze the *evolution* of the Moroccan–Polisario contest since 1975. Whereas chapter 1 deals exclusively with the war (1975–91), chapters 2 and 3 discuss the regional and international dimensions of the conflict, respectively. Chapters 7, 8, and 9 also examine the international influence on the conflict, although that influence is mediated through the UN. This influence becomes even clearer in the final two chapters, where U.S. and French interests are clearly exercised in Security Council chambers.

Central to our understanding of the conflict's evolution is our examination of nationalism in Western Sahara, the subject of part two. Chapter 4 provides the deep history, and the other two chapters in this part are preoccupied with the parallel evolution of Western Saharan nationalism in exile (chapter 5) and under Moroccan occupation (chapter 6) since 1975. We believe that one of this book's main contributions to the literature is our critical portrayal of Western Saharan nationalism. We say more on this point later.

The third objective of this study is to analyze the conflict's *resilience*. Here we seek to answer a simple question: Why, after more than twenty years of Security Council intervention, is the Western Sahara conflict still unresolved? This third component is obviously the most dependent on and builds on the previous two. Understanding the UN's failure in Western Sahara first requires looking at the conditions of the conflict when peacekeepers arrived in 1991. The subsequent fifteen years of the peace/decolonization process, which consumed the UN mission's efforts in Western Sahara, is the subject of the final two chapters. Chapter 8 is concerned primarily with the abandonment of the 1991 Settlement Plan, which sought to hold a referendum on independence first proposed by Spain in 1974, then by the OAU in the late 1970s, and finally by the UN Security Council in 1988. Chapter 9 deals with the more recent Baker proposals to settle the conflict and diagnoses their fatal flaws. This discussion leads into a larger assessment of the failed peace process in Western Sahara, tying together the local and extraregional forces prohibiting a resolution.

Although these three analyses form the superstructure of this study, two overarching corrective theses likewise guide and frame it. One thesis is the claim that Western Saharan nationalism—the belief among many Sahrawis that the territory of Western Sahara should and will become an independent nation-state—is an accomplished fact. Although this assertion might seem trivial to some, the dimension of Western Saharan nationalism is often totally absent from daily reportage and scholarly works on the conflict. In other accounts, it is flatly denied. An inverse, although equally naive, tendency is a patronizing idealization of Western Saharan nationalism, especially among explicitly leftist observers. For example, one early analysis of the war characterized the population of Western Sahara as "[p]rimitive and poor." The Western Saharans had "slumbered for centuries, recently under Spanish rule," only to be rudely awakened by the "historical process [of capitalist] appropriation and accumulation" (Lalutte 1976, 7).

In this study, we correct these two tendencies—elision and romanticization—by simply treating the Western Saharans as we would any other people, nation, and country while respecting their spatial, cultural, and historical specificities. Doing so means correcting the colonialist bias in many other accounts of the Western Saharans, which have characterized them as a primitive and undeveloped people until Western ideology swept them into history (on this bias, see chapter 4). Although Western Saharan nationalism is clearly the outcome of the European encounter, the same can be said of Algeria, Morocco, and Mauritania, if not all of Africa, Southwest Asia, and other colonized areas of the world. The reality of a nationalism depends less on its age than on its motivating capacity. Given that so many people have been willing to live and die for a free Western Sahara and that many more are apparently still willing to sacrifice their lives for it, nationalism among Sahrawis cannot be ignored, either analytically or practically.

The other thesis that guides this study is the claim that extraregional actors have made substantial contributions to the conflict, in particular the governments of France and the United States. We are not arguing that the Franco–American consensus sufficiently—on its own—explains the eruption and persistence of the Western Sahara conflict. We are, however, making the case that Western interventionism is a necessary component in (1) a historical understanding of the evolution of the conflict and (2) an analysis of why the Western Sahara conflict has been so difficult to resolve. We see this thesis as corrective in that it challenges many analyses of the Western Sahara conflict. These studies either place too much emphasis on the role of Algeria in the conflict (at the expense of extraregional factors) or totally elide the direct relationship between the Western Sahara conflict and the interests of the United States and France.

An understanding of the Moroccan role is likewise a necessary ingredient. However, we take issue with the argument that Western Sahara simply represents a power vacuum that ought to be filled by Morocco or Algeria. At the very least, this idea proposes that the Western Sahara conflict is a localized dispute whose internal logic is dominated by Moroccan–Algerian antagonisms. At worst, it suggests that Algeria's role in the conflict has been equal to, if not greater than, that of Western Saharan nationalism. We do believe that there is a regional component to the conflict, primarily pitting Moroccan irredentism against Western Saharan nationalism, with Algerian support for the latter. We argue, however, against overemphasizing Algeria's role, which we detail in chapter 2, and repeatedly demonstrate this point throughout the book. Indeed, the second part makes clear that Western Saharan nationalism is an independent, powerful force to be taken seriously both in analysis and at the negotiating table. For the sake of this introduction, we simply restate two facts that should help disabuse readers of the idea that the Western Sahara conflict is essentially a Moroccan–Algerian contest: Algeria did not create Western Saharan nationalism, nor can Algeria make it disappear by kicking Polisario out of Tindouf. Algeria has done much to sustain Polisario, but the cases of East Timor and Eritrea demonstrate that nationalism is often self-sustaining in even the hardest and most desperate conditions.

By now, readers will have sensed a certain tension between cynicism and idealism in our description and analysis. Certainly, this study is tempered by our appreciation of and advocacy for basic international norms of behavior. Although the rational and often not-so-rational pursuit of power is a useful tool to explain the actions of individuals (or agents) and states (or structures), the horrors of the twentieth century demonstrate that the "law of the jungle" is clearly not a desirable way of ordering world affairs or of analyzing relationships. To live in a world of ethics, rights, and laws, both observers and critics of power—academics, journalists, nongovernmental organizations, and so on—should treat such basic norms as central, not peripheral or incidental, to world affairs. In international-relations circles, this confession of ours would quickly earn us the label *liberal* or *progressive,* although we do not identify as such. As good pragmatists, we deny differences that do not make a difference. The distinction between realist and liberalist analysis well serves hermetic cliques, catechist myth, and human misery.

It is not academic labels that concern us, but rather the false distinction between "disinterested" observation (which allegedly produces accurate, nonpartisan truths) and a perspective that takes legal and ethical norms as realities (which allegedly produces biased beliefs). The idea that academics can opt into or out of social and political *engagement* ignores the fact that they are *embedded* in—and thus benefit from—those very social and political networks. Description and analysis take place within, not outside of, history and relations of power. Nor does it follow that engagement upsets objectivity (i.e., the capacity to discern, weigh, and adjudicate the justification of claims). We would not expect passengers on a sinking ship to be disinterested about their situation, yet does that involvement rule out their ability to utter true statements about their situation?

Furthermore, we reject the other definition of objectivity by which observers are commanded to balance the facts between predetermined sides. The determination of what is an appropriate "balance" of facts and who are the official "sides" in a contest already belies a prejudice. It seems that the purpose of this kind of objectivity is to cause as little offense as possible rather than to aim for some kind of useful understanding. Although this "objectivity" might be couth for diplomats, it serves as a poor model for observation. The point of having scholars in a society is to discuss the inappropriate facts, to say what has not been said and cannot be said. Our aims in writing this book are not only to convince the reader that our analysis is correct, but also in some way to influence those whom we think are best placed to affect the situation in Western Sahara: an informed citizenry and civil society.

## A NOTE ON TRANSLITERATION AND TRANSLATION

Naming is a political act, whether of conquest or of resistance. Naming with regard to Western Sahara presents several challenges, not the least of which is the inconsistent usage of names across Spanish, French, and English transliterations and transcriptions of Arabic. Western Sahara's undecided fate also means that there are no internationally recognized standard place-names. For most Western Saharan places, we have opted to use a direct transliteration of the standard Arabic if possible; if not, we have attempted to present the closest equivalent in the Arabic dialect, Hassaniyyah, using a modified version of the *International Journal of Middle East Studies* transliteration system (i.e., without diacritical marks in the main text). There is, however, one major deviation from this rule. For the capital city of Western Sahara, we use "al-'Ayun," which is closer to both dialectical versions (Moroccan Darijah and Sahrawi Hassaniyyah) of the name, instead of the formal "al-'Uyun," which would appear rather alien to most readers familiar with the French and Spanish variants (Laâyoune, Laayoun, El-Ayoune, El-Aaiún, etc.). With respect to Moroccan, Mauritanian, and Algerian places and names, we have used the most internationally recognized forms. As for personal Sahrawi names, we have tried to use whichever form the person uses herself or himself; lacking that information, we have opted for whichever form of a name is most frequently used.

Because Spanish is an official language of the Polisario and its government in exile, we have opted, for the most part, to present Polisario-related names in Spanish first, then an English translation, with the abbreviation based on the Spanish. We give Algerian, Mauritanian, and Moroccan government and organization names in French first, then in English, with abbreviations based on the French version.

PART ONE

# War

Politics is war by other means.
—MICHEL FOUCAULT, *"Society Must Be Defended"*

# 1

# The War for Western Sahara

The Western Sahara conflict has outlasted the 1975–91 war between Morocco and the Western Saharan independence movement, led by the Frente Polisario. Yet an examination of the war for Western Sahara—its origins, its evolution, and its nonconclusion—is an important first step toward an understanding of the broader conflict. To that limited end, this chapter's main concerns are the proximate causes of the Morocco–Polisario war, its trajectories of development, and some of the factors behind its termination. In terms of immediate or trigger causes, this chapter focuses on Morocco's November 1975 invasion of Spanish Sahara, but it also discusses some of the war's background causes and analyzes Polisario's strengths and weaknesses, strategies and tactics as an insurgent movement. (See chapters 2 and 3 for a much broader and deeper discussion of the conflict's root causes and sustaining dynamics. In chapters 4 and 5, we deal with the most important underlying cause, the rise of Sahrawi nationalism, including Polisario's war against Spain [1973–75].)

The course of the war, like this chapter, begins in November 1975, when Polisario aimed its guns at the new occupiers rather than at Spain. With support from Algeria, Polisario drove Mauritania out of Western Sahara by 1979 and greatly embarrassed Moroccan forces. Yet just when it seemed that Polisario was on the edge of military victory in the late 1970s, Morocco overhauled its strategy and turned the tables on Polisario's Ejército de Liberación Popular Saharaui (ELPS, Saharan People's Liberation Army). Although the war had quickly become unbearably expensive for Hassan II's regime, Morocco's allies soon began providing arms and financing to help turn the tide against Polisario. The participation of foreign actors on Morocco's behalf receives greater attention in chapter 3, but this chapter does analyze their sustaining and ultimately decisive influence on the war.

Following Mauritania's withdrawal in 1979, and with increased external support, King Hassan's Forces armées royales (FAR, Royal Armed Forces)[1] successfully switched to a defensive posture instead of wasting energy hunting down the ELPS's highly mobile units. With generous foreign support, Morocco painstakingly built a series of earthen walls ("berms"). At first, the berms served to defend Morocco's tenuous purchase on the territory. Yet by patiently increasing the walls' size, FAR was also gradually able to deny Polisario its key asset—freedom of movement. The result was, by the end of the 1980s, a military stalemate. Polisario was not powerful enough to break the siege, nor was

3

Morocco daring enough to invade Algeria to smash Polisario's main base near Tindouf. With no viable military solution left, the conflict moved to the UN. However, the relationship between the war in Western Sahara and the peace process that followed is not one of simple cause and effect. The peace process has been a political extension of the war, as the third part of this study explains. In concluding this chapter, we thus consider the political and military prospects of a return to armed conflict.

A PREMEDITATED INVASION: THE 1975 SAHARA CRISIS

For Polisario, the war against Morocco was a continuation of the liberation struggle launched in 1973 (see chapter 4). For Morocco, the war against Polisario was an unexpected consequence of invasion and occupation. It is not known precisely when Hassan II made the decision to use force to capture Spanish Sahara. What is known is that since mid-1974 Morocco had stationed one-quarter of its military forces in its southern regions in anticipation of a possible military confrontation. Hassan was applying more pressure on Madrid on the diplomatic front in early 1975 by reviving the issue of the long-held Spanish enclaves of Ceuta and Melilla on Morocco's Mediterranean coast. Although Hassan had promised Spanish dictator Generalissimo Francisco Franco in 1963 that the issue would not be discussed in their lifetimes, in January 1975 the Moroccan government requested that the UN declare the largely Spanish-populated presidios non-self-governing territories.

By the summer of 1975, the Spanish government had good reason to believe that Morocco was willing to go to war over Western Sahara. For months, both regular Moroccan troops and pseudo-Saharan insurgents, under the guise of the prointegration Frente de Liberación y de la Unidad (FLU, also Front de libération et de l'unité, Front for Liberation and Unity), had carried out military and terrorist attacks against targets in Spanish Sahara and the Spanish presidios in northern Morocco. On March 26, Moroccan agents allegedly laid a bomb targeting Spanish military posts in the presidio of Ceuta in northern Morocco (U.S. Embassy Madrid 1975). In late May 1975, a bomb planted in a café in Melilla caused numerous injuries, which was followed by an explosion in Ceuta on June 19 and another failed attempt the following day in Melilla, killing both Moroccan terrorists (Hodges 1983b, 203). Starting in April, the Moroccan navy harassed Spanish fishing vessels off the northwestern African coast. On June 8, forty-six regular Moroccan troops penetrated the Saharan frontier but surrendered to Spanish troops without a fight. Two days later more Moroccan regulars attempted to take a Spanish outpost in the territory's Northeast but fled when they found it defended (U.S. Central Intelligence Agency 1975). Moroccan antiaircraft batteries attacked two Spanish reconnaissance planes over the Sahara at the end of June, resulting in a retaliatory strike by Spanish forces. Around the same time, a mine laid by a small Moroccan force killed five Spanish soldiers during another raid on Tah. Then on August 2, some forty miles inside the colony, Spanish forces repulsed a Moroccan attack against the small town of Hawzah (Hausa), which resulted in three casualties (*Africa Research Bulletin,* June 1975, Aug. 1975).

Tensions mounted as the international community awaited the mid-October release of the ICJ advisory opinion. Hassan himself had requested the opinion in 1974, which was to address Morocco and Mauritania's territorial claims to Western Sahara. Yet on August 20, 1975, he stated in a royal speech that, regardless of the ICJ's judgment, "Morocco will liberate its Sahara region, whatever the price," by the end of the year (*Africa Research Bulletin,* Aug. 1975). Around that time, Hassan apparently initiated secret preparations to use civilians to claim Western Sahara (Hodges 1983b, 211). A week before the ICJ's opinion was read, Hassan and his military staff moved to Marrakech, from where he had directed the 1963 border war with Algeria (U.S. Embassy Rabat 1975b). A day later the U.S. Embassy in Rabat reported a massive movement of troops and armor to areas near the Saharan–Moroccan border, including all thirty-five of Morocco's T-54 tanks in the Southern Command (U.S. Embassy Rabat 1975a). Even in the face of these threats, the Spanish government informed the UN on October 1 that a referendum would be held sometime during the first half of 1976 (Hodges 1983b, 207).

The ICJ's awaited opinion, released October 16, 1975, largely dismissed Morocco and Mauritania's historical claims to Western Sahara. What minimal ties existed, the court highlighted, were not sufficient grounds to deny the Western Saharans their right to self-determination. (For details on the court's opinion, see chapter 4.) Despite this ruling, Hassan declared to his people only hours later that the court had ruled in Morocco's favor. He then announced that he would lead 350,000 unarmed Moroccan civilians into Spanish Sahara at the end of October to "reclaim" it. This "Green March," named after Islam's holy color, would force Spain either to fire upon unarmed civilians or to enter into negotiations with Morocco. The former would surely galvanize nationalist sentiments for a war against Spain, so Hassan had apparently engineered a no-win situation for Madrid.

The announcement of the Green March triggered a flurry of diplomatic activity in the UN Security Council and behind the scenes in the national capitals of the western Mediterranean. Hassan's gambit owes its success as much to luck as to its shrewdness. Franco became incapacitated on October 17, and the Spanish cabinet appeared to split into two factions, those favoring negotiations with Morocco and those favoring UN intervention to stop the Green March. By the end of October, with the UN failing to act resolutely against Morocco's announced invasion, the pro-Moroccan factions apparently prevailed. The leaders of Spain and Morocco came to an agreement whereby a small portion of the Green March would symbolically cross only several kilometers into the frontier. The march began on the morning of November 6, 1975, when a small contingent of the 350,000 Moroccans who were gathered near Tarfaya penetrated the Spanish Sahara frontier. Hassan called back all his marchers three days later.

With Mauritanian and Moroccan delegates present in Madrid on November 12, the final negotiations got under way. The basics of the arrangement were released two days later. The Madrid Agreement instituted a tripartite transitional administration until February 28, 1976, giving Spain enough time to withdraw. The Moroccan and Mauritanian division of the territory was announced much later, in April 1976—roughly a straight line running from just north of Dakhla to the border near Zouerate, Mauritania. Mauritania named its new province Tiris al-Gharbiyah (map 1). The Madrid Agreement also contained secret aspects covering Spanish economic interests, including fishing rights and a continued 35 percent stake in phosphate production (*Africa Confidential,* Jan. 7, 1976; Hodges 1983b, 224).

Mostly unknown to the outside world was the fact that a new conflict was brewing in Western Sahara. On October 31, 1975, elements of the Moroccan military crossed into the northeastern corner of the territory (map 2), where they soon met resistance from Polisario guerillas (*Africa Research Bulletin,* Oct. 1975). Few then would have guessed that these shots were the first in a war that would last for more than fifteen years.

THE SAHRAWI INSURGENCY

When the war in Western Sahara started in late 1975, many observers were quick to dismiss the nationalists' fighting abilities. The U.S. ambassador in Rabat, for example, concluded as much after two of his deputies visited the territory in December 1975. "Polisario," he wrote to Washington, "even though [the] guerillas' needs [are] probably few, would not seem capable of standing up for long against relative Moroccan military might and in a highly inhospitable environment where spotting from [the] air [is] relatively easy" (U.S. Embassy Rabat 1975b). The International Institute for Strategic Studies also predicted a tough road for Polisario: "[G]uerilla operations are difficult in the open desert of Spanish Sahara, where it is relatively easy for a defender to control movement" (1976b, 47).

In little time, such predictions proved shortsighted. The geographical assumption that the former Spanish colony is a flat wasteland, like the *hammadah* of Tindouf, is simply false. Western Sahara contains an array of terrains well suited to guerilla warfare: the deep gullies of the Saqiyah al-Hamra', the rises of the Zammur Massif, the ready shelter of the Ouarkaziz Mountains, the rugged, cliff-lined coast, and even the shade of weathered Saharan trees.

As is often the case with indigenous insurgencies, observers also failed to understand the advantage of generations of place-based knowledge. For centuries, the peoples of the westernmost Sahara have lived and warred across its vast stretches, alternately vying and cooperating for mastery of trade routes and scattered pastures. The memories, traditions,

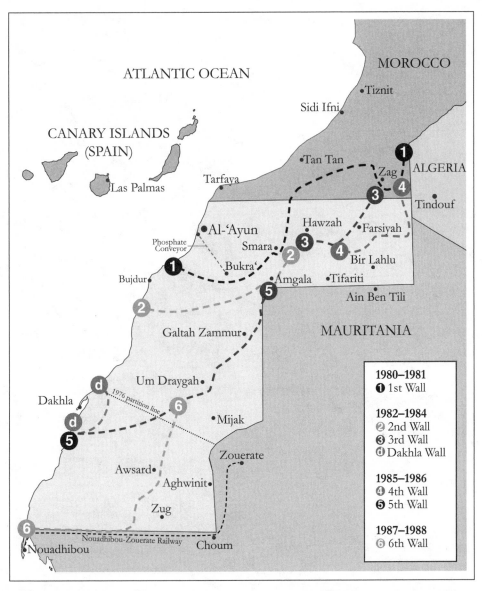

Map 1. Approximate location and development of Moroccan barriers (berms) in Western Sahara and Morocco, 1980–1988. Based on maps in Tusa 1988, 41; *Le Monde,* reprinted in *Saharan Peoples Support Committee (SPSC) Newsletter,* June 1981, 1; *SPSC Newsletter,* Nov. 1983, 1, Apr. 1985, 1, Apr. 1985, 3, Feb.–May 1987, 1; UN map no. A4-010 (May 4, 2007).

and practices of armed resistance, discussed further in chapter 4, were thus an inheritance that nationalist fighters exploited to the full.

The ELPS thrived in the initial years of the war by avoiding face-to-face battles and operating between the wide gaps in Morocco and Mauritania's fixed positions. Early in the war, a Sahrawi fighter explained this strategy to a Western journalist:

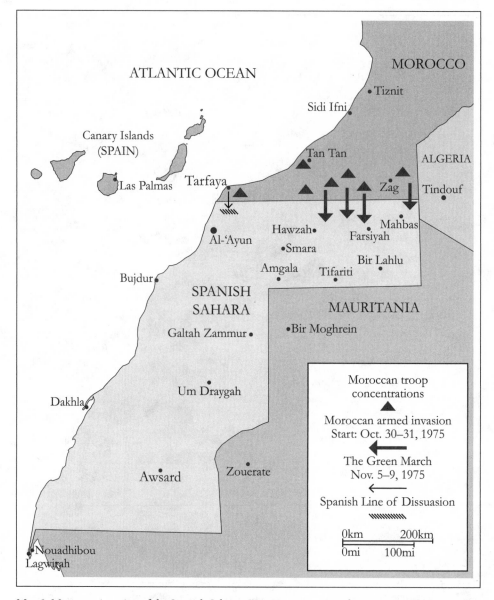

Map 2. Moroccan invasion of the Spanish Sahara, Oct.–Nov. 1975. Based on maps in Aguirre 1988.

"It isn't enough to hold the post—the land in between has to be occupied, and if it isn't, it will be hell for them."

[Journalist:] "But in between, there is nothing . . ."

"That is where we are at home," he replied. (Weexsteen 1976, 3)

The "in between" included the highly porous borders of Mauritania and Algeria, which the ELPS used to slip away from pursuing enemies, much to the Moroccan army's annoyance. Following the initial Moroccan–Mauritanian onslaught in 1975–76, Polisario's forces harassed the occupying forces into a few pockets inside Western Sahara. They even took the war to the Mauritanian capital and deep into Moroccan territory.

The Sahrawi guerillas also benefited early on—in both skill and arms—from mass defections of Sahrawi soldiers from the colonial military unit Tropas Nómadas (Nomad Troops). Some departing Spanish troops also donated arms and supplies and readily abandoned positions to the Sahrawis they had commanded. The massive Sahrawi refugee exodus in 1975 and 1976 provided Polisario with a huge reservoir of more-than-willing recruits. Soon most fighting-age men were either soldiers in the ELPS or workers in supporting roles. Sahrawi women were empowered to take charge of the refugee camps, although some even received arms training for camp defense.

Polisario made good use of captured arms from Spain, Morocco, and Mauritania, but it received fresh arms and ammunition as well. Libya and Algeria provided material support, the latter readily offering its own guerilla expertise. Especially useful was Algeria's knowledge of French military technology and counterinsurgency tactics that the Moroccans were now trying to put to use in Western Sahara. The ELPS effectively combined Algerian training and knowledge with Sahrawis' natural mastery of the terrain and a modified version of their centuries-old practice of *al-ghazi,* the raid. The use of quick assaults and retreats, often from different directions, allowed for a high level of surprise and minimized losses. The ELPS also made good use of inclement weather (e.g., sandstorms) and the cover of night.

Although Algeria's role in the Western Sahara war was certainly significant, it is easily overstated. The only time Algeria ever directly intervened was to help transport Sahrawi refugees in late 1975 and early 1976. Following a clash at the Amgala oasis on January 29, 1976, when Moroccan forces captured several Algerian soldiers, Algeria withdrew all its "humanitarian" troops (*Africa Research Bulletin,* Jan. 1976).

Nevertheless, Polisario's decisive advantage has always been its ultimate refuge in Algeria. With that extraterritorial home base, where nearly half of Western Sahara's population came to reside, Polisario's political and military health was virtually guaranteed by Algeria. This relationship also created two significant disadvantages for Morocco. First, in order to defeat the insurgency, Morocco would have to invade another country—one that would certainly fight back. Second, Morocco could not use the civilian Sahrawi population under its control against Polisario. In other words, any Moroccan resort to systematic brutality—a "dirty war"—would have little effect on Polisario's capability. To use a common counterinsurgency analogy, Morocco could not drain the sea to kill the fish. Although the Moroccan government's hands were by no means clean in the occupied Western Sahara, its army would have to apply different tactics to defeat Polisario.

DEFEATING MAURITANIA

From the start, Mauritania had trouble upholding its end of the Madrid Agreement. The postcolonial Mauritanian state was fragile, which Polisario knew firsthand. Mauritanian dissidents of ethnic Sahrawi extraction formed a significant core of Polisario's leadership. These leaders included Ibrahim Hakim and Ahmed Baba Miské, former Mauritanian diplomats turned renegade opposition leaders (Damis 1983, 40). Mauritania's army was so weak that Moroccan forces ended up defending many positions in the Mauritanian-administered section of the territory. For a time, the Moroccan government even found it necessary to send troops to the Mauritanian capital of Nouakchott (*Africa Research Bulletin,* Dec. 1975).

Having achieved independence from France in 1960, Mauritania was wrought with the same problems that faced countries across the Sahara–Sahel: politically fragmented populations within arbitrary boundaries; a ruling elite instituted to serve the former colonizer's continued interests; and weak states poorly equipped to deal with the demands of late global capitalism. In Mauritania, this situation was aggravated by the small population, the vastness of the territory, and the limited means with which to build an economy capable of supporting rapid sedentarization. At independence, Mauritania's number one asset and economic backbone were the iron mines at Zouerate, controlled by the multinational corporation Société anonyme des mines de fer de Mauritanie (Corporation of Iron Mines of Mauritania).

Independent Mauritania faced not only steep internal challenges, but also significant external threats. Morocco had claimed all of Mauritania as a part of Greater Morocco, pursuing this claim on the international scene and within Mauritania's domestic politics. When Mauritania had emerged as a free nation-state in 1960, President Mokhtar Ould Daddah (1960–78) and his Parti du people mauritanien, "the closest collaborators of French neo-colonialism" (Bennoune 1977, 8), won out against pro-Moroccan elements (i.e., Rabat's well-paid "reintegrationists"). That same year King Mohammed V and Crown Prince Hassan, commander of Morocco's armed forces, began secretly preparing for an invasion of Mauritania. Yet they deemed an air–sea invasion too difficult and a land invasion impossible with Spanish and French colonial forces still in Western Sahara and Algeria, respectively. Then King Hassan's failed 1963 war to redraw Morocco's border with Algeria further proved that Mauritania was under military threat from the north. Throughout the 1960s, Morocco pursued its claim to Mauritania diplomatically, notably at the UN (where it attempted to block Mauritania's admission) and the Arab League. Morocco finally recognized Mauritania in 1969 in order to further Rabat's ambitions for Spanish Sahara.

Ould Daddah first articulated Mauritania's irredentist claim on Western Sahara in 1957. Whereas Morocco's notions of sovereignty were based on the Sahrawis' alleged fealty to past Moroccan sultans, Mauritania's claim was based on ethnic congruity (e.g., language and social structures). For this reason, until 1974 Mauritania unconditionally supported the Western Saharans' right to self-determination, believing that most Sahrawis would naturally choose unity with their kin. Should self-determination lead to independence, at least Mauritania would have a buffer between it and Morocco. Mauritania's vulnerability was especially acute along its shared border with the Spanish Sahara, which runs parallel to the country's economic lifeblood—the iron mines near Zouerate and the rail line that connects it to the Nouadhibou port. Poor and sparsely populated, Mauritania knew it would be unable to defend itself from far larger Moroccan forces along the thousand-mile border (Kilgore 1987, 158–59). Security interests also led Ould Daddah to gravitate toward President Houari Boumedienne's (1965–78) Algeria (Gretton 1976, 23). When the unlikely Moroccan–Mauritanian alliance emerged in the early 1970s, it was with Algeria's blessing. That changed in mid-1975, however, when Boumedienne decided to back Polisario. Ould Daddah's final break with Boumedienne came in November 1975, when he refused to succumb to the Algerian president's pressure to side against Rabat. That fateful choice ended up costing Ould Daddah his regime, nearly destroying the Mauritanian state in the process (Pazzanita 1992, 286).

Indeed, the weakest part of the Mauritanian state was its military, which had only 2,550 soldiers and paramilitaries in 1975. These forces were tasked to protect a country nearly twice the size of France, yet with minimal logistical and communications capabilities (International Institute for Strategic Studies 1976a, 47). Polisario, in contrast, had at least as many fighters, better motivation, and backing from Algeria and Libya.

In the first half of 1976, Polisario demonstrated its willingness to take the fight to Moroccan and Mauritanian soil, hitting Tan Tan in southern Morocco and the vulnerable Zouerate mines in Mauritania. Then on June 8, 1976, the ELPS launched a major operation on the Mauritanian capital, Nouakchott. In an assault deploying more than five hundred fighters, Polisario was able to get within range to carry out a sustained shelling of the capital. At nearly a thousand miles from the ELPS's main bases in Algeria, the attack proved that the ELPS could carry out complex operations requiring extensive logistical preparation. The Mauritanian response, however, dealt a severe blow, its forces chasing the ELPS back into the desert and destroying a large part of the expeditionary force during the retreat. More important, the counterattack killed the Polisario's inspirational leader, El-Ouali Mustapha Sayed.

In order to bolster its defenses, the Mauritanian regime quickly drafted 13,000 men in 1976. But these conscripts were drawn mostly from the minority black population, which was generally treated as second-class citizens in Mauritanian society and thus not well motivated. Nouakchott also signed a joint defense and cooperation agreement with Rabat. The percentage of government expenditures dedicated to the military increased from less than one-tenth to more than one-half of the country's still meager budget.

Polisario strikes on Moroccan and Mauritanian positions continued unabated into 1977, the most noteworthy being a May 1 raid on Zouerate that disabled the mining facilities. In the attack, the ELPS killed two French citizens and took several others captive. Mauritania agreed to allow Morocco to move 9,000 soldiers into its territory so that it could redeploy its own forces to the besieged mining complex. Mauritania also benefited from financial aid from Arab monarchies in the Persian Gulf and increased French military aid. Yet Polisario responded to the increased security at the mines by attacking the railway, which was the only means of exporting the iron ore (*Africa Research Bulletin,* May 1977).

Polisario's Zouerate raids also triggered direct Western intervention. The French air force attacked ELPS positions in December 1977, flying out of bases in Senegal. The French government said that the air strikes had come in response to a Mauritanian request, yet the French were also punishing Polisario for its seizure of eight French citizens in the attacks on Zouerate and the railway. One of the hostages later said that his government had exploited the situation as a pretext for military engagement, and he seemed to be right. In fact, the UN and the Algerian government had already secured the hostages' release prior to the French air strikes. French fighter aircraft and military advisors remained in the area afterward, though, to aid the counterinsurgency effort. Morocco's military presence in the Zouerate area also increased significantly (*Africa Research Bulletin,* Dec. 1977; Disney 1976).

To help further stabilize France's client regimes in Rabat and Nouakchott, French military participation in the conflict—both direct and indirect—increased markedly in 1978. This participation included the deployment of sophisticated electronic missile countermeasures and airborne detection equipment in Mauritania. French military personnel on the ground did everything from advising to mapping Mauritania's Saharan hinterlands. Likewise, France supplied Morocco with advanced fighter aircraft, sent paratroopers to the main Moroccan air base near Benguerir, and worked jointly on air strikes against Polisario, with French planes offering air support for Moroccan raids. The French secret service even began recruiting mercenaries to fight alongside the Moroccans and Mauritanians. The extent of French military aid was so great that, as Keith Somerville concludes, by 1978 "France was more or less running the Mauritanian armed forces" (1990, 117). When French assistance resulted in increased Polisario casualties, the ELPS responded by limiting the size of its operations and its daytime operations (Chaliand 1980, 107).

In the end, close military cooperation from France and Morocco failed to save Ould Daddah. A quiet coup d'état led by his own chief of staff, Lieutenant-Colonel Mustafa Ould Salek, removed Ould Daddah from power on July 10, 1978. The new military leaders suspended the Constitution, disbanded the Parliament, and dismissed many government officials—all without protest from the general population. The war had never been popular with the Mauritanian people and was even less so with the black conscripts doing most of the fighting. Images of teenage prisoners of war (POWs) held by Polisario underscored the desperate measures the Mauritanian government had been taking. Unlike Moroccans, Mauritanians never felt much enthusiasm for seizing the Spanish Sahara. And as the war drained the economy, popular support waned. Compounding these issues, when the conflict erupted in 1975, drought was already pushing Mauritania into a severe economic recession, with inflation reaching 33 percent. Crop shortfalls left 75 percent of domestic need unmet, forcing food prices skyward and more nomads into the two major coastal cities, Nouadhibou and Nouakchott. To help cover the country's fourfold increase in debt, Ould Daddah had instituted a very unpopular war tax of three days' wages per month.

Yet with 10,000 Moroccan troops in Mauritania, the new regime would have to walk a fine line between domestic and regional pressures. The new sixteen-member government led by Ould Salek, the Comité militaire de redressement nationale (Military Committee for National Recovery), attempted to reassure Morocco's top general, Ahmed Dlimi, that Mauritania's military cooperation would continue against Polisario. However, there were indications that Ould Salek's group had seized power before pro-Moroccan elements could stage their own coup (*Africa Confidential*, Aug. 4, 1978; *Africa Research Bulletin*, July 1978). Furthermore, the new Mauritanian regime began pursuing diplomatic initiatives, via Africa and Europe, to settle the conflict with Polisario only a month after the coup. Polisario reciprocated the goodwill by providing a welcomed respite from attacks against Mauritanian targets. Offers of aid from Libya and warming relations with Algeria coaxed Mauritania into discussing a peace agreement with Polisario directly. Once these initiatives became known, King Hassan warned that he could not accept an independent state in Tiris al-Gharbiyah, Mauritania's third of Western Sahara, which would have given Polisario a foothold in Western Sahara. For a time, Ould Salek tried to seek a global resolution to the entire conflict that would satisfy all sides, although in early 1979 he also kindly asked all Moroccan troops to leave Mauritania.

Polisario eventually grew impatient and resumed attacks in the first months of 1979. Mauritanian lieutenant-colonel Ahmed Ould Boucief reined in Ould Salek's powers in April and reconstituted the regime as the Comité militaire de salut national (Military Committee for National Salvation). He was helped by Colonel Mohammed Khouna Ould Heydallah and Lieutenant-Colonel Mahmoud Ould Ahmed Louly (Pazzanita 1992, 287–88). However, it was Ould Boucief's death in a plane accident in the summer of 1979 that finally paved the way for a bilateral Mauritania–Polisario peace deal. Following three days of negotiations in Algiers, an agreement was signed on August 5, 1979. Mauritania, then led by Ould Heydallah, renounced all claims to Western Sahara and secretly agreed to hand over Tiris al-Gharbiyah to Polisario within seven months. The Moroccan government and press condemned the agreement, and Morocco's FAR quickly took control of Dakhla, the largest Western Saharan city under Mauritanian control. Morocco formally annexed the whole area as its thirty-seventh province, Oued Eddahab (Arabic for Río de Oro). Considering Morocco's already sizable military presence in Tiris al-Gharbiyah, the annexation amounted to little more than a change of flags. Mauritania, however, has since maintained control over the southwestern entire peninsular tip of Western Sahara, including a small garrison in the largely abandoned settlement of Lagwirah (La Agüera/

La Güera/Lagouira) south of Nouadhibou. For all intents and purposes, Morocco has ceded control of this area of Western Sahara to Mauritania.

Following its reconciliation with Polisario and Algiers, Mauritania tried to assume a lower profile in the conflict. An allegedly pro-Moroccan coup that failed to depose Ould Heydallah on March 16, 1981, only deepened the rift between the two former allies. Several Moroccan "hot pursuits" of Polisario into Mauritania further increased tensions. Faced with these provocations and Morocco's refusal to cooperate with OAU efforts to end the war, Ould Heydallah formally recognized the Polisario's RASD on February 27, 1984, the ninth anniversary of Polisario's declaration of independence. Ould Heydallah, however, was himself deposed on December 12 of that year when nationalist officers accused him of authoritarianism, unilateralism (e.g., in recognizing RASD), corruption, and bad management. The new regime, under the leadership of Colonel Maaouya Ould Sid Ahmed Taya, opposed his predecessor's strong support for Polisario and took a more neutral stance, restoring relations with Morocco but without rescinding recognition of RASD (Pazzanita 1992, 290–92). Since then, Mauritania—under both Ould Taya and the short-lived regime that finally removed him in 2005—has successfully balanced relations with Morocco, Polisario, and Algeria. The August 2008 military (counter)coup that overthrew President Sidi Mohamed Ould Cheikh Abdallahi a little more than a year after his election had little effect on Mauritania's attitude toward Western Sahara (for background, see Bullard and Tandia 2003; International Crisis Group 2005a, 2005b, 2006).

Since exiting the war, the Mauritanian government has appeared somewhat indifferent to whether Morocco or Polisario prevails in Western Sahara. Although Mauritania recognizes RASD, its behavior throughout the peace process indicates a real attempt to be nonpartisan. On the one hand, if Polisario were to win, Mauritania would still benefit, likely becoming one of Western Sahara's closest allies and trading partners. Polisario's leadership already has familial ties to figures in Mauritania's government and civil society, and these ties would undoubtedly lay the foundation for friendly relations between the two countries. On the other hand, with Morocco's age of aggressive expansionism likely at an end, Mauritania would no longer face an existential threat should Rabat win Western Sahara. A genuine peace—whether independence, integration, or something in between— would likely open up the region to more trade and tourism. Either way, Mauritania would win.

THE EARLY WAR AGAINST MOROCCO

As Western Sahara sunk into war in late 1975, few observers, as noted earlier, would have predicted a Moroccan defeat. On paper, Morocco was clearly dominant. Whereas Polisario started with 1,000 to 2,000 lightly armed guerillas, Morocco started it with 80,000 soldiers. Morocco's air force and army, which were still being modernized, had been well supplied with weapons from the United States, western Europe, and the Eastern bloc. The FAR also had practical knowledge from the anticolonial struggle against France, as members of the UN team sent to the Congo in 1960–61, in the brief 1963 war with Algeria, and on the Syrian front in the 1973 Arab–Israeli war.

Yet the ELPS was able to deliver successive humiliating defeats to Morocco that suggested otherwise. Captured Moroccan officers admitted that their morale had been "badly shaken." By 1977, Moroccan losses were rumored as high as one to two hundred men a month (*Middle East International*, Oct. 1977). One problem for Morocco when confronting Polisario was the Moroccan military's highly centralized command structures, which was an effect of the military's attempted coups against Hassan II in the early 1970s. For example, defensive air support from the Forces royales air (Royal Moroccan Air Force) would have to be cleared from Rabat. Such lag time is one reason Polisario's hit-and-run raids were so successful.

As Mauritania began withdrawing in mid-1978, Polisario attacks against Morocco became more audacious. The ELPS intensified its attacks on Moroccan convoys on the Tan Tan to al-'Ayun road, disrupted the Bukra' phosphate conveyor belt, and on October 17 lobbed rockets into the center of al-'Ayun. In one of the most spectacular battles of the war, on January 28, 1979, the ELPS launched a two-hour invasion of the Moroccan city of Tan Tan, a town with a predominantly ethnic Sahrawi population. This operation was one of the more brazen in Polisario's 1979 "Boumedienne Offensive," named in honor of the recently deceased Algerian leader. Although such raids in southern Morocco and northern Western Sahara failed to draw FAR out of Tiris al-Gharbiyah, they were a clear message from Algeria that support for Polisario would continue (*Africa Research Bulletin,* Jan. 1979). Even more impressive than the Tan Tan raid was an August 24, 1979, attack in which 5,000 ELPS fighters overran a Moroccan garrison in Lebouirate and then ambushed a relief force coming from Zag. Journalists taken by Polisario to these sites as late as September 12 witnessed documents revealing "widespread demoralization among Moroccan troops." Similarly, on October 6 the ELPS dared a three-sided attack on the heavily defended Western Saharan city of Smara. Both sides asserted widely divergent narratives of the battle. Morocco claimed that the guerillas were repulsed by FAR's French-built Mirage F-1s, whereas the ELPS claimed that it entered the city, freed hundreds of political prisoners, and left with minimal losses (*Africa Research Bulletin,* Nov. 1979).

Military analyst William H. Lewis later identified the main failure of FAR's strategy: "The Moroccans had ignored the famous dictum of Frederick the Great: 'He who attempts to defend too much defends nothing'" (1985, 125). Lewis explains that Moroccan forces had become too widely dispersed, which hampered their ability to fight and provide logistical support. However, as he charts, the FAR was learning from its mistakes and began implementing a new strategy based on concentrated firepower and the slow consolidation of control. Morocco began sending out heavily armored clear-and-hold operations to drive ELPS out of its forward bases in southern Morocco and northern Western Sahara. In late 1979, 1,000 armed vehicles and 6,000 soldiers in a thirty-kilometer-wide Moroccan detachment named "Ouhoud" left Tan Tan to bolster the Dakhla garrison. The mission took three weeks to reach its goal. Another Moroccan unit, named "Zellaka," headed via the Dra'a (Drâa) Valley toward ELPS safe havens in the Ouarkaziz Mountains and to reinforce the isolated outpost at Zag. The greener Zellaka troops fared poorly against the ELPS, and only after the redeployment of soldiers from the Ouhoud detachment to the south of Morocco was FAR able to secure the Ouarkaziz Mountains and Zag. That August (1979), a third large Moroccan deployment called Larak tried to secure the region between the Zini Mountains and Smara, which would block Polisario's access to the road from Tan Tan to al-'Ayun. Coupled with improved *cordons de sécurité* (defensive barriers), Morocco's new tactics signaled the opening of a new phase in the war over Western Sahara.

Instead of directly countering Morocco's shift in strategy, Polisario simply changed its primary areas of operation. During this period, Polisario sought out undefended targets. On January 25, 1980, the ELPS attacked Akka, a small oasis town just across the Moroccan–Algerian border, and raided Tarfaya along the Moroccan coast. The attack on Akka was repeated that September, with Polisario's fighters pushing all the way to the administrative capital, Tata. Polisario also focused on its naval operations, attempting to reduce the profitability of commercial fishing off Western Sahara's coast. Targeted ships included Spanish and other European vessels as well as Eastern bloc vessels, such as a Romanian trawler that Polisario sunk in 1986.

LINES OF SUPPORT: ARMS, AID, AND EXTERNAL ACTORS

The war for Western Sahara was heavily influenced by external actors' indirect participation. As is often noted, Algeria heavily subsidized Polisario's military and diplomatic campaigns and the refugees' livelihood. Polisario's safe haven in Algeria accounts for a great deal of the ELPS's success and longevity. In addition to the arms it captured, the ELPS had light and medium armaments provided by Algeria and, for a time, Libya. Though the ELPS never received direct aid from the Soviet Union or other Warsaw Pact countries, most of its sophisticated hardware was of Soviet manufacture, including SA-6 and SA-7 surface-to-air missiles, ZSU-23 self-propelled 23-millimeter antiaircraft guns, antitank weapons, artillery, BMP-1 armored cars, and a small number of T-54 and T-55 tanks (International Institute for Strategic Studies 1988, 109, and 1990, 95–96). Neither Algeria nor Libya has provided figures as to its outlays for Polisario, though providing such equipment was easily affordable for both oil-rich countries. From 1977 to 1991, the Algerian government imported $10.2 billion in arms; Morocco brought in only $3.9 billion worth. In the same period, the Libyan government took in more than $26 billion in arms (Volman 1999, 220).

As it became increasingly difficult for Sahrawis in the Moroccan-occupied areas to join Polisario in the late 1970s, the ELPS's ability to recruit more fighters peaked. The only way Algeria could help escalate the war was by providing more sophisticated arms. The most striking example was at the battle of Galtah Zammur (Guelta Zemmour) on October 13, 1981. In one of the largest confrontations of the war, Polisario attacked with several units—all having tanks—from multiple directions, including from Mauritania. However, what made the battle devastating for Morocco was Polisario's potent use of Algerian-supplied, Soviet-made SA-6 surface-to-air missiles. In the course of the battle, the ELPS downed five Moroccan aircraft: two F-1s, an F-5, a C-130 command plane, and a troop carrier. These losses were quite heavy for the Moroccan air force relative to its size. Polisario—and apparently Algeria—had hoped that the raid would prove to Hassan that it could match Morocco's tactics and technology. A major effect of the battle, however, was to galvanize Western support for Morocco.

Although Algeria's support for Polisario's war effort cannot be ignored, external support for Morocco played a more decisive role. Only two factors can account for the fact that the war turned against Polisario in the early 1980s: Morocco's strategic adaptation and a massive increase in foreign military and financial aid to Rabat. Polisario, in contrast, continued to receive comparatively steady levels of support and used the same tactics throughout the war.

The most dramatic increase in foreign aid to Morocco was in the period from 1978 to 1982, leveling off only when these weapons and financing had helped create the conditions for a military stalemate, or what some officials called "balance" (Neuman 1988, 1064–65; see also Neuman 1986) (figure 1). The majority of Morocco's hardware came from France and the United States, and Saudi Arabia offered generous financing. French arms included sophisticated jet aircraft (e.g., Mirage F-1s), helicopter gunships, light tanks, armored cars, artillery, and radar equipment. France and the United States even competed directly for the Moroccan market. A 1979 sale of twenty-four U.S. Hughes Model 500 helicopter gunships was never completed when Morocco opted for French Gazelle helicopters instead. France also provided significant training and intelligence to Morocco derived from its colonial experience in the Sahara.

Upon coming to office, the Jimmy Carter administration (1977–80) initially toned down the overtly pro-Moroccan stance that had marked the Gerald Ford administration (1974–77). At first, Carter conditioned arms sales to Rabat on the latter's willingness to negotiate a resolution to the conflict. Then, as a result of Polisario's attacks inside Moroccan territory, the White House revised its policy. The new position was that ELPS operations inside Morocco constituted acts of aggression that warranted "defensive" arms sales to Rabat. Despite domestic legal measures that should have restricted these transfers, the State Department approved the sale of a $200 million ground sensor system in May 1979 (Wenger 1982, 24). The unexpected fall of Iran's shah in 1979 further motivated the Carter administration to tighten relations with its remaining clients in the Middle East and

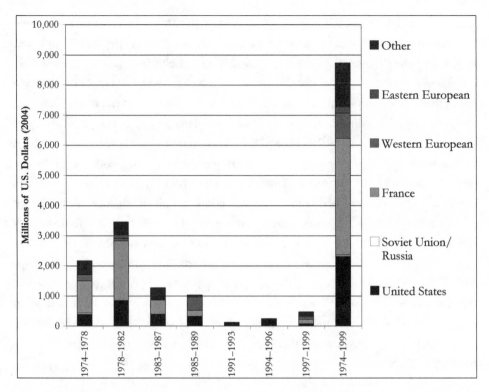

Fig. 1. Value of arms imports to Morocco by supplier, 1974–1999. Based on data compiled from U.S. Department of State 1980, 161; 1984, 95; 1989, 111; 1993, 131; 1996, 153; 1998, 55; 2001b, 158.

Africa, Morocco foremost among them. In October 1979, the White House announced that the United States would be providing $230 million in aircraft and helicopters for Morocco's counterinsurgency effort, including twenty F-5 jets, Cobra attack helicopters, and OV-10 spotter planes (Damis 1986, 15). Thus, direct U.S. arms sales deliveries grew from $33 million in 1977 to $86 million in 1978 and then to $133 million in 1979 (U.S. Department of Defense 1984, 10–11). By 1980, the United States had supplied close to $1 billion in arms to Rabat, mostly in the form of sales financed by Saudi Arabia (Volman 1980, 10). This support included clandestine shipments of U.S. arms through third parties. As early as February 27, 1976, the United States had arranged arms transfers from Jordan (twenty F-5As) and Iran (six F-5A fighter jets and sixteen 155-millimeter artillery pieces) (Kamil 1987, 31; U.S. Department of State 1976).

Unlike Carter, the Ronald Reagan administration (1981–89) did not hesitate to support Morocco. In fact, during his first week in office, Reagan approved the controversial sale of 108 M-60 battle tanks to Morocco (Damis 1986, 16). Following the October 1981 debacle in Galtah Zammur, a string of high-level U.S. officials visited the troubled Moroccan military, including Secretary of Defense Caspar Weinberger and his assistant, Francis West, along with Central Intelligence Agency (CIA) officials, Secretary of State Alexander

Haig, and General Vernon Walters. As the *New York Times* noted, "If the United States suddenly unleashes a cascade of Cabinet members on a friendly Arab nation, two possibilities suggest themselves. One is that the country is extremely important. The other is that its regime is in trouble" (Dec. 20, 1981). In the case of Morocco, it was both.

During the Reagan years, Morocco received specialized military hardware. Large C-130 aircraft with side-looking airborne radar were supplied, along with K-130 tanker planes for midair refueling, which enabled the Moroccan air force to track ELPS units for longer and farther. Morocco reportedly had some success using C-130s, thus denying the ELPS its treasured freedom of movement in the open desert (Dean 1986, 45). Morocco's C-130s also performed the vital task of resupplying isolated bases. In addition, Morocco received an increased supply of antipersonnel ordinance, including large amounts of CBU-58 and CBU-71 cluster bombs. Unlike U.S. shipments of such weapons to Israel, which carried stipulations as to their use (albeit rarely enforced), there were no such special restrictions for Morocco (*New York Times,* July 22, 1982; Sahrawi Red Crescent 1983). Although the Moroccan air force received the very expensive AGM-65 Maverick air-to-ground missile, this ordinance was used with only "limited success" on two known occasions (U.S. Central Intelligence Agency 1988, 45–46).

Between 1976 and 1984, the U.S. government spent an average of $1 million annually training Moroccan military officers, including specialized counterinsurgency commandos and pilots (Hodges 1985, 269; U.S. Department of Defense 1984, 82–83). By 1982, there were approximately 130 U.S. military advisors working with the Moroccan armed forces, including members of the U.S. Army's Special Forces and U.S. military attachés sighted in Moroccan uniforms in battle zones (Wright 1984, 167). By the end of the war, more than 1,500 Moroccans went to U.S. military bases for training through the International Military Education and Training Program for combat flying, counterinsurgency warfare, military command and control, and the use of American-supplied hardware (U.S. Department of Defense 1989, 86–87, 94–95; U.S. Department of Defense and U.S. Department of State 1990, 19).

In particular, the U.S. military worked closely with the Moroccan air force and FAR to provide intelligence. In testimony before the U.S. Congress in 1982, Moroccan officials acknowledged that the United States was providing Morocco with "technical assistance regarding Polisario movements and bases in the Western Sahara" (U.S. House 1982, 11). According to one study by the U.S. military, U.S. Air Force training for Moroccan pilots (especially in missile countermeasures and evasion) was coupled with "a concerted effort to locate the position of SA-6s operated by Polisario." At "considerable expense, US forces obtained specific intelligence data" on the location of Polisario antiaircraft missiles and provided it to the Moroccan government. The United States also sent a team to train a special battalion-size unit to launch commando-style raids against Polisario's SA-6 positions. Despite this assistance, "Morocco did not use efficient procedures to disseminate the information properly" and "[f]requently the timely intelligence obtained by the United States did not reach the south in time to do any good" (Dean 1986, 69).

Morocco had other arms suppliers as well: Egypt, pre-revolutionary Iran, Belgium, Italy, Jordan, Libya, Iraq, and Brazil. Even the former colonial administrator, Spain, provided military training and arms transfers to Polisario's foe. South Africa was one of Morocco's most controversial arms partners. Although Morocco did not boast about its relations with the apartheid government, in March 1980, at the battle of Ouarkziz, the ELPS captured six South African–built MK-6 armored reconnaissance vehicles, with visible markings in English and Afrikaans. Also captured were a number of AML-90MM armored vehicles also believed to be South African in origin because of technical characteristics different from the original models. Moroccan POWs captured in the same battle admitted being ordered to erase South African inscriptions from their weapons and reported that eight South African advisors had accompanied the equipment when it had arrived. In addition, there were other reports of South African advisers and technicians in Morocco, experienced in desert counterinsurgency warfare in Namibia (Harrel-Bond 1983, II:12–13). Such relations did little to advance Morocco's case against Polisario inside the OAU.

Foreign aid did not win the war for Morocco, but it had an impressive effect. As the war turned against Polisario in early 1980, Morocco was benefiting from a large influx of foreign support, especially from the United States. Yet, as shown earlier, the Moroccan military did not always use its arms, training, and intelligence with success. Although FAR grew to 130,000 soldiers by 1984 (International Institute for Strategic Studies 1986, 36), with more than half stationed in Western Sahara, it still could not absorb and utilize all the aid on offer. Between 1974 and 1985, for example, U.S. arms agreements with Morocco exceeded deliveries by $275 million (Damis 1986, 13). As we argue in chapters 2 and 3, the major effect of foreign aid has been to make Morocco's war and occupation affordable but not necessarily winnable. The military stalemate in Western Sahara, which came about by the mid-1980s, owes as much to Morocco's simplistic clear-and-hold strategy as to the billions of dollars in arms lavished on the kingdom.

TURNING THE TIDE: THE WALL

In 1981, Polisario reported that it had engaged Moroccan forces constructing a large "earthwork defense system." During the fight, the ELPS had blown up several "earthmoving machines" that were digging a double-walled trench (*Africa Confidential*, July 1, 1981). What Polisario was describing were the early phases in Morocco's revamped counterinsurgency effort. Instead of directly confronting Polisario, Morocco switched to an entirely defensive strategy. After making several strategic withdrawals in order to concentrate forces, it decided to build off of previous gains by slowly clearing land and holding it with well-defended barriers. Morocco had implicitly come to accept in the best case a long war of attrition or in the worst case total stalemate. A defensive posture, however, would minimize casualties and material losses. The war would become more affordable, while also allowing for the gradual establishment of a functional civilian administration in the most important parts of Western Sahara.

The use of barrier defenses in antiguerilla warfare has a long history, particularly in North Africa. The Italians used it during the subjugation of Libya in the early twentieth century in order to cut off Egyptian supplies and sanctuary in Egypt. The French had copied this tactic during the Algerian war of liberation (1954–62), attempting to separate the colony from support in the independent states of Morocco and Tunisia. The United States had set up a slightly different version along the demilitarized zone in Vietnam, and in a more conventional setting Israeli forces had established the Bar Lev line that was broken by the Egyptians in 1973 (Tusa 1988, 36). In the Western Saharan war, Morocco's defensive approach worked quite well. Whereas French and Italian barriers attempted to cut off the insurgents' extraterritorial supply lines, Morocco's Western Saharan barrier effectively kept the insurgents out and protected vital interests.

The foundation of Morocco's new strategy was primitively simple: sand, dirt, and stone embankments from three to six feet in height. The berms were then heavily mined on the Polisario side, topped with barbed wire, monitored by sophisticated electronic sensing devices, and guarded by an estimated 100,000 to 150,000 Moroccan soldiers, either in frontal guard positions or in rear rapid-reaction bases. So even if the walls were successfully breached, autonomous reaction forces would counterattack while the berm was resealed, making escape difficult for Polisario. At its final length, fifteen hundred miles, Morocco's "great wall" is the largest functional military barrier in the world, giving Morocco more or less absolute control over 80 percent of Western Sahara, leaving roughly twenty thousand square miles to Polisario (Copson 1994, 60). Furthermore, Moroccan forces have continually upgraded the wall, even under the auspices of a UN cease-fire since 1991.

Starting in 1981, successive walls were constructed in roughly six stages, until the final berm was completed in April 1987. The overall growth of the wall was outward from the useful triangle, but also down from southern Morocco into Western Sahara's eastern panhandle. The last two berms sealed off Dakhla and then reached the southern border with Mauritania. The wall stretches from near Akka, in southern Morocco, to Lagwirah at the Mauritanian border on the Atlantic. For two main reasons, Morocco did not build the wall directly on the border. First, whenever possible, Morocco used hilltops and ridges so as to have command of the highest ground possible. Second, FAR wanted to have small pockets of territory where it could engage Polisario units without violating international borders. However, the wall does cross into Mauritania at two points: along the southern border of Western Sahara and north of Bir Moghrein, the latter effectively separating the northern and southern Polisario-controlled zones (maps 1 and 3).

Map 3. Western Sahara, 2009. Based on UN maps.

The wall was not without its problems for Morocco. Attacks inside defended areas were possible after small ELPS units removed mines, stripped away the wall's barbed wire, and subverted its electronic detection devises. Indeed, the highly touted radar systems and electronic sensors provided by the United States and France tended not to work in the searing heat and the frequent sandstorms.[2] Sahrawi fighters would sometimes simply dig up mines and move them to the Moroccan side. If the wall was secretly penetrated, the ELPS could attack Moroccan posts from their undefended rear. The fixed Moroccan positions on the edge were also vulnerable to Polisario bombardment and unable to withdraw or mount an assault without leaving portions of the wall undefended. Polisario would often attack different areas of the wall simultaneously, thus diverting Morocco's rapid-reaction forces so that the ELPS could carry out an attack inside Western Sahara.

Overall, though, the wall worked, and Morocco's combat engineers—often working under fire—became the unsung heroes of the war. Troop and material losses were minimized, giving FAR a desperately needed morale boost. Conversely, the wall demoralized the ELPS's fighters, although Polisario denied that the berms were an impediment. Despite such boasting, it was clear that Morocco had won an advantageous position, even if neither side achieved outright victory. The economic costs continued to be high for Morocco, but Rabat's grip on Western Sahara was firmer than it had ever been (Copson 1994, 61).

Between the construction of the outer berm in the early 1980s and the 1991 UN cease-fire, the war in Western Sahara was far less intense. As the armed struggle began to take the form of a stalemate, there were numerous cessations of hostilities to create space for diplomatic initiatives. Following King Hassan's 1981 announcement that he would allow an OAU-organized referendum on independence, a truce held throughout 1982. When the political situation deteriorated in mid-1983, Polisario resumed attacks in July, first hitting Lamsayyad (Lemseied) in southern Morocco. During the month-long engagement, the ELPS barraged Moroccan positions with Soviet-made rockets. This bombardment was followed by a massive, fifty-kilometer-wide mechanized ELPS assault near Smara in September. A month later the ELPS downed a Moroccan F-1 mirage. All the while, Morocco patiently worked to expand its berms.

Although RASD's 1984 ascension into the OAU was a major political coup for Polisario, Morocco countered by signing the Treaty of Oujda with Libya, in which Libya agreed not to challenge Morocco's claim on Western Sahara and to continue a previously self-imposed embargo on arms to Polisario (*Africa Report,* Nov. 1984). In fact, the most substantial arms transfers had been between 1979 and 1982. During peak Libyan support for Polisario, Mu'ammar Qadhdhafi's role in the conflict was still less than Algeria's. Libya even refused to recognize RASD until April 1980, presumably because support for pan-Arab unity contradicted the idea of supporting a new state. Even when Libya did formally recognize RASD, Qadhdhafi still expressed his preference for a voluntary union between Mauritania and Western Sahara (*Africa Confidential,* July 25, 1981; Hodges 1983b, 326–27). A 1983 seven-nation study by a U.S. congressional group acknowledged that even during the height of Libyan aid to Polisario, it was "under the general supervision of Algeria" (U.S. House 1983, 37). One Polisario leader claimed, albeit after the Oujda Treaty, that the Libyans "would promise a lot and give little" (quoted in *Newsday,* May 12, 1987). Although King Hassan later revoked the treaty in August 1986—much to the Reagan administration's relief—there was no evidence of renewed Libyan military support of Polisario.

Two years after the Oujda Treaty, Algeria was also forced to reduce aid to Polisario. When global hydrocarbon prices collapsed in 1986, the Algerian economy—already faltering after years of poor management—took a nosedive. Algerian arms purchases fell substantially from their 1982 high. Because Algerian state spending was cut across the board, aid to Polisario was reduced as well. ELPS had done some stockpiling, but the quantitative and qualitative decline in Algerian and Libyan material support limited the number of active fighters and military initiatives Polisario could support. During the same period, internal strife within Polisario led to some high-profile defections in the late 1980s and poor morale in the lower ranks (Zunes, briefing with U.S. military attaché, Rabat, Morocco, June 1990).

By 1984, the effect of the berms on the ELPS was noticeable. Early in the war, Polisario was able to run many political and military operations inside Western Sahara, even seating a provisional capital as deep as Hawzah. By the late 1980s, however, Polisario could no longer risk such a presence. Its freedom of movement was severely constrained tactically. Although the ELPS could still choose when to engage, Morocco had drastically shrunk the number and value of targets as well as options for retreat. Polisario attacks in the last few years of the war were clearly timed for political rather than military effect.

The ELPS's 1984 initiatives against FAR included areas around Dakhla and Argoub in southern Western Sahara and intense fighting in southern Morocco near Zag before a berm sealed it off. Polisario was able to down another F-1 in early 1985, and in August it hit Moroccan positions close to Mahbas and Awsard, which were not yet behind the berm. In 1986, the ELPS reportedly attacked near Galtah Zammur, Farsiyah, Hawzah, and Jdriya. An early 1987 ELPS offensive in the Mahbas–Farsiyah region mobilized more than one hundred armored personnel carriers and SA-6s, resulting in two hundred Moroccans dead. This battle would, however, be the only major one of the year, ending with a temporary cease-fire to allow a UN fact-finding mission. The calm ended in early 1988 when the ELPS attacked the berm near Um Draygah (Oum Dreiga), which was repeated in September. The following year started with another cease-fire, during which Morocco and Polisario held their first direct talks in January. That truce was off by March, yet Polisario attacks later in the year were exclusively against the wall near Galtah Zammur and Amgala. The 1990s began with a cease-fire that managed to hold. With the creation of the UN referendum mission in April 1991, the calm held until that August, when Morocco launched a series of attacks to destroy several Polisario facilities in its section of Western Sahara. To keep the conflict from escalating, the UN secretary-general decided unilaterally to declare a cease-fire, which both sides have chosen to respect since September 6, 1991.[3]

THE IMPACT OF THE WAR

The war in Western Sahara was over long before the 1991 cease-fire. By 1986, Polisario's leader, Mohammed Abdelaziz, admitted that victory by arms was "more than difficult, if not impossible" (quoted in *Africa Report,* May–June 1986). Geography and norms largely structured the stalemate. Without a radical revision of strategy, neither side could possibly assert total military victory. The only options left were largely unthinkable. For Rabat, destroying the ELPS would require an invasion of Algeria and Mauritania. For the Sahrawi guerillas, urban warfare and terrorism were possibilities, but they rejected these tactics.

The relatively "clean" or conventional nature of the warfare in Western Sahara also helped engender international ignorance and indifference to the situation. Estimates of the total deaths in the war, including civilians, range from 6,000 to 16,000 (Copson 1994, 59; *Los Angeles Times,* Mar. 7, 1992). In 1988, Morocco claimed it had lost only 2,500 men (*Christian Science Monitor,* Aug. 12, 1988). There are no reliable estimates for Polisario casualties, although one prominent defector claimed as many as 3,000 deaths (Zunes, interview with Omar Hadrami, Madrid, 1990). Compared to other asymmetric conflicts of that period (e.g., in Africa and Latin America), the war in Western Sahara was relatively bloodless and so rendered uninteresting by an international media environment driven by spectacular images of horror and misery.

For both Morocco and Polisario, however, the war in Western Sahara had lasting effects that shaped the subsequent peace process. During the war, the Moroccan regime discovered that it would not be punished internationally for its belligerent and intransigent behavior in Western Sahara. Since 1975, its actions have been variously tolerated, condoned, and even supported by its allies. King Hassan, assured of his bases of support in the West, entered into a UN peace process feeling assured that his two friends on the Security Council—France and the United States—would never hold him accountable for attempting to subvert the referendum, not to mention for invading Western Sahara in the first place. The same has held for Hassan's successor, King Mohammed VI.

The second lasting consequence of the war was its galvanizing effect on Western Saharan nationalism. During nearly twenty years of armed struggle, first with Spain and then with Morocco, Western Saharan nationalism transformed from an idea into the lived practice for thousands of Sahrawis, who found in it a reason for living and dying. For some time to come, the war will be a source of meaning and memories that will fuel the drive for independence. Polisario's refusal to compromise on the question of a referendum on independence is largely justified by the fact that the project of Western Saharan nationalism continues to grow in strength.

Through 2008, the stalemated peace process in Western Sahara owes much to the stalemated war. By the mid-1980s, the war was intractable, but this intractability was highly sustainable for both sides. It can be contrasted with a situation of unsustainable intractability, where both sides grow weaker (i.e., William Zartman's [1989] distinction between hurting and nonhurting stalemates). Under the latter conditions, there is a compelling incentive to make concessions at the negotiating table because the cost of compromise is less than the costs incurred from fighting. In 1991, the Western Sahara situation was the opposite. The war had obtained sustainable intractability, with both sides becoming stronger as the war became more protracted. There was thus little incentive to make fundamental concessions because the heavy cost of such compromise was nowhere near the relatively light cost of waging war. The only reason Polisario and Morocco entered into the UN peace process was the offer of a winner-take-all solution: a referendum on independence or full integration. Victory by arms had become impossible for Morocco and Polisario, yet the UN proposed victory by other means. The two sides' acquiescence to the 1991 peace process could rightly be described as a case of deescalation. As Louis Kriesberg has theorized, however, "Those decreases [i.e., in severity of means] are not always a prelude to a conflict's ending" (1998, 181). William Zartman and Johannes Aurik have also noted that "a decision to de-escalate . . . may mean the continuation of the conflict more cheaply" (1991, 156).

FAREWELL TO ARMS?

The cease-fire in Western Sahara has held steady since its enactment in 1991. The closest the two sides have come to firing angry shots at each other was almost ten years later. The year 2000 held major setbacks for Polisario, which was angry at the UN for abandoning the long-promised referendum on independence. Polisario's leadership soon warned that if the UN did not put the referendum back on track, then they would have to consider a return to fighting. In April 2000, Polisario official Brahim Mokhtar cautioned, it "will be a matter for the Polisario and Morocco to deal with and it will be worse than anything the western countries are expecting" (*The Middle East,* April 2000, 22). Since 1991, Polisario had made similar claims when things were not going its way, so the UN had little reason to take Polisario seriously then. During the 1990s, most observers and policymakers assumed that Algeria, debilitated by internal armed conflict, would not support a return to war in Western Sahara.

In early 2001, however, Polisario unilaterally mobilized all of its forces, almost overnight. The reason for this mass deployment, as numerous media reports claimed, was the planned route for the 2001 Paris–Dakar Rally, which would take the race from Moroccan-occupied Western Sahara to Mauritania via a Polisario-controlled area. The rally planned to cross from the Moroccan zone through a gate in the berm near Smara on January 7. Although previous rallies had gone through Western Sahara with Polisario's permission, organizers in 2000 made the mistake of consulting only the Moroccan government and the UN mission in Western Sahara.

Polisario's mobilization, however, was really for a much more substantial reason. In preparation for the rally's crossing, the Moroccan military sent a special demining unit into the UN-mandated five-kilometer buffer zone between the berm and Polisario's side of the territory. The Moroccan deployment's mission was to search for landmines and clear a route for the rally. In the process, however, FAR fired warning shots toward

Polisario positions and thus seriously violated the cease-fire. Polisario demanded that the UN halt the rally and reprimand the Moroccan government. When the UN failed to act, Polisario warned that it had no other recourse but to resume military operations to protect its territory.

Shortly before the January 7 deadline, Polisario mobilized the majority of its fighting force in a twenty-four-hour period, catching UN military observers off guard. The UN could no longer account for any elements of the ELPS. Polisario's forces had moved to positions near the berm, spaced at thirty-kilometer intervals along the entire length. According to Polisario officials and military officers, once media outlets reported the Polisario's mobilization, dozens of Western Saharans living in Europe began flying to Tindouf. The Moroccan military responded by mobilizing a large number of its forces and called in units from as far as Agadir. Polisario was apparently so serious that it prepared some of its settlements for Moroccan aerial bombardment; the hospital in Tifariti, for example, was cleared of its expensive equipment (Bhatia 2001, 293).

A spate of high-level diplomatic activity involving the French and U.S. governments as well as the African Union and UN secretary-general Kofi Annan put pressure on the Algerian government to stop Polisario. The crisis came to an end when Algerian chief of staff General Mohamed Lamari intervened directly with Polisario's leader Mohammed Abdelaziz. Shortly thereafter, Polisario backed down, officially citing the rally's cooperation as its reason (Mundy, interviews with ELPS commanders, Tifariti, Western Sahara, Sept. 5–6, 2003). Since then, neither Polisario nor the Moroccan government has come nearly as close to a resumption of armed fighting, although calls for war within Polisario grew considerably between the 2003 and 2007 national congresses.

With the further deterioration of the peace process in recent years, the prospects for a new war in Western Sahara have likely increased. Yet, for the Moroccan regime, there would be little to accomplish from any military action except to extend total control over the rest of Western Sahara. Especially since 2005, Morocco's diplomatic approach has been tactically concessionary under Rabat's autonomy proposal, formally presented in 2007. Any armed aggression would undermine the positive diplomatic gains Morocco has made in recent years. This is not to suggest that Morocco is not in a position to fight back if Polisario fires the first shots. Although Morocco's military is idle in Western Sahara, it is still estimated at roughly 100,000 strong and increasingly modernized.

A new war in Western Sahara will likely depend much more on the Sahrawi nationalists' political willingness for such a war. For Polisario, the Algerian government's consent seems requisite; for now, though, such consent seems far from forthcoming. Without Algerian backing, Polisario would still be able to wage basic guerilla warfare, procuring supplies on the black market. In recent years, West Africa and North Africa have seen their share of small wars, and there are plenty of weapons that might easily find their way into Polisario hands if needed. Self-financing, also, is an option for Polisario, given the growth of a market economy in the refugee camps and the importance of remittances from the Sahrawi diaspora in Europe (see chapter 5).

More important than arms, however, is motivation. After years of false promises from the international community, the Western Saharan refugees seem more than willing to contemplate returning to armed struggle. One finds—in the refugee camps and among some Polisario officials—a widely held belief that the Moroccan regime will surrender only if forced to do so militarily. Polisario's high-level leaders, in contrast, spend much of their domestic energies trying to convince the refugees that diplomacy can still work and that the time is not yet right for war.

Despite the militancy of the protest movement spawned in May 2005—the Sahrawi intifada—many Western Saharan nationalists, especially Polisario's elite, realize that the nonviolent nature of the movement has the potential to bring heavy international scorn upon Morocco, given the brutal manner in which the Moroccan security forces have historically reacted to free expression (see chapter 6). A new war would likely undermine the intifada by giving Morocco an excuse to repress the demonstrations, organizations, and activists with impunity. However, the intifada has also created a potential flashpoint that may trigger a new war. The more Morocco resorts to blunt coercion to control nationalists, the more sentiments in the camps favor armed struggle in defense. As tensions have increased in the occupied territory, they have also increased across the berm, with Polisario's leadership finding itself hard pressed to restrain its forces. Furthermore, in the context of a new war, radicalized Sahrawi youths, facing sure Moroccan repression, might become a new urban front, which may easily slip into terrorism. The potential for a self-reinforcing dynamic leading to terrorism and a dirty war in Western Sahara exists.

If there has to be war, Polisario's military wing feels that it is still up to the challenge.[4] Cease-fire observers with the UN mission in Western Sahara likewise feel that the ELPS should be taken seriously, given the seamless transfer of knowledge between veterans and new recruits. Even under the UN cease-fire, Polisario's forces are allowed to train on a daily basis. Newer and less-experienced soldiers train with battle-tested veterans, often their own relatives. At any given time, two-thirds of Polisario's forces are on "active duty" in positions parallel to the berm, either training or watching the Moroccan forces on the other side.

The current estimated size of the ELPS is at least 3,000 to 6,000 soldiers (International Institute for Strategic Studies 2003, 113), although a 2001 survey noted that the number of possible fighters might be "an order of magnitude greater" (Bhatia 2001, 294). If the ELPS were indeed able to mobilize most of its fighting-age males sixteen years of age and older, then the total strength would potentially be 15,000 to 20,000, based on camp and referendum registration figures. The ELPS also maintains a number of heavy armaments and numerous types of surface-to-air missiles (International Institute for Strategic Studies 2003, 113). For these reasons and not for any lack of willingness, Polisario officials, military leaders, and soldiers on the ground are confident that they can successfully pursue a military option in the future.

It is difficult to see where Polisario's optimism comes from, though. The most important factor in a new war—the Western response—will likely be unfavorable. As will be seen in coming chapters, France and the United States have never truly deviated from their pro-Moroccan stance, always prioritizing Morocco's stability above other considerations. Should the toxic status quo erupt into a new war, what role will Paris and Washington assume? Will the West come to Morocco's aid, as it did in the 1970s and 1980s, supplying critical arms and diplomatic support to the Moroccan occupation? Based on recent and historical trends, these questions should be answered in the affirmative.

# 2

# Arab Maghrib Disunity

*Algeria and Morocco*

For the purposes of this study, it is useful to consider how the Western Sahara conflict has operated within three frames. At the local level, there is the fundamental conflict between Morocco and Western Saharan nationalists. At the regional level, preexisting tensions between Rabat and Algiers have been exacerbated by Algeria's support for Polisario. At the international level, certain states and international bodies have attempted to influence the conflict, either directly or indirectly. Although sometimes useful, these frames are not hard realities. In this chapter, we are most concerned with the middle frame: Morocco and Algeria. Here we examine the historical origins of their enmity, the development of their respective roles in the conflict, the logics behind their positions, and the effects of the conflict on them. Looking at Morocco and Algeria through the optic of Western Sahara and looking at Western Sahara through the prism of Algiers and Rabat are important steps toward any understanding of the evolution and perpetuation of the conflict, although they by no means tell the entire story.

In our explication of the Moroccan and Algerian dimensions, we devote much more attention to Morocco, both domestically and internationally, than to Algeria. The prime reason for this bias is obvious: Western Sahara is more important to Morocco than it is to Algeria. In many ways, the history of Morocco since independence has become intricately intertwined with the fate of the former Spanish Sahara. We believe that our detailed study of Morocco's internal politics is warranted by the interrelationship between the Western Sahara conflict and Morocco's troubled development as an independent nation-state. Morocco's instability vis-à-vis Western Sahara—both real and perceived—is a major consideration at the international level, especially in Paris and Washington, and thus deserves serious attention.

Assessing Algeria's role in the conflict has always been highly politicized. For many Moroccans and their partisans, the Western Sahara conflict is fundamentally a Moroccan–Algerian conflict. In its most grotesque form, this argument asserts that Polisario is a mere device of Algeria's strategic interests. In a more sophisticated variant, it claims that Western Saharan nationalism would not exist if not for generous Algerian aid. For this reason, among others, Morocco has sought to negotiate with Algeria, not Polisario, over the fate of Western Sahara. We reject this argument for several reasons. First, although Algeria has played a major role in the dispute between Western Saharan nationalism and Morocco, Western Saharan nationalism predates Algeria's support for it. Second, far weaker nationalist movements have survived and sometimes succeeded without strong backing from a neighboring state (e.g., in East Timor and Eritrea). Finally, this argument not only aims to undermine the legitimacy of Western Saharan nationalism, but also elides the importance of Morocco's backers as well. The Western Sahara conflict owes as much to the influence of Morocco's supporters as to the influence of Algeria, if not more. As the previous chapter argued, Algeria did not start the war, and as will be seen in the final chapters, a Moroccan–Algerian agreement is not sufficient for the conflict's resolution.

We begin here by recounting Moroccan–Algerian relations before the war in Western Sahara, followed by an in-depth look at the material and ideational facets of Morocco's interest in Western Sahara. The idea of Greater Morocco, coupled with the unremitting socioeconomic and political crises of legitimacy, power, and government in postcolonial Morocco, lie behind Morocco's seizure and occupation of Western Sahara. We juxtapose this analysis with an explanation of Algerian support for Western Saharan nationalism, which has its own reasons. We then take a look at Morocco's domestic and international policies during the war and recount the efforts to build a transnational North African union, how those efforts played into the peace process in the late 1980s, and how they have so far failed to achieve a North African confederation and peace in Western Sahara. We then return to Morocco following the 1991 cease-fire, to the death of Hassan II in 1999, and the years under the new king. We conclude the chapter by analyzing at the regional level the dynamics that contribute to the irresolution of the Western Sahara conflict.

## MOROCCAN–ALGERIAN RELATIONS BEFORE THE WAR

Tension between Algiers and Rabat predated King Hassan's seizure and occupation of Western Sahara. Twelve years before Algeria decided to back Polisario in 1975, Morocco went to war against Algeria over a disputed border region. As discussed more fully later, Morocco has never accepted its colonially inherited frontiers, especially those with Algeria. This problem is most acute in the Sahara. The colonial border was clearly demarcated from the Mediterranean coast to the Figuig–Bechar area; south of that, the French administrations in Morocco and Algeria never established clear divisions of sovereignty until very late. The Dra'a River was sometimes treated as one of Morocco's "natural limits" (Reyner 1963, 317–18), yet the long-standing Moroccan 'Alawi dynasty had originated from just beyond that river, in the oases of southeastern Morocco and southwestern Algeria.

French colonial maps were often inconsistent, and administrative divisions were regularly mistaken for delineations of sovereignty. Often as an effect of competition between the French "colony" of Algeria and the "protectorate" of Morocco, the Moroccan–Algerian frontier suffered numerous adjustments and readjustments after its first demarcation in 1845 through the Treaty of Lalla Marnia. Later modifications included the 1901 and 1902 Franco–Moroccan protocols, which extended Morocco's border southward; the 1912 administrative line, drawn by Maurice Varnier, high commissioner for eastern Morocco; the five North African Conferences in the 1920s, which aimed to resolve border issues; the 1929 Confins algéro–marocains (Algerian–Moroccan Borders), which provided for a joint security-administration arrangement along Morocco's southeastern Saharan border (without addressing definitive sovereignty); and then the final Limite opérationnelle (Operational Limit) set in 1958—two years after Moroccan independence—during heavy guerilla activity emanating from Morocco, Spanish Sahara, and Algeria. The result was a balance that clearly favored Algeria over Morocco, engendering resentment and irredentist desires in the latter.

In particular, the Tindouf plain was central to the dispute, which first came under French control in 1934 when a Colonel Trinquet (first name unknown), arriving from Morocco, occupied it. The only sizeable oasis in the area, Tindouf was seen as a necessary strategic point for policing the wide-ranging Sahrawi confederation of the Rgaybat al-Sharq, whose raids (al-ghazi) frequently harassed colonial interests in Morocco, Algeria, and Spanish Sahara. The ambiguity of the 1929 Confins and the French occupation of Tindouf later provided Moroccan irredentists with several useful facts: Tindouf was administered from Agadir, Morocco, until 1952; Moroccan colonial soldiers manned posts around Tindouf until 1950; and colonial salaries were paid in Moroccan currency as late as 1960 (Damis 1983, 17).

In early 1956, as Paris was preparing to quit Morocco, there was an effort to solidify the 1929 boundary. This border was a rough compromise to meet the demands of French administrators in Rabat and Algiers and roughly corresponded to a line *proposed* by Trinquet in the 1930s. An early study of Morocco's postcolonial borders noted, "Although the French Government rejected this proposal to enlarge Morocco, *le projet Trinquet* became the basis of Moroccan territorial claims against Algeria" (Reyner 1963, 316–17; see also Trout 1969, 317–23). However, following the outbreak of the Algerian war for independence in 1954 and a 1957–58 trans-Saharan uprising, the French army in Algeria assumed positions on Morocco's side of the 1929 line. With reservation, independent Morocco stayed behind this Limite opérationnelle as France fought the Algerians (see Joffé 1987).

At that time, French motivations went beyond security. In the early 1950s, high-grade iron ore deposits and potential oil and gas reserves were discovered in western Algeria. French authorities made sure that the area between Bechar and Tindouf was more clearly incorporated into Algeria. Because Morocco was a protectorate, eventual independence was a given by the 1950s; but Algeria, as a province of France, would remain French. Ironically, as the Algerian war for independence became more intense, French authorities offered Rabat the Bechar–Tindouf region, with all its mineral wealth, in exchange for security cooperation against Algerian guerilla bases in Morocco. Instead, the Moroccan regime supported the Algerians, led by the Front de libération nationale (FLN, National Liberation Front), who had promised to renegotiate the border in exchange for Moroccan support. Rabat went as far as to back Algeria's territorial integrity against a cynical French proposal to cede northern Algeria to the FLN while retaining the resource-rich South as a "French Siberia." However, as soon as Algeria achieved independence in July 1962, President Ahmed Ben Bella refused to discuss its border with Morocco.

The irredentism of Greater Morocco had suffered a huge blow following Mauritania's independence in 1960, and King Hassan, who had inherited all his country's problems but little of his father's legitimacy in 1961, was in need of military credentials and a national diversion. Border clashes, expulsions, and small land grabs between Morocco and Algeria commenced in the summer of 1962. The situation boiled over in September 1963, when a large Moroccan force invaded Tindouf. Algeria responded by seizing vulnerable Moroccan lands around Figuig. Had Egyptian president Gamal Abdul Nasser not rushed aid to Algeria, the Moroccan conquest might have been successful. At an October conference in Mali, Ethiopian emperor Haile Selassie, through the auspices of the OAU, convinced the two sides to return to their prewar positions. Although Morocco claimed military victory on the battlefield, the Algerian government easily won the diplomatic war. Status quo ante was restored through an OAU arbitration commission. Algeria made its final feelings on the matter quite clear in November 1963. Foreign Minister Abdelaziz Bouteflika stated, "Our borders are incontestable for we have paid for them with our blood" (quoted in Trout 1969, 426–28).

Moroccan–Algerian relations were quickly "normalized" in 1964 and diplomatically rehabilitated over the following decade. A January 1969 treaty of solidarity and cooperation signed in Ifrane, Morocco, was the first major step, followed by a 1970 joint communiqué announcing a border commission. With Morocco's belated recognition of Mauritania in 1969, King Hassan, President Boumedienne of Algeria (who had seized power in a 1965 coup), and President Ould Daddah of Mauritania held a trilateral summit in Nouadhibou, Mauritania, in September 1970. All three backed UN calls for the decolonization of Spanish Sahara. A Moroccan–Algerian border was finalized in a June 1972 treaty. Although based on the Limite opérationnelle, it offered joint exploitation of the resources around Tindouf. Another trilateral summit was held in Agadir, Morocco, in 1973, where all sides again called for respect for the right of self-determination in Spanish Sahara. King Hassan, who withheld final ratification of the border, likely made these territorial "concessions" to gain Algerian support on Western Sahara (Joffé 1987).

When Spain announced in 1974 that it was preparing for a referendum in Western Sahara and setting up an interim autonomous regime, Morocco and Mauritania were forced to reconsider their support for self-determination. King Hassan, with Mauritania's president in tow, demanded that the ICJ consider Morocco's historical claim. Algeria, at first, did not distance itself from Rabat's repudiation of self-determination. At the October 1974 Arab League summit in Rabat, Hassan and Ould Daddah apparently reached an understanding on a division of Spanish Sahara, with Boumedienne's blessing. At that time, Algeria did not seem enthusiastic about Polisario, having even deported its leaders on occasion, thus leaving it with just Libya as its primary support. Morocco also continued to withhold final ratification of the 1972 border treaty with Algeria. Then, at an April 1975 ministerial of the Arab League, Algeria's foreign minister, Bouteflika, contradicted the Moroccan position on Western Sahara. Two months later, as Bouteflika and his Moroccan counterpart, Ahmed Laraki, were shuttling between Rabat and Algiers to hammer out the border agreement, Boumedienne reaffirmed that Algeria's foreign policy was guided by self-determination. By July, however, Bouteflika believed he had won Moroccan ratification of the 1972 border, and so it seemed that Boumedienne had once again given his blessing to a Moroccan–Mauritanian takeover (Parker 1987, 110–11). Yet in front of the ICJ that summer, Algeria argued forcefully for self-determination and the right of other states to intervene in favor of that principle.

As the situation in Western Sahara deteriorated in October 1975 with the announcement of the Green March, the previous decade of Moroccan–Algerian détente was undone. Boumedienne attempted to block the Moroccan invasion of Western Sahara, pressing Spain and even personally threatening Ould Daddah as the Green March was under way. When that failed and the Madrid Agreement was concluded, Boumedienne decided to back Polisario's war. From his point of view, Western powers had conspired to help King Hassan redraw the map of North Africa and had done so without consulting Algeria. This was too much of an affront for a respected Middle Eastern and African country, an aspiring regional hegemon, and a leader of the Nonaligned Movement to ignore. As a matter of face saving and international credibility, Algeria could no longer retreat from self-determination. Yet the war in Western Sahara also provided it with a golden opportunity to pursue its strategic interests indirectly. As one Algerian official claimed in early 1976, "We're going to bleed Hassan white" (quoted in Parker 1987, 113).

IRREDENTIST DREAMS, INTERNAL CRISIS:
BEHIND THE MOROCCAN OCCUPATION

Western Sahara's significant phosphate reserves are often cited as Morocco's primary, if not only, motivation for invading Western Sahara. King Hassan rejected this suggestion, though (Hassan II 1978, 163, cited in Shelley 2006, 19), and there are credible reasons to believe him. At the time of the 1975 invasion, Morocco was already the world's preeminent exporter of phosphates, which, among other uses, is a key ingredient for modern agriculture. Morocco has eleven billion tons in working phosphate reserves and potentially fifty-eight billion more, giving it between half (Rosemarin 2004, 31) and three-quarters of the world's known reserves (Economist Intelligence Unit 2005, 39–40). The addition of Western Sahara's high-grade deposits has only slightly enhanced Morocco's already dominant position in the world market.

Western Sahara's phosphates cost Morocco much more in terms of protection than their initial worth. The isolated Bukra' mine and the even more vulnerable conveyor belt connecting it to the port of al-'Ayun were initially very difficult to guard. By 1977, Polisario attacks had stopped all production. Adding insult to injury, world phosphate process collapsed in the late 1970s, which hit the Moroccan economy hard. Following improvements in the berms, the mines finally returned to normal service in 1982. Yet Morocco's state-owned phosphate company, Office chérifien des phosphates (Sharifian Phosphate Office), failed to turn a profit in Western Sahara between 1986 and 1996. Shortly after the cease-fire, it was reported that Morocco kept the Bukra' mines open just to keep the workers employed (*Los Angeles Times,* Nov. 9, 1991).

Although phosphates do not sufficiently explain Morocco's desire to seize Spanish Sahara, they now provide Morocco with ample motivation to hold on to it. According to the UN Environmental Program (2008), satellite imagery taken between 1987 and 2007 reveals that Morocco has expanded the size of the mine more than three times. The Europe-based organization Western Sahara Resource Watch believes that, with annual exports from Bukra' estimated between 1.5 to 3.0 million tons, Morocco is possibly earning $80 to $150 million from Bukra' each year (personal communication from Western Sahara Resource Watch to Jacob Mundy, Oct. 10, 2007). The price of raw phosphate quadrupled globally over the course of 2007 and 2008, a trend driven by increasing need for fertilizers to grow alternative fuels. When the world's largest consumer of phosphates, the United States, exhausts its domestic reserves in three decades, and as global populations rise, demand will only increase.

Western Sahara's fisheries are just as important. With some of the richest grounds in all of Africa, fishing has been the most profitable aspect of Morocco's occupation, contributing significantly—perhaps two-thirds—to the almost $1 billion earned by Rabat annually from this sector (Shelley 2006, 18). For the Moroccan government, Western Sahara has become more and more lucrative as the status quo ossified under the 1991 UN cease-fire. Likewise, the prospect of oil and gas in Western Sahara, amidst a global scramble for previously unprofitable hydrocarbon sources, has only added further incentive to control Western Sahara. Mauritania's 2006 entry into the world of hydrocarbon-exporting countries highlighted this fact.

Although economic motivations have changed through time, ideational and political rationale have remained constant. In other words, Morocco was willing to invade Western Sahara—and then has been willing to occupy it for years at great cost—because of a postcolonial national identity based on irredentism and the regime's need to consolidate itself, especially the monarchy. Regarding the former, the postcolonial Moroccan state has been predicated on the idea that Spain and, mainly, France excised large parts of Morocco's territory during the protectorate. The dangers of this belief were apparent early on to scholar Douglas Ashford, who noted in 1962 that "[t]he major shortcoming of the irredentist appeal, in terms of the long-run development of the new nation, is its irremovable and irreconcilable character. Almost any other political issue offers more opportunity for compromise and adjustment to new circumstances. In the Moroccan case one finds that the more remote the chances of fulfilling the goal became, the more intense and widespread were the demands" (650). The drawback, as Ashford well predicted, was that Morocco would commit its postcolonial national identity to a "quixotic venture" marked by "futility and costliness" (1962, 651).

"Greater Morocco" did not originate with the monarchy, but with Moroccan nationalist leader 'Allal al-Fassi. As Morocco was approaching independence from France (and Spain) in 1956, al-Fasi asserted that colonialism had truncated the "real" extent of Morocco. In July of that year, a map of "Greater Morocco" appeared in the newspaper of al-Fasi's Istiqlal (Independence) Party, the right-wing heir of the independence movement. This map showed Morocco with a border encompassing large parts of western Algeria, a section of northern Mali (150,000 square miles), all of Mauritania, and, of course, Spanish Sahara (see map 4). The paper also ran an article explaining the strategic and economic value of the natural resources in the areas that Morocco should annex (Reyner 1963, 314). Al-Fasi successfully pushed the issue to center stage in Morocco's foreign relations. In February 1958 near the Algerian border, in the small Saharan town of M'hammid, south of Zagora, Mohammed V declared that Morocco should work toward "the return of the Sahara in accordance with respect for our historic rights and the will of its inhabitants" (quoted in Zartman 1963, 46). That same year in Tangier, delegations from Tunisia and French-occupied Algeria recognized, with respect to French Mauritania and Spanish Sahara, Morocco's "historic and ethnic unity" (Ashford 1962, 647). King Mohammed V even created the Direction des affaires sahariennes et frontalières (Directorate of Saharan and Border Affairs), which protested Mauritania's independence in 1960. Yet in a world where colonial borders were being treated as sacrosanct, such claims were entirely rebuffed.

Following the death of his father in 1961, King Hassan II continued to champion the thesis of Greater Morocco. However, in the period between his botched seizure of Tindouf in 1963 and his 1974–75 campaign to take Western Sahara, his actions were mostly symbolic, aimed at pleasing elite domestic constituencies. The claim on northern Mali was never seriously pursued, and good relations with Spanish dictator Franco, stemming from a 1963 summit in Spain, were given priority, muting any claims to Spanish Sahara. Substantively, Hassan did create a ministry for Mauritanian and Saharan affairs in 1965, but it was soon abandoned in 1969 when Morocco recognized Mauritania. In parallel, Hassan

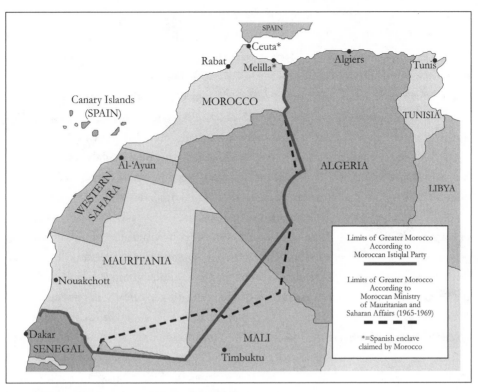

Map 4. Greater Morocco. Based on U.S. CIA map.

repaired relations with Algeria and began hammering out a border agreement. Morocco, having abandoned most of its claim for territory it considered part of Greater Morocco, felt that such compromise entitled it to Western Sahara.

Like the Greater Morocco thesis, the fractured Moroccan polity dates to the transition from colony to independent nation. The amicable union between Moroccan nationalists under Istiqlal and traditionalist elements led by King Mohammed V soon fell apart. Elements of the anticolonial struggle contested the shape of the country's first government, especially the king's role in that government. Although King Mohammed V incorporated members of the Istiqlal and the older Parti démocratique et de l'indépendence (Democratic Independence Party) into his first cabinet, he resisted holding elections or implementing a constitution. Following large labor strikes amidst stagnating economic conditions in 1958, the progressive wing of Istiqlal broke off to form the Union nationale des forces populaires (UNFP, National Union of Popular Forces), under the leadership of Mehdi Ben Barka and with the support of the country's largest trade federation, the Union marocaine de travail (Moroccan Labor Union). Although the monarchy tolerated the socialist-leaning UNFP, the Moroccan Communist Party was banned in 1959 (but later regrouped into the Parti de libération et socialisme [Liberation and Socialism Party]).

As the threat posed by the socialist opposition became too strong to ignore, Mohammed's regime arrested sixty members of the UNFP for allegedly plotting to kill Prince Hassan and expelled all UNFP members from government. Subsequent UNFP victories in local elections drove King Mohammed to declare himself prime minister.

In some rural areas, small but notable uprisings plagued the consolidating regime. The first, in 1957, took place in the province of Errachidia in southeastern Morocco. This uprising was followed by one in the North, in the Rif Mountains from 1958 to 1959. In 1960, there was a smaller uprising in the Middle Atlas, near Beni Mellal. In all cases, the Moroccan military quickly repressed the agitation, stepping up its efforts to disarm the popular militias that had previously fought the colonial occupiers (Hart 2000, 84–101).

Following the death of Mohammed V in February 1961, Hassan II assumed control of the throne, the premiership, and several ministries. A year later a new constitution was passed by national referendum. The UNFP and Union marocain de travail staged an electoral boycott because of the broad powers the Constitution granted the monarchy and the surreptitious manner in which it was drafted. The king became commander-in-chief of the military, the country's spiritual leader *(amir al-mu'minin)*, and head of state with the power to dismiss government unilaterally. The Constitution provided for a House of Representatives (elected by universal suffrage) and a Chamber of Councilors. Morocco held its first election for the legislature in May 1963. Promonarchist parties, such as the Front pour la défense des institutions constitutionelles (Front for the Defense of Constitutional Institutions), won 66 of 144 seats even though they had garnered only 24 percent of the vote. Shortly after the UNFP denounced the elections and threatened to boycott upcoming local elections, the Moroccan government repressed the socialists further. More than one hundred UNFP members, including twenty-one parliamentarians, were arrested for allegedly conspiring against the king. The Moroccan government handed down eleven death sentences and sentenced others to five to twenty years in prison, thus forcing Ben Barka into exile. Shortly before he mysteriously disappeared in October 1965, the Moroccan government sentenced him to death in absentia.

Popular dissatisfaction fueled by Morocco's deteriorating economy—the government had raised taxes and cut federal spending—spilled out onto the streets in the spring of 1965 when thousands of Moroccans joined ongoing strikes and protests. Hassan's regime responded violently, killing upwards of three hundred civilians. In June 1965, King Hassan dissolved the government, suspended the Constitution, and declared a state of emergency that would last five years, although he finally allowed elections in the countryside and some municipalities in 1969. The outcome of such elections, however, was rank with obvious manipulation (Seddon 1989, 242). A year later the UNFP and Istiqlal, which had unified their efforts as the Kutla Wataniyya (Nationalist Bloc), contested the 1970 national referendum on a new constitution and the elections for the new single-chamber legislature. Hassan's unilateral promulgation of a new constitution in 1972 only served to alienate the opposition further.

By the 1970s, threats to the regime were no longer limited to the opposition parties. In July 1971, a coup attempt by the Moroccan army in the Skhirat royal palace was foiled. Hassan's regime summarily executed ten officers and imprisoned a thousand others. Among those imprisoned were 193 UNFP members; they received sentences ranging from several months to death (Amnesty International 1977, 3). A second coup attempt, this time led by air force officers, failed to shoot down King Hassan's personal jet as it was flying home from France in August 1972. Not only was a different branch of the military involved, including the head of the air force, but ultimate responsibility was laid at the feet of King Hassan's right-hand man, the minister of defense General Mohammed Oufkir. More than two hundred members of the air force received punishment, and eleven were put to death in January 1973. General Oufkir (the alleged mastermind of Ben Barka's "disappearance") ostensibly committed suicide. Six months later the Moroccan regime exposed yet another plot on the king's life. The Moroccan government executed sixteen alleged conspirators; dozens of UNFP members were imprisoned without trial (Amnesty International 1977, 4).

The depth of the problems facing Morocco was reflected in the radicalization of university campuses in the early 1970s (the same milieu that inspired some of Polisario's founders). The dominant student unions, the Union nationale des étudiants marocains (UNEM, National Union of Moroccan Students) and the Syndicat national des lycéens (SNL, National Union of Secondary Students), were the primary targets of state repression, along with Ila al-'Amam ("Forward," made up of Marxists from the defunct Parti de libération et socialisme) and the 23 Mars group (a leftist UNFP splinter). The regime charged that UNEM and SNL had been taken over by "Frontists," activists who sought to infiltrate unions and political parties in order to overthrow the 'Alawi regime and institute a socialist government. Following almost three years of continuous student unrest, Hassan's regime banned the UNEM in early 1973 and later gave its members fifteen-year sentences (Amnesty International 1977, 4).

Widespread dissatisfaction among the populace and not just the educated political elites had an economic dimension too. As one observer noted, "The disparities of the colonial era, so outrageous to Moroccan nationalists, were reproduced and even exceeded within post-colonial Morocco." Indeed, social inequity was so extreme that by 1978 just four Moroccan families controlled more than one-third of the private domestic capital invested in Moroccan industry (Clément 1986, 16).

It was under these crisis conditions that the "liberation" of Spanish Sahara presented itself as a way for the monarchy to disarm its opponents and redirect national attention. By playing on still potent anticolonial sentiments, a politics of diversion (i.e., focusing national discontent on a foreign "enemy") would allow Hassan to buttress his rule.

Furthermore, the campaign to take Spanish Sahara also afforded Hassan the opportunity to make amends with the opposition at little cost. Repression decreased, some political prisoners from the UNFP and UNEM were freed, and new elections were promised for 1976. However, the regime rounded up two hundred Frontists in November 1974 because of their support for self-determination in Western Sahara, and members of Ila al-'Amam were targeted for supporting Polisario. Yet, in contrast, proannexation socialists from the outlawed Communist Party, led by Ali Yata, were allowed to form the Parti du progrès et du socialisme (PPS, Party of Progress and Socialism).

The popular response to the Green March vindicated Hassan's gamble. Three days after his initial announcement of the march on October 16, 1975, Moroccan volunteers—drawn from all provinces based on quotas—reportedly exceeded demand by 50 percent. In some cases, local officials claimed that volunteers for the march had exceeded their quota by 800 percent. All notable members of the elite, including heads of political parties, rededicated themselves to Hassan's leadership, just as every level of civil society—including newspapers, Moroccan Jewish organizations, and the religious establishment, al-'ulama'—expressed its support (see Mundy 2006, 285; Weiner 1979, 27–31). Following the Madrid Agreement of November 1975, Hassan's popularity was at its zenith.

King Hassan's intent regarding Western Sahara was not a classic land grab for natural resources, but a way to reassert royal legitimacy, which would afford him more political leeway domestically. He was able to mobilize the country behind him by tapping into a powerful idea—Greater Morocco—that had become central to the national identity. Furthermore, because the apparent target of the Green March was Spain, not the Western Saharans, it also played on the still palpable resentment of colonialism and the ideals of the struggle for independence. Although Hassan succeeded in taking Western Sahara, the unforeseen effects of a costly war and occupation would soon deepen the crisis that had pushed Morocco into Western Sahara in the first place. In order to maintain the diversion, a new national enemy would have to be put forward. Algeria fit the bill, given its support for Polisario.[1]

ALGERIAN SUPPORT FOR WESTERN SAHARAN NATIONALISM

What really motivates Algerian support for Polisario is, like many aspects of Algerian politics, difficult to investigate directly. The ideational factor is obviously crucial when it comes to understanding Algeria. This factor not only extends to the ideal of self-determination, which played a key discursive role in Algeria's struggle for independence, but also covers other affinities the Algerian regime has with Polisario. Support for Western Saharan resistance is consistent with Algeria's own history and its form of nationalism. Algeria's revolutionary heritage, anti-imperialist credentials, and advocacy of socialism gave it a particularly strong reputation in the Third World. This was especially so in the mid-1970s, at the height of Algerian ambition and influence in the post-Nasser Third World. As one Moroccan official complained, Algerians had *"l'aura"* that provided them more credibility in international forums (Zunes, notes from a briefing, Moroccan Foreign Ministry, Rabat, 1990). Part of this credibility was rooted in Algeria's effort to champion a third way in the Cold War, neither pro-Western nor pro-Soviet. A leading American scholar of Algeria describes nonalignment, the "centerpiece" of Algeria's foreign policy, as "a vigilant anticolonialism that finds unswerving Algerian support for movements of national liberation; the organization of the struggle against imperialism, which assumes a simultaneous struggle for the creation of a new global economic order involving the solidarity of all 'exploited' states; and determined action in favor of maintaining world peace" (Entelis 1986, 201). President Boumedienne's wholehearted adoption of Polisario in November 1975 fit with these core Algerian values. Dismissing the idea that their support for Polisario has been and is a cynical effort to destabilize Morocco and gain regional supremacy, Algerian officials often boast that they had good relations with Indonesia and nevertheless still called for its decolonization of East Timor.

Norms, however, do not sufficiently explain Algeria's actions. As shown earlier, the regime's unbridled support for Western Saharan nationalism followed the Moroccan invasion. Nor was support for Western Saharan nationalism shared across the regime; some leading Algerian figures, including Mohamed Boudiaf, a founding member of the FLN, supported Morocco (International Crisis Group 2007, 12). For Boumedienne, the most offensive part of the Moroccan takeover was Algiers's exclusion from the decision-making processes and the way in which Western leaders sided with Moroccan expansionism on Algeria's southern flank. Before then, also as noted earlier, the Algerian position on Western Sahara seemed to vacillate between accommodating Morocco and backing self-determination. What support Algeria rendered to Polisario starting in mid-1974 was minimal. Furthermore, given the history of tense relations between postcolonial Morocco and Algeria, it is difficult to believe that Algeria's interest in Western Sahara was and is based on national self-image. Last, Algeria has supported Polisario's drive for statehood and independence, not just for self-determination—the right to *choose* independence.

The other component of Algeria's Western Sahara policy is hegemonic competition (see Zoubir 1997). As the region emerged from colonialism in the 1950s and 1960s, the balance of power there was not clear. Algeria had distinct advantages given its territorial size, the diversity of its resources, and the intensity of its colonization (e.g., infrastructure and education). Indeed, one aim of the Greater Morocco plan was to correct this imbalance. Thus, Hassan's attempt to consolidate the postcolonial Moroccan state through the annexation of Western Sahara simultaneously threatened to tip the regional balance of power, which had favored Algeria up to November 1975. In Polisario, the military-dominated Algerian regime saw a legitimate vehicle to reverse the situation or at least keep Morocco in check.

Finally, it goes without saying that a simpatico state in Western Sahara would further Algerian interests.

It is often suggested that Algeria's support for an independent Western Sahara is based on resources. More precisely, Algeria wants access to the Atlantic to ease export of its hydrocarbons and minerals to the Americas. This suggestion has even found its way into the peace process. A 2001 draft autonomy proposal (see chapter 9) came with the suggestion that there should be a special corridor to connect Tindouf to the Atlantic through Western Sahara. This side offer, however, had no effect on Algeria's position; Algeria backed Polisario's rejection of the plan. Indeed, according to surveys, the most geographically feasible route from Tindouf to the Atlantic is not through Western Sahara, but through southern Morocco to the port of Tarfaya (Damis 1983, 35). Furthermore, Algeria already exports gas to Europe using a pipeline that runs through Morocco, strongly suggesting that "both sides are quite capable of separating economic and political interests" (Zoubir 1997, 50). And finally, the profitability of Atlantic access has to be reconciled with the steep costs of constructing a port that can handle oil, gas, or minerals, whereas Algeria already has such processing facilities on the Mediterranean.

For these ideational and strategic reasons, Algeria, more than any other country, has worked to sustain and further the cause of Western Saharan nationalism. And like Morocco's, Algeria's Western Sahara policy has changed little since 1975. Algerian presidents from Boumedienne to Bouteflika (1999– ) have remained faithful to Western Saharan nationalism and the ideal of self-determination. The cost to Algeria has never been estimated, although supporting Polisario has certainly not been cheap. For more than three decades, Algeria has supported the diplomatic activities of Polisario/RASD and offered significant material aid to the tens of thousands of refugees near Tindouf. Throughout the years of both Boumedienne's (1965–78) and Chadli Bendjedid's (1979–92) administrations, Algeria provided military material to the ELPS, including advanced weaponry. During the 1990s, Algeria—embroiled in its own internal conflict—seemed to take a more hands-off approach. Yet Algeria has used either its own seat or those of various allies on the UN Security Council to protect and advance the cause of self-determination in Western Sahara. At the General Assembly and associated bodies, Algeria's backroom lobbying for Polisario has continued to pay dividends.

One of the major false assumptions regarding Algeria's role in the conflict is the idea that because Algeria is only indirectly involved, its motivations are cynical, weaker, and more susceptible to change. For example, the election of Abdelaziz Bouteflika to the presidency in 1999 and the death of King Hassan shortly thereafter were thought to herald a new era in Moroccan–Algerian relations, especially on Western Sahara. As one African diplomat noted in 2003, "On Western Sahara, Boumedienne had one language, Bouteflika had another" (BBC Monitoring Service, Feb. 5, 2003). Bouteflika's pragmatism of early 1975, when he was Algeria's foreign minister—apparently acquiescing to Hassan's planned invasion of Spanish Sahara in exchange for a border agreement between Algeria and Morocco—was on minds at the UN. Indeed, at the earliest opportunity (February 2000), the Security Council, under pressure from France and the United States, effectively abandoned the long-awaited referendum on independence. Throwing nine years of work out the window, the council opened the door for an alternative approach that precluded independence, thinking that Algeria would go along with the new plan.

In fact, quite the opposite happened. In recent years, Algeria has shed its pariah status and returned to the international stage as an important regional and international player. An important factor behind this reemergence is Algeria's reinvigorated economy owing to high global hydrocarbon prices. Another important factor is the corresponding decline in the levels of political violence, which peaked in 1997–98 and have steadily decreased ever since. With the retirement of several key generals and President Bouteflika's reelection in 2004 (without overt backing from the military), stronger civilian control over the government has not translated into less support for Polisario. Contrary to predictions made in 1999, Algeria has become more, not less, strident in its support for Western Saharan nationalism. Algeria under Bouteflika has also shown little interest in normalizing relations with Morocco. As Algeria positions itself as the regional powerhouse, Polisario remains more central to its strategy.

## CONTINUED CRISIS: THE COST OF WAR AND OCCUPATION TO MOROCCO

During the early years of the war in the Western Sahara, King Hassan used his newfound political capital to reassert control. "For at least ten years," notes one academic observer, "the king portrayed the campaign to retain the Sahara as a prolonged national emergency, a period of crisis that he used as the justification for postponing promised internal reforms and liberalization of the regime . . . to distract public attention from domestic problems and stifle political dissent" (Damis 2000, 28). The occupation of Western Sahara instantly became a double-edged sword. On the one hand, it was the monarchy's greatest achievement since independence, the means by which Hassan secured his throne. On the other hand, the monarchy's legitimacy became predicated on Western Sahara's remaining Moroccan, even though retaining it would become a burden Morocco could not easily bear.

Between 1972 and 1978, Morocco's biannual military expenditures increased rapidly from $270 million to $367 million to $755 million to $770 million (1978 dollars) (Stork and Paul 1983, 6). In the mid-1980s, estimates put the average cost of war and occupation at $1.5 million a day (*Africa Report*, May–June 1986). A 1990 estimate of Morocco's annual military expenditures, including elaborate infrastructure investment in Western Sahara, put them as high as $430 million (Damis 1990, 167). The major suppliers for Morocco were

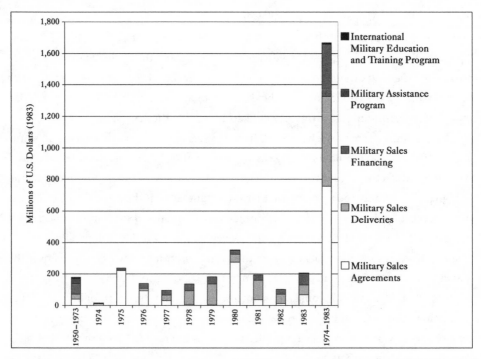

Fig. 2. U.S. military aid to Morocco, 1950–1983. Based on data compiled from U.S. Department of Defense 1983.

the United States and France, which from 1975 to 1987 supplied one-third and two-thirds of Moroccan military needs, respectively (Volman 1993, 159–62) (see figure 1 in chapter 1 and figures 2 and 3 here).

Citing Moroccan-supplied numbers, one study concluded that the cost of the war to Morocco was "quite bearable." At a cost of $1.17 million a day between the critical years from 1976 to 1986, this amount accounted for only 3 percent of government spending and 9 percent of gross domestic product (GDP). However, as the author of this study indicates, Morocco received generous aid from Saudi Arabia, to the tune of $1 billion per year from 1979 to 1981 and nearly one-quarter of that per annum thereafter (Damis 2000, 25). Saudi Arabia effectively paid for the war. Other studies have suggested, however, that the war was far more expensive for Morocco even with Saudi grants. Starting from the claim that the Saharan war cost Morocco between $2 and $5 million per day in 1979, David Seddon calculated that Moroccan defense spending "accounted for no less than 40 per cent of the consolidated national budget" (1989, 245). Citing World Bank figures, Mark Tessler noted that Morocco's total defense spending had risen from 13 percent in 1975 to 23 percent of all government expenditures in 1977. Based on a figure given by the U.S. Embassy in Rabat, this study then went on to claim the same 40 percent figure (of Morocco's budget) given by Seddon (1985, 47). In the early 1980s, the World Bank claimed that

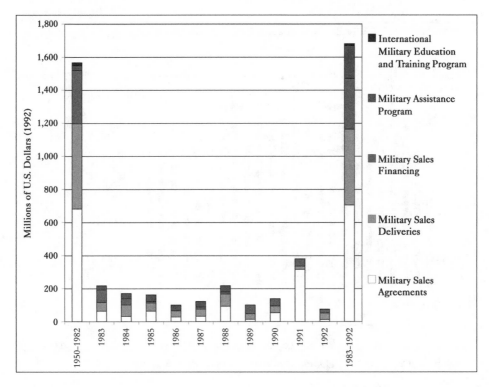

Fig. 3. U.S. military aid to Morocco, 1950–1992. Based on data compiled from U.S. Department of Defense 1992.

foreign grants and loans, especially from Saudi Arabia, covered upward of 60 percent of the cost of military imports for Morocco (Hodges 1983b, 294–95). The war was affordable for Morocco, but only after the fact. In 1991, Morocco's debt to Saudi Arabia was written off, a gesture of gratitude for Moroccan participation in the first U.S.-led war against Iraq (Economist Intelligence Unit 2003b, 46). The war effort was also made possible domestically through "national solidarity taxes" and bonds (Zoubir 1990a, 29). Yet even after the 1991 cease-fire, occupying Western Sahara has remained expensive for Morocco. From 1975 to 1999, Morocco's daily military expenditures averaged $4.1 million (adjusted to 2004 dollars). What made the war more exceptionally expensive were, obviously, arms imports. From 1975 to 1991, Morocco imported $529 million in arms annually, whereas from 1992 to 1999 it imported $145 million annually (see figure 4).

By the late 1970s, the Moroccan state was forced to cut spending drastically in order to finance the war, implementing the 1978 austerity plan (Leveau 1997). Export revenues had taken a hit following a drop in phosphate prices, with profits dropping 50 percent between 1974 and 1978. A growing reliance on imports and a sizeable debt burden expanded Morocco's trade deficit. Major imports included petroleum, which rose in cost in 1979. Furthermore, Moroccan under- and unemployment, estimated at 35 percent in

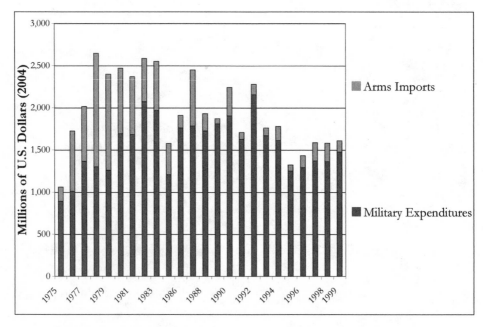

Fig. 4. Moroccan military imports and expenditures, 1975–1999. Based on data compiled from U.S. Department of State 1980, 59, 143; 1987, 86; 1989, 96; 1995, 75, 123; 2001b, 85, 137.

1971, grew throughout the 1970s. The agricultural sector was also in trouble when rainfall fell below average in the late 1970s, reducing crop yields and herd stocks, forcing Morocco to import half of its cereal needs. In the same period, food costs rose much more quickly than personal income (Seddon 1984, 12). In response to the 1978 austerity plan, major labor strikes led by the Confédération démocratique des travailleurs (CDT, Democratic Confederation of Workers) and a relegalized UNEM were launched, which eventually won some concessions from the government. Founded in 1978, the CDT had close ties to the Union socialiste des forces populaires (USFP, Socialist Union of Popular Forces), a breakaway from the UNFP.

Facing an untenable economic situation, the Moroccan government accepted an International Monetary Fund (IMF) economic rescue package in October 1980. At that time, the plan amounted to the second largest of its kind for a developing country. One of the conditions of the package was that the Moroccan government would have to reduce basic subsidies, which caused steep rises in food prices. Both student and labor unions reacted by calling for strikes in June 1981. The Moroccan regime's rejoinder to the widespread discontent was to call in the army. After two days of unrest, Moroccan officials claimed that sixty-six people had been killed and two thousand had been arrested; other sources claimed that six hundred to one thousand had been slain. The Moroccan regime subsequently arrested and tried members of the USFP, the CDT, and the UNEM, and it banned publication of the USFP's two papers, *Libération* and *Al-Muharrir*. Later, in September 1981, the Moroccan government arrested USFP secretary-general Abderrahim Bouabid and several other members for criticizing King Hassan's support of OAU initiatives on the Western Sahara conflict (Amnesty International 1982, 4). The Moroccan government pushed ahead with the announced economic reforms but held off on additional measures. In the face of obvious and massive economic discontent, the IMF and the World Bank still criticized the Moroccan government for not pushing ahead with "more stringent policies" (Seddon 1989, 247).

Although the war in Western Sahara was starting to turn in Morocco's favor in the early 1980s, the country's political and economic situation was still dire. In 1983, the Moroccan monarchy thwarted another military-led conspiracy to overthrow Hassan, which was followed by the suspicious death of General Ahmed Dlimi, chief of the Sahara campaign. The Moroccan regime also caved in to IMF and World Bank pressure and quickly implemented the demanded economic reforms, which included a devaluation of the Moroccan dirham, cuts in government spending, and a reduction in barriers to international trade. In return for these structural adjustments, Morocco was able to renegotiate its $530 million in commercial debt, and the IMF agreed to offer further loans and credit. Again, though, the burden fell on poor Moroccans. The price of tea—a Moroccan staple—rose 77 percent in August 1983 (Seddon 1984, 13, 15). While unemployment hovered around 35 to 40 percent, half of national income went to 10 percent of the population. Access to wealth and opportunity in Morocco were largely determined by one's access to the center of power, the monarchy (Tessler 1985, 45). When initial education cuts and further price hikes—affecting nearly all basic foods by as much as 20 percent— were announced in early 1984, a wave of strikes and demonstrations broke out. They were similar in scope to the 1981 unrest, although the number of demonstrators killed by the government was somewhat lower, estimated at approximately two hundred. Reported arrests numbered in the thousands, though; fifteen hundred were eventually brought to trial, and many were given sentences of ten years (Amnesty International 1991a, 2). Legislative elections in September 1984 helped to diffuse some of the political discontent, although promonarchist parties under the banner of the Union constitutionelle (Constitutional Union), formed in 1983, took two-thirds of the seats, allowing for the exclusion of both Istiqlal and USFP from the new government. Yet one of the most popular movements in Morocco, the Islamist al-'Adl wa al-'Ihsan (Justice and Charity Spirituality), was barred from forming a political party. Having cynically used the Islamists as a foil against the leftists in the 1970s, Morocco was forced to reconsider this policy in the 1980s owing to the increasing popularity of political Islam. On Moroccan campuses, the regime repressed al-Shabibah al-Islamiyyah (Islamic Youth), founded in 1970. In 1984, it tried more than seventy Islamic activists for purportedly conspiring against the throne; several received death sentences (Amnesty International 1991b, 7). Despite such ongoing repression, international lenders, impressed with Morocco's resolve, rescheduled more than $1 billion in debt (Seddon 1989, 253–54).

By the late 1980s, the war in Western Sahara had reached a stalemate. The construction of the berms had placed a significant damper on Polisario's activities, although it precluded Morocco from winning outright. In 1988, Hassan, by agreeing to a UN referendum, had succeeded in moving the issue to the Security Council, which was more sensitive than the OAU to Moroccan interests. Nevertheless, the domestic picture in Morocco was one of continuing social discontent. At the end of 1990, the CDT called for a general strike in Fez. The state again resorted to violence to quell the riots when they spread to other cities, notably Tangier, where two hundred protesters died. This unrest took place within the context of the first U.S.-led war against Iraq, in which Moroccan forces participated in the liberation of Kuwait. Although many of these demonstrations were ostensibly pro-Iraqi, some observers considered them thinly veiled "bread riots" in the tradition of 1981 and 1984. Despite the fact that the early 1990s saw growing GDP per capita, a falling budget deficit, and increasing exports, there were still strong indications of an economy in trouble: real wages had decreased; the gap between rich and poor had widened; and unemployment, inflation, and national debt had risen, the latter going from $8.47 billion in 1980 to $20.66 billion in 1993 (Layachi 1998, 20–21). Even a personal advisor to King Hassan, Ahmed Reda Guedira, took the regime to task for relying "solely on means of coercion" (Demir 1990, 38).

However, because of continuous and growing international pressure on the regime to address its human rights abuses, the Moroccan government took several dramatic steps following the creation of the royal Conseil consultatif des droits de l'homme (CCDH, Human Rights Advisory Council) in 1990. The regime also allowed an anti–Gulf War demonstration to take place in Rabat on February 3, which saw three hundred thousand Moroccans in attendance. In addition to releasing dozens of Sahrawi "disappeared" in 1991, the regime freed notable dissidents it had held since the 1970s for crimes of opinion. Among them were prominent members of Ila al-'Amam: Abraham Serfaty, Abderrahmane Nouda, and Mohammed Srifi. Yet when Serfaty continued to refuse to recognize Moroccan sovereignty over the Western Sahara, he quickly lost his citizenship and was forced into exile in Europe (Human Rights Watch 1992).

THE ARAB MAGHRIB UNION

Although the war in Western Sahara had polarized and poisoned relations across the Maghrib, by the mid-1980s the entire region recognized several threatening realities that united them. On the socioeconomic front, all faced rapidly growing populations, daunting unemployment numbers, staggering foreign debt, increasing calls for political pluralism, and rising political Islamism. The situation was made worse following the 1986 fall in world oil prices and the collapse of Soviet support. Although the authoritarian governments of the Maghrib were quite disparate ideologically, they all had come to the realization that economic instability was breeding much of the surfacing political challenges facing them. The international free-trade consensus, unchallenged at the end of the Cold War, promised political stability through economic liberalization.

In the late 1980s, Algeria took the lead in the early negotiations between the five North African states—Mauritania, Morocco, Algeria, Tunisia, and Libya. Rabat had broken off relations with Algiers in 1976, when Algeria became the first state to recognize RASD, but eventually the two countries summit meetings in 1983 and 1987. Saudi Arabia brokered the latter summit, at the Algerian border town of Akid Lotfi, with King Fahd present. At the 1988 Arab League summit in Algiers, Rabat demanded the reestablishment of formal diplomatic relations with Algeria before it would attend. To present a united Arab front in support of the first Palestinian intifada, which had recently broken out in the West Bank and Gaza Strip, Algeria worked hard to facilitate Moroccan participation.

Early meetings to discuss a regional union in North Africa were possible only because Western Sahara was excluded from the agenda, and Algiers for a time did soften its criticisms of Morocco's occupation (*New African,* June 1989). The Algerian government staunchly denied any lessening of support for Polisario, though, arguing that mutually beneficial economic and political relations have nothing to do with the right of self-determination. In February 1989, following the UN adoption of the Western Sahara conflict, the Union du Maghreb arabe (UMA, Arab Maghrib Union) was created at a summit in Marrakech (the acronym for the French name, UMA, is also the Arabic word for community or nation, *al-'ummah*). The agreement called for the easing of visa restrictions (designed to help trade, tourism, families, and migrant workers); tariff reductions or eliminations; expanded rail links; and the establishment of a single regional airline. Although generally vague in its phrasing on some economic issues, the UMA sought reciprocity in industry and agriculture, while encouraging countries with surpluses of certain resources to trade with those lacking them.

Any improvement in Algerian–Moroccan relations came with speculation that support for the Polisario would decline in Algiers. In the late 1980s, however, the Algerian and Moroccan governments were able to separate the Western Saharan track from all other diplomatic initiatives, which was one of the benefits of the UN's push to resolve the Morocco–Polisario conflict. The exclusion of RASD—recognized by three of the five states in UMA—was a victory for King Hassan. Yet a UMA Charter clause allowing the admission of new member states left open the possibility of later adding RASD as well as Egypt, which was given observer status, and Sudan, which has not shown any interest in the UMA.

Polisario welcomed the Moroccan–Algerian rapprochement, reading it as Moroccan capitulation. As a joint Moroccan–Algerian communiqué in 1988 stated, their normalization of relations sought "a just and definitive solution to the Western Sahara conflict, through a free and regular referendum for self-determination held without any constraints whatsoever and with utmost sincerity" (quoted in Zoubir 1990b, 227). To Polisario, which had been fighting for, at the very least, a self-determination referendum, such language was comforting. The statement also paved the way for the first (and only) meeting between King Hassan and Polisario officials in January 1989.

The UMA held several summits until 1994, when Morocco and Algeria again broke off relations and closed their mutual border. The Algiers–Rabat détente had been a troubled one, anyway. A brief escalation of Morocco–Polisario fighting in the fall of 1989 led to further charges and countercharges from both governments and their allied media. Yet it was the issue of terrorism that undid the UMA. As the Islamist insurgency in Algeria grew more and more violent, Algiers frequently charged Morocco with both passive and active complicity in the rebellion. An August 1994 attack on a hotel in Marrakech that left two Spanish tourists dead was followed by new salvos in the Rabat–Algiers verbal war, resulting in the closing of the border, which held at least through 2008.

The UMA has survived, but only at the technical level and with some support from the EU's Barcelona Process, or Euro-Med Dialog, initiated in 1995 to facilitate cooperation between the EU and its neighbors along the southern Mediterranean basin. Nevertheless, year after year, the Western Sahara conflict has managed to undermine the revival of the UMA by spoiling Rabat–Algiers relations. More than in any other year since 1994, in early 2005 the prospects for a summit seemed particularly good. Several months beforehand, Morocco had dropped its visa requirement for Algerians, and that March, at the Arab League summit in Algiers, Bouteflika and Mohammed VI met on the sidelines. As a warm gesture, Mohammed decided to extend his stay past the meetings. Yet the UMA summit, set for May 2005 in Tripoli, fell apart when Morocco protested a letter from Bouteflika to Polisario leader Mohammed Abdelaziz. This reportedly private letter for the thirty-second anniversary of the Polisario's founding, later published by RASD's press service, swore unwavering Algerian support for Western Saharan independence. Morocco's Foreign Ministry denounced the letter and questioned the utility of a summit where Algeria would be supporting Polisario. Algeria shot back that Western Sahara was not on the agenda. In the end, Libya was forced to cancel the meeting when Morocco said it would no longer attend. Where Western Sahara was once deliberately excluded from the UMA process, it has since become central to that process.

MOROCCO AFTER THE CEASE-FIRE

Following the 1991 armistice, which lifted the burdens of war making from Morocco, Hassan's regime took several measures to stabilize the domestic situation. A September 1992 constitutional referendum, which passed by an implausible 99 percent, was undermined by charges of corruption. Opposition leader Abderrahmane Youssoufi of the USFP called for the resignation of Interior Minister Driss Basri, Hassan's right-hand man (Daoud and Ouchelh 1997). Morocco finally held a parliamentary election in June 1993, the first in nine years. The opposition democratic bloc—USFP, Istiqlal, and PPS—took 45 percent of the first-round vote but earned only 20 percent in the second round, leading to new charges of tampering. In the face of an opposition boycott, Hassan simply appointed technocratic clients and royalist center-right parties to governing posts.

Hassan then offered up another constitution, passed by national referendum in September 1996. It contained provisions for a bicameral parliament elected every six years. The lower house, or House of Representatives, would be elected by direct universal suffrage, and the upper house, the Chamber of Councilors, composed of regional representatives and advisers, would be elected indirectly by electoral college. The opposition accepted these minor changes, although the king still remained far beyond any real checks and balances. One observer suggested that besides addressing the official aspects of the monarchy's unqualified power (e.g., control over the premiership, the Interior Ministry, and all security forces), real reform would have to "separate out the financial relationship between the monarchy and the state." This relationship included the throne's control over "major state contracts," "public corporations such as the Office chérifienne des Phosphates," and the holding company Omnium nord africain, "the personal vehicle of the king's economic and commercial interests"—not to mention "the fact that the monarch is Morocco's greatest landowner" (Leveau 1997, 110–12). At the same time, the referendum in Western Sahara was four years past due and going nowhere.

Following elections under the new constitution in 1997, USFP came out the decisive winner with fifty-seven seats; Istiqlal took thirty-two. The rightist promonarchy bloc, Wifaq (Concord), composed of several rural-based parties, garnered seventy-nine seats. For the first time since independence, the will of the electorate was respected, and Hassan nominated Youssoufi for the premiership. Yet in the December 1997 elections for the Chamber of Councilors, the monarch's rural powerbase reasserted itself, giving royalist parties the control over the upper house. Although supporters of the regime were quick to applaud the new government and the USFP's break with its policy of "noncooperation" dating from 1959, King Hassan still retained control over the Interior, Foreign, and Defense ministries (Daoud and Ouchelh 1997). "Driss Basri would continue as interior minister," one academic observer has noted, "ostensibly because his responsibility for the Western Sahara portfolio made him indispensable" (Sweet 2001, 24).

One of the effects of the socialist opposition's entrance into the government was its political delegitimization. Many hopes were pinned on the USFP, yet its capacity to make reforms was as much internally constrained by the regime as it was externally constrained. Not only did the monarchy still control the key ministries, but Morocco's IMF structural adjustment program and agreements with the EU allowed heavy foreign control of the economy. With its hands tied, the USFP would be unable to address the pressing socioeconomic issues it had long promised to tackle, especially the 20 percent unemploy-ment rate (*The Economist,* Mar. 21, 1998). These debts, however, stemmed from years of failed policies, war, and occupation of Western Sahara—factors that the opposition had little control over. By creating the impression that the regime was sharing power with the USFP, though, the monarchy was cleverly spreading the blame for poor governance.

With the regime's definitive co-optation of the Left, the only viable and organized alternative was political Islam, although the Parti de la justice et du développement (PJD, Justice and Development Party), the sole legal Islamist party, earned only nine seats in the 1997 elections. Since the early 1980s, the Moroccan government had worked to curb the emergence of an articulate Islamic social movement. Whereas repression in the immedi-ate postcolonial period was marked with measures against leftists, the 1980s saw a con-certed effort to control the growth of Islamic parties and associations. Even as late as 1995, the Moroccan state "disappeared" Islamic activists, a practice thought abandoned in 1991 (Human Rights Watch 1995, 10). Leaders in the most popular Islamist organiza-tion, al-'Adl wa al-'Ihsan, worked under the constant fear of arrest and detention; its head, the charismatic Shaykh 'Abdessalam Yacine, lived under house arrest for more than ten years starting in 1989, the same year the government outlawed his organization. Before then, Yacine had served a long prison sentence for writing an open letter to King Hassan in 1974, challenging his legitimacy and calling on him to embark on a program for his own "redemption and salvation." Yet the regime realized that political Islam, given its popularity, had to be brought slowly onto the playing field, starting with the 1997 elections (Layachi 1998, 53–58). The genius of Hassan's strategy at that time was his co-optation of the Left before it could make common cause with the equally marginalized Islamists (Leveau 1998).

Upon his death in June 1999, Hassan left his heir, Mohammed VI, a legacy of unapolo-getic authoritarianism, failed development, and illegitimate occupation. The UN Develop-ment Program's 2000 Human Development Index ranked Morocco 125 out of 174 countries. Within North Africa, Algeria, Tunisia, Libya, and even Egypt ranked higher—107, 101, 72, and 119, respectively. Adult literacy (47 percent) and school enrollment were incredibly low relative to Morocco's neighbors and the wider Middle East. Literacy among women, at 34 percent, should have been a particular embarrassment. Furthermore, Morocco had the lowest life expectancy (sixty-seven years), the highest infant mortality (3.7 percent), and the highest percentage of the population without access to safe water (35 percent) and health services (38 percent) (UN Development Program 2000, 158–59, 70). More than 50 percent of the rural population had neither electricity nor running water (Ramonet 1999). At that time, 7 percent of the Moroccan population—more than two million people—lived on less than one dollar a day, and more than seven million existed below the national poverty level (UN Development Program 2000, 158–59). Among the working-age urban population, the unemployment rate was officially at 20 percent, although the actual figure was suspected to be higher (Daoud and Ouchelh 1997). In a country where 50 percent of the labor force was still agricultural, the difference between a year with "very heavy" and "extremely poor" rainfall was the difference between 12 percent growth in GDP or a 6 percent decrease in GDP respectively. In the last full year of Hassan's rule, 1998, Morocco ran a trade deficit of $2.3 billion; overall international debt was $20.5 billion; and debt servicing, at $2.7 billion, consumed nearly 23 percent of earned export income (Economist Intelligence Unit 2003b, 29, 63–64).

King Hassan's power had derived from as many corrupt, concealed, and informal aspects as from official and formal ones. A 1997 report claimed that Morocco's parallel and illegal economies, including human and commodity smuggling, earned upward of $3 billion a year; drug production and export earned $2 billion a year (Leveau 1997, 99). Under Hassan, Moroccan hashish had come to dominate the global market, supplying upward of 70 percent of Europe's demands. In 1996, *Le Monde* charged that drug-related corruption had reached the royal palace itself, although the monarchy had ostensibly launched an antinarcotic campaign in the 1990s under pressure from the EU (Ketterer 2001, 31).

Although Hassan's regime could easily dismiss accusations leveled by the French press, it had more difficulty covering up domestically exposed fraud. In one of the most startling cases revealed to the Moroccan public, it was found that officials appointed by Hassan had misappropriated an amount equivalent to 80 percent of the nation's foreign debt. The government's response, as one Moroccan scholar laments, was to "put before parliament a law to improve the 'management' of public enterprises, utterly marginalizing the question of political accountability that was at the root of the scandals" (Maghraoui 2002, 30). Ironically, the Hassan II mosque in Casablanca, one of the world's largest religious monuments, finished in 1993 and costing between $500 and $800 million, stands as a symbol of the former regime's corruption: Moroccans later learned that most of the money they were forced to pay in a special tax for its construction was either misappropriated or extorted. However, no one was ever held accountable—a trend that continued into Mohammed VI's reign. In 2004, the Moroccan Parliament looked into a $1.3 billion loan scandal, but when the investigation came close to "the seat of power," it was dropped. In 2005, it was revealed that some Moroccan generals responsible for policing the coast and regulating fishing were also large stakeholders in fisheries businesses that they had failed to regulate. One result was the near total collapse of the Morocco and Western Sahara costal ecosystems from overfishing (Transparency International 2006, 204–6).

The effects of widespread official corruption on the Moroccan population and on its perceptions of the state's legitimacy were quite measurable. In a poll by a prominent Moroccan magazine, nearly 97 percent of Moroccans said they did not trust politicians, and 96 percent said they did not trust the police. In a subsequent poll, conducted shortly before parliamentary elections in 2002, 90 percent of those polled did not know either the names or orientation of the major parties (cited in Entelis 2002). Using citizens' opinions of their own country's transparency, the Switzerland-based World Economic Forum ranked Morocco the most corrupt country in North Africa in 2004 (*afrol News,* Aug. 2, 2003).

Where the Moroccan state failed to serve the governed, a pervasive informal sector filled in the large gaps. Such gaps had become most noticeable in the exploding urban areas. In 1971, Moroccans living in urban areas accounted for only 31 percent of the total population. By 1995, however, more than half of Moroccans lived in the cities, many of them moving into the ever-expanding improvised and ungoverned neighborhoods on the metropolitan peripheries (Sweet 2001, 23). The rate of growth shows no sign of decreasing, and each year these cities absorb almost half a million Moroccan economic refugees. The level of rural poverty at the turn of the millennium was estimated to be 27 percent versus 12 percent in the cities, thus fueling the population drift to the urban centers. By 2002, the combined population of Casablanca and Rabat was officially five million. Casablanca's estimated ten thousand homeless children, although paling in comparison to the number in some of the world's megacities, is twice the number in São Paulo, Brazil, despite the fact that Casablanca has less than half São Paolo's total population (Maghraoui 2001, 16). From 1997 to 1999, urban unemployment grew from 17 percent to 22 percent, although the labor unions dispute these figures as being far too low. Given these conditions, few are surprised that nearly 75 to 90 percent of young Moroccans, who now compose more than 50 percent of the total population, want to emigrate. Because of the high level of remittances from Moroccans working abroad, however, there is little incentive for the government to discourage either legal or illegal emigration, despite the effects of losing skilled workers (the "brain drain"). In 2001, remittances totaled nearly $4 billion, which was equivalent to 50 percent of Morocco's export earnings (Economist Intelligence Unit 2003b, 31, 46, and 61).

At first, King Mohammed VI attempted to distance himself from his father's governing style. Only weeks after his ascension to the throne, he gave a speech in which he admitted that his father's regime had committed grave human rights abuses, including "disappearances," and promised that the victims and their families would be compensated. King Mohammed also invited notable dissidents back to Morocco, including the exiled leftist Abraham Serfaty and the son of Amazigh legend Abdelkarim Khattabi, leader of a short-lived breakaway republic in the Rif Mountains during Spanish colonial rule. King Mohammed even visited that drought-stricken region, which his father had visited only once—in 1959, to crush a rebellion.

With respect to Western Sahara, the new king's most breathtaking act occurred in early November 1999 when he summarily dismissed Driss Basri, the longstanding minister of the interior. Already gone was Mohammed Azmi, Basri's deputy in the Western Sahara, and secret-service head Benbrahim Allabouche; both had been dismissed in

September that year. The new king also used the state media to publicize his charity efforts as the head of the Mohammed VI Foundation. Not only did these efforts boost his popularity in some rural locations, where his father never set foot, but they aimed to counter the Islamic charities' grassroots activism (Ramonet 2000). The promonarchy press soon dubbed Mohammad VI the "king of the poor." Despite the moniker, his inherited wealth was estimated at $30 billion in 1999 owing to his father's direct control of more than 20 percent of Morocco's best agricultural land and the phosphate industry as well as to large investments in Europe and the United States (*Africa Confidential,* Aug. 6, 2000). With this promising start, Mohammed VI not only earned widespread international praise, but also won a huge favor from the UN Security Council. In February 2000, France and the United States backed an effort to scrap the referendum process so that Morocco would not have to suffer the inevitable vote for independence in Western Sahara (see chapter 8).

Despite being spared a referendum in Western Sahara, King Mohammed VI failed to produce the substantive change his population and international backers had hoped for. Although the international community hailed the 2002 parliamentary vote as Morocco's first genuinely free and fair elections, voter turnout was a dismal 50 percent. And although USFP won a majority of seats, it was denied the premiership. In a move reminiscent of his father, Mohammed VI instead appointed his interior minister, technocrat and former industrialist Driss Jettou, as prime minister. Turnout in the 2007 elections was even worse at 38 percent. The PJD, which ran at full strength for the first time ever, won a majority of votes, yet owing to a new convoluted electoral law it was awarded fewer seats than Istiqlal, which won the premiership. Most surprisingly, USFP fell to fifth (see Storm 2008).

The most serious challenge to Mohammed VI came in May 2003, when coordinated suicide bombings struck "Western" targets in downtown Casablanca, killing forty-five people. The May 16 bombings, according to the king, signified "the end of the era of leniency." With that, the government quickly made moves to crush clandestine Islamic organizations. The number of Moroccans charged with criminal offences after the attacks was 2,112, and as many as 5,000 were arrested—to which should be added the at least 400 people already in detention at the time of the bombings. Moroccan courts sentenced more than 900 individuals in connection with the events and gave 17 death sentences. A year after the bombings, Human Rights Watch, remarking on Morocco's human rights backsliding, warned that "the broader freedoms that Moroccans have enjoyed during the last decade-and-a-half were never institutionalized and can thus be easily removed" (2004, 25; see also Amnesty International 2004, 2). Although King Mohammed had initially tried to distance himself from his father's methods (torture, political imprisonment, and secret detention centers), his new regime soon found them indispensable.

Since 2000, Morocco has been spared the realistic threat of losing Western Sahara to a referendum on independence. In that period, it has not achieved the long-promised economic and political stability; indeed, it has continued to play up its virtues and its weaknesses to extract continued patronage from Paris and Washington. After September 11, 2001, amidst the U.S. "global war on terror," the presence of radical Islamic militants in Morocco has worked to Mohammed VI's favor. Before 2001, the Moroccan regime prided itself on the lack of violent Islamic activism inside its borders and often went to great lengths to contrast Morocco with the alarming bloodbath in 1990s Algeria. In the years since May 2003, however, Morocco has been willing to exploit signs of an internal "terrorist" threat in order to gain more sympathy from Washington and Paris.[2]

Former French president Charles de Gaulle once described Morocco as a country whose revolution was still to come. Although the Morocco regime has made peaceful change nearly impossible, it has managed to hold off the inevitable alternatives by carefully manipulating more than fifty years of sustained instability. The transmission and transformation of crisis in Morocco, from independence to recent years, has ironically become as central to the regime's existence as the occupation of Western Sahara. Reforms that would bring transparency, democracy, and accountability to Morocco are unfeasible because the government is not yet strong enough to implement them. Yet it is the lack of those qualities that undermine the Moroccan government and justify regime robustness that inhibits reform.

What Morocco's international supporters have failed to realize is that the relationship between Western Sahara and Morocco is a vicious catch-22. A solution to the Western Sahara conflict is a precondition for Morocco's stability. Yet a solution to the Western Sahara conflict first depends on Morocco's stability. For advocates of democratic reform, it might be worth noting that if political power and responsibility were more diffuse in Morocco, the loss of Western Sahara would not fall on the shoulders of one person. The Moroccan monarchy—considered a cornerstone of Middle Eastern, African, Mediterranean, and even global stability from the Cold War to the war on terror—cannot bear the loss of Western Sahara, however. Peace efforts have so far failed to address (openly) the fact that Western Sahara's fate is tied to the internal legitimacy of the occupying regime—a regime of significant strategic importance to at least two permanent Security Council members. The problem of authoritarianism is not just a problem for Morocco; it is central to the irresolution of the Western Sahara conflict.

## DURABLE AUTHORITARIANISM AND THE DOMESTIC (NON)POLITICS OF THE WESTERN SAHARAN DISPUTE

The Western Sahara deadlock was born out of three mutually reinforcing consensuses. At the international level, there is the pro-Moroccan consensus of the United States and France (chapter 3). At the local level, there is the Western Saharan nationalists' consensus and their aspirations for independence (see part two). Finally, at the regional level, there are the contrasting consensuses within Morocco and Algeria.

From 1975 to the present, the actors and structures of the regimes in Algeria and Morocco exhibit a clear continuity. Both have survived war, widespread domestic unrest, periodic economic rupture, and minimal reforms. Yet both have come away largely unchanged. Adversity and crises of legitimacy have tended only to reinforce the dominant political actors' control rather than to diminish it. Underneath this layer are populations whose views toward the Western Sahara conflict are unlikely to change their political leaders' attitudes, either because of enforced consensus (Morocco) or apathetic indifference (Algeria). As with all major policy matters in Morocco and Algeria, Western Sahara is essentially a nonissue among domestic constituencies because there are no means for the population at large to have input. In Algeria, most citizens know that the key decisions affecting the conflict are made at the highest levels in the regime, far outside of their limited input into the constrained democratic processes. In Morocco, it is *assumed* that popular support for the annexation of Western Sahara remains high, yet there is likewise no means for the population either to question or to voice real democratic support for it.[3]

For all the superficial differences between the postcolonial states in Morocco and Algeria, there is one striking and important similarity. Although both countries have regular, internationally monitored elections as well as other structures of representative government, real power has remained highly concentrated since independence. The political economy that actualizes the rule of the regimes in Morocco and Algeria is fairly straightforward. Following independence, the Moroccan and Algerian states bought political obedience by placing few demands on the people. The government provided a wide array of services to the general population, albeit on a limited basis (i.e., enough to keep dissent to manageable levels). Rather than through taxation, income earned from exports and other sources of state revenue formed the basis of the economy. One regional expert has described this state-led economic model in the following way: "As it is sometimes put, there is 'no representation without taxation.' Rather than make themselves beholden to their people, the regimes use their externally generated income to buy acquiescence to their rule. Thus have the governments of North Africa provided generous consumer subsidies, education, health care, and other services to their people, becoming, in essence, preindustrial welfare states" (L. Anderson 1997, 130). The durability of such rentier regimes is evidenced in their ability to adapt to gradual economic liberalization. Instead of dovetailing with political liberalization, economic liberalization was simply placed more pressures on the general population while removing many economic burdens and thus blame from the government by displacing it to the private sector.

With regards to the Western Sahara conflict, the demonstrable continuity of these robust regimes bodes ill for any change in their attitudes—not only because of their rigidity, but also because popular opinion is disengaged from the functioning of power. The broad historical trend of the postcolonial period suggests that this will be the case for some time to come, barring an unforeseen chain of events (e.g., an economic collapse, an Islamic revolution, an international intervention) that might radically alter what has become a static regional politics. Likewise, the extraregional states most involved in the conflict have exhibited a parallel continuity of interests, to which we turn next.

# 3

# The Franco–American Consensus

Ever since the UN first addressed the question of Western Sahara in the early 1960s, a broad international consensus has supported that territory's right to independence through self-determination. Standing opposed to this consensus is not only Morocco, but also France and the United States, Rabat's primary bases of international support. This mutual understanding—implicitly shared by other states, notably Spain—is grounded in the belief that Morocco's and perhaps the entire region's stability hinges on the 'Alawi monarchy. Morocco's control of Western Sahara, in turn, is believed to be a necessary condition for the regime's survival. Given the fact that Western Saharan nationalism threatens Morocco's control over Western Sahara, it is therefore a threat to the regime and, by extension, to Morocco. One noticeable and obvious effect of this counterconsensus has been tacit support for Morocco's occupation and colonization of the former Spanish colony.

The background to this logic is simple enough. There has long been a fear among French and U.S. strategists that without the monarchy, Morocco could slide into chaos or be taken over by elements that might not ensure continuity of Western interests. During the Cold War, left-wing nationalists were the threat. Now it is political Islam. The Moroccan monarchy has been more than willing to play up its alleged vulnerabilities—"après moi, le déluge!"—to win over support. Although the popular Moroccan political imaginaire is not as limited as the West fears, the country's pivotal location at the mouth of the Mediterranean prioritizes stability over all other considerations. Considering the histories involved and the geopolitical context of the mid-1970s, it is clear that France and the United States were already predisposed to support Morocco's takeover of Spanish Sahara in 1975. Analyzing the intractability of the Western Sahara conflict, one group of scholars compare it with the equally deadlocked situation in Cyprus, where "mediation exercises tend to become embedded in broader geopolitical policies." In the case of Western Sahara, they note that "neither the United States nor France, the most important external powers in Maghrebi politics, has been prepared to make the fate of the Sahrawis the defining touchstone of its relations with Algeria and Morocco" (Crocker, Hampson, and Aall 2004, 33). Yet these authors do not go far enough. In this chapter, we show how the actions of the U.S. and French governments have profoundly determined the conflict's overall contours to such an extent, we believe, that one can hardly understand the past and present of Western Sahara without first incorporating this crucial dimension.

The French and U.S. governments consider themselves juridically neutral in the Western Sahara dispute. This self-avowed stance is based on two superficial facts: neither has formally recognized Moroccan sovereignty over Western Sahara or recognized the RASD. But to claim neutrality while arming and providing critical diplomatic support for only one side is a very twisted conception of impartiality. The French and U.S. governments have never shied away from the fact that they support the Moroccan monarchy, do not trust in Algeria, and see Polisario as another destabilizing force in Africa and the Middle East. Since the outbreak of war in 1975, the United States and France have been among the most important supporters of the Moroccan occupation, providing significant political, economic, and military backing for Rabat's conquest. At times, the support has been direct and overt; at other times, it has been more passive and seemingly neutral. The overall trend, however, has been a clear bias toward Morocco, from the Green March in 1975 to the negotiations in Manhasset, New York, in 2007–2008.

In this chapter, we focus largely on the United States and, to a lesser degree, France, but we also make an effort to describe the ways in which Spain and other regional and continental powers and interests have affected the Western Sahara conflict.[1] We start from the beginning, examining the U.S. response to Morocco's invasion of Spanish Sahara. We then trace U.S. policy during the war and the peace process, provide an analysis of U.S. policy that aims to understand Washington's thirty years of support for Morocco in Western Sahara, and bring in the French and Spanish dimensions. Concluding this chapter, we look at the roles other actors have played, arguing that transnational civil society is best placed to affect a positive outcome in Western Sahara.

### THE U.S. ROLE IN THE MOROCCAN INVASION

The first intervention the United States made in Morocco's favor in Western Sahara was arguably the most profound. The United States had officially adopted a position of "neutrality" on the question of Spanish Sahara, reflected in the U.S. abstention on most General Assembly votes on the issue. Both Spain and Morocco were important allies in the Cold War, and the U.S. government was as concerned about Spain's expected transition to democracy as it was about Hassan, who had narrowly escaped two attempted coups. So when Hassan declared his intent to seize Spanish Sahara, the Ford administration was placed in a difficult situation.

Yet the U.S. CIA had warned Secretary of State Henry Kissinger of Hassan's intent two weeks before the Green March was announced. On October 3, 1975, the CIA claimed, "King Hassan has decided to invade the Spanish Sahara within the next three weeks." The agency worried that "a serious conflict could develop" leading to the "downfall of the present government in Rabat" as well as to "a political crisis in Madrid" if the fighting went on for too long. These concerns were echoed in the CIA's October 5 and 8 *National Intelligence Daily* (Mundy 2006, 292–94). It is disputable whether this warning was the U.S. government's first knowledge of a planned Moroccan invasion or not. Speeches by King Hassan and his earlier troop movements in the South should have raised concern. It is also possible that Kissinger might have approved Hassan's invasion beforehand. The U.S. ambassador in Algiers during the 1975 crisis, Richard Parker, later claimed that "[t]he official record will never reveal the full truth, but Secretary Kissinger, intentionally or otherwise, may have given Hassan what the latter took to be a green light during a conversation in the summer of 1975" (1987, 126).

Another aspect of the still secret "official record" is the role played by then CIA deputy head Vernon Walters. Three years after the invasion, Walters refused to discuss his role because "[i]t would look like the King of Morocco and the King of Spain are pawns of the United States, and that wouldn't be in anybody's interest" (quoted in *Africa News,* Nov. 2, 1979). In 1981, Walters's ambiguous statement was given some background when the *New York Times* wrote, "One of Mr. Walters's last missions in the C.I.A. was a trip in late 1975 to Spain, where in meetings with King Hassan II of Morocco and Spanish officials he convinced Spain to give up control of Western Sahara" (Dec. 6, 1981). In fact, Walters's contacts with the Moroccan monarch went back to World War II, when he served as an intelligence officer in Vichy-controlled North Africa. He had met the young Prince Hassan following the Allied landing in Morocco and had reportedly given him a ride in a tank. Writing in 1978, Walters said, "Thus began a friendship which was to endure until the present" (1978, 52). So close was the friendship between Hassan and Walters that from 1972 to 1976 Walters (as CIA deputy director) "was almost considered the [Moroccan] King's case officer" (Woodward 1987, 308).

Although the official record is patchy, it is now known that on October 5, 1975, Kissinger sent a private letter to King Hassan asking him to avoid drastic measures in Spanish Sahara. King Hassan's response to Kissinger, received October 14, reassured Kissinger that Morocco would not attack Spain. Two days later Hassan II announced that he would lead 350,000 Moroccan civilians into Spanish Sahara to take it. This announcement came only hours after the ICJ published its rejection of Morocco's claim to Western Sahara. The day before that, October 15, a General Assembly Visiting Mission had reported that the population was largely in favor of independence.

On October 17, President Ford and National Security Advisor Brent Scowcroft met with Kissinger, who, deliberately or not, misrepresented the ICJ finding in Morocco's favor: "Morocco is threatening a massive march on Spanish Sahara. The ICJ gave an opinion which said sovereignty had been decided between Morocco and Mauritania. That basically is what Hassan wanted" (quoted in Mundy 2006, 294). Nevertheless, on October 19 Kissinger sent another message to Hassan II asking him to avoid escalating the situation and to let diplomacy take its course through the UN.

On October 22, the UN Security Council responded to the crisis by calling on the secretary-general to enter into consultations. Yet that same day U.S. assistant secretary of state for Near Eastern affairs Alfred Atherton met with Hassan II in Marrakech. He came away with the impression that Spain and Morocco had already achieved some kind of understanding. The Green March would be symbolic only, but Spanish Sahara would not achieve independence. This understanding complemented the secretary-general's thinking, which was based on the "West Irian precedent." In that case, the UN had simply handed West New Guinea (or Papua New Guinea), a Dutch colony, over to Indonesia in 1963, a turnover that was followed six years later by a dubious act of self-determination.

In the final days of October, the Hispano–Moroccan understanding seemed to have fallen apart, blamed on Algerian pressure. Meanwhile, the Moroccan army secretly crossed into Spanish Sahara on October 30. Spain's Prince Juan Carlos's defiant November 2 trip to al-'Ayun underscored the increasing tension, even though the Spanish withdrawal secretly began the next day. Kissinger sent a message to King Hassan on November 2 drawing his attention to the Spanish government's concerns that the Green March might spark a wider conflict. Kissinger did not call on King Hassan to halt the march; he only asked him to pursue the UN's "bilateral and multilateral diplomatic efforts" (U.S. Department of State 1975a).

President Ford, Scowcroft, and Kissinger met on the morning of November 3. Discussing the Spanish Sahara crisis, Kissinger made the following proposal, which Ford agreed to:

> KISSINGER: . . . On the Spanish Sahara, Algerian pressure has caused the Spanish to renege. Algeria wants a port and there are rich phosphate deposits. The Algerians have threatened us on their Middle East position. We sent messages to the Moroccans yesterday. I think we should get out of it. It is another Greek–Turkey problem where we lose either way. We could tell Hassan we would entirely oppose him; that might stop it but it would make us the fall guy. Or we could force [UN secretary-general Kurt] Waldheim forward.
>
> PRESIDENT: I think the UN should take on more of these problems. God damn, we shouldn't have to do it all and get a bloody nose.
>
> KISSINGER: The UN could do it like West Irian, where they fuzz the "consulting the wishes of the people," and get out of it.
>
> PRESIDENT: Let's use the UN route. (quoted in Mundy 2006, 297–8)

Kissinger's policy was clarified during a November 5 meeting with his deputies. Atherton began by reporting,

> Things are continuing to move towards the crunch in the Sahara. Tomorrow is the outside day on which the march will probably start.

There is a lot of diplomatic activity. The Moroccan Prime Minister flew into Madrid. We have a report in from [Ambassador] Wells [Stabler] about the Spanish account of this, in which the Spanish seem to have made a fairly reasonable suggestion, but there is no indication—

Kissinger, interrupting Atherton, interjected, "Just turn it over to the UN with the guarantee it will go to Morocco." Responding to a question about letting members of the Green March into the Spanish Sahara, Atherton said, "Let the marchers go into it ten kilometers, and let a token number go all the way to [al-'Ayun], and having done this turn around and go back. And to do all they can to see that the UN self-determination procedure comes out in favor of Morocco. This has been carried back to [Moroccan king] Hassan." He then said, "Hassan's problem is that if he seems to cave very much, he is in difficulty at home, of course." When Kissinger asked, "But he is going to get the territory, isn't he?" Atherton replied,

Well, he wants it 100 percent guaranteed. I think he is getting less than that—but he is getting probably the most he can hope for now in the position that the Spanish have taken. He may . . .

[Interrupting] SECRETARY KISSINGER: He is getting the most he can hope . . .

MR. ATHERTON: In the way of a promise that it will come out in the end the way he wants, after going through the UN procedure. It isn't a 100 percent guarantee. But I don't see that there is any more he can hope for or will have any support from anybody else.

Arthur Hartman, head of European affairs, added that the Spanish government was "very explicit" about "what they would do in influencing" the referendum for Morocco (U.S. Department of State 1975b).

That same day Spain notified the UN that Moroccan civilians were crossing into Western Sahara. At three in the morning on November 6, the Security Council called on King Hassan to stop the march, an order that was ignored. The Security Council then passed Resolution 380, which called upon the Government of Morocco to "immediately withdraw from the Territory of Western Sahara all the participants in the march" (UN 1978, 182 and 187). The next day Spain accused the United States of "watering down" the resolution's language, from *condemn* to *deplore*. A State Department North Africa analyst during the crisis later noted that in "all these 'toothless' resolutions, it was reportedly the United States and France that successfully resisted more forceful actions by the Security Council" (Damis 1983, 64). Confirming this speculation, then U.S. ambassador to the UN Daniel Patrick Moynihan, in reference to Security Council inaction on the almost simultaneous invasions and occupations of Western Sahara and East Timor, explained a few years later that "[t]he United States wished things to turn out as they did, and worked to bring this about. The Department of State desired that the United Nations prove utterly ineffective in whatever measures it undertook. This task was given me, and I carried it forward with no inconsiderable success" (1978, 247). The Security Council's weak response to the Green March achieved Washington's desired effect. On November 8, 1975, Spain was forced to pursue direct talks with Morocco, and on the following day Hassan announced the withdrawal of the Green March. Yet there was some uncertainty before Madrid and Rabat announced their agreement on November 14. Kissinger, Scowcroft, and Ford met in the Oval Office on the morning of November 10 to discuss the retreating Green March. According to the notes of the meeting, Kissinger told the other two, "Hassan has pulled back in the Sahara. But if he doesn't get it, he is finished. We should now work to ensure he gets it. We would work it through the U.N. [to] ensure a favorable vote." The following day Kissinger again told Ford: "It has quieted down, but I am afraid Hassan may be overthrown if he doesn't get a success. The hope is for a rigged U.N. vote, but if it doesn't happen . . ." (quoted in Mundy 2006, 300, ellipses in original).

The U.S. intervention was only a half-success. It had helped deliver Spanish Sahara to Morocco but failed to make it legal. The November 14 Madrid Agreement provided for a referendum at the end of the four-month tripartite transitional administration. However, by February 1976, with large numbers of Western Saharans fleeing to Algeria and the war heating up, the UN deemed a self-determination vote impossible, "rigged" or otherwise. The Ford administration had played a key role in creating the Western Sahara conflict; subsequent administrations would play a supporting role by sustaining it.

## THE UNITED STATES AND THE WAR FOR WESTERN SAHARA

Some modern diplomatic historians have attempted to contrast Kissinger's realpolitik, the Carter administration's "idealism," and the subsequent Reagan and George H. W. Bush (1989–92) administrations' hawkish approach. In the case of Western Sahara at war, the differences were minute. The only perceptible changes have been in terms of the quality and quantity of support the U.S. government has afforded Morocco. Support for the Moroccan regime and thus for its expansionist campaign in Western Sahara was never questioned. The same general pattern carried itself into the peace process of the 1990s and early 2000s under Bill Clinton (1993–2000) and George W. Bush (2001–2009).

In the period between the Moroccan takeover of Western Sahara and the latter half of the Carter administration, U.S. military aid to Morocco remained at modest levels (see figure 2 in chapter 2). The Carter administration's initial reluctance to become more openly involved stemmed from two constraints. A bilateral 1960 agreement prohibited use of U.S. arms by Morocco outside of its internationally recognized borders. Supplemental to that agreement was the U.S. Arms Export Control Act, which notionally aims to limit the use of U.S. weaponry by recipient countries to defensive purposes only. However, the Carter administration was not concerned about the use of weapons for illegal expansion; the major concern was that Morocco would use U.S. weapons in Algeria during a "hot pursuit" raid, which Hassan often threatened. Inside Western Sahara, Carter officials largely tolerated the use of U.S. weapons. Deputy Assistant Secretary of State for Near Eastern and South Asian Affairs Nicholas Veliotes testified that Morocco was violating its agreements with the United States and would likely continue to do so, but that the Carter administration still favored increased military aid (U.S. House 1977; see also U.S. House 1978). The State Department subsequently claimed that Morocco's deployment of U.S.-supplied F-5 aircraft in Western Sahara was not a "substantial violation" of U.S. law (U.S. House 1980a). Despite concerns expressed by some congressional liberals, Congress bowed to administration pressure and refused to block further sales.[2]

When Polisario commenced a series of attacks in 1979 that brought the war to southern Morocco, the U.S. government had a new excuse to sell more "defensive" arms to Morocco. The increase was dramatic. In 1980, the Carter administration proposed $250 million in new arms sales agreements, whereas the two previous years had seen a mere $10 million in such agreements (U.S. Department of Defense 1984, 3). Secretary of State Cyrus Vance and the Arms Control and Disarmament Agency favored increasing the shipment of defensive weapons but questioned the *scale* of President Carter's buildup of military support for Morocco. The president's inner circle never considered cutting off aid to Hassan's war of aggression. At times, there was even explicit opposition to Polisario's winning the war for Western Sahara (U.S. House 1980a, 3).

Only a handful of congressional liberals questioned the implications of U.S. policy in Western Sahara for international law, human rights, and relations with the Third World. Morocco attempted to counteract these voices by hiring the public-relations lobbying firms DGA International in late 1978 for $900,000 for six months' work and Hill and Knowlton at $100,000 per year (Houser 1980, 50).

This increase in arms shipments to Morocco also came at a time when the Carter administration was reassessing many of its prior foreign-policy stances, especially with respect to arms transfers. The contemporaneous revolution against the shah in Iran, one of the U.S. government's key allies in the Middle East, led the administration to shore up support for its regional allies. Ironically, as critics observed, the Iranian shah fell despite— and in part because of—his reliance on U.S. support.

When it came to supporting U.S. associates in the Cold War, Ronald Reagan did not share the same trepidations as his predecessor. The seriousness with which his administration would back King Hassan was clearly stated early on when in March 1981 Morris Draper, deputy assistant secretary of state for Near Eastern and South Asian affairs, told a congressional subcommittee, "It would not be in the spirit of this administration's policy if support for America's traditional and historic friends—to meet reasonable and legitimate needs—were to be withheld or made conditional other than under extraordinary circumstances" (quoted in Hodges 1985, 268). President Reagan, in one of his first major ambassadorial appointments, designated Joseph Reed, a friend of King Hassan, to serve in Morocco as the only noncareer ambassador in the Middle East. Reed had worked closely with David Rockefeller—another friend of Hassan—as his executive assistant and as vice president of Chase Manhattan Bank from 1969 to 1981. Reed later stated that "[as ambassador] [m]y mandate is to illustrate to our friends around the globe that the Reagan Administration wanted to single out Morocco as the primary example of how America supported a proven ally and friend" (quoted in *New York Times,* February 1, 1983). Ambassador Reed presented his credentials to King Hassan on November 6, 1981—the sixth anniversary of the Green March.

Only weeks before the anniversary, Polisario fighters, using heavy armor and sophisticated weaponry, had decimated the Moroccan garrison at Galtah Zammur, downing several Moroccan aircraft. CIA director William Casey afterward hand delivered a request for support from Hassan to Reagan. "We want to back him," Casey reportedly told Reagan. In November 1981, nearly two dozen U.S. military, intelligence, and diplomatic officials were sent to Morocco to help, led by Assistant Secretary of Defense Francis West (Woodward 1987, 170). This support came on the heels of a September visit by Lieutenant General James Williams, director of the Defense Intelligence Agency, and was followed by December meetings between Hassan and Secretary of Defense Casper Weinberger and then Senate Foreign Relations Committee chairman Charles Percy. In the following year, a series of meetings between the two countries' officials took place: Secretary of State Alexander Haig met King Hassan on February 12, 1982, promising greater U.S. economic assistance; Hassan met with President Reagan in May 1982, and their visit was complete with a photo op on horseback; Vice President George H. W. Bush visited Morocco in September 1983; and Jeanne Kirkpatrick, U.S. representative to the UN, visited Moroccan-occupied Western Sahara that same month (*Inquiry,* Apr. 12, 1982; *Washington Post,* Nov. 5, 1981; Zunes, interview with Steve Weissman, staff of House Subcommittee on Africa, Washington, D.C., Mar. 25, 1988).

U.S. moral support for Hassan's cause was matched by a sizable increase in U.S. military aid. Within the first weeks of the Reagan administration, a substantial tank sale to Morocco, proposed by the Carter administration in 1980, was pushed forward. The delivery of these weapons was originally based on Morocco's alleged "willingness to help achieve a cease-fire to negotiate the relevant Western Sahara issues, and to cooperate with international efforts to mediate the dispute" (U.S. House 1980b, 15). The Reagan administration defended the tank sale on the grounds that Morocco needed the tanks to balance the region strategically vis-à-vis Algeria, despite the fact that Algiers had just played a key role in the release of U.S. hostages held by Iran.

Throughout the Reagan administration, military sales agreements with Morocco averaged $50 million, a large percentage subsidized by grants (Damis 1993, 226) (see figure 3 in chapter 2). In 1983, the White House had proposed $100 million in loans for U.S. arms purchases, half of which would be given to Morocco at subsidized rates of interest. On May 11, 1982, the House Foreign Affairs Committee proposed a bill that would cut that figure in half and eliminate the interest-rate subsidy. Furthermore, it would prohibit U.S. military advisors from "performing official functions in the Western Sahara" or engaging in "any training which has as its principal purpose improving the ability of the Moroccan armed forces to carry out offensive counterinsurgency military activities in the Western Sahara" (quoted in Wright 1984, 165–66). The bill never reached the floor, though; foreign aid passed as part of a continuing resolution, with Senator Robert Kasten slipping in the administration's $100 million—$75 million in guaranteed military loans and $25 million in military grants. Besides snubbing the Foreign Affairs Committee, this last-minute move had the effect of forcing a reduction in aid to other countries. In general, economic and development aid to Morocco was also on the rise, even as aid to poorer African countries was cut back. Assistance in this form also helped to defray the costs of waging war by freeing up more funds in the Moroccan budget.

On the diplomatic front, the Reagan administration cut off the limited contacts made with Polisario during the Carter administration. A House Committee on Foreign Affairs Staff Study Commission to the region in 1982 criticized the administration for "prohibiting even discreet and low-level diplomatic contact with the Polisario" and its "over-reliance on the military component in United States–Moroccan relations" (U.S. House 1982, 5, 9).

Aid from the United States to support the Moroccan war effort, especially during the Reagan administration, prolonged the fighting and delayed the peace process. As early as 1979, Representative Stephen Solarz correctly predicted that arming Morocco would "encourage intransigence rather than flexibility" and "prolong the war rather than shorten it" (Solarz 1979, 295–96). The Carter administration had made some efforts to tie military aid to Moroccan peace commitments, stating in early 1980s that the supply of counterinsurgency weapons would "give Morocco a sense of support that can contribute toward negotiation of a solution which reflects the wishes of the inhabitants" (U.S. House 1980a, 3).

The Reagan administration, in contrast, made no such demands. As Deputy Assistant Secretary of State for Near Eastern Affairs Morris Draper stated in a hearing before the House Subcommittee on Africa, "We will not . . . make decisions on military equipment sales explicitly conditional on unilateral Moroccan attempts to show progress toward a peaceful negotiated settlement" (U.S. House 1981, 5). This position was taken despite the fact that the House had mandated in its 1980 foreign-aid legislation that U.S. arms "should be related to Morocco's willingness to help achieve a cease-fire, to negotiate the relevant Western Sahara issues, and to cooperate with international efforts to mediate the dispute"

(U.S. House 1980b, 15). Military aid to Morocco had the opposite effect; it helped provide the means with which Morocco could turn the tide against Polisario and walk away from the OAU's settlement efforts. The 1982 Foreign Affairs Committee Staff Study Mission warned that U.S. military assistance, by sending the wrong message and emboldening Hassan, would likely have a detrimental impact on the peace process (U.S. House 1982, 11–12, 18). Indeed, Hassan was not willing to accept UN mediation until stalemate had been achieved on the battlefield.

### THE U.S. GOVERNMENT IN THE SEARCH FOR PEACE

The years 1988 to 2000, which coincided with the George H. W. Bush and Clinton administrations, also saw the strongest UN push to hold a referendum on independence in Western Sahara. The end of the Cold War ushered in a monopolar world, what the elder Bush would christen the "New World Order" of U.S. hegemony. In a realignment of U.S. priorities, conflicts were no longer seen as opportunities to advance interests, but rather as blockades to those interests. During this period, the international community felt it was time to end many conflicts sustained by the Cold War. In this context, U.S. policy appeared to drift back toward believable neutrality. Although U.S. military aid to Morocco remained high until the end of the war, overtly pro-Moroccan statements were toned down and low-level channels to Polisario were reopened. More important, the United States offered strong backing to the UN settlement effort, suggesting that Washington had come to accept the possibility of an independent Western Sahara. When Hassan II visited President Bush in Washington just weeks after the 1991 cease-fire, Bush declared his support for the UN plan. In reality, as will be seen in chapter 8, the United States supported the referendum effort only as long as Morocco did.

The UN was able to achieve a cease-fire in Western Sahara in September 1991, but plans for the referendum that was supposed to follow just months later faltered from the start. The UN had decided to push forward with the partial implementation of MINURSO, the UN Mission for the Referendum in Western Sahara, despite any formal or signed agreement on its particulars. The major stumbling block, which would ultimately capsize the entire project in 2000, was a late Moroccan demand to triple the size of the voter list. In the face of Moroccan efforts to subvert the referendum's legitimacy, the U.S. response was ambivalent. Although some elements of the State Department did not see Hassan's effort to flood the vote with Moroccans as a threat to the referendum's "integrity" (Bolton, 1998), other officials stated privately to Stephen Zunes that relations would be "seriously affected" if Morocco did not cooperate with the fair implementation of the referendum (Zunes, briefing, U.S. Department of State, Washington, D.C., Jan. 1991). The State Department also refused to allow U.S. colonel Albert Zapanta—deputy military commander of MINURSO's peacekeeping force and the highest-ranking U.S. soldier in the mission—to testify before a congressional committee hearing that Morocco was preventing MINURSO from carrying out its mission and that the U.S. government needed to support the peace process more strongly. In that same hearing, Undersecretary for International Organizations John Bolton admitted that Morocco had been "unhelpful," but he also stated that Morocco's role in supporting U.S. foreign policy had to be taken into account in determining the U.S. response (*New York Times*, Mar. 1, 1992). The U.S. House nevertheless passed a strongly worded resolution (269) supporting MINURSO in early 1992, despite vigorous lobbying against it by the Moroccan embassy.

When the Clinton administration came to power in 1993, the U.S. profile in the referendum effort increased somewhat, first with the creation of the Security Council's "Group of Friends" for Western Sahara: the United States, France, Russia, Great Britain, and Spain. Behind the scenes, the United States tried to keep the peace process on the right track, using its influence in July 1993 to keep Morocco–Polisario negotiations going in al-'Ayun (Jensen 2005, 42) and convincing Hassan to reduce sentences for Sahrawi political prisoners arrested during recent protests (Chopra 1997, 57). Once MINURSO was able to start registering voters for the referendum in 1994, some upper-level positions in the mission were given to former U.S. officials, explicitly as a sign of U.S. commitment to the referendum.

The Republican takeover of the U.S. Congress in 1994 saw a strong anti-UN mood settle into Washington. Congress criticized many aspects of UN operations and their budgets and even Secretary-General Boutros Boutros-Ghali personally. As news surfaced in 1995 that the UN mission in Western Sahara had been compromised by Morocco, congressional conservatives began to use MINURSO as an example of the supposed UN incompetence. These allegations were supported by reporting from the *New York Times*, Human Rights Watch, and the congressional testimony of Frank Ruddy, former head of MINURSO's identification unit. Looking into some of the issues plaguing the referendum, the United States took part in a special Security Council mission to Western Sahara in June 1995. The U.S. government decided afterward to take a harder line with Morocco and requested that Rabat preprocess the tens of thousands of additional voters it wanted included in the referendum. It also tried to moderate Security Council resolutions on Western Sahara, whether introduced by France on behalf of Morocco or introduced by Argentina and Germany for Polisario's benefit (Chopra 1997, 57). The Clinton administration, fighting for reelection in 1996 and heavily involved in the conflict in former Yugoslavia, also considered abandoning the costly, ineffective, and heavily criticized referendum in Western Sahara. The "limited sympathy" between Secretary of State Madeleine Albright and Boutros-Ghali, according to a former head of MINURSO, did not help either (Jensen 2005, 74). The United States later vetoed Boutros-Ghali's reappointment late in 1996.

In early 1997, a different kind of U.S. intervention saved the referendum in Western Sahara: the secretary-general's appointment of former U.S. secretary of state James

Baker as lead negotiator. Although acting as a UN envoy, Baker brought with him explicit backing from the Clinton administration, a key asset that the new UN secretary-general, Kofi Annan, was undoubtedly banking on. Within months of his appointment, Baker had obtained the first and so far only signed agreement between Morocco and Polisario—the Houston Accords.

The death of King Hassan II and the ascension of Mohammed VI in mid-1999 changed the rules of the game. Where a referendum on independence under Hassan seemed plausible, under the young and untested Mohammed it seemed dangerous. At the first possible opportunity, February 2000, the United States helped put the Houston Accords aside. Although MINURSO had just completed the provisional voter list after six years of work, the Franco–American consensus reasserted itself to protect the new monarch. Looking into the delayed referendum, the U.S. House Subcommittee on Africa held hearings in September 2000, the waning days of the Clinton administration. Deputy Assistant Secretary of State for Near Eastern Affairs Allen Keiswetter, questioned on the status of the referendum, refused to blame Morocco for the failed implementation of the Settlement Plan, opting instead to spread blame equally. Reaffirming the main reason behind the referendum's demise, Keiswetter confirmed, "The United States opposes any solution being imposed on the parties" (U.S. House 2000, 4).

This policy of nonimposition carried into the George W. Bush administration. Although Baker had helped win Bush the election in Florida in 2000, by 2004 Bush was undermining Baker's efforts to resolve the conflict. The events of September 11, 2001, had again changed the rules of the game; and like Reagan before him, Bush saw Morocco as a crucial ally in a global struggle. Morocco's geostrategic positioning remained the same, but Morocco under King Mohammed VI was also able to present itself as a rampart against radical Islamist ideas, an active ally in the global war on terror and a vehicle for Bush's "transformative" democratic vision for the Middle East. The 2003 suicide attacks in Casablanca and several "terrorist" incidents thereafter underscored Morocco's vulnerabilities and further justified U.S. support for the regime. It was in this context that Bush sided with Morocco against Baker in 2004, thus scuttling seven years of peacemaking efforts.

For Polisario, only a few positive developments emerged following Baker's departure. In ratifying a free-trade agreement with Morocco in 2004, Congress forced the explicit exclusion of Western Sahara from the agreement. Grassroots U.S. pressure helped to convince the Oklahoma-based Kerr-McGee Company to withdraw from oil exploration in Western Saharan for Morocco in early 2006. And Polisario's congressional supporters set up hearings on the Western Sahara issue in November 2005 (U.S. House 2005).

While Polisario struggled to maintain its bipartisan support in Congress, support for Rabat grew in the White House, especially from Elliot Abrams and other neoconservatives among the national-security elite. The Bush administration ramped up support for Morocco following Baker's departure in 2004, yet the short tenure of John Bolton as U.S.

representative to the UN (2005–2006), who favored carrying out MINURSO's mandate to hold a referendum, moderated this policy briefly. Bush administration support for Morocco took more and more the form of backing autonomy as the optimal solution to the conflict. In a June 2008 letter to Mohammed VI, Bush stated that autonomy is the only realistic solution to the conflict, a sentiment later endorsed by Secretary of State Condoleezza Rice several weeks later. In the Bush administration's waning months, a new UN envoy was named, former U.S. ambassador and Middle East expert Christopher Ross (*Alhurra,* Sept. 25, 2008). Although these statements and Ross's appointment suggested that the United States was going to take a more active role in the conflict, the radical swing toward a pro-Moroccan position—if not de facto recognition of Moroccan sovereignty—had so alienated Polisario and Algiers that the prospects for peace were dismal.

## UNDERSTANDING U.S. POLICY

Morocco's 'Alawi dynasty was in fact the first government to recognize the United States as an independent nation, in 1777. Ten years later, during the heyday of the Barbary pirates, the two nations signed a friendship treaty that has become one of the longest sustained by the United States. In more recent times, Morocco's usefulness can be traced to World War II with the Allied landing at Casablanca led by General Dwight D. Eisenhower, which helped cement a new era in relations between the Moroccan monarchy and Washington. Then, as the Cold War began to take shape, the 'Alawi regime aligned itself with Western interests, even after France terminated its protectorate there in 1956. As either a "moderate" voice in the Arab–Israel conflict or a proxy force in African intervention, Morocco not only became key to U.S. policies in the Middle East and Africa, but also helped implement them. It also has immense strategic value to the United States. Its shared control of a key global chokepoint, the Strait of Gibraltar, with Spain and Great Britain makes it one of the world's "pivotal states"—a geographical blessing and curse. Western interest in Morocco's stability, despite the fact that Morocco is a relatively resource-poor land, is in line with treatment of similar geostrategic linchpins (e.g., Turkey, Egypt, Indonesia, and Panama).

As a sign of its commitment to Morocco, the United States gave Rabat $3.53 billion in economic and military aid between 1946 and 2006, the majority in the form of grants. Apart from Egypt, Morocco has received more U.S. aid—especially military—than any other country in Africa before September 11, 2001. In the Middle East, apart from Egypt and Israel and Iraq after 2003, Morocco is second only to Jordan ($9.46 billion) in terms of aid received (United States Agency in Development 2002, 2006).

For the first fifteen years of the conflict, the U.S. government's support for the Moroccan occupation of Western Sahara was articulated in the context of the Cold War. However, unlike the situation in Afghanistan or Vietnam, the war in Western Sahara was never a true proxy war between the United States and the Soviet Union, although at times King Hassan tried to create this false impression in order "to strike a responsive chord in Paris and Washington" (Damis 1985, 146–47). In no way were the Soviets using Polisario to attack a Western client; indeed, the Soviets had excellent relations with Morocco. Furthermore, as demonstrated earlier, U.S. support for Morocco's conquest has outlasted and transcends Cold War rationale. Furthermore, the war with Polisario was an unintended consequence of the Green March in 1975. Kissinger and the CIA's primary concern at that time was the threat to Hassan's regime posed by either a war with Spain or a failure to take Western Sahara. Washington was simply blind to the existence of Western Saharan nationalism.

Moroccan stability has been important to United States not only because of Morocco's geostrategic face value, but also because of its instrumental value. From the Cold War to the war on terror, Morocco has both supported and, more important, furthered U.S. interests. Even before the war with Polisario, Hassan's reign had benefited from a CIA "assistance program." In exchange, Hassan allowed U.S. intelligence agencies "virtually free run of his country" (Woodward 1987, 308). Although the U.S. military has close relations with its Moroccan counterparts, the United States closed the last of its four air bases in Morocco in 1963 and its last communications station there in 1978. Nevertheless, it has held on to emergency transit, staging, and refueling rights at the four former U.S. bases (Wright 1984, 176–77). Similarly, two telecommunications centers, although operating under the pretext of civilian functions, apparently also serve military and intelligence purposes. Morocco's location is important to the U.S. Central Command both for refueling rights and for the use of airspace, but King Hassan reportedly expressed his unwillingness to have the United States use Morocco in any military operation against any "Arab country friendly to Morocco." Under the 1982 U.S.–Morocco Agreement, Rabat made the military part of Casablanca's international airport and the Sidi Slimane military air base available to U.S. forces (Damis 1983, 127), and the latter also served as one of the emergency landing facilities for the U.S. space shuttle. The U.S. Navy also regularly calls at Moroccan ports; the port at Tangier is able to accommodate the largest ships in the U.S. fleet.

As a close ally of the U.S. government in the Cold War, the Moroccan regime had been deputized with certain regional responsibilities under the Nixon or "Guam" Doctrine (i.e., the doctrine was announced in Guam), otherwise known as the "surrogate strategy." Following the disastrous U.S. war in Indochina, the surrogate strategy became a cornerstone of U.S. foreign policy toward the Third World; direct U.S. intervention in Third World conflicts had become politically prohibitive. Instead, day-to-day control over the spread of "communism" or even unsympathetic democratic governments was outsourced to Western-aligned states and organizations. Morocco was a member of an elite group of Middle Eastern states called the "Safari Club," whose main task was to uphold Western interests in Africa. Following South Africa's failed 1975–76 intervention in Angola, the French intelligence agency, with Kissinger's approval, built a secret alliance among Washington, Paris,

Saudi Arabia, Iran, Egypt, and Morocco in September 1976. The group's goal was to counteract Soviet influence on the African continent. Twice in the late 1970s, Moroccan forces helped suppress uprisings against the pro-Western dictator Mobutu Sese Seko of Zaire (Democratic Republic of the Congo). In April 1977, the U.S. and French governments coordinated deployment of troops from Morocco and Egypt to Zaire's Shaba Province, the center of a rebellion threatening European mining operations. In 1978, the U.S. Air Force airlifted another fifteen hundred Moroccan troops as the mainstay of an "African Defense Force" (also consisting of token contingents from Togo, Gabon, Senegal, and the Ivory Coast) to suppress a second uprising. Yet there were some failures, such as when the U.S. government did not come to Somalia's aid following the Soviet Union's switch to Ethiopia's side in the Ogaden conflict in 1977 (Hodges 1983b, 250–51; Mamdani 2004, 84–86). According to several accounts, by going through Morocco as a means to circumvent the 1976 U.S. Clark Amendment, which prohibited direct American support of Angolan opposition groups, the United States was able to arm a rebel movement in southern Angola (Wenger 1982, 25). Morocco was also the base for U.S.-backed Libyan exiles opposed to Muʻammar Qadhdhafi's regime, and Rabat played a role in the overthrow of the Chadian government in 1982 (*Inquiry*, Apr. 12, 1982). In 1979, King Hassan dispatched one hundred troops to Equatorial Guinea in support of Colonel Teodoro Obiang Nguema Mbasogo after his successful coup d'état, and this contingent grew into a permanent force of four hundred (Ruf 1987, 94). Hassan also dispatched security personnel to support conservative Arab monarchies in the Persian Gulf region (Parker 1987, 159).

In the Middle East, Morocco had to be more cautious to balance Arab–Islamic and Western concerns, but it nonetheless has been generally supportive of U.S. interests. Despite sending three combat brigades to fight Israel in the Golan Heights during the 1973 war, Morocco has been considered one of Israel's closest contacts in the Muslim world. Hassan acted as a go-between for Egyptian representatives and Israeli officials and other Jewish leaders before Anwar Sadat's 1977 trip to Jerusalem. Although in secret helpful of Egypt's peace initiatives with Israel, Morocco, under pressure from its Saudi benefactors, publicly opposed the Camp David Accords and temporarily broke relations with Egypt. In the early 1980s, clandestine meetings with high Israeli officials were reported periodically, culminating with the July 1986 meeting between Hassan and Israeli prime minister Shimon Peres in Rabat. Given the fact that Israel has become more and more central to U.S. Middle East policy since then, whether under Clinton or George W. Bush, Morocco's good relations with Israel have only earned Morocco more clout in Washington.[3]

Given the logic of the Cold War, it seems reasonable to assume that the United States also supported Morocco to prevent Western Sahara from becoming independent. As an ally of Algeria and with Polisario espousing radical Third World socialist nationalism, an independent Western Sahara would have caused friction against U.S. interests in the region. For France, a pro-Algerian state in Western Sahara would have disrupted

Paris's West African sphere of influence by cutting Morocco off from Mauritania. Yet the only direct evidence of such an attitude is a quote from Kissinger—"the United States will not allow another Angola on the East flank of the Atlantic Ocean"—that has no firm source (quoted in Kamil 1987, 10). In the official record of Oval Office conversations cited earlier, there are no indications that U.S. policymakers feared a power vacuum if Western Sahara became independent. If it was a concern, it was at best only a secondary interest. Moreover, U.S. policy has been so consistently focused on the survivability of Morocco's regime that it is reasonable to assume that Washington would support Western Sahara's independence if that became necessary for Morocco's stability.[4]

However, the question of Western Sahara's viability has gained more currency in recent years. After September 11, 2001, the Sahara–Sahel region of Africa became a major front in the U.S. global war on terrorism. In 2004, the United States announced the multi-million-dollar Pan-Sahel initiative, which aimed to increase border security in the poor Saharan states of Chad, Niger, Mali, and Mauritania. In 2006, the initiative's budget was increased to $500 million, and the program was expanded to include Morocco and Algeria and renamed the Trans-Saharan Counter Terrorism Initiative/ Partnership. According to the State Department's 2007 budget, its aim was "supporting the U.S. national security interests of waging war on terrorism and enhancing regional peace and security" (U.S. Department of State 2006, 247). Not only were U.S. troops involved in training activities, but they also appeared to be actively involved in counter-terrorism operations in many of the participant countries (see Keenan 2004, 2006).

The new U.S. security concerns in the Sahara–Sahel region have been based on the impression that weak states and porous borders define the region. It is believed that in such an environment, terrorist organizations will find not only safe havens (as al-Qaida did in Central Asia), but also willing recruits. An independent Western Sahara came to be seen not only as a threat to U.S. interests in Morocco, but also as a threat in and of itself. Fears flourished that an independent Western Sahara would be weak, unstable, and open to anti-U.S. influences. Thus, in June 2008 President Bush announced U.S. support for autonomy as the only solution for Western Sahara because "an independent state in the Sahara is not a realistic option" (Agence France Presse, May 1, 2008).

This is not to suggest that Morocco's stability is no longer the overriding priority for the United States. The Bush administration's 2005 Congressional Budget Justification noted, "As the May 16, 2003 terrorist attacks in Casablanca demonstrated, Morocco is on the front lines in the global war against terrorism. . . . It is in the United States' interest that Morocco—a moderate Arab state, whose leadership is committed to a democratic transformation—succeed" (U.S. Department of State 2004, 426). In 2003, King Mohammed stole a page from his father's book and quickly learned to use Western fears and prejudices—this time, in regard to radical Islam—to justify a more authoritarian mode of rule and a harder line on the Western Sahara. A year after the May 16 bombings, the

United States declared Morocco a "major non-NATO ally," adding it to a list including Australia, Egypt, Israel, Japan, Jordan, Kuwait, New Zealand, and South Korea. For Western Sahara, the effect of the new war on terror has been eerily similar to the effect of the Cold War. The peace process has all but collapsed as U.S. moral and military support for Morocco has increased.

FRANCE AND THE MAGHRIB

French policy toward Western Sahara has largely complemented U.S. policy, yet it is founded upon a richer, more direct historical experience with the region. The conquest of Algiers in 1830 heralded the birth of a century of French control in Northwest Africa. By 1912, which saw the final establishment of a French protectorate over Morocco, France had laid claim to the majority of North and West Africa, with Algeria considered a territorial extension of mainland France. One hundred thirty-two years after the invasion of Algiers, most of these territories had achieved independence: Tunisia and Morocco in 1956; Chad, Mali, Mauritania, Niger, and Senegal in 1960; and finally Algeria in 1962. With respect to Algeria, the experience for both colonizer and colonized was much more profound, especially the final eight years, which witnessed one of the bloodiest wars of national liberation in the twentieth century. Hundreds of thousands of Algerians were killed, and millions of French settlers fled back to France. Whereas France was able to leave Morocco on relatively amicable terms, the Algerian War (1954–62) created feelings of mutual animosity that resonate to the present. Yet the ties between France and Algeria—the most intensely colonized French possession—have only become more complex since independence, facilitated by the roughly one-million-strong Algerian community in France (see Naylor 2000).

When Hassan announced his invasion of Spanish Sahara in October 1975, France was already predisposed to help Morocco (and Mauritania) for its own reasons as well as for the same Cold War, geostrategic reasons shared with the United States. And like Washington, Paris played a more behind-the-scenes role, blocking an effective UN Security Council response to Moroccan aggression against Spain. However, months before the Madrid Agreement, in May 1975, France's conservative president, Valéry Giscard d'Estaing (1974–81), met with King Hassan, a meeting in which many old and outstanding issues were settled and an agreement was apparently reached—the "Marrakech Plan"—to fast-track arms deliveries to Morocco, including fifty F-1 fighter-jets, Puma helicopters, AMX tanks, and various light weapons (Hodges and Pazzanita 1994, 272). President Giscard d'Estaing, in opposing the creation of an independent Western Sahara, also let it be known that he was against "the multiplication of microstates" (quoted in Naylor 1987, 211), even though he had supported independence for the Comoros Islands that same year and was to do so for Djibouti in 1977, two French colonies with populations roughly equal to that of Western Sahara (Damis 1983, 117).

During the early years of the Morocco–Polisario war, the French government trans-ferred some $1.5–2.0 billion worth of arms to Moroccan forces—at a time when the Carter administration was restricting some arms transfers (Damis 1983, 116). The French gov-ernment also reinforced its relations with embattled Mauritania. On September 2, 1976, the two governments signed an *accord d'assistance militaire technique* (technical military assistance agreement), "which provided for French aid in the organization, equipping, and training of the national armies and police forces." Of the roughly 14,000 French military personnel in Africa in 1978, 100 were posted in Mauritania, 250 in Morocco, and 1,300 in Senegal, the latter a major staging point for operations in the western Sahara and in the Chadian conflict (which involved 1,800 French personnel already). The French base at Dakar was home to eighteen Jaguar and twelve Mirage III fighter-jets, reconnaissance aircraft, and KC-135 airborne fuel tankers (Lellouche and Moisi 1979, 109, 114–15, 127).

France also has the distinction of being the only third party to intervene militarily into the Western Sahara conflict. From its positions just south of the Western Sahara war, France launched Operation Lamantin (Manatee) against Polisario in late 1977, purportedly as a punitive measure for its killing of two French nationals and taking of several others as hos-tages at the iron mines in Zouerate, Mauritania. In reality, the hostages had provided only a pretext for the French government to strike back at Polisario, which had seriously desta-bilized its client regime in Mauritania and was increasingly threatening Morocco. Direct French intervention, however, could do nothing to counteract the low morale in the Mau-ritanian forces, which eventually led to the overthrow of President Mokhtar Ould Daddah in mid-1978. The French government then reverted to a behind-the-scenes position and reportedly played a part in expediting the Polisario–Mauritanian peace accord of August 1979 (Price 1979, 69–70).

Even before the French intervention against Polisario, tensions between Algiers and Paris were running high. France had laid the blame for the killing of its nationals and the hostage crisis squarely at the feet of Algeria. The Algerian populace reacted with the "largest anti-French demonstration since the War of Liberation," and, following the airstrikes, Algerian president Houari Boumedienne nationalized several French hold-ings. Although Giscard d'Estaing was the first French head of state to visit independent Algeria, in April 1975, his support for the Moroccan–Mauritanian takeover of Western Sahara earned him public derision from Boumedienne, who accused the French leader of deliberately misleading him on the issue. Giscard d'Estaing's response was to call for the "banalization" of the heated Franco–Algerian relations, which only earned further scorn from Boumedienne. The French government's relations with Algeria had soured earlier that decade when Boumedienne nationalized all French petroleum interests in Algeria in 1971 (Balta 1986, 242–43). The conservative French president's ambitious efforts to maintain France's neocolonial relationship with most of its former African colonies and France's defiance of the UN arms embargo against the apartheid regime in South Africa also ran counter to Algeria's left-leaning nationalistic vision for Africa (Lellouche and Moisi 1979, 119).

For obvious reasons, Polisario and the Algerian government, then under President Chadli Bendjedid (1979–92), welcomed the election of the Socialist Party in France in May 1981. Before the vote, the Socialists had stated strong support for the Western Saharans' right to self-determination and "privileged ties with non-aligned countries of the Mediterranean zones and the African continent, especially Algeria" (quoted in Naylor 1987, 214). Shortly after the Socialist victory, the French foreign ministry met with a Polisario official in August and later allowed Polisario to open an office in Paris as a national liberation movement, comparable to the status given the Palestine Liberation Organization (PLO). President François Mitterrand (1981–95) also moved quickly to repair relations with Algeria. France's trade surplus with Algeria quickly disappeared when deliberately overpriced gas imports were allowed onto the French market. Then, in early 1982, an announcement was made that Algeria had accepted more than $3 billion in large-scale project contracts with French firms and $2.43 billion in major infrastructure-development support (*Africa Report,* May 1983).

President Mitterrand's courting of Algeria coincided with a marked diplomatic turn away from the French government's uncritical support for King Hassan. Following the Moroccan military's June 1981 massacre of more than five hundred demonstrators in Casablanca who were protesting against the economic effects of an IMF structural adjustment program, the French government condemned the killings. Paris also called for the release of Moroccan Socialist leaders who had been jailed for criticizing the king's proposal to hold a referendum in Western Sahara. It also apparently used whatever influence it could on the Moroccan regime to get the latter to acquiesce to the idea of a referendum in Western Sahara, which King Hassan had accepted at the 1981 OAU summit in Nairobi (Balta 1986, 246). Yet Morocco was still the third-largest African destination for French goods, purchasing $1.2 billion in 1981; and France was still Morocco's number one export market (*Africa Report,* May 1983). Shortly before the Socialist victory, France had entered into an agreement to invest more than $10 billion in Moroccan industry. King Hassan visited Mitterrand in Paris in January 1982; three months later the French government agreed to an aid package for Morocco, including military debt rescheduling, followed by an increase in annual aid from $192 to $266 million starting in 1983 (Damis 1983, 116; see also Balta 1986).

Nevertheless, there was a time during this period when France seemed less pro-Moroccan than the United States. When asked to access the possibility of a French mediation role, U.S. ambassador to France Evan Galbraith concluded that Paris did not want to be associated with Washington's position on the issue "because the French believe that we are operationally involved with the Moroccan military effort." He added, "The French, seeing the risks in terms of appearing to Algeria as lining up with an ally of Morocco, would not be likely to agree to any sort of coordinated approach to solving the problem of the Sahara" (U.S. Embassy Paris 1984). Whereas Reagan and his Cold Warriors were perfectly willing to fall firmly behind their Moroccan surrogate, the French government's ambivalent interests kept it from making an important contribution to resolving the conflict. The French government was hesitant to push either side toward making any concessions that might have led to an early peace and perhaps resolution.

As long as the Quai d'Orsay (French Ministry of Foreign Affairs) prioritized the delicate balance in its web of relations, it had no freedom of movement on the Sahara issue. All the idealist rhetoric regarding self-determination and ending France's role as Africa's gendarme amounted to nothing more than talk. Indeed, the French government was more than willing to provide arms to support the Moroccan government's war effort and to offset Algeria's Soviet-made sophistication of Polisario. During the war for Western Sahara, French military equipment comprised 50 percent of the arms obtained by Morocco, costing nearly $4 billion. The major French arms transfers to Morocco from 1975 to 1988 included twenty-four F-1CH and fifteen F-1EH Mirage fighter aircraft, twenty-four SA-341 Gazelle helicopter gunships, twenty-four Alpha-Jet counterinsurgency aircraft, thirty AMX-13 light tanks, almost four hundred VAB armored personnel carriers, and more than one hundred AMX-F-3 155-millimeter self-propelled howitzers (Volman 1999, 212–13). However, near the end of the war, France scaled back its military aid to Morocco for financial reasons, but not ethical or legal ones. When it did so, the U.S. government stepped up, providing Morocco with $183.8 million in military loans between 1987 and 1992, $159.8 million of which were forgiven starting in 1989 (U.S. Department of Defense 1992, 32–33). By the mid-1990s, U.S. arms would come to dominate Moroccan imports, and France's share would fall to 10 percent (Volman 1999, 218).

As the Western Sahara conflict came under the UN's purview in the late 1980s, the French government's influence was instead channeled through its permanent seat on the Security Council. Reinvigorated French support for King Hassan came about after the election of the conservative center-right Jacques Chirac (1995–2007) to the presidency. Throughout the existence of the UN mission in Western Sahara, France generally joined with the council on the need to maintain consensus, to keep the parties talking, and to move the referendum process forward. However, more than any other permanent member, France has defended Morocco's position on the Security Council.

France's influence on the peace process is well illustrated in the 2001 Framework Agreement proposed by UN envoy James Baker. The agreement called for the signatures not only of Morocco and Polisario, but also of France and the United States to "guarantee performance." Later, in 2003, Baker called on Chirac, via Secretary-General Annan, to use his influence with King Mohammed so that a new peace proposal would be well received. However, when Rabat decided to reject the Baker Plan, France used its position on the Security Council to block wholeheartedly any effort to endorse the 2003 proposal. Likewise, following Baker's 2004 resignation, the French government largely supported Morocco's posture. As many European and American diplomats were willing to note, President Chirac's personal relationship with a member of the Moroccan royal family had reinforced in a staunchly pro-Moroccan French policy. Indeed, the French president saw himself as a kind of godfather to Mohammed VI, charged to protect the young king during his early reign. Conservative president Nicolas Sarkozy, elected in May 2007, has not altered France's policies. Sarkozy declared during his first visit to Morocco that October, "France will stand shoulder to shoulder" with Morocco on the question of Western Sahara. The only signs of French dissent tend to come from civil society; like Spain, France boasts a number of nongovernmental organizations (NGOs) and Western Saharan support groups. As in Spain and the United States, these groups have not been able to reshape France's Western Sahara policy.[5]

Meanwhile, France's relations with Algeria remained rocky. French support for the Algerian regime's military coup and bloody counterinsurgency in the 1990s was not lost on Algiers, especially after many other countries, including the United States, reduced overt ties with Algeria. The election of Abdelaziz Bouteflika as president in 1999 was followed by several years of improving relations between Algiers and Paris, including a visit from Chirac in 2003. However, the expected signing of an Algerian–French treaty of friendship in 2005, which aimed to put certain historical issues behind the two countries, failed to occur when, among other tensions, France decided to highlight the positive aspects of colonialism in its school textbooks. Mitigating this problem, though, is the fact that Algeria has recently refused to use significant leverage to change French policy on Western Sahara. A recent instance of such refusal occurred at the founding summit of Sarkozy's Mediterranean Union, originally proposed as a regional alliance, separate but equal to the EU. The idea, riding roughshod over the existing Barcelona Process or Euro-Med Partnership, was initially seen as a cynical attempt to stop the spread of the EU to Turkey and provoked serious skepticism in the major non-Mediterranean European capitals that were being asked to finance the new union. In the lead up to the July 2008 summit, there was a blur of diplomatic activity as France attempted to persuade Algiers to attend. Amidst all the horse trading, Algeria apparently never put the issue of Western Sahara on the table, despite the fact that Sarkozy had staked his foreign policy on the summit's success.

SPAIN AFTER THE MADRID AGREEMENT

As the former colonial power in Western Sahara and Morocco's closet European neighbor, Spain holds a special position in relation to the conflict. Although Madrid attempted to wash its hands of Western Sahara on February 28, 1976, following a tumultuous and incomplete decolonization process, Spain has never been able to extricate itself fully from the Morocco–Polisario dispute. Like France and the United States, Spain shares a strong interest in Moroccan stability, perhaps more so given their proximity across the Strait of Gibraltar. And like France, Spain has a significant colonial legacy in North Africa that ties it to Morocco, whether historically in the protectorates of northern and southern Spanish Morocco or currently in the Spanish presidios Cueta and Melilla on Morocco's Mediterranean coast. However, a powerful cross-section of Spanish civil society and politics strongly support Western Sahara's right to independence through self-determination.

Indeed, one of the most enduring questions in the history of the Western Sahara conflict is: why did Spain bow to Moroccan pressure and abandon the Sahrawis to whom Spain had recently promised self-determination? The politics behind the Spanish government's dramatic reversal during the 1975 Sahara crisis—from promising Polisario independence in October to meeting Rabat's demands in November—were unclear in the years immediately thereafter. A 1978 Spanish parliamentary inquiry attempted to answer this question. Its conclusion, which had been suspected early on (e.g., Franck 1976), was that amidst the chaos following Franco's collapse into a coma on October 17, 1975, a small group of pro-Moroccan "ultraconservatives," led by Prime Minister Carlos Arias Navarro (1973–76) and Minister José Solís Ruíz, cut a secret deal with Hassan behind the back of the more moderate foreign minister, Pedro Cortina y Mauri, who favored UN mediation. Not only were the ultras sympathetic to Morocco, but they also feared Polisario's radical nationalism, which was quite different from the moderate nationalism Spain had tried to cultivate. One concrete fear was that a Polisario-led government might provide a base for the Canary Islands Independence Movement, which was based in Algiers (Damis 1983, 65). (Algeria also served as a refuge for several Basque Euzkadi Ta Askatasuna activists, although the Algerian government agreed to trade information on these terrorists in 1986 in exchange for Spanish intelligence on Algerian exiles, notably the deposed Algerian president Ben Bella [Segal 1991, 259].) Some colonial officials thought avoiding war with Morocco was worth the price of abandoning the Sahrawis, but Governor-General Federico Gómez de Salazar and Secretary-General Colonel Luis Rodríguez de Viguri y Gil abhorred the idea. For General Gómez de Salazar, the indigenous population was "unanimous" in its "desire for independence" (quoted in Hodges and Pazzanita 1994, 185, 375). Viguri even claimed that Spanish businesses, including the Banco Ibérico, had intervened to protect their investments in Morocco, but he also suspected French and U.S. hands in these affairs (Zunes, interviews with former Spanish colonial officials, Madrid, 1990).

Since then the Spanish government has maintained an uneasy balance between its moral obligations to the Western Saharans and its political, economic, and strategic interests in both Morocco and Algeria. In 2000, Spain consumed $2.5 billion of Algeria's petroleum-dominated exports, facilitated by a gas pipeline running through Morocco and under the Strait of Gibraltar (Economist Intelligence Unit 2002, 63). Trade with Morocco was more symmetrical, with exports and imports to and from Morocco adding up to around $1 billion in 2001. Spain also gave Morocco $119.2 million in development assistance from 1996 to 2000, compared with $44.5 million in aid for the same period to Algeria (Economist Intelligence Unit 2002, 67, 2003b, 61–65). The Spanish government, which ranked number seven for worldwide arms export agreements between 2000 and 2003 (Grimmett 2004, 78), has also become a major supplier to Morocco since the end of war in Western Sahara, including one Descubierta frigate, four Lazaga missile-equipped patrol ships, and seven CN-235 transport aircraft (International Institute for Strategic Studies 2002, 112–13). Spain has also participated in joint military maneuvers with Morocco (Segal 1991, 255). Unlike much of the French and U.S. arms sales to Morocco, however, Spain's arms transfers were not specifically tailored for antiguerilla operations.

The two Spanish coastal enclaves Ceuta and Melilla as well as the disputed islets Peñón de Vélez de la Gomera, Peñón de Alhucemas, and Islas Chafarinas continue to represent a major aspect of Hispano–Moroccan relations. More than 120,000 Spaniards reside in Ceuta and Melilla, which have been under Spanish control for more than five hundred years. Following independence, the Moroccan government laid claim to them as a part of Greater Morocco. The Moroccan regime, however, has never pressed as hard for the presidios and islets as King Hassan successfully did for Western Sahara. In fact, as a Moroccan concession in the Madrid Agreement, Hassan agreed not to raise the presidios and islets' status so long as Gibraltar remained under British control (Segal 1991, 256). In the hands of the Moroccan monarchy, the status of the Spanish possessions has been as much a tool for leveraging Spain as it has been for irritating Spain when relations are not going Rabat's way. It also remains a convenient jingoist prop, capable of diverting the Moroccan people's attention from domestic issues, as when King Mohammed VI, in order to manufacture militarist credentials he still lacked, sent several gendarmes to occupy a Spanish islet about the size of a soccer field in the summer of 2002, only to be quickly removed by Spanish Special Forces.

Good Hispano–Moroccan relations are necessary, yet they are often strained by the fact that Morocco is a major jumping-off point for illegal immigrants and trade destined for Europe. Spain and the rest of Europe are heavily dependent on migratory workers for agricultural labor, other poor-wage jobs, and population growth; for African countries, remittances form a vital aspect of many economies, including Morocco's. Yet along with immigrants seeking a better life, Morocco produces a considerable amount of the illicit drugs consumed in Europe. Not only is it in Spain's own interest to maintain good relations with Morocco, but Spain is often pressured by other European states to do so for these reasons.

Besides the security of its mainland and presidios, Spain's interests in Morocco also extend to the Canary Islands and the rich fishing grounds around them. In the 1960s,

Spain trawled off the coasts of Africa and the Americas with the world's third-largest fishing fleet, pulling in 1.5 million metric tons a year, much of it going to feed Spain's enormous appetite for seafood. By the end of the 1970s, however, the new Law of the Sea Treaty, which allowed countries to extend their economic zone from seventy miles to two hundred miles from their shores, severely curtailed Spain's previously unlimited access to the Moroccan littoral. Before then, the Moroccan government had initially exercised its right to an insignificant twelve-mile limit, but by 1973 it had expanded its excursions to the seventy-mile limit, which incorporated the best fishing areas. Although a deal was reached in 1977 that allowed Spanish fishermen to continue but with catch limits, Morocco withheld ratification. In the meantime, Morocco regularly seized Spanish vessels in its waters and even attacked one, killing seven sailors. Several interim agreements diffused tensions and allowed Spanish fishermen to work under Moroccan constraints, such as catch limits (Meltzoff and Lipuma 1986, 682, 691–92). Morocco's own fishing industry, which grew substantially in the late 1970s and 1980s with the help of $300 million in foreign investment, was by 1990 employing half a million Moroccans (Damis 1995, 64). Unfortunately, all of the fishing off the Atlantic coast of Northwest Africa has stressed the undersea environment and curbed the numbers of the most lucrative catches, which has only complicated subsequent fishing deals with the EU. Morocco decided in 2001 not to renew its agreements with the EU, which hit the Spanish fishing industry the hardest. A new agreement was eventually negotiated and passed in 2005–2006, but it brought on international criticism for including Western Saharan waters.

During the early years of the war, Morocco's tenuous grasp on Western Sahara meant that Spanish fishing interests in the Atlantic were exposed to attack. Polisario regularly carried out threats to protect its territory from foreign exploitation. In one of these attacks, it took eight Spanish fishermen hostage but later released them to Spanish politician Javier Rupérez in 1978. Upon accepting the hostages, Rupérez, who had attended Polisario's fourth General Congress, agreed to recognize Polisario as the legitimate representative of the Western Saharans in his capacity as a representative of Spain's ruling Unión del Centro Democrático (Union of the Democratic Center). A later meeting between Spanish prime minister Adolfo Suárez (1976–81) in his role as the head of the union, not as prime minister, and RASD president Mohammed Abdelaziz provoked a strong reaction from Morocco. Rabat again broached the issue of Ceuta and Melilla and withheld ratification of the 1977 fishing agreement. King Juan Carlos subsequently visited Morocco to smooth things over (Naylor 1993, 25–27).

Polisario and the Algerian government looked forward to the government of the Partido Socialista Obrero Español (PSOE, Spanish Socialist Workers' Party), victorious in the October 1982 Spanish elections, as they had to the coming of the French Socialists. The new prime minister, Felipe González (1982–96), had traveled to the Western Saharan refugee camps in 1976 and had joined calls for his government's formal renunciation of the 1975 Madrid Agreement. The PSOE also worked to gain formal recognition of Polisario and supported the 1978 hearings into the 1975 Sahara crisis. In another similarity with the French Socialists, however, the PSOE quickly toned down its pro-Polisario rhetoric after taking office. A new fishing agreement was signed with Morocco in 1983, resulting in resumed attacks by Polisario against Spanish fishing vessels in the waters off the Western Sahara. Despite a visit from Algerian president Bendjedid in 1985, the Spanish government expelled Polisario's representative in Madrid that September after the ELPS attacked a Spanish vessel flying a Moroccan flag (Naylor 1993, 25, 28–29).

The numerous Western Saharan solidarity groups in Spain have attempted to challenge close Hispano–Moroccan relations. Although one would expect Spanish civil society support for Polisario to come from left-wing organizations, it actually tends to be nonpartisan. Former members of the Spanish Sahara's colonial and military administration, including conservative Francoists, have been particularly outspoken on the issue of self-determination. Their devotion to the independence cause rests on paternalist colonial sentimentalities and present-day contacts with former native soldiers now in the refugee camps. They have expressed a deep feeling of betrayal by some civilian politicians in Madrid who had long promised the Western Saharans self-determination and a feeling of humiliation from having to back down in the face of the smaller and weaker Moroccan forces. At a more grassroots level, Spanish families host ten thousand Sahrawi refugee children each summer, offering them a welcome respite from the intense conditions near Tindouf (see Mundy 2007b, 289). Yet this level of civic engagement with the Western Saharan cause has hardly affected Spanish foreign policy, suggesting once again the powerful nature of Morocco's strategic importance to the West.

In July 2003, Spanish–Moroccan relations, always tenuous, suffered heavily when it became clear that the conservative government of Prime Minister José Maria Aznar (1996–2004) vigorously supported the U.S. push to impose the Baker Plan in the Security Council. The Moroccan and Spanish governments had only recently repaired the damage from the Parsley Islet fiasco a year earlier, which had included a withdrawal of ambassadors. Some sources in Spanish intelligence predicted as early as fall 2001 that King Mohammed needed to improve his image as a military commander through a minor show of force against Spain's lingering possessions in Morocco. However, in addition to the two Spanish presidios Ceuta and Melilla in Morocco, tensions also had their roots in King Mohammed's first visit to Western Sahara in 2002, during which Moroccan security agents escorted a Spanish reporter back to Madrid when he attempted to cover the royal visit. Shortly thereafter, the Moroccan ambassador was recalled from Madrid as unfavorable news reports turned up in the Spanish press. The role of Spanish vessels in the overexploitation of fishing stocks in the waters off Morocco and Western Sahara were also a source of friction between the Aznar government and Mohammed VI (for background, see González 2002). Holding a seat on the Security Council in July 2003, Madrid fully supported the Baker Plan, which led to accusations in the Moroccan press of neoconservative collusion between the Spanish government and the George W. Bush administration to reshape the Middle East. However, it is also possible that Aznar's domestically unpopular support for the U.S. invasion and occupation of Iraq in 2003 may have helped provoke devastating terrorist attacks on commuter trains in Spain by Islamist extremists in March 2004, leading to PSOE's return to power.

Spain's current prime minister, José Luis Rodríguez Zapatero (2004– ), made improved relations with Morocco his priority. His first foreign trip was an April 2004 meeting with King Mohammed. In July, Spanish foreign minister Miguel Ángel Moratinos warned that a referendum in Western Sahara could destabilize the region, but in October, after meeting with Algerian foreign minister Abdelaziz Belkhadem in Algiers, Moratinos back-peddled: "The desire of the Spanish government is to apply the Baker Plan" (Agence France Presse, Oct. 26, 2004), which called for the holding of a referendum. The Spanish media and the opposition accused Zapatero's government of having two positions on the Baker Plan, one for Algiers and one for Rabat. But in the wake of Baker's departure, with a UN mediator lacking since June 2004 and with tensions rising, Spain took a leadership role in the peace process that no one else wanted to own. Spain first attempted to stage trilateral talks with Morocco, Polisario, and Algeria. Toward this end, Zapatero met Polisario head Mohammed Abdelaziz at the end of November 2004, although this meeting was quickly balanced by a fence-mending visit by King Juan Carlos to Morocco in January 2005. Spain's push for negotiations outside the UN framework ultimately failed because Polisario continued to demand Morocco's acceptance of the Baker Plan as a precondition for talks. The failure was also a reflection of the solidifying support for Morocco from France and the United States. With the outbreak of the Sahrawi intifada in May 2005 and Spain's failure to arrange any semblance of Morocco–Polisario dialog, Madrid pushed the hardest for a new UN envoy when many other states felt Morocco and Polisario should be left to stew. Following the appointment of a new UN envoy in late 2005, Spanish diplomacy again took a back seat to the UN while relations among Rabat, Algiers, and Polisario were balanced. Spain's Western Sahara policy, echoing the Franco–American consensus but for more ambivalent reasons, drifted back to supporting UN initiatives through the reelection of Zapatero's PSOE in March 2008.

ROOM FOR NEW INTERESTS?

Although it is clear that the United States, France, and Spain have profoundly shaped the Western Sahara conflict, other international interests have either played minor roles or may conceivably come into play. One of the first that comes to mind is Russia, which holds a Security Council veto and a seat in the council's Group of Friends for Western Sahara. The latter position suggests that Russia has some interest in the conflict, although it has historically shown little real interest in either mediating or voicing support for either side.

One would expect, given the logic of the Cold War, that the Soviet Union would have naturally supported Polisario. The Soviets, however, kept a careful distance from the dispute and maintained important trade relations with both Algeria and Morocco. Since 1962, Algeria has been almost exclusively equipped with Soviet/Russian arms, yet because of its ideological independence and Muslim population, the Algerian regime shunned close ties with the "atheist" Soviets. The Soviets had a strategic interest in good relations with Algeria's ports, which would allow them to outflank the NATO forces aimed at eastern Europe (Parker 1987, 149). Yet the Soviets never recognized RASD, nor did any other Warsaw Pact country; Polisario was one of the few African national liberation struggles that never received arms from the Soviet bloc directly. On several occasions, Polisario forces even attacked Soviet fishing vessels operating off the coast of Western Sahara.

The Moroccan government's wartime relations with the former Soviet Union were surprisingly comfortable despite its pro-Western pronouncements abroad and its aggressive anti-Communist behaviors at home. The Moroccan Communist Party, which was Hassan's backchannel to Moscow, consistently supported the takeover of Western Sahara and lobbied Moscow to support Morocco's claim. Morocco was also one of the Soviet Union's most important trading partners in Africa, with nonmilitary assistance to Morocco the third highest among non-Communist countries (Zindar 1988). At the time of the Madrid Agreement, Morocco received 60 percent of its oil from the Soviet Union, and the two nations had important agreements in fishing and agriculture. In 1978, Morocco signed what Hassan called the "deal of a century"—a thirty-year agreement to supply phosphates to the Soviets in exchange for $2 billion in investments for a new mine (Harrel-Bond 1983, I:10; Zoubir 1993, 109).

In the Western Sahara peace process, Russia has continued to play a neutral role on the Security Council, balancing its interests in Algeria and Morocco while displaying concern through its membership in the Western Sahara Group of Friends. Under President Vladamir Putin (2000–2008), Russia returned to the international stage as a prominent player, largely on the wings of soaring oil and gas prices that revived the Russian economy. As will be seen in chapters 8 and 9, Russia has sometimes played a tiebreaker role on the Security Council, whether countering French and U.S. attempts on behalf of Morocco or more inexplicably siding with France in 2003 and against the United States in order to water down support for the Baker Plan. Indeed, Russia's silence on Western Sahara stood in sharp contrast to its vocal opposition to Kosovo's 2008 independence and, only months later, to its military intervention under recently elected President Dimitry Medvedev (2008– ) on behalf of the breakaway regions of South Ossetia and Abkhazia in pro-NATO Georgia.

Like Russia, Great Britain has been a member of the Group of Friends for Western Sahara on the Security Council but has shown little interest in the conflict, partisan or otherwise. Sharing trade ties to both Morocco and Algeria, yet without either the historical baggage of France and Spain or the superpower onus of the United States, the United Kingdom, it is often remarked, does not have a dog in the fight, apart from the issue of Gibraltar, which mirrors and is often tied to the issue of Spain's presidios in northern Morocco.

In Europe, the overriding interests of France and Spain have kept—and will keep—the EU from assuming an active role in the Western Sahara conflict. The EU formally has no foreign policy unless such is mandated by the member states; in the case of Western Sahara, some European countries complain that the EU is not allowed to address the issue because of France and Spain. Outside of a small group of activist members of the European Parliament, who lobby to support the right of self-determination, the EU has been only tangentially caught up in Western Sahara owing to trade agreements with Morocco, most notably the 2006 EU–Morocco fisheries agreement. The EU focuses primarily on economic issues in the southern Mediterranean basin. Morocco was also the first North African nation to sign an association agreement with the EU in 1995, mostly economic in nature (see Damis 1998). A regionwide initiative was inaugurated in the Euro-Med Partnership signed at Barcelona Conference in 1995. The initiative's primary goal was improving non-EU economies, although Euro-Med also called for a "common area of peace and stability" (Carapico 2001, 25). However, when Euro-Med's ten-year anniversary came around in 2005, there was little progress to report, partially owing to tensions between Arab states and Israel. Both Morocco and Algeria, however, had refrained from bringing the Western Sahara issue into the forum, demonstrating that the two countries could prioritize issues on which there is common ground. The Western Sahara issue was likewise nowhere to be seen when French president Nicolas Sarkozy's Mediterranean Union initiative held its first summit in July 2008.

The Middle East and Africa have been disabled from playing a constructive role in the conflict owing to their polarization. In Africa, Polisario receives the strongest support; in the Arab world, Morocco has the upper hand. More than any international organization besides the UN, the OAU played a significant role in the effort to resolve the Western Sahara conflict (see chapter 7). For many African states, Morocco's Western-backed violation of self-determination and disrespect for colonially inherited boundaries (*uti possidetis*) has provided a self-interested reason to back Polisario. Much of the credit, however, goes to Algeria, whose traditional leadership on Third World issues has played a major role in RASD's diplomatic successes in Africa. The OAU's successor organization, the African Union, continues to recognize RASD as the legitimate government of Western Sahara, and so the Moroccan government continues to boycott that African forum as well. In an effort to counteract Polisario's success in Africa, Rabat—with the support of France, which has considerable economic leverage over most of its former colonies—has convinced several African nations to rescind or suspend their recognition of RASD since the cease-fire of 1991. South Africa's recognition of RASD in 2004 reminded Morocco that the Western

Saharan independence movement still had powerful friends on the continent, although the effect of this recognition was to disable further any possible African mediation role.

Morocco has received the most sympathy from other Arab states for its occupation of Western Sahara, originally owing in large part to Hassan's credibility and support from the powerful monarchies of Saudi Arabia, Jordan, and the Persian Gulf. In the Middle East, the Western Sahara issue is generally seen from the Moroccan point of view as a problem between Rabat and Algiers. Polisario's pull with Arab states outside North Africa is weak, although it is also the case that Algeria has not lobbied as vigorously in the Arab world as it has in Africa. King Hassan served as head of the Arab League and other international Islamic organizations more often than any other Middle Eastern leader (Stork 1990, 4). He also sent Moroccan troops to fight on the Syrian front during the 1973 Arab–Israeli war. Such good relations and a history of leadership enabled Morocco to receive the acquiescence of the Arab League on the Western Sahara issue. Until the United States was able to ship offensive weapons directly to Morocco for the Western Sahara war, Egypt forwarded some of its own U.S.-supplied arms, as did Jordan and Iran under the shah.

One exception to the general support for Morocco in the Middle East was the Arab Steadfastness Front, composed of Middle Eastern states opposed to U.S.-sponsored peace negotiations with Israel in the late 1970s (Algeria, Libya, South Yemen, Syria, and the PLO). This group endorsed Polisario's cause as a means of retaliating against Morocco's facilitation of the Israeli–Egyptian dialog during that period, although that endorsement meant little in terms of practical support. The late Egyptian president Anwar Sadat had supported Morocco's ambitions in the Sahara early on, and Morocco returned the favor by "facilitating Sadat's trip to Jerusalem in 1977" (Balta 1986, 246). Although Libya had frequently blasted Morocco as an obstacle to pan-Arabism and the Palestinian cause, in 1984 Qadhdhafi signed an agreement with Morocco that terminated Tripoli's support for Polisario. In exchange, Morocco withdrew support for the Chadian government in the dispute against Libyan-backed rebels over the Ouzou Strip. Although Morocco called off the Oujda Treaty with Libya just two years later, the treaty had served its purpose by denying Polisario arms. Algeria's efforts in the Arab world to link Polisario's struggle to that of the Palestinians has otherwise fallen on deaf ears, except for in Syria. Comparisons with Iraq's 1990 invasion of Kuwait have been equally unsuccessful. Indeed, in the fall of 1990, Morocco dispatched a token two-thousand-man force to Saudi Arabia following Iraq's takeover, creating significant domestic tension but earning significant debt forgiveness from the Saudis.

Outside the traditional state-based framework of international relations, it is worth considering whether transnational civil society might potentially play a positive role, as was the case with activism against apartheid in South Africa. The yearly conference of the European Coordination Conference of Support to the Sahrawi People, which held its thirty-fourth annual meeting in 2008, historically organized efforts in Europe for the

Sahrawis. International human rights organizations also brought pressure to bear, albeit indirectly, during the early years of the conflict. From the beginning of the Moroccan occupation, the work of groups such as Amnesty International, Human Rights Watch, and International Federation for Human Rights, although neutral on the question of sovereignty, have monitored Moroccan abuses in the occupation of Western Sahara. Amnesty International in particular helped bring to light the issue of the hundreds of Sahrawis whom Morocco had "disappeared" following the 1975–76 invasion (see chapter 6).

In the years following the demise of the peace process in 2004 and the outbreak of a Sahrawi intifada in 2005, transnational activism has increased. The Internet has been key to the coordination of activists from Australia to Norway to the occupied Western Sahara. One area that has received special attention, with some success, is Morocco's ongoing illegal exploitation of natural resources in Western Sahara. After Morocco announced petroleum exploration contracts in Western Sahara, several successful divestment efforts in Europe and the United States have resulted in companies' walking away from or avoiding Western Sahara oil. If victories in the areas of human rights and natural resources can be multiplied and amplified, the conflict may be as affected by grassroots activism as by powerful states. Transnational solidarity also has the potential to change the policies of key democratic states such as France, the United States, and Spain. However, the limited success of Spanish activists—the most engaged in the world—in changing their country's policies speaks to the powerful interests behind the Franco–American consensus.

# PART TWO

# Nationalism

Some nations have certainly emerged
without the blessings of their own state.
—ERNEST GELLNER, *Nations and Nationalism*

# 4

# The Historical Formation
# of Western Saharan Nationalism

In the 1990s, the site of the Western Sahara conflict shifted from the desert hinterlands to the voter-identification centers of the UN mission. From 1994 to 1999, the effort to resolve the conflict, the arduous process to establish an electorate for a referendum on independence in Western Sahara, became the conflict. The weapons were no longer guns but memories, claims of blood, lineage, habitation, ancestry, and colonial documents. These difficulties faced by the UN mission resulted from Morocco's politicization of the identification process, made possible given the contested and often confused nature of Western Saharan identities. Spanish colonialism had provided the UN referendum with clear spatial and temporal boundaries. What colonialism had failed to provide were clear boundaries of blood.

The correspondence between the frontiers of Spanish Sahara and the social boundaries of groups attributed to it was largely imagined. Spanish colonialism and Western Saharan nationalism posited the Sahrawi people as an ethnos, a consanguineous identity previously rooted in family and "tribe." At the same time, the Sahrawi people had become a nation, a people with a new sense of place resulting from nearly a century of direct European intervention. In the ambiguous space between blood and land, Morocco successfully challenged the idea that Spain had counted all indigenous Western Saharans in 1974. By opening up debate on the question "Who is a Western Sahrawi?" (Dunbar 2000), the Moroccan government caused the very idea of a Sahrawi people to come into question. In any understanding of the Western Saharan conflict, it is thus necessary to delve into questions of nationalist identity, its historical formation in Western Sahara, the conditions from which a Sahrawi people became possible, and the consequences of exposing these factors.

The idea of a Sahrawi people, like the idea of nationalism, is recent, and, like many nationalisms, the Sahrawi idea is the outgrowth of the colonial dialectic. It is in the nature of such processes of domination to create social boundaries as well as geographical ones. In colonialism, settlers differentiate themselves from natives; natives are differentiated into castes, classes, races, tribes. Identities become fixed into hierarchies until liberation movements invert them, often creating new modes of rule by perpetuating old ones. These operations of power, discussed more fully later, have been a major force shaping identity formation throughout history. Spanish Sahara is not exempt. Likewise, it is in the nature of nations to warrant histories. Historicity provides legitimacy, grounding, meaning, purpose, telos. National self-construction must therefore constantly write and rewrite its history. As Benedict Anderson notes, the nation narrates its history and thus creates itself in reverse (1991, 205). As the nation progresses, its history regresses countertemporally; a nation's forefathers are its progeny, unwitting ancestors are descendants, its makers are its products.

With these arguments in hand, this chapter delves into the historical formation of the Sahrawi people. First, we examine the concept of "Sahrawi" and try to come to some understanding of its origins via a critique of the ways in which Saharan populations have been conceptualized in colonial historiography and ethnography. These insights allow us to consider the historical formation of identity in the westernmost Sahara without repeating some of the mistakes of past observers. Working in three stages, we advance from the long Arabization of the western Sahara to the rise and fall of regional empires and then to the latter stages of European domination in the late twentieth century, right to the precipice of the Moroccan invasion of 1975. Next we take a slight detour and consider in depth the ICJ's 1975 opinion regarding Morocco and Mauritania's historical claims to Spanish Sahara. We think this topic worth excavating for two reasons: the opinion reveals not only the weakness of the Moroccan claim on Western Sahara and thus further underscores the illegitimacy of the takeover, but also elucidates the Western Saharans' sovereignty over their own land. From the foundation provided in this chapter, the following two chapters explore the Western Saharan nationalist movement's contribution to the ethnogenesis of the Sahrawi people from 1975 onward. Coupled with the political and historical background supplied in part one, these three chapters—dealing with the origins, developments, and mutations in the Western Saharan nationalist movement—form a crucial basis for part three.

## CONCEPTUALIZING THE SAHRAWI

The idea of a Sahrawi people is central to Western Saharan nationalism and thus to the Morocco–Polisario dispute. The term *Sahrawi* (normally *Saharaoui/Sahraoui* in French and often *Sahraui* in Spanish) is often used to mean "indigenous Western Saharan," although this equivalent is not accurate. Indeed, it is sufficient on most accounts that an "ethnic" Sahrawi only has to claim descent from one of the recognized major or minor social groupings—"tribes" or "confederations"—in or overlapping the former Spanish Sahara. A member of the Rgaybat al-Sharq confederation, the most populous Sahrawi group, could be Sahrawi by blood and yet never have set foot in Western Sahara. Thus, any definition of *Sahrawi* that limits the category to persons native to the territory of Western Sahara (i.e., only Western Saharans are Sahrawi and not vice versa) is overly restrictive given normal usage of the term. Such a definition would, for example, exclude many proindependence activists native to southern Morocco but who identify as ethnically and nationally Sahrawi.[1] The most pragmatic definition of Sahrawis is that they are the Hassaniyyah-speaking peoples who claim membership among at least one of the social groupings found in and around the area now known as Western Sahara.

Linguistic and cultural affinity with Mauritanians has led some to categorize the Sahrawis as a subgroup of the Bidan ("Moors") of the greater western Sahara. H. T. Norris explains that the term *Bidan* "is used by the Saharan Moors, both Arab and Berber speakers, to distinguish themselves from the negros [al-Sudan]. The term, meaning 'the whites' is found in quite early writings" (1986, 245). The division of Saharan peoples into "black" Africans (al-Sudan) and "white" Arabs/Berbers (al-Bidan) was the product of earlier imperialisms and colonialisms, later refined in Islamic epistemology by geographers and conquerors (Lydon 2005, 295–96). Romans had differentiated themselves from the "Others" of Northwest Africa by naming them "Maurus," derived from the late Greek *mauros* (black) and from which we have inherited the term *Moor*. Although Sahrawis could claim membership within the Bidan, it still does not prove that the Sahrawis constituted a distinct self-identifying group before colonialism. If this was the case, it should have registered before colonialism, not during the midst of it. Yet the term *Sahrawi* as the native people of Spanish Sahara did not exist before the mid–twentieth century.[2]

This is not to say that the term *Sahrawi* was neither used nor meaningless before Spanish colonialism. What is interesting, however, is the way in which the term gained its new ethnonationalist meaning. In 1962, David Hart used the term in his study of the Rgaybat, but only to mean "Saharan Bedouins" (516). This meaning is in fact closer to the most basic sense of the term *Sahrawi,* Arabic for "Saharan"—a person or thing of the Sahara (*al-Sahra'*). Because most people of the Sahara would be Bedouin, this reported definition makes sense. However, in a revision of the same article more than thirty-five years later, Hart altered his definition to mean "the generic term for Western Saharan nomads" (1998, 31). He does not explain, however, why he abandoned his earlier definition in favor of the later, geographically constrained meaning. The best explanation is that in the preceding three decades, the term *Sahrawi* earned a new meaning. Indeed, in order to make any argument for the category Sahrawi as Western Saharan, one has to rely on premises provided by colonialism in the first place.

Yet in making this suggestion, that the idea of a Sahrawi people is a relatively recent development, we need to avoid haphazardly repeating the mistakes of colonialism. Most studies of the Western Sahara conflict—this one included—have relied heavily on descriptions of the peoples and events of the western Sahara that were derived from studies conducted during colonialism. Yet the models of "traditional" societies that were refined during European colonialism in the nineteenth and twentieth centuries often tell us much more about colonial interests than about the colonized. French anthropology in North Africa in particular sought to divide Maghribis into distinct categories so as either to solidify existing power relations or to "divide and rule"—in both cases, to serve colonial interests. In Morocco, ethnic manipulation sought to weaken the monarchy and eventually impose a new political structure based on influential Amazigh ("Berber," indigenous North Africans) leaders in the High Atlas. In Algeria, such colonial practices took the form of the "Kabyle Myth," which saw the Imazighen (the plural form of Amazigh) as a civilizable Mediterranean people lost in a sea of barbarian Arabs (Lorcin 1999).

In the western Sahara, European ethnography applied the same basic oppositional model—Amazigh/Arab—except in a different context. Colonially supported anthropology divided Saharan tribes into "castes" and attributed to them Amazigh or Arab ancestry and qualities. The colonial model held that the Arab Hassan constituted a warrior cast ("guerriers"), the direct descendants of the Banu Ma'qil (Arab Bedouins who had come to North Africa from the Arabian Peninsula in the eleventh century). Imazighen, in contrast, composed a scholarly class (Zawaya), remnants of the Zenagah-speaking "true" natives. Within the caste system, as colonial anthropologists understood it, the Zawaya were allegedly subordinate to the Hassan. In 1971, Philip Curtin challenged the neatness of these categories when he pointed out that both the Hassan and the Zawaya groups maintained "military capability," "forced others to pay tribute" and "contained inferior endogamous casts of minstrels and artisans as well as a class of slaves, 'abid or haratin" (1971, 13). Despite the well-known shortcomings of this model, scholars have continued to employ it for some time. Timothy Cleaveland (1998), however, has insisted that the static colonial model should be abandoned in favor of a more dynamic conception of Saharan societies.

Colonialism generally tended to view the "primitive" and "underdeveloped" societies it colonized as more rigid and fixed (i.e., "traditional"), whereas Western nation-states were seen as places of change and rapid development (i.e., "modern"). The pervasiveness of this worldview has meant that many anthropologists and historians in the twentieth century were almost totally blind to the dynamics within a variety of different societies, especially the ones under their domination. Beyond this general problem, Cleaveland specifically takes to task the "[colonial] politics of the model's construction" in Mauritania, highlighting the fact that its use benefited not only the colonial occupiers, but also the native elites, who eagerly espoused its veracity. These elites, typically male, could also (ab)use "tradition" to buttress patriarchal social relationships, much to the detriment of the colonized women and youth (see Ranger 1983). Cleaveland's alternative is a constructivist approach, which he argues can accommodate an understanding of the ways in which Saharans perceived, accepted, and sometimes resisted social relations in their societies (1998, 370–71; see also Cleaveland 2002).

The colonial administration in Spanish Sahara utilized ethnographic knowledge as well, especially when applying governing powers. In 1962, Spain created a system of indirect control grafted onto their understanding of the indigenous model of decision making. "Tribal" fractions (*fracciones nómadas* or *afkhadh*) represented the basic division from which members would send representatives to a council, the Jamaʻa (Djemma). The Jamaʻa handled, as it had before Spanish formalization, the aspects of life left largely untouched by the colonial apparatus outside of the major cities. Spanish administrators, however, regularly made sure that those selected to this larger body were sympathetic to the colonial interest (Hodges and Pazzanita 1994, 151–52). In 1967, Madrid established a larger Jamaʻa (Asamblea General del Sahara), composed "overwhelmingly of Sahrawis who were openly prepared to collaborate with the colonial authorities" (Hodges and Pazzanita 1994, 117).

Bringing these skepticisms of colonial knowledge to bear will help guide us to the modest goal at hand, which is to identify the historical and epistemological conditions that make the Sahrawi possible. Starting from the premise that identities are made, not found, we aim to understand how a group of people on the western edge of the Sahara came to see themselves as a people, a nation, and, eventually, a country under occupation. As is the case with many colonized peoples, the ways in which the inhabitants of Western Sahara imagined themselves before and after their subjugation by Europeans are markedly different. Spanish domination specifically and regional colonization generally played a profound role in shaping the Western Saharans' self-conception. By imposing new boundaries—real and imagined—on the peoples of Western Sahara, Spain, with substantial aid from France, provided the material and ideational grounds upon which an indigenous nationalist movement could gain traction.

THE ARABIZATION OF THE WESTERN SAHARA

The Sahrawi identity is a unique and complex regional hybrid—a mixture of autochthonous, Arab, and sub-Saharan African factors. The Arab layers, of course, come into play with the Islamic conquest of North Africa, which had reached the Atlantic by the early eighth century, although it failed to reach beyond the coastal plains. When Islam finally found the Sahara, it was not by sudden conquest, but after several centuries by coursing its way through the networks of everyday life. By the eleventh century, sub-Saharan West Africa had joined the Islamic sphere (Brett and Fentress 1996, 82; Lapidus 1988, 491).

The rise and fall of regional Islamic empires played an important role in the transformation of local identities. The largest of these, al-Murabitun (the Almoravids), a political and religious movement originating in mid-eleventh-century Mauritania and Western Sahara, would come to claim most of Northwest Africa in a very short time. By 1090 C.E., the Murabitun had taken the important northern Saharan "port" of Sijilmasah, sacked the Ghanaian kingdom's capital of Kumbi-Saleh and its Saharan stronghold of Awda-ghust, crossed the High Atlas, founded Marrakech, and penetrated deep into Spain and Algeria. The empire of the Almoravids, however, was short-lived.[3] A new movement, al-Muwahhidun (the Almohads), surged out of the High Atlas in the middle of the twelfth century, easily overtaking the crumbling Almoravid empire. Although the Muwahhidun reached as far as Tunis by 1200 c.e., their rule was likewise insecure and was driven out of Spain fifty years later. The empire was later lost when a new challenger, the Banu Marin (Merinids), composed primarily of Zenatah Berbers, took the Maghrib. To assert control in some areas, the Merinids worked closely with a group of Yemeni invaders coming from the east, the Awlad Hassan.

Also known as the Banu Ma'qil, this coalition of the six sons of Hassan ibn 'Aqil had joined with the Banu Hilal invasion of North Africa. The Fatimid Caliphate in Egypt in the eleventh century had sent these groups reportedly as a punishment. Reaching the western Maghrib by 1200, they took Sijilmasah and followed the Wadi Dra'a west, then went south along the Atlantic coast in the next century. The nomadic Ma'qil easily took to the Sahara in the thirteenth and fourteenth centuries and quickly colonized areas in present-day Western Sahara and Mauritania: Zammur, Tiris, and Adrar. Some of the Zenagah Berber groups (Sanhajah in Arabic) resisted the invasion, but their last stand, the War of Shur-bubba, ended with their defeat at Tin Yifdad around 1674 (Norris 1986, 36, 244, 246).

The broad Arabization of the western Sahara included two major features: the reconstruction of lineages and the ascendancy of Arabic as the dominant regional language. As the fourteenth-century Islamic historian Ibn Khaldun noted, the Zenagah, as early as the tenth century, claimed ancient Yemeni ancestry for reasons of political legitimacy (Brett and Fentress 1996, 131). Zenagah claims of Southwest Asian ancestry had become "myth-ical genealogy concocted by non-Arab Muslims of Africa for social or ethnical prestige" (Norris 1962, 318). Four hundred years later this process accelerated rapidly. According to Norris, "[Between] 1400 and 1500 many of the Western Saharan peoples redesigned their lineages and genealogies. This may have taken place with a marked switch from semi-matrilineal kinship nomenclature to that of patrilineal eponyms, many of them alleged descendents of the Prophet himself or one of his Companions, or else family trees which illustrated later ties with eponyms of the Ma'qil bedouin." Norris argues that this timeline might be too early, but the process, later "perfected," was certainly under way before the Awlad Hassan completed their conquest of the western Sahara (1986, 44–45). This wide refashioning of their past also coincided with "vast social changes in the region, both social and cultural," facilitated by the establishment of "the Hassaniya dialect of Arabic as the lingua franca from the Wadi Draa to the Senegal and from the Atlantic to Timbuktu" (Norris 1986, 2). Over the course of the next three centuries, Arab identities had achieved hegemony in the western Sahara, with the Zenagah dialect marginalized to a few areas in Mauritania by 1900.

At the onset of colonialism in Western Sahara, there were several major and minor social groups in and around the region that would later become Spanish Sahara (map 5), most of them claiming Arab origins. The two Rgaybat confederations formed the largest groups by population and territorial spread. Based on their geographical tendencies, there was Rgaybat al-Sahil (coastal) and Rgaybat al-Sharq (eastern). All Rgaybat have constructed their lineages around the figure Sidi Ahmad Rgaybi, who arrived in the Dra'a region in the sixteenth century. From him, almost all Rgaybat gain status as *shurafa'*,

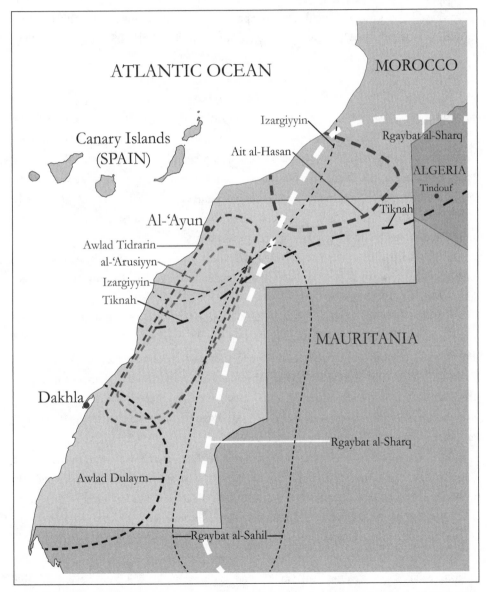

Map 5. Approximate geographical distribution of major Western Saharan social groups before 1975. Based on maps in Barbier 1982; Damis 1983; Ibn 'Azuz Hakim 1981; Vilar 1977.

descendents of the Prophet Muhammad (Norris 1986, 250). In the southern Río de Oro region, the Awlad Dulaym (Dalim), taking their name from one of the six original Ma'qil groups, had established themselves along the southwestern coast and into Mauritania. Directly north of the Dulaym, the Awlad Tidrarin and the al-'Arusiyyn maintained overlapping ranges near the coast. Straddling the northern border of the Spanish Sahara, the dominant subgroups of the Tiknah confederation, the Ait al-Hasan and the Izargiyyn, inhabited the Spanish territory, but also as far north as the Sus River and the Anti-Atlas Mountains. There were also dozens of other minor groups all across the region. Not only were these latter groups difficult for the Spanish to classify ethnographically, but they would later complicate UN efforts to hold a referendum in Western Sahara in the 1990s.

COLONIAL ENCOUNTERS, IMPERIAL AMBITIONS

For European powers, the Sahara initially had little value in itself, yet it stood between them and their economic interests—slaves, gold, and spices—south of the desert. The overland trade routes were well known before the Renaissance, yet improvements in seafaring techniques meant that Europeans could finally circumvent trade or forcibly alter the flow of goods through the Sahara to their advantage. Following the conquest and genocide in the adjacent Canary Islands in the 1400s, Spanish interest in the Saharan coast, mostly in the late fifteenth and early sixteenth centuries, was short-lived. The contemporaneous "discovery" of the Americas had diverted attention. Along the Mediterranean, however, Spain occupied Melilla in 1497 and was granted Ceuta from Portugal almost two centuries later (Woolbert 1946, 725).

At the same time, West Africa saw the rise and fall of several local empires. Following the disintegration of the Malian Empire of the thirteenth to fifteenth centuries, the Kawkaw assumed prominence in the western Sudan as the Songhay kingdom. Its leader, Sunni 'Ali, took Timbuktu in 1486, and subsequent generations secured uncontested control over the Saharan trade routes (Lapidus 1988, 494). The greatest challenge to Songhay dominance over the Sahara came from the Sa'di dynasty, which succeeded the Banu Wattas (Wattasids, 1472–1549) as the hegemonic power north of the Sahara in 1554. With substantial material aid from European powers, the Sa'dians charged down into the Sahara and drove the Songhay out of Timbuktu. The Sahara soon slipped out of the Sa'dians' grip when their proxies in the southern Saharan "ports" declared independence in Timbuktu and Gao around 1632 (Mercer 1976b, 92–93). Saharan trade subsequently shifted to eastern routes and to the emerging Ottoman power on the Algerian coast.

The current Moroccan dynasty, the 'Alawi from areas near Sijilmasah in the Tafilalt region, replaced the weakened and fragmented Sa'dians in 1664, yet it has never been able to resurrect an empire of such vast scope. The most adventurous 'Alawi, Mawlay Isma'il (1672–1726), ventured as far as Mauritania, yet his interest was slaves for his personal army more than imperial domination. A 1767 Hispano–Moroccan treaty subsequently noted that the 'Alawi sultan's "sovereignty does not extend as far to there [to the Dra'a River]." Indeed, one member group of the Tiknah confederation, Ayt Mussa wa 'Ali, established their own independent "principality" around Goulemine in the region of Nun, appearing on an official 1844 French map as "L'État de Sidi Hecham" (the State of Sidi Hicham). In 1875, the Moroccan sultan Hassan I reiterated to Britain that his influence did not extend to Cap Juby, where an English trading post was established. Yet this combined British–Tiknah threat to Moroccan trade influence spurred Hassan I to launch two expeditions to his southern flank in 1882 and 1886. In the process, he formed relations with the Ayt Mussa wa 'Ali among other Tiknah groups, but other members of the confederation ignored him. The largest confederations in the region, the two Rgaybat groups, always rejected the sultan's suzerainty, as did the emirs of Mauritania at that time (although later French encroachment changed some minds). After Moroccan attacks, the British trading fort was abandoned in an 1895 treaty in which the British recognized the land from the Dra'a to Cap Bojador (Boujdour) as an area of Moroccan interest, if only to counter Franco–Spanish ambitions in the region (Trout 1969, 139, 143, 150–63, 478–79).

Following Hassan I's expedition to the Nun in 1886, he named a Saharan deputy (*khalifah*), Shaykh Ma' al-'Aynayn. Then approximately fifty-six years old, Ma' al-'Aynayn was highly educated and religiously passionate as well as a prolific writer. With substantial aid from the 'Alawis, he started organizing attacks to halt French intrusions into the Mauritanian interior in the late 1890s. In 1904, Ma' al-'Aynayn founded the city of Smara as a center for learning and, of course, Saharan trade, but he later moved to Tiznit, where he launched an attempt to drive the French from Morocco and depose the complicit 'Alawi regime. Yet the French, with their modern weaponry, easily defeated Ma' al-'Aynayn's forces; he died later that same year, 1910, back in Tiznit. With Mauritanian help, the French subsequently sacked Smara and burned the hundreds of books in its library (Norris 1964, 6). One of Ma' al-'Aynayn's sons, El-Hiba, continued the resistance, attempting again to face the French forces head on, but he later turned to guerilla warfare in the Anti-Atlas, dying near Kerdous in 1919. His brother, Merebbi Rebbu, continued the struggle against European domination until his surrender in 1934, the year Spain forcefully occupied the territory's interior. It was also in that same year that the French military connected key positions in southeastern Morocco, Algeria (Tindouf), and Mauritania (Zouerate), thus surrounding the Spanish colony, strangling guerilla movements, and making the "pacification" of the greater western Sahara possible (Mercer 1976a, 503).

MAKING THE SAHARA SPANISH

From the fifteenth century onward, Europeans continually raided the Saharan coast, but it was Europe's nineteenth-century scrambling of Africa that renewed Spanish interest in the African littoral off the Canaries. Spain was already well established in its two enclaves in northern Morocco, Ceuta and Melilla; there was also a brief occupation of Tétouan in 1860, and in 1893–94 a large force was sent to defend the expansion of Melilla (Woolman 1968, 31–35). Southward occupation commenced when the Spanish government obtained Ifni—then believed to be the site of the fifteenth-century outpost of Santa Cruz de Mar Pequeña—as a result of the 1860 Treaty of Peace and Amity with the Moroccan sultan (Reyner 1963, 324). In 1884, the Compañía Comercial Hispano–Africana established Villa Cisneros (present-day Dakhla) and by the end of the year had the Spanish government declare a protectorate over a region to be called "Río de Oro." At the Berlin Conference, the 1884–85 meetings of European colonial powers that formally carved up the African continent, Spain's minimal coastal occupation was recognized as extending into the interior (Damis 1983, 10).

Southward expansion along the coast, which started to rub against French interests in Mauritania, led to the Franco–Spanish convention of June 27, 1900, setting the southeastern boundary of Río de Oro. Four years later Spain and France marked the northern limits, including the separate enclave of Sidi Ifni. This demarcation came shortly after an agreement between France and Great Britain that allowed the latter a free hand in Egypt in exchange for the former's domination of the other end of North Africa. A Franco–Spanish convention signed in 1912 demarcated the final borders and clarified their powers in their respective possessions. This came shortly after the sultan in Fez, Mawlay 'Abd al-Hafiz, allowed a French "protectorate" over Morocco. The last Franco–Spanish convention reduced Spain's overall holdings, yet it firmly recognized Saqiyah al-Hamra' as a Zona del Libre Ocupación (Zone of Free Occupation) because it resided outside of known 'Alawi control. However, in a small region directly north of Saqiyah al-Hamra', now internationally recognized as a part of the Kingdom of Morocco, Spain administered "on behalf of the [Moroccan] Sultan" (Woolbert 1946, 730) the Zona del Draa, also known as the Tarfaya Strip, Tekna Zone, or Dra'a Zone (Zona del Draa) (see map 6).

Spain's presence was initially limited to the coast, setting up minimal garrisons at Tarfaya (1916) and Lagwirah (1920). In 1934, the French government, which had been pursuing far more aggressive policies in the Sahara, pressured Madrid to take action against anticolonial forces based in Spanish territory. So for the first time Spanish forces set up positions in the interior and at Ifni. Madrid also centralized control of its North African territories in Tétouan, but later, in 1946, it created the independent entity Africa Occidental Española for Ifni, Saqiyah al-Hamra', and Río de Oro and juridically separate from its protectorates in northern and southern Morocco. The newly founded city al-'Ayun became the regional administrative headquarters, and the governor-general remained at Ifni. Small garrisons were maintained farther inland, including a large post at Smara. In 1958, following a brief native insurgency, Spain relinquished the Sahrawi-populated Zona del Draa to Morocco, two years after ceding northern Spanish Morocco to Rabat following

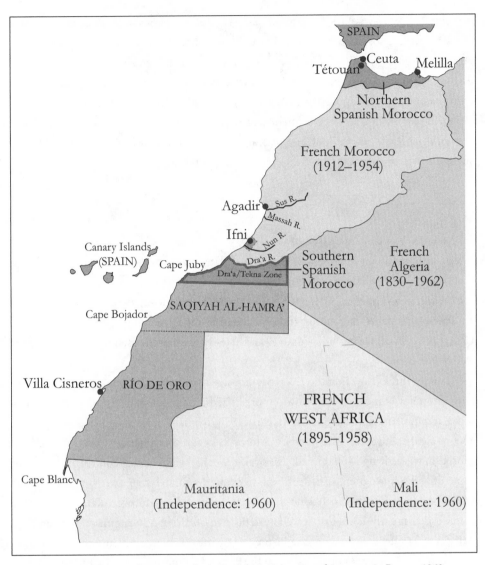

Map 6. Spanish Sahara and Spanish-administered Morocco. Based on maps in Reyner 1963.

Morocco's independence from France in 1956. Spain declared both Ifni and the Sahara to be its "provinces," hoping to circumvent pressure from the UN to decolonize.

Although Ifni was eventually given to Morocco in 1969, Spain held on to the Sahara as long as possible, investing in the territory and its population. Settlement in the metropolitan centers, however, resulted from drought as much as from material enticements (e.g., employment, housing, schools, and hospitals). By the 1974 census, the Spanish administration claimed that well more than half of the counted population was sedentary in or near the three major cities, Dakhla, Smara, and al-'Ayun (Aguirre 1988, 612). In 1967, Spain had taken a step toward creating the appearance of local consultation by creating a council of eighty-two Sahrawi elites, the Jama'a. In the late 1960s, Spain also started making heavy investments in phosphate-extraction capabilities, connecting the mines at Bukra' to the port in al-'Ayun. When the system came on-line in 1972, it seemed possible that Fosfatos de Bu-Craa (Fosbucraa) could become the world's second-largest exporter of high-grade phosphate rock, challenging Morocco's dominant position in the global market (Gretton 1976b, 21–22). Such a large investment clearly added a disincentive for Spain to cede the territory—at least, not without first making sure its interests would be respected by the successor regime, whatever form that regime should take.

RESISTANCE, NATIONALIST, AND INDEPENDENCE MOVEMENTS

In 1966, the UN General Assembly passed its Resolution 2229, reaffirming the right of self-determination for Spanish Sahara. Six years later it adopted Resolution 2983 (XXVII), reaffirming "the inalienable right of the people of the [Spanish] Sahara to self-determination and independence" (UN 1975, 580). However, the idea that Spanish Sahara could constitute an independent nation-state, an equal among its neighbors, was not born at the UN in 1972. The drive for independence had already manifested itself within the territory well before then.

Twenty-three years after the 1934 "pacification" of the western Sahara, a group of militants from newly independent Morocco organized an anticolonial insurgency in Mauritania, Algeria, and Spanish Sahara. In early 1956, Benhamou Mesfioui, leader of guerilla actions against the Spanish in northern Morocco, began coordinating actions in southern Morocco, where King Mohammed V's royal forces had yet to assert control. The fighters, some of them Imazighen, were from the informal Jaysh al-Tahrir (Army of Liberation), which had come together in 1955 to fight for an independent Morocco. Raids into Algeria commenced as early as 1956, followed by actions in northern Mauritania and Ifni in 1957. Attacks were often staged from the ill-policed Spanish Sahara and from remote areas of southeastern Morocco. When pressed on the matter by France and Spain, the new Moroccan regime claimed that the insurgents were "uncontrolled and difficult to control," even though they were often operating from well within Moroccan territory (quoted in Hodges 1983b, 77). In the Spanish Sahara, colonial forces withdrew to the important coastal cities as the frequency and intensity of attacks grew.

By the end of 1957, French and Spanish commanders had agreed to a massive joint counterinsurgency campaign. A combined force of fourteen thousand French and Spanish troops deployed for Operation Ouragan (Hurricane) in February 1958, quickly breaking the back of the rebellion in Spanish Sahara (Hodges and Pazzanita 1994, 53–57; see also Aguirre 1988, 338, 392, 296). As a result of the repression, thousands of Sahrawis fled into southern Morocco. This refugee situation was aggravated by a severe drought in the following years, causing large numbers of Sahrawis to seek shelter in the cities of southern

Morocco, southwestern Algeria, and Mauritania. The social and environmental conditions also accelerated sedentarization of Sahrawi nomads in Spanish Sahara. Although there existed ambiguities and contradictions in the intent of the Saharan participants in the brief insurgency of 1957–58, out of this brief uprising would come the first explicitly proindependence movement.

In the history of Western Saharan nationalism, Mohammed Sidi Ibrahim Bassiri is recognized as the first activist to press publicly for independence. Like many Western Saharan nationalists to follow him, he had attended primary and secondary school in Morocco. He later studied journalism in Cairo and Damascus. Returning to Spanish Sahara in the late 1960s, Bassiri started organizing the Harakat Tahrir Saqiyah al-Hamra' wa Wadi al-Dhahab (Liberation Movement of the Saqiyah al-Hamra' and Wadi al-Dhahab). Obviously inspired by contemporary Arab and African liberation movements, the Harakat Tahrir called for the dissolution of traditional social structures as a step toward building national consciousness. The organization drew some of its strength from veterans of the 1957–58 conflict. The nationalist movement announced itself when it staged a sizable demonstration on June 17, 1970, in al-Zamlah Square in al-'Ayun. Spanish forces summarily killed between two and twelve of the protestors on the spot. The Harakat Tahrir was quickly suppressed, and Bassiri was arrested, never to be seen again (Hodges 1983a, 47–49). Some Western Saharan nationalists call this the Intifadah al-Zamlah, their first uprising.

Yet not all of the movements calling for the liberation of the Spanish Sahara have called for its independence. Following the creation of a ministry to implement Greater Morocco in 1965 (i.e., the Ministère des Affaires Mauritaniennes et Sahariennes), Morocco's weight was put behind a group of anticolonial militants under the banner of the Frente de Liberación del Sahara bajo Dominación Española (Liberation Front of the Sahara under Spanish Domination), but the effort soon petered out after Spain ceded Ifni and then Morocco and Mauritania reconciled in 1969. Three years later Bashir Figuigi (a.k.a. Edouard Moha) founded the Mouvement de Résistance "les Hommes Bleus" (Blue Men's Resistance Movement). Moha set up his group in Morocco but moved to Algiers in 1973, rejecting Moroccan claims on Spanish Sahara. The Moroccan government then attempted to support a group calling itself the Mouvement du 21 août (August 21 Movement), but it also was very short-lived.

The Spanish colonial administration belatedly followed suit in early 1975 with the establishment of the Partido de la Unión Nacional Saharaui (PUNS, Party of Sahrawi National Unity). With the Jama'a's legitimacy in question and left-leaning Polisario's popularity increasing, Madrid hoped PUNS could co-opt nationalist sentiment to Spain's favor (Hodges 1983b, 112–13; Mercer 1976b, 243–44).

The Moroccan government countered PUNS and Polisario with the FLU, an irregular branch of the Moroccan army that carried out limited terrorist and guerilla attacks against Spanish targets. The FLU virtually disappeared upon the signing of the Madrid

Agreement in November 1975. After that, the Moroccan government supported the Association des originaires du Sahara anciennement sous domination espagnole (Association of Natives of the Sahara Formerly under Spanish Domination), an organization whose acronym, AOSARIO, was deliberately meant to reflect "Polisario." The short-lived AOSARIO was led by none other than Bashir Figuigi, who had again switched sides. Although the group turned out to be politically and numerically insignificant, it continued to agitate into the late 1970s for a guerilla movement that would "rescue" the refugees at Tindouf (Hodges and Pazzanita 1994, 173–75).

Almost three years after the Zamlah massacre, a small band of poorly armed Sahrawi insurgents attacked a Spanish outpost at al-Khanga in the northeastern corner of Saqiyah al-Hamra' on May 20, 1973. This new movement had been founded just ten days earlier, and few even knew of its existence. Manning the outpost was a small unit of Sahrawis serving in the colonial army's indigenous Tropas Nómadas. The element of surprise, however, was almost lost when a patrol of the Tropas Nómadas caught two of the rebels searching for water, including one of the movement's key founders, El-Ouali Mustapha Sayed. Once the other insurgents realized what had happened, they decided to attack the post that night. Without a drop of blood spilled or a bullet spent, the guerillas took the garrison, freed their comrades, confiscated all the Spanish weapons, and lectured the Tropas Nómadas on the philosophy of their anticolonial movement (see Hodges 1983b, 160–61).

Like Bassiri's movement, this group drew its strength from experienced veterans of the 1957–58 uprising. Its core was also composed of young Sahrawi refugees from that conflict who had come of age in southern Morocco and had studied in Moroccan universities. There they had come in contact with the Moroccan political Left, learning about the recent and ongoing movements in the Third World for national self-determination. This biography was especially true for the movement's founder, El-Ouali Mustapha Sayed. A reportedly charismatic and tireless organizer, El-Ouali was born of impoverished nomads who had sought refuge in southern Morocco. His new independence movement called itself the Frente Popular para la Liberación de Saguia el-Hamra y Río de Oro—the Polisario Front. Its 1971 founding or "embryonic" leadership included El-Ouali's brother, Bachir Mustapha Sayed, as well as Mohammed Lamine Ould Ahmed, Mohammed Salem Ould Salek, and Mohammed Ould Sidati (Hodges and Pazzanita 1994, 135–37). As Polisario approached neighboring states for assistance, the group maintained a strategic ambiguity regarding its final aims (i.e., independence or integration with Morocco or Mauritania). At one point, El-Ouali allegedly nurtured some sympathy for the idea of a Moroccan takeover of Spanish Sahara—or at least a Moroccan-backed insurgency. However, he later broke with Rabat following the regime's crackdown on leftists in the 1970s and its violent reaction to anti-Spanish demonstrations in southern Morocco. El-Ouali and company received only a tepid response from Libya and Mauritania and were rebuffed by Algeria. Frelisario, as the group first called itself, was able to mount a series of raids on Spanish forces and interests between 1973 and 1975 while also carrying out diplomatic activities abroad and propaganda work within the territory.

In May 1975, only two years after the raid on al-Khanga, an official UN visiting mission witnessed the startling growth of indigenous nationalism in Spanish Sahara. Composed of diplomats from the Ivory Coast, Cuba, and Iran, the mission toured the Spanish Sahara between May 12 and May 19. According to the mission's report, Sahrawi support for Spain's PUNS paled in comparison to the support for Polisario. Indeed, during the UN visit, two units of Spain's native Saharan Camel Corps rebelled against their Spanish officers and joined the Polisario's ranks. The report, released in October 1975, detailed what had happened that May:

> Within the Territory, the Mission noted that the population, or at least almost all those persons encountered by the Mission, was categorically for independence and against the territorial claims of Morocco and Mauritania. . . .
>
> The Frente POLISARIO, although considered a clandestine movement before the Mission's arrival, appeared as a dominant political force in the Territory. The Mission witnessed mass demonstrations in support of the movement in all parts of the Territory. (UN General Assembly 1977, Annex, p. 7, par. 19, 21)

Seeing which way the wind was blowing, PUNS's leader, Khalihenna Ould Rachid, defected to Morocco during the mission, although the bulk of his organization later backed Polisario. The Moroccan-backed FLU, however, made much more of an impression on the UN mission, carrying out several terrorist attacks in al-'Ayun.

A week after these dramatic and unexpected nationalist displays in May 1975, the Spanish cabinet admitted that "Polisario is a reality." The colonial administration then moved to reconcile PUNS, the Jama'a, and Polisario (Hodges 1983b, 204). Throughout the summer, Madrid ceded several small settlements and remote military stations to Polisario in exchange for a cessation of attacks. The growing goodwill between colonial authorities and Polisario led to prisoner exchanges and a September 9 meeting between Spanish foreign minister Pedro Cortina y Mauri and Polisario secretary-general El-Ouali Mustapha Sayed. There, according to El-Ouali, they reached an understanding whereby Madrid would hand over control of the territory to a Polisario-led government in exchange for economic concessions on phosphates and fisheries. More prisoner releases, including a high-level exchange on October 21 in Mahbas, Western Sahara, followed. The following day—nearly a week after Hassan announced the Green March—the governor-general of Spanish Sahara, Federico Gómez de Salazar, agreed to let some Polisario leaders move into al-'Ayun in preparation for the territory's independence. However, less than a week later Spain abruptly turned its back on Polisario and abandoned its colony to Morocco and Mauritania (Hodges and Pazzanita 1994, 49, 103, 133, 166; see also Aguirre 1988, 756, 760).

SELF-DETERMINATION AND SOVEREIGNTY: THE ICJ OPINION

On November 14, 1975, Spain, Morocco, and Mauritania announced that they had reached an agreement on the fate of Western Sahara. This announcement came nearly a month after the ICJ released its opinion on Morocco and Mauritania's claims on Western Sahara. Most observers have noted The Hague's unqualified endorsement of Western Sahara's right to self-determination and simultaneously its stiff rejection of Moroccan and Mauritanian claims of historical right. However, if one goes beyond the ICJ's final conclusion and examines the breadth of its opinion, it is clear that under international law the sovereign power in the former Spanish Sahara is the Sahrawis native to it. When juxtaposed against the weakness of the Moroccan case, the claim for Sahrawi sovereignty becomes even stronger.

On September 30, 1974, Morocco put a request to the UN General Assembly for an ICJ ruling on whether Spain had occupied Moroccan territory when it established its colony in Western Sahara. The Spanish delegation at the UN, however, would not submit to binding arbitration. Instead, Madrid supported an advisory opinion, but only as long as it also considered the questions in the context of the UN charter and applicable resolutions. On December 13, 1974, the UN General Assembly Resolution 3292 called for an ICJ advisory opinion on the following questions:

> I. Was the Western Sahara (Rio de Oro and Sakiet El Hamra) at the time of colonization by Spain a territory belonging to no one (*terra nullius*)?
> If the answer to the first question is in the negative,
> II. What were the legal ties between this territory and the King of Morocco and the Mauritanian entity? (UN 1977, 794–95)

The first hurdle that the court had to clear in answering the two questions was to determine whether Western Sahara was a "no man's land" or not at the start of Spanish colonization in 1885. The ICJ determined that Western Sahara did belong to someone, but that someone was neither Morocco nor Mauritania. It found that the lands were "inhabited by peoples which, if nomadic, were socially and politically organized in tribes and under chiefs competent to represent them." The fact that early Spanish colonial officials had made agreements with the indigenous inhabitants reinforced the idea that the land was far from *terra nullius*. The court was able to proceed to the second question, not because Morocco or Mauritania ever held sovereignty over Western Sahara, *but in spite of it* (ICJ 1975, par. 81–83).

The Moroccan case had several aspects. The first argument, "immemorial possession," was historical, starting from the Islamic conquest of North Africa in the seventh century. The court remarked that the evidence for this claim was based on events that were "far-flung, spasmodic and often transitory," rendering "the historical material some-what equivocal as evidence of possession." Morocco also underscored the "geographical continuity" between their nation and Western Sahara, citing an ICJ precedent set in *Legal Status of Eastern Greenland,* where Denmark's possession of a part of Greenland trans-lated into sovereignty over the whole. The ICJ found this argument unviable given Green-land's status as *terra nullius* in that case, in contrast to Western Sahara. Overall, the court expressed dissatisfaction with Morocco's "indirect inferences drawn from events in past history" (ICJ 1975, par. 90–93).

Before presenting its evidence for "internal" and "external" displays of sovereignty, the Moroccan delegation explained the nature of the "Sherifian State." Whether certain areas in the western Sahara fell under the sultan's direct rule or not, all people in the region acknowledged his "spiritual authority" as a descendant of the Prophet Muhammad (i.e., a *sharif*) and the commander of the faithful *(amir al-mu'minin).* Lands under de jure cen-tral control (Bilad al-Makhzan) were as much a part of the country as lands outside of it (Bilad al-Siba), a de facto sovereignty. The ICJ, however, was obviously uncomfortable with the idea of indirect or passive sovereignty. It noted that Morocco could not demonstrate sovereignty within internationally recognized parts of Morocco. The region between the Sus and the Dra'a rivers in southern Morocco, for example, was in "a state of permanent insubordination and part of the [Bilad al-Siba]." This example, the court felt, "implies that there was no effective and continuous display of State functions even in those areas to the north of Western Sahara" (ICJ 1975, par. 94–97).

Regarding "internal" displays of authority, Morocco argued that ties of allegiance existed between the Moroccan sultan and certain Saharan leaders *(qa'ids),* particularly of the Tiknah confederation, inhabiting the region from the Nun River (southern Morocco) to Saqiyah al-Hamra' (Western Sahara). Furthermore, Morocco claimed, Shaykh Ma' al-'Aynayn, a recognized and powerful leader in the western Sahara, became the Moroccan sultan's deputy in the late nineteenth century, later leading a resistance movement against colonial domination. Most important of all, King Hassan I personally visited the region in 1882 and 1886, where some Saharan tribes reaffirmed allegiance *(baya'ah).* Morocco concluded that through internal displays of sovereignty, Western Sahara had "always been linked to the interior of Morocco by common ethnological, cultural and religious ties" that had been severed by European colonization (ICJ 1975, par. 99).

The court, however, felt that the evidence presented "appears to support the view that almost all the dahirs [decrees by the sultan] and other acts concerning caids [*qa'ids*] relate to areas situated within present-day Morocco itself" and therefore "do not in themselves provide evidence of effective display of Moroccan authority in Western Sahara." The ICJ also said that none of the evidence was convincing enough to conclude that the Moroccan sultan had imposed or levied taxes in Western Sahara. "As to Sheikh Ma ul-'Aineen," the court added, "the complexities of his career may leave doubts as to the precise nature of his relations with the Sultan." Indeed, history suggests that Shaykh Ma' al-'Aynayn sought to take the Moroccan throne for himself, not to defend it. The court was well aware of this alternate narrative: "Nor does the material furnished lead the Court to conclude that the alleged acts of resistance in Western Sahara to foreign penetration could be considered as acts of the Moroccan State." Hassan I's expeditions to the South before colonial domination, the court noted, "had objects specifically directed to the Souss [Sus] and the Noun [Nun]." For the court, none of the evidence supported "Morocco's claim to have exercised territorial sovereignty over Western Sahara." The court did not "exclude authority over some of the tribes in Western Sahara," but it felt that such authority was limited to the Tiknah; ties to "other independent tribes living in the territory could clearly not be sustained" (ICJ 1975, par. 103–7).

The third aspect of the Moroccan case, international or "external" acknowledgment of sovereignty, was made through four specific materials. These materials included several treaties with foreign governments dealing with the recovery of shipwrecked sailors; an 1895 treaty with Great Britain relevant to the region between the Dra'a River and Cape Bojador; the 1860 Treaty of Tétouan with Spain; and a Franco–German correspondence in 1911 (Ibid., par. 108).

For Morocco, the eighteenth article of the 1767 Spanish–Moroccan Treaty of Marrakech recognized the sultan's ability "to have the power to take decisions with respect to the 'Wad Noun and beyond.'" Yet the Spanish text of the treaty was different from the Arabic version presented by the Moroccan delegation. It stated unambiguously, "His Imperial Majesty refrains from expressing an opinion with regard to the trading post which His Catholic Majesty wishes to establish to the south of the River Noun, since he cannot take responsibility for accidents and misfortunes, because his domination [*sus dominios*] does not extend so far" (ICJ 1975, par. 109–10). Spain was also able to provide pertinent diplomatic exchanges that verified the authenticity of the language in the Spanish version.

Moving closer to the time of Spanish colonialism in 1885, the court examined a shipwreck clause (Article 38) of the 1861 Hispano–Moroccan Treaty of Commerce and Navigation and, as a case example, the recovery of nine sailors from the *Esmeralda,* a ship taken captive more than 180 miles south of the Nun. Morocco argued that Article 38 was explicit Spanish recognition of the sultan's sovereignty over Saharan tribes, a sovereignty later exercised in the safe delivery of these sailors back to Spain. The Spanish delegation, however, provided documents showing that a prominent local *qa'id* in the Nun region, "Sheikh Beyrouk," negotiated directly with the Spanish consul at Mogador for the release of the sailors. Furthermore, from Spain's point of view, the Moroccan sultan simply "negotiated with local powers, he could not give orders." In the court's opinion, all the documents relating to the treaty and the shipwreck in question did not "warrant the conclusion that Spain thereby also recognized the Sultan's territorial sovereignty." It simply confirmed that the sultan could exercise his "personal authority or influence" on

Tiknah *qa'id*s of the Nun, although this influence could not "be considered as implying international recognition of the Sultan's territorial sovereignty in Western Sahara" (ICJ 1975, par. 112–18).

Morocco also tried to argue that an 1895 Anglo–Moroccan agreement constituted British recognition of the sultan's authority as far south as Cape Bojador. Yet the court found the Moroccan interpretation of the agreement "at variance with the facts as shown in the diplomatic correspondence" and that "the position repeatedly taken by Great Britain was that Cape Juby [Tarfaya] was outside Moroccan territory." To the ICJ, the agreement represented a British agreement "not to question in future any pretensions" of the sultan in that area rather than "recognition by Great Britain of previously existing Moroccan sovereignty over those lands [i.e., Tarfaya]" (ICJ 1975, par. 119–20).

However, the court could not adjudicate on the 1860 Treaty of Tétouan and a crucial corresponding 1900 protocol on Ifni because the Spanish delegation denied that the 1900 agreement had ever existed. The court was left with a 1911 Franco–German understanding implying that Saqiyah al-Hamra' was a part of Morocco but that the Río de Oro fell outside of Morocco. Spain countered by pointing out that the 1904 and 1912 Franco–Spanish conventions, which had established the colonial borders of Spanish Sahara, clearly recognized Saqiyah al-Hamra' as falling outside of Morocco. The court ultimately found it difficult to read into the 1911 exchange of letters any more than an acknowledgment of France's "sphere of influence" and saw the exchange rather as "constituting recognition of the limits of Morocco" (ICJ 1975, par. 121–27).

In the three arguments the Moroccan delegation made before the ICJ and the materials it presented, whether historical cultural, regional, or international, the court could not find "any legal tie of territorial sovereignty between Western Sahara and the Moroccan State." In its final opinion on both Mauritanian and Moroccan claims, it found that "the materials and information presented to it do not establish any tie of territorial sovereignty between the territory of Western Sahara and the Kingdom of Morocco or the Mauritanian entity [i.e., Bilad Shinqiti]." Yet the court admitted that there was "a legal tie of allegiance between the Sultan and some, though only some, of the tribes of the territory" (i.e., Tiknah subgroups). In its final conclusion, it explained the significance of these minimal "legal ties": "Thus the court has not found legal ties of such a nature as might affect the application of resolution 1514 (XV) in the decolonization of Western Sahara and, in particular, of the principle of self-determination through the free and genuine expression of the will of the peoples of the Territory" (ICJ 1975, par. 129, 162). The sixteen ICJ judges voted fourteen to two against Morocco and fifteen to one against Mauritania. The common dissenting vote in the two instances was an ad hoc judge appointed by Morocco under a special ICJ rule. The other dissenting vote on Morocco's claim, Judge José Mara Ruda, felt that the ICJ had not gone far enough to denounce Morocco's claim (Franck 1976, 711). Unable to convince the world court or the international community that Western Sahara belonged to Greater Morocco, Hassan set out to make the latter a reality nevertheless.

## SAHRAWIS AND/AS WESTERN SAHARANS

To be Sahrawi is an ambivalent if not undecided and ambiguous mixture of claims—claims of blood and land. This ambiguity became utterly clear in the 1990s, when the UN mission in Western Sahara attempted to establish a Sahrawi electorate for the proposed referendum on independence (see chapter 8). The UN was looking for Sahrawis native to Western Sahara, not just Sahrawis generally. It was looking for Sahrawis who could prove both ties of blood and land rather than for any persons claiming descent from a predominantly Hassaniyyah-speaking social group once found in the area of former Spanish Sahara. Proof of Sahrawi-ness was not enough; a prospective voter had to prove Western Saharan-ness. The idea of a Sahrawi people based on a one-to-one correspondence with Western Sahara proved far too simplistic in the 1990s.

The development of the idea of a Sahrawi people, coterminous with the former Spanish Sahara, found its greatest champion in the Western Saharan nationalist movement. Polisario claimed in its first manifesto, issued shortly after the group's founding congress on May 10, 1973, that it was a "unique expression of the masses, opting for revolutionary violence and the armed struggle as the means by which the Saharawi Arab African people can recover total liberty and foil the maneuvers of Spanish colonialism" (quoted in Hodges and Pazzanita 1994, 162). More than two years later, on November 28, 1975, less than a month after Spain announced that it would abandon its colony to Morocco and Mauritania, Polisario unveiled the Galtah Zammur declaration. Signed by the vast majority of the native representatives from the colonially instituted bodies (i.e., PUNS and the Jama'a) as well as by dozens of other Sahrawi leaders (*shuyukh*, or shaykhs, and other notables), the declaration named Polisario as "the sole legitimate authority of the Saharan people" (quoted in Hultman and Larkin 1985, 32). Three months later, on February 27, 1976, at Bir Lahlu (Bir Lehlou/Lahlou) in the territory's northeastern region, Polisario declared Western Sahara an independent, albeit largely occupied, nation. Although it might seem that the Sahrawis thus transitioned from a people to a nation, it is the nation that made the people possible.

The name of Polisario's republic, al-Jumhuriyah al-'Arabiyah al-Sahrawiyah al-Dimuqratiyah (República Árabe Saharaui Democrática, Sahrawi Arab Democratic Republic), elucidates this ambivalence. In Arabic, *Sahrawi* and *Sahrawiyah* are adjectival forms *(nisbah)* of *Sahara (al-sahra')*. As noted earlier, the adjective *Sahrawi* can modify a person, a place, or a thing to make it Saharan in the generic sense. But in what sense is the republic Sahrawi: an ethnic sense (Sahrawi Republic), a territorial sense (Saharan Republic), or both? Yet most nationalists among themselves simply refer to their country as "al-Sahra'," reserving the name "Western Sahara" (al-Sahra' al-Gharbiyyah) for deliberate delineations, formal settings, and Western audiences.

Only when we look to colonialism do we find some answers. The colonial subjects of Spanish Sahara (al-Sahra' al-Asbaniyyah), imbued with their own a sense of nationalism, were no longer—if ever—Spanish Saharan (Sahrawi Asbani), but just Saharan (Sahrawi). The term *Sahrawi,* as nationalists used it and as observers adopted it, was born of an act of symbolic resistance and partial negation: Sahrawi ~~Asbani~~ (i.e., ~~Spanish~~ Saharan). Their country was no longer "al-Sahra' al-Asbaniyyah," but simply "al-Sahra'" (the name "Western Sahara" was applied by the international community in the early 1970s, not by the native inhabitants). The great thrust of Western Saharan nationalism was to assert that the people of the Western Sahara were not colonial subjects of Spain (i.e., Spanish Saharans), but simply Saharans, free of oppressive qualifiers. Their land likewise was not El Sahara Español, but simply El Sahara. Although the terms have changed since 1975, the oppositional operations are still the same. Sahrawis are Sahrawi, not *darijah*-speaking Maghribi (Moroccan or, broadly, North African). Their country is still al-Sahra, but not al-Sahra' Maghribiyyah (Moroccan Sahara).

None of this argues that the Sahrawi identity is ephemeral, that the Sahrawis constitute a false nation, or that the Spanish Sahara should have been absorbed into Mauritania for reasons of ethnic congruence. All identities in this case—Algerian, Moroccan, and Mauritanian as well—are not given; they are the outcome of the historical interaction of dominant and subordinate social forces. One should not forget that the Sahrawi identity is very real to those who have lived and died for it. Willingness to sacrifice for blood and land is the sine qua non of nationalism (Anderson 1991, 7), as will be seen in chapters 5 and 6, which explore the continuing project of nation building among Sahrawis in the camps and, more recently, the Moroccan-occupied Western Sahara.

# 5

# Expressions of Nationalism

*The Polisario Front, the Sahrawi Arab Democratic*
*Republic, and the Sahrawi Refugee Camps*

Since the beginning of the conflict, nearly half the native population of Western Sahara has lived in four refugee camps in southwestern Algeria. The Moroccan government has long claimed that these are Polisario-run "prison camps" holding "Moroccan citizens" against their will—nothing short of a Potemkin village of a few thousand nomads propped up by the Algerian government to garner sympathy for Polisario. Given the chance, the Moroccan government claims, these refugees would happily return to Morocco. To make its case, Rabat produces well-paid Sahrawi defectors.

Such claims have been recently put to the test by a refugee-exchange program administered by the UN High Commission for Refugees (UNHCR) with help from the UN mission in Western Sahara, MINURSO. By the end of 2006, almost three thousand Sahrawis—equal numbers coming from each side of the berm—had participated in the exchange program. For the first time since 1976, Sahrawi families were able to see what reality was like in the occupied territory and in the camps, yet only a handful of refugees opted not to go back to the camps.[1]

The camps, however, are not paradise. Although the claims made by the Moroccan government and its proxies (e.g., the Moroccan American Committee for Policy in the United States) are normally far from realistic, the descriptions given by supporters of Polisario's nationalist project—often characterizing the camps as a viable self-contained nation-state in exile, if not an ideal democratic community, forged out of harsh circumstances that include dispossession, war, and an unforgiving natural environment—are sometimes overly enthusiastic. After visiting the camps, African specialist George Houser raved,

> I have visited many refugee camps in Africa over the years, but never have I seen a group of people more self-reliant or better organized. Indeed, I found it impossible to think of them as refugees. They have turned to other countries for food and clothing, to be sure, but politically they are independent of outside control. Their camps are not administered by Algerians, the United Nations, or technicians from other countries—the people have

organized themselves according to their own way of life. In the camps, I had a feeling I was visiting a nation in exile. (1989, 309)

In 1982, noted peace researcher and sociologist Elise Boulding concluded that the refugee camps represented one of the greatest "intentional experiments in creating peaceable gardens that exist today" ([1982] 2000, 131). Seduced by the camps' highly self-sufficient organizational structure, the wide deployment of women, and Polisario's lofty rhetoric, however, some Western observers have tended to blur the lines between the members of the nationalist vanguard elite and Polisario as a multifaceted popular movement—between the republic as government in exile and daily self-managed life in the camps. All of these things are interrelated, but important distinctions should be made among them.

The aim of this chapter is to clarify the relationship between the camps, Polisario, and the Sahrawi republic, RASD. In the process of this analysis, we first examine the development and interplay of Polisario's elite and of its broader political project, the RASD. Second, we attempt to describe the camp's quotidian administration in relation to the refugee population's political engagement in the RASD as a grassroots national-consciousness-building project. Our larger goal is to demonstrate that Western Saharan nationalism, as a political identity, is a powerful force that needs to be taken seriously in any deliberation or intervention in the conflict. Indeed, Western Saharan nationalism will undoubtedly remain an important dimension in the persistence of the dispute for some time to come, even if the conflict takes on different forms, such as those examined in chapter 6.

## FORMATION OF THE CAMPS

Shortly after the tripartite agreement in Madrid was inked in November 1975, ending Spain's presence, Moroccan and Mauritanian forces attempted to establish control quickly over the areas of Western Sahara already being vacated by Spain. Some Sahrawi civilians started moving away from the ever-expanding scope of the new occupation, especially from the more numerous and violent Moroccan forces. By December 20, 1976, Spain had handed over control of Smara and al-'Ayun to Moroccan forces, and the U.S. ambassador in Rabat described the two towns as "virtual armed camps." The same report, stemming from an official visit by the U.S. Embassy's political counselor and press attaché, indicated that the "[c]ivilian population of these towns has obviously diminished considerably from last year's Spanish census" (U.S. Embassy Rabat 1975c).

Moroccan and, to a lesser extent, Mauritanian military attacks on Polisario-controlled areas in the hinterland were by all accounts quite brutal, thus laying the conditions for the refugee exodus to Algeria. Occupying forces encircled towns with barbed wire and placed them under a state of siege (Harrel-Bond 1981, II:5). Testimonies by refugees, Western journalists, and the International Red Cross reported widespread atrocities during the opening phases of the Moroccan occupation. Many fleeing refugees were attacked from the air; others perished in the difficult desert crossing to Algeria. Reports indicated systematic violations of the Geneva Conventions and other laws of war. Several reputable human rights groups, such as the International Federation for the Rights of Man, published detailed accounts of extensive attacks against civilian populations (noted in Weexsteen 1976, 6). According to testimony before a U.S. congressional subcommittee, such attacks were part of a wider Moroccan strategy. American scholar Ann Lippert, who engaged in extensive interviews with refugees in the years immediately following the exodus, characterized the situation in the following way in her testimony: "The refugees who were in the Western Sahara at the end of January 1976 and the beginning of February through mid-February 1976 were bombed, strafed, and napalmed. There was a decided attempt by the Moroccan invading forces to eliminate these people" (U.S. House 1979, 22). A February 1976 report by the International Federation of Human Rights similarly noted that

> [t]he invasion has been accomplished by innumerable exactions on persons of all ages and conditions. . . . [T]he soldiers of the two occupying countries have butchered hundreds and perhaps thousands of Sahrawis, including children and old people who refused to publicly acknowledge the king of Morocco. . . . [S]ome have seen their children killed in front of them by way of intimidation. . . . [W]omen described to us how they have been tortured and how soldiers had cut off young men's fingers to make them unable to fight. . . . 80 percent of the inhabitants of [the capital city of] El Aioun have left . . . [and] defenseless refugee camps have been bombarded. (quoted in Harrel-Bond 1981, II:5–6)

Perhaps the worst atrocities of the war took place in February 1976 near the northeastern towns of Galtah Zammur and Um Draygah, where thousands of refugees had congregated. It was there that the Moroccan air force bombed civilian refugee encampments, resorting to the use of napalm on four known occasions. Late in January that year, Moroccan forces had attacked an Algerian military unit assisting Polisario with refugee needs at Amgala. By that time, the International Committee of the Red Cross claimed that tens of thousands of Sahrawis had fled their homes and cities in Spanish Sahara, with the majority of them heading for Algeria (Hodges 1983b, 232–33; see also maps in Aguirre 1988, 830). In the coming years, the number of refugees camped outside of Tindouf, a town with a large sedentary population of ethnic Sahrawis, would exceed the initial influx of twenty to fifty thousand refugees. Polisario and its supporters claimed that most of the Sahrawis had voted with their feet. The Moroccan government would claim and still does so today that most of the refugees are detainees held against their will by Algeria and Polisario.

In the early months of the exodus, life in the refugee camps was harsh for the men, women, and children who were not on the front lines in Western Sahara, Morocco, and Mauritania. Yet in only a matter of months, the refugees would transform the camps into one of the most interesting social experiments in the postcolonial world. Within a small area granted by the Government of Algeria to the exiles, Polisario worked to establish a space in which it could encourage the Sahrawi refugees to reimagine themselves as a nation, to make the transition from stateless nomads and colonial subjects to exiled citizens of an occupied republic.

## POLISARIO FRONT IN WAR AND PEACE

Polisario is a coalition of Sahrawi nationalist political tendencies, spanning Western notions of a Left–Right, progressive–conservative spectrum. Although several of its founders were young radicals, reflecting the ideals of national self-determination and socialism that swept through Africa, Asia, and the Americas in the late colonial period, Polisario quickly learned that it would have to appeal to a wide variety of backgrounds and interests to unite Western Saharans under one big tent. Early Polisario propaganda portrayed a secular-modernist movement along the lines of Algeria's early democratic-socialist nationalism, with touches of 1950s pan-Arabism not unlike the original PLO and hints of Libyan leader Mu'ammar Qadhdhafi's unique brand of socialism. Many observers initially identified Polisario with the early FRELIMO (Frente de Libertação de Moçambique/Liberation Front of Mozambique), under Eduardo Mondlane, or with Amílcar Cabral's PAIGC (Partido Africano da Independência da Guiné e Cabo Verde/African Party for the Independence of Guinea and Cape Verde) in Guinea-Bissau. And of course, Polisario's founder, El-Ouali Mustapha Sayed, was reportedly inspired by the writings of Frantz Fanon while studying in Morocco.[2]

Polisario's Algerian tutelage, Libyan-supplied Soviet arms, and relations with Cuba and other Third World Communist regimes quickly earned it a bad reputation in the West, though. As early as January 1976, for example, Polisario met with Vietnamese defense minister Vo Nguyen Giap. Likewise, the symbolic imagery of Polisario—an emblem with a Soviet-like hammer over a Kalashnikov, a flag reminiscent of the PLO—set against the geopolitical backdrop of the 1970s and 1980s translated into wide misunderstanding of the Polisario's ideological orientation. Morocco readily manipulated such perceptions to gain Western governments' favor. Yet Polisario refused to identify itself as Marxist, saying that the nation's ideological direction was up to the Western Saharans themselves, not to a vanguard party (from Polisario's third General Congress, quoted in Barbier 1982, 205). For most Sahrawis, Polisario is a very simple idea. Ali Habib Kentaoui, a former RASD ambassador to India, described Polisario in the following way: "To be a Polisario means to be committed to the liberation of your country. It is only such a concept as national liberation for which one can expect such total identification from the people. You cannot get that kind of commitment to a party or ideology" (Zunes, interview, Rabouni, Algeria, June 17, 1987). Although observers often remarked on the cohesiveness of Polisario's core leadership through good times and bad, the overall contours of its high-level internal politics remained largely obscure, especially in the ways in which it interfaced with Algeria's regime. During most of the war, Polisario's top echelon quietly managed its own internal politics outside of the democratic constraints placed on it by its own constitution, often through frequent redistributions of power. A political crisis in its top leadership in the late 1980s and discontent in the camps led to efforts to change this configuration of power. Democratic reforms were enacted to eliminate the schism between the grassroots and the seven-member executive in the early 1990s, but immense decision-making capacity still appears to rest at the top, not at the bottom.

Shortly after Spain's capitulation to Rabat and Nouakchott, Polisario brought together nearly a supermajority of the Sahrawi representatives of the colonial Jama'a at Galtah Zammur, where on November 28, 1975, the Jama'a endorsed Polisario and dissolved itself. The early forms of a government in exile also took shape with the establishment of the Provisional Sahrawi National Council with M'hammed Ould Ziou as its president—a respected leader from the 1957–58 uprising and an early supporter of Polisario's ambitions (*Africa Confidential,* Jan. 14, 1981). This body later became the Sahrawi National Council following the declaration of the RASD at Bir Lahlu on February 27, 1976. The RASD's first government was announced in early March.

Polisario's most important long-term strategic decisions have been made at the General Congress. The first congress was the group's founding meeting on May 10, 1973; the second General Congress was held more than a year later, in late August 1974. During its first two years, Polisario's basic structure included the Political Bureau, the ELPS, and the mass organizations—national unions for women, students, and workers.

The third General Congress, held in Algiers, August 26–30, 1976, and composed of representatives elected from the Base Congress in the camps, approved the RASD's first constitution, elected a twenty-one-member Political Bureau (including the nine-member Executive Committee) and the Sahrawi National Council (*Africa Research Bulletin,* Sept. 1976). Under the 1976 RASD Constitution, members of the Executive Committee also served as the Consejo del Mando de la Revolución (CMR, Council for the Command of the Revolution), which held day-to-day control over political and military matters. Polisario's head of information, Mohammed Salem Ould Salek, described the political process in the following way: "One month before the Congress, Primary Popular Congresses were held in every local area. Everyone, including old women and young people, came to discuss the political and military situation, social and economic problems, ideological issues, all in a mature way. Finally, they elected representatives, who went on to meet at the Congress of the Wilaya, the next level. And finally all went on to the General Congress" (Paul and Paul 1976, 17). The 1976 congress also elected Mohammed Abdelaziz, a refugee of the 1957–58 conflict and a tested guerilla leader against Spain, as Polisario secretary-general to replace the late El-Ouali Mustapha Sayed, who had recently died in battle. According to some accounts, the Algerian regime handpicked the relatively unknown Abdelaziz as their "yes man" over Bachir Mustafa Sayed, El-Ouali's brother. Other Sahrawis counter that Abdelaziz was chosen to avoid single-family rule, citing Bachir's reputation for unilateralism, which was incompatible with Polisario's consensus-based processes. Although initially not as famous as other early members of Polisario or even among its founding fathers, Abdelaziz has had three decades of leadership based on his ability to moderate all the tendencies within Polisario rather than to dominate them.

During the war against Morocco, the CMR Executive Committee made most of the key political, diplomatic, and military decisions. The main body of the RASD, the Sahrawi National Council, combined the Polisario's Political Bureau and the district representatives from the camp subdivisions. During its time, the Political Bureau included RASD ministers, heads of the camps, and the leaders of the mass organizations. The size of the Political Bureau jumped to twenty-seven when more ministries were added to the RASD government in the mid-1980s; the total number was later cut back to twenty-three (Lippert 1992, 642–43) (see figure 5).

Polisario held a secretive fifth congress "somewhere" in the largely "liberated" Western Sahara in mid-October 1982 to discuss "internal issues." It allowed delegates from Libya, Mali, Mauritania, and Algeria to attend the congress, but no other foreigners or press. The congress reduced the Executive Committee to seven members, made amendments to the Constitution, and conjoined Polisario's secretary-generalship with the RASD presidency, both positions held by Mohammed Abdelaziz since then. The congress got rid

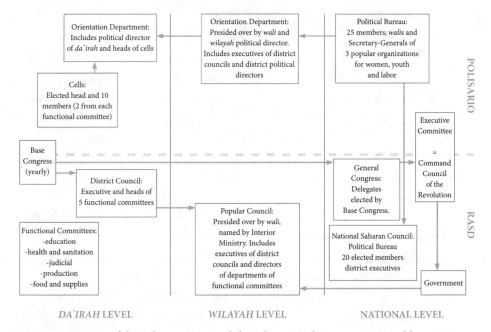

Fig. 5. Organization of the Polisario Front and the Sahrawi Arab Democratic Republic, c. 1982.

of the deputy secretary-general position, held by Bachir Mustafa Sayed. In another notable shakeup, Mahfoud Ali Beiba (1982–85, 1988–93, 1995–99) replaced longtime prime minister Mohammed Lamine Ould Ahmed (1976–82). Joining Beiba, Mohammed Lamine, Bachir Mustafa Sayed, and Mohammed Abdelaziz on the Executive Committee were Ibrahim (Brahim) Ghali, Ayoub Ould Lahbib, and Mohammed Lamine Ould Bouhali (*Africa Research Bulletin,* Oct. 1982). Mohammed Lamine Ould Ahmed, one of the Polisario Front's original members, having met El-Ouali in the late 1960s in secondary school, took over the education seat. Brahim Ghali retained the defense post he had manned since joining the Front in 1973. Ghali proved his worth to the early Polisario because of his former high rank in the Spanish territorial police and his contacts in the colonial nomadic corps (Hodges and Pazzanita 1994, 220–21). Ayoub Ould Lahbib and Ghali's later successor, Mohammed Lamine Ould Bouhali, served Polisario as important military commanders during the war. At the next congress, December 7–10, 1985, Mohammed Lamine Ould Ahmed took back the premiership, and Mahfoud Ali Beiba took over the foreign-affairs portfolio from Ibrahim Hakim, who was demoted to the information and culture post.

As Polisario's efforts shifted from war making on the battlefield to diplomacy at the UN in the late 1980s, there were several high-profile defections. The first was Omar Hadrami, whose status within Polisario elite diminished after his ejection from the Executive Committee in 1982. Well rewarded by the Moroccan government for his change of heart, Hadrami later claimed that members of the Rgaybat dominated Polisario, which echoed a statement given by a previous defector, Ramdane Ould Nass. A member of the Rgaybat himself, Hadrami, who claims to have been imprisoned in solitary confinement for seven months by Polisario, stated that independence had become unrealistic. The defectors also claimed that widespread dissention in the camps had been suppressed on several occasions. Parallel charges made by Moroccan-based human rights groups have included imprisonment, physical mistreatment, psychological abuse, and even extrajudicial killings of political prisoners. Hadrami's defection came after the seventh Polisario General Congress and a high-level reshuffling in August and September 1988, which saw Mahfoud Ali Beiba, of the Izargiyyn tribe, take over the premiership and the justice and interior posts. Several top members were reported absent from the congress, where Mohammed Abdelaziz spoke openly against "tribalism" within the nationalist movement (*Africa Research Bulletin,* June 1989).

The question of tribalism—that is, whether certain social groups, especially the Rgaybat, have dominated leadership positions—has been a vexing one for Polisario because such a practice would undermine its claims of being egalitarian, democratic, and socialist. Early assertions that tribal identities had been superseded by nationalism veiled the fact that power was not distributed evenly across the population. Polisario officials' reluctance to talk about tribalism or to let researchers investigate such power relationships suggests that the issue is both very much alive and sensitive among Sahrawi nationalists.

However, claims from defectors and Morocco that Polisario had become a Rgaybat mafia not only were contradicted by the number of high-level Polisario officials from minority tribes, given the need for tribal unity among Polisario's leadership, but were also clearly emphasized to attack Polisario's democratic credentials. Aside from these facts, the two Rgaybat confederations, according to the 1974 Spanish census, constituted half the native Sahrawi population. One would thus expect to find a large number, if not a majority, of Rgaybis in any Sahrawi institution. Polisario's hesitance to allow research into tribal politics has more to do with the political purposes of such knowledge than with having any secrets to hide.

For the refugees, the problem was not so much tribalism but authoritarianism within Polisario. In the early 1990s, with the war subsiding and the expectation of a referendum, the serious discrepancies between Polisario's egalitarian rhetoric and the reality of an established elite was a problem that had to be addressed. Outside of routine administrative affairs in the self-managed camps, Polisario's Executive Committee made all of the major decisions affecting the nationalist struggle on the battlefield and in the diplomatic arena. Although the needs of waging war and the dictates of solidarity had required an elitist political structure to carry the movement during the military conflict, the expectation of independence meant that after the war Polisario could no longer act as the vanguard it claimed it had never been (table 1).

Following large protests in the camps, what some nationalists would call the revolution in the revolution, reformers won a series of victories in the eighth General Congress. Held from June 18 to June 20, 1991, in the camps, this congress was the largest ever and

TABLE 1. LEADERSHIP OF THE POLISARIO FRONT, 1971–1989

| *"Embryonic Movement" (1971–1972)* | *Polisario Executive Committee, 1976–1989* |
| --- | --- |
| El-Ouali Mustapha Sayed (d. 1975, secretary-general, 1973–1975) | Mohammed Abdelaziz (secretary-general, 1976 to present) |
| Bachir Mustapha Sayed | Bachir Mustapha Sayed |
| Mohammed Lamine Ould Ahmed | Mohammed Lamine Ould Ahmed |
| Mohammed Salem Ould Salek | Mahfoud Ali Beiba (Mahfoud Laroussi) |
| Mohammed Ould Sidati | Ibrahim Ghali |
| | Mohammed Lamine Ould Bouhali |
| | Ayoub Ould Lahbib |
| | Omar Hadrami (Mohammed Ali Ould El-Ouali)* |
| | Batal Sidi Ahmed* |

*1976–1982 only.

was the first to include Sahrawi representatives from the Moroccan-occupied territory. It successfully overhauled Polisario, eliminating the Executive Committee, CMR, and the Political Bureau. These bodies were replaced with an elected National Secretariat. A new constitution was adopted with checks and balances, including a bill of rights that guaranteed freedom of expression, association, and movement as well as the rights of privacy, private property, and equal justice before the law; presumption of innocence until proven guilty; and explicit prohibitions against torture and unlawful detainment (Lippert 1992, 644). The congress also adopted a platform calling explicitly for multiparty democracy and a free-market economy following independence. The new constitution called for an extraordinary Polisario congress, once independence was obtained, to elect a "government of national unity" until regular multiparty elections for the RASD could be organized.

Despite the 1991 reforms, another high-ranking defection racked Polisario in 1992. That year Ibrahim Hakim (a Rgaybi), who had been serving as the RASD's ambassador in Algiers, joined King Hassan in August. From the safety of Morocco, where he attained high political office, Hakim claimed that even Algeria no longer believed in the struggle for Western Sahara. He claimed that Khalid Nezzar, one of Algeria's top military leaders and the leader of the January 1992 coup against President Bendjedid, had said, "You should stop dreaming about a state in the Sahara, because the establishment of such a state is not in Algeria's interest and is against its wishes" (quoted in *The Guardian,* Aug. 18, 1992). Even with the highly lucrative enticements offered by the Moroccan regime, however, the only major crossover since then was the unexpected 2002 defection of one of the movement's founding members, Ayoub Ould Lahbib, then serving as the RASD's minister of occupied territories. After pledging allegiance to Mohammed VI, he claimed that his disenchantment stemmed from the Algerian intelligence agencies' alleged control over Polisario (Pazzanita 2006, 38–40).

Shortly before the tenth General Congress, the RASD's prime minister Mahfoud Ali Beiba was ousted in a vote of no confidence by the 101-member Parliament in February 1999 (*The Guardian,* Feb. 11, 1999). At the September 1999 congress, the popular Parliament was reduced to 51 members, and an ill-defined Consultative Council of Shaykhs was added, making RASD a bicameral system. The creation of the wise-men council stemmed from the power that the Sahrawi *shuyukh* (shaykhs) had gained in the 1990s as key players in the UN voter-identification process (see chapter 8). In the 1970s, elements of Polisario had tried to free Sahrawi society of such "traditionalism" not only for ideological reasons, but also because of some Sahrawi shaykhs' complicity with Spanish colonialism via the Jamaʻa. Although Polisario had received backing from the Jamaʻa and had learned to make compromises within Sahrawi social traditions, its core cadres nevertheless represented a younger generation. However, by 1999, Polisario's founding members had become respected elders.

The eleventh (2003) and twelfth (2007) General Congresses took place in Tifariti, located in the "liberated" Saqiyah al-Hamra'. On both occasions, Mohammed Abdelaziz was reelected as secretary-general of Polisario and thus as RASD president. Although four other candidates contested the 2003 presidential election, calls for national solidarity in the face of increasing Moroccan obstinacy led to Abdelaziz's running as the sole candidate in 2007. The 2003 congress, from October 12 to October 19, 2003, saw an enlarged National Secretariat that incorporated twelve undisclosed delegates from the Moroccan-occupied Western Sahara. The congress also amended the RASD's 1991 Constitution, giving it more than 130 articles.

The most pressing topic of debate at the 2003 meeting was the new peace proposal, the second "Baker Plan," supported by the UN Security Council and endorsed by Algeria and Polisario months earlier. Before the congress, there was widespread ignorance in the camps about the latest UN offer. The new Baker Plan proposed a limited four-year period of autonomy for Western Sahara followed by a referendum polling both native Western Saharans and Moroccan settlers on the choice of continued autonomy, integration, or independence. Many observers were surprised that Polisario had accepted a plan that allowed the majority Moroccan settlers to participate in the self-determination process, and there was a double shock when Morocco flatly rejected the Baker Plan.

When the Baker Plan's details were understood in the camps, there was dismay that Polisario had accepted it without popular consultation. Many refugees insisted that they would never return to Western Sahara unless Morocco had totally vacated the land. After long and acrimonious debate at the 2003 congress, the Sahrawi body accepted the Baker Plan. However, the congress pressed its diplomats to make sure that they obtained security and protection guarantees from the international community during the proposed transitional four-year autonomy period. Polisario's diplomats were later somewhat vindicated by Morocco's rejection of the Baker Plan. From late 2003 through 2005, Polisario clearly held the high ground internationally. In its internal workings, however, many nationalists were deeply concerned that their leadership had taken such a risk without popular consultation. The reforms of the late 1980s and early 1990s had gone some way toward increasing democratic control over the movement. However, the leadership's dangerous unilateral actions in 2003 revealed that the party and the government needed further separation. Of particular concern to many nationalists was Polisario's foreign-diplomat corps, those with the most influence over the peace process. There was a growing sense that they had become too comfortable and too out of touch with the people and that they had maintained their long-held positions without accountability.

In mid-2004, a reform movement within Polisario, Khatt al-Shahid (Line of the Martyr), went public. Claiming support in the camps, among young Sahrawi militants in the occupied territory, and in the diaspora community in Europe, Khatt al-Shahid became the first overt faction within Polisario. It claimed elected RASD officials among its members, and its top leaders were mostly in European exile (e.g., Mohammed Bennou, a refugee in Switzerland). After failing to achieve reforms quietly, Khatt al-Shahid, usually through the voice of dissident Salek Mahjoub, called for a return to the basic principle of the movement (i.e., "all the homeland or martyrdom"), more changes and new faces in the political leadership (especially among the diplomats and ambassadors), and a complete separation of Polisario from the RASD, especially at the top. Its militant rhetoric appealed to the youngest elements of the intifada in the occupied territory. Democratic reformers, who had long sought to subordinate Polisario under the RASD, were also sympathetic to its program. To more mature activists, however, Khatt al-Shahid was like a ghost, often speaking but without having an open constituency or core membership. Other nationalists attacked the new faction for its public criticisms of Polisario, which the Moroccan media cynically and selectively used to assail Polisario.

This challenge to Polisario's leadership was amplified following the outbreak of the May 2005 intifada. As Moroccan repression increased inside the occupied territory, Polisario's leaders appeared increasingly impotent to their constituents. On several occasions, Mohammed Abdelaziz threatened that he would call for MINURSO's withdrawal from Western Sahara and the resumption of armed struggle unless the UN restrained Morocco. Yet several MINURSO rollovers have since passed with little more than verbal posturing from Polisario's leaders. The timing of a new armed initiative was becoming less and less ripe for Polisario's leaders but more and more demanded in the camps. All of the diplomatic gains Polisario had made in 2003 by embracing the Baker Plan were slowly eroded in the UN Security Council under pressure from France and the United States. With a U.S.-backed Moroccan autonomy proposal on the table in early 2007, and the UN Security Council and secretariat pushing for direct talks without preconditions, Polisario found itself backed into a corner.

In this context, the 2007 Polisario General Congress followed the first two rounds of Morocco–Polisario negotiations in Manhasset, New York. The negotiations had made little headway, further convincing the Western Saharan nationalist movement that Morocco understood only the language of force. Although Polisario's diplomatic wing was able to temper calls for war, the 2007 congress resolved to improve ELPS's war footing in case the negotiations with Morocco failed. The drawn-out diplomatic stalemate was still far from a sufficient casus belli internationally, but domestic pressures on Polisario to fight had become increasingly impatient. Western Saharan nationalism in the camps was drawing its strength more and more from the Sahrawi activists in Moroccan jails and the Sahrawi youth throwing stones in the streets of Western Sahara. The exiled Polisario founding fathers in the Rabouni camp administration center could do little more than offer verbal support and find ways to maintain their legitimacy in the face of increasing Moroccan repression and international indifference. Nevertheless, the proliferation of organizations within the occupied territory and the emergence of a new generation of militants (detailed in chapter 6) signaled a shift in Western Saharan nationalism's center of gravity from the refugee camps to the streets of al-'Ayun.

THE RASD'S FOREIGN RELATIONS

The Sahrawi republic sees itself as an independent state under illegal occupation, not as a government in exile. Polisario officials emphasize that the refugees are in Algeria for security and humanitarian reasons only, although after the cease-fire many refugees now freely transit between the camps and the "liberated" territory. The Sahrawi republic attempts to carry out as many governmental functions in the territory as possible, especially the Polisario congresses and national celebrations, such as RASD's anniversary celebrations in February, normally staged in Tifariti. As discussed later, even small daily acts create a sense of statehood and nationalism in the camps, such as when the RASD's first postage stamps were issued in July 1990 (Lippert 1991, 13).

Modeled after Algeria's struggle for independence, Polisario's major foreign-policy goal has been to maintain the internationalization of the Western Sahara conflict, for a couple of reasons. First, this approach seeks to counter Moroccan attempts to reduce the conflict to an internal matter of "separatism" or a bilateral dispute with Algeria. Second, internationalization seeks to frame the conflict in terms of international law and human rights norms that are in Polisario's favor. For example, in early 2001 Polisario led a successful challenge to the Moroccan government's efforts to exploit possible oil reserves off the coast of Western Sahara. Using an ally on the Security Council, Polisario obtained an official opinion from the UN legal counsel that forbade petroleum exploitation in Western Sahara. At the same time, the RASD signed similar oil concessions with different companies as a counterassertion of sovereignty, although these concessions would be actionable only after independence.

One of Polisario's main diplomatic strategies at the international level has been the pursuit of bilateral recognition from other states. At one time or another, more than eighty nations and the African Union (formerly the OAU) have recognized the RASD as the legitimate government of an otherwise Moroccan-dominated Western Sahara. Recognition in most cases has not always entailed an exchange of ambassadors or a RASD embassy, though, and has little more than symbolic value in the case of small and poor nations. The precise number of governments who recognize the RASD's sovereignty over Western Sahara is difficult to obtain because several states have withdrawn recognition over the years; some have gone back and forth; others have ambiguously suspended recognition pending a referendum. The reasons for these cancellations and suspensions of recognition range from external diplomatic pressure from France and Spain, economic incentives offered by Morocco, and regime change resulting in ideological antipathy toward Polisario. Yet among international legal scholars, there is a debate about whether derecognition and suspension are even possible unless the state ceases to exist. For example, the 1933 Montevideo Convention on the Rights and Duties of States, which is often treated as reflecting customary international law, states unambiguously that recognition is unconditional and irrevocable. Thus, there is significant support to back Polisario's claim that RASD is considered an independent (albeit occupied) nation-state by a significant number of the world's governments. During the war, Polisario officials argued that were it not for the Security Council's control over the nomination process (i.e., the threat of French or U.S. veto), the RASD would likely have become a full member state of the UN (Zunes, interview with Mouloud Said, Rabouni, Algeria, June 25, 1987).

Most of the countries that recognized the RASD early on were Third World countries, including both left-leaning and conservative African governments (e.g., the former regimes of Togo and Rwanda), as well as moderate Latin American states such as Mexico and pre-Chávez Venezuela. Several international forums, most notably the Nonaligned Movement, endorsed Polisario, and the OAU/African Union recognizes RASD. More progressive European governments have tended to offer Polisario the most sympathy (e.g., Ireland, Norway, and Sweden), yet the only European countries ever to recognize the RASD were the nonaligned Communist states of Yugoslavia and Albania. A current map of RASD recognition shows that the strategy of seeking bilateral recognition has been most successful in Africa, followed by Latin America and Asia. The RASD has been unsuccessful in its attempts to break Morocco's stranglehold of support in the Middle East apart from the endorsements it has received from Iran, Afghanistan, and Syria.

Overall, the RASD claims that it has sought good relations and support from almost every nation. The only exceptions to this pattern in RASD's foreign relations have been apartheid South Africa, Israel (despite a lack of PLO reciprocation), and, while under military rule, Chile (Zunes, interview with Mouloud Said, Rabouni, Algeria, June 25, 1987). The Sahrawi republic's support for national liberation struggles, however, has been a little less than principled. Good relations with India—even after New Delhi's 2000 derecognition of RASD—kept Polisario largely quiet regarding Kashmir. Despite some important parallels with the Eritrean struggle for independence, which finally triumphed in 1991, Polisario did not openly support the Eritrean People's Liberation Front so as to preserve good relations with Ethiopia, where the OAU was based and where the RASD maintains an embassy. Some Polisario members readily call this neglect a "dark spot" in their history. The Unión Nacional de Mujeres Saharauis (UNMS; National Union of Sahrawi Women), however, did unilaterally create ties with Eritrean women activists because both were a rare example of armed politically active women within an African liberation movement.

The Sahrawi republic has also promised to be neutral in regional conflicts, including those between Morocco and Algeria; has agreed not to enter into any treaties or alliances that would be hostile to Morocco; has pledged not to be a base of attacks on Morocco; and has offered to be cooperative in economic relations (*Africa Report,* May 1989). Polisario actually welcomed the 1989 North African economic cooperation agreement, the UMA, as "a regional platform furthering peaceful resolution through negotiations and dialogue" and hoped that it would be incorporated in the regional process after independence. Since then, the RASD has continued to play an important role in the African Union as a full member state and even as a contributing member to peacekeeping efforts.

One of the charges Polisario has had to confront is whether, as an independent state, it will work to undermine the Moroccan regime or not. Ali Yata, a Moroccan Communist leader in the 1970s, claimed that El-Ouali Mustapha Sayed saw an independent Western Sahara as a platform for a wider war against the ʿAlawi-dominated Morocco. On paper, however, Polisario claimed the opposite in its General National Program, adopted at the fourth General Congress in 1978. The program read, "[O]ur fight is a liberation war, for national independence, and is not intended to overthrow foreign regimes" (quoted in Hodges 1985, 261). Polisario has pledged that it will not raise a counterirredentist claim on the contiguous Sahrawi-populated areas in southern Morocco formerly under Spanish administration along the Draʿa (the "Tekna Zone,"; see map 6 in chapter 4), especially the cities of Tan Tan, Tarfaya, and Assa), although some resistance leaders inside the occupied territory believe that this increasingly rebellious region will perhaps seek to join an independent Western Sahara if Morocco maintains its regressive development and human rights policies.

In Africa, Polisario has suffered some significant setbacks since the height of its movement in 1984, the year RASD entered the OAU as a full member state. Derecognitions from French clients such as Chad, Burkina Faso, and Madagascar, along with continued major nonrecognitions (e.g., Sudan, Egypt, and the Democratic Republic of the Congo) have eroded support for the RASD in Africa. However, support from African powerhouses such as Algeria, Ethiopia, Libya, Nigeria, and South Africa form a strong base in the face of Moroccan demands that the African Union reconsider its recognition of the RASD.

The Sahrawi republic's strongest support has recently come from the African National Congress in South Africa. Former South African president Nelson Mandela has been particularly outspoken in support of Polisario and has visited the refugee camps and even Polisario-controlled territory in the Western Sahara. Thabo Mbeki, Mandela's successor until September 2008, was equally supportive. In 1996, the African National Congress majority in the Parliament pushed President Mandela to recognize the RASD. At the same time, South Africa offered to mediate the deadlocked referendum process. Its foreign minister was scheduled to visit Rabat and Algiers in February 1996. Morocco, however, refused to receive him; in response, he went to Tindouf. Pressure from UN secretary-general Boutros Boutros-Ghali and even from Palestinian president Yasir Arafat (given Morocco's support of the Palestinian cause) convinced South Africa to withhold formal recognition for a time. The United States, France, and the United Kingdom also advised South Africa not to take that step; otherwise, Rabat would never accept it as a mediator

(Zunes, interviews with UN diplomats, UN, New York, June 1997). Yet in September 2004 Pretoria finally recognized the RASD, claiming that Morocco's rejection of Baker and the peace process required this recognition. It was followed by recognitions from Kenya and Uruguay in 2005, although the former's was "frozen" under unclear circumstances.

The Sahrawi republic has also scored recent victories in Latin America, where more and more progressive governments have come to power as U.S. hegemony in that region wanes. Polisario has received strong support from Venezuelan president Hugo Chávez since his election in 1999, although not from Brazil under the center-left government of Luiz Inácio Lula da Silva, elected in 2003. Likewise, the elections of socialist-leaning presidents in Bolivia (2006) and Paraguay (2008) have increased the RASD's standing in the Western Hemisphere, especially following Paraguay's subsequent re-recognition of RASD.

In Asia, one set of relationships that has been especially important for Western Saharan nationalists is with the East Timorese. Less than six weeks following Morocco's invasion of Western Sahara in 1975, Indonesia followed suit with its U.S.-approved invasion of East Timor. East Timorese president Jose Ramos-Horta, who won the 1996 Nobel Peace Prize for his advocacy on behalf of his then-occupied homeland, worked out of the RASD's unofficial UN mission during his early years of exile in the late 1970s (Zunes, interview with Dr. Juan Federer, Porto, Portugal, July 1997). In exchange, East Timor, following its independence vote in 1999, has been one of the more recent nations to recognize the RASD. However, the loss of recognition from India in 2000 was an indisputable blow to RASD.

## A REPUBLIC IN PRACTICE: THE SAHRAWI REFUGEE CAMPS

The Sahrawi camps were initially a sea of tents spread across a single location. Their division and organization into three and then four separate and well-defined spaces happened later (map 7). In the beginning, each family (i.e., women, young children, and elderly males) had a single tent. Now most families live in mud-brick dwellings alongside their tent. Although the brick rooms serve the refugees well during sandstorms, heavy rains can quickly reduce them to mud. Rains in early 2006, for example, left tens of thousands of refugees with only their tents, destroying years of hand-built infrastructure in several hours. Indeed, the weather is among the most severe in the entire Sahara—very dry, with frequent sandstorms, freezing temperatures on winter nights, and some of world's highest recorded temperatures in summer. During the height of summer and winter, refugees often sojourn inside the Polisario-controlled areas of Western Sahara, where there is more vegetation and moderate temperatures.

When the refugees started arriving in the Tindouf area in late 1975, it was also already well populated by ethnic Sahrawis. Amidst the chaos of the 1957–58 French–Spanish counterinsurgency operations, many Sahrawis fled to the region (as well as to southern Morocco and Mauritania), where the Rgaybat had been a dominant presence

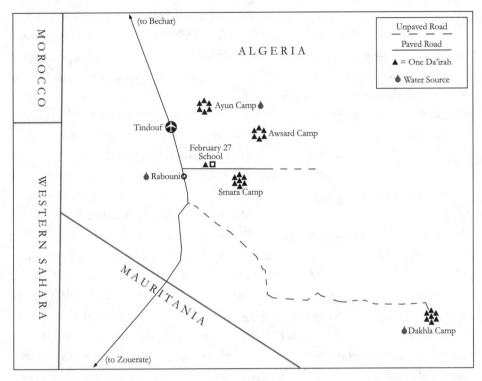

Map 7. Western Saharan refugee camps (schematic). Based on authors' notes and UN maps (UNHCR and MINURSO).

for at least a century. As much for logistical as ethnic reasons, Tindouf was a natural place for Polisario to establish itself. At eight hundred kilometers from the nearest Algerian city, but with an airport, Tindouf is Polisario's regional administrative and military center in southwestern Algeria.

The percentage of those living in the camps who are native to Western Sahara—as opposed to ethnic Sahrawis from Algeria, Morocco, or Mauritania or possibly to Arabic-speaking Malians—is a matter of ongoing debate. Polisario's Sahrawi Red Crescent, which oversees humanitarian affairs in the camps, and Algeria claim that their population figures are based on accurate data, yet with no external verification, no international oversight, no transparent record keeping in the food-distribution process, no accounting for additional bilateral aid from NGOs, and reports of donated food being sold in Mauritanian markets, aid donors have become increasingly unhappy in recent years.

The international community has traditionally accepted, with some skepticism, the figure of 165,000 refugees, first provided by Algeria in 1976, although Polisario apparently claimed that the number was only 110,000 in 1979 (Knight 1979). Starting in 1982, the UNHCR agreed to provide aid for 80,000 of the most "vulnerable" refugees without directly challenging the 165,000 figure. Following reports and studies indicating widespread malnutrition, aid was increased to 155,000 persons in 2000 and again to 158,000 in 2004. In 2005, however, the UNHCR and UN World Food Program reduced the number to 90,000 persons. The World Food Program claimed that it was again helping only the most "vulnerable" refugees. UN officials long suspected that the real population was far less than 165,000 and realistically closer to 100,000 in the mid-1990s (Zunes, briefing, UN, June 1996). The World Food Program's own internal estimates, based on satellite images of the camps, put the population in the range of roughly 100,000 in 2005.

A UNHCR repatriation "census," conducted between 1998 and 2000 to prepare for the then expected referendum, arrived at a figure of 129,863 refugees. Yet the accuracy of this count is questionable because it relied solely on the testimony of male heads of households rather than on a direct count of the population. The results of MINURSO's voter-identification process, completed in 2000, suggest that roughly 40 percent of native Western Saharans are in the camps. The UN voter list was based on the 1974 Spanish census, which counted roughly 75,000 Western Saharans. Assuming an initial camp population of some 30,000 in 1976, an extremely high average annual growth rate of 3.5 percent yields more than 70,000 refugees in 2000, whereas a more reasonable 2 percent growth rate produces a population of 50,000. Given these wide-ranging figures, there is either a significant number of non–Western Saharan Sahrawis in the camps or serious problems with the MINURSO voter list or the UNHCR census or a combination thereof. (See chapter 8 for further demographic analysis.)

Regardless of the exact refugee population figures, the camps are still unique in the world of forced migration. Unlike in other refugee situations, in these camps multigovernmental organizations and NGOs do not play a direct role in daily management. Such organizations must work through the Sahrawi Red Crescent or a relevant RASD ministry. The camps are entirely self-managed, with locally elected functionaries acting as the capillaries of aid distribution. However, there is no hope for self-sufficiency in such a hostile environment. The refugees have always been heavily dependent on outside aid for their survival. In the mid-1980s, one estimate claimed that the Algerian government had allocated as much as $100 million in assistance (Chichini 1985). In more recent years, international donor fatigue and reports of misappropriated food has led to food crises in the camps requiring frequent stopgap measures. The recent development of a small market economy in the camps, following the 1991 cease-fire, has also given the false impression of self-sufficiency.

The Sahrawi refugees are additionally at a disadvantage in terms of their international status. The UNHCR deals with two types of refugee situations: short-term emergencies during crises and long-term postconflict resettlement. The Western Sahara conflict is still treated as an "emergency" situation because a solution has not been found. This designation means that UNHCR is limited in the activities it can carry out in the camps, especially long-term development projects. Indeed, the quantity of food aid is minimal precisely because Western Sahara is treated as an ongoing crisis: a minimum basic caloric requirement aimed at keeping a person alive during a short-term crisis, not at sustaining them for thirty years. It is heavy in flour and rice but also includes oil, sugar, salt, and beans or lentils. Algeria, as the host country, is not willing to resettle the refugees formally on its soil barring a solution to the conflict, nor have the refugees expressed a willingness to return to Western Sahara while it is still under Moroccan occupation. Thus, they remain in a thirty-year-old state of emergency.

As the refugees became more settled in 1976, they began to implement a system of self-management. This system was fully in effect by the time of the second popular Base Congress in the spring of 1977. The grassroots level of decision making and management resides at the *hayy* (neighborhood or barrio); each *hayy* comprises around two hundred tents. Below this level, each refugee is officially a member of a local twelve- to fifteen-person cell *(khaliyah),* an organizational structure dating back to Polisario's founding. The *khaliyah* organizes the subneighborhoods for specific activities (e.g., neighborhood cleanup), deals with emergencies (e.g., the floods in 2006), and discusses political or social initiatives to be brought to the *hayy* or the functional committees.[3]

Four *hayy*s come together to form a *da'irah* (district). Each *da'irah* has a council *(majlis)* composed of the elected representatives *(mas'ul)* from the *hayy*s, ministry representatives, and an elected executive who represents the *da'irah* at higher levels. The *hayy mas'ulah*—a position typically held by a woman during the war—is responsible for food distribution and all other matters in her *hayy*. On a yearly basis, the six to seven districts within each camp hold a Base Congress to elect the *da'irah* executive and to assign positions on the local committees *(lajnah)*. These committees cover five areas of social life: children's education, health/sanitation, justice, food/provisions, and production/crafts. The districts also set objectives for themselves and propose objectives for the national bodies to consider (Bontems 1987, 174).

The four camps are the *wilayah* (provincial) level, each named after the four *wilayat* of RASD's envisioned, independent Western Sahara: Dakhla, Smara, al-'Ayun, and Awsard. Both Dakhla and Smara are currently composed of seven *da'irat,* and al-'Ayun and Awsard have six. Smara, the largest camp by population, currently houses some forty-two thousand Sahrawis, according to Bushraia Baiun, the camp *wali* (governor). Each *wilayah* has six primary schools and a hospital, and there is a medical clinic/dispensary in each *da'irah*. At the "national" level, there is a women's school, the February 27 School. It is home of the UNMS and has its own small camp so that families can remain together while women attend classes and training courses. There are also two national secondary schools for boys and girls (the October 12 and June 9 Schools), although there is no postsecondary capability except for the training programs available at the February 27 School for women. The national hospital and most of the national government, military, and foreign NGO offices are located in a central area called "Rabouni."

The refugees developed this decentralized management structure in the camps as much out of necessity as out of choice. Polisario leaders boast that their system is simply the most pragmatic and efficient means of governance and self-management given the situation. Controlling disease epidemics was also a major concern behind the large distances between the first three *wilayat* that were established (al-'Ayun, Smara, and Dakhla). Access to water resources was another issue. The camps of al-'Ayun and Dakhla were established on underground water sources, but water has to be trucked in from Rabouni to Smara. The creation of the fourth camp in 1985, Awsard, has placed further strain on the Rabouni source.

Although communication between camps was limited during the war, this is no longer the case. Freedom of movement was not hindered by policy, but by a shortage of means. During the height of the armed conflict, with almost every available vehicle devoted to the war effort, Polisario provided only a limited number of flatbed trucks for civilian transportation needs. Since the beginning of the cease-fire and the demobilization of a large part of the ELPS, transit between camps has been greatly enhanced by the number of vehicles now put to civilian use. Personal car ownership has also greatly increased in recent years, a sign of the growing internal economy. Some Land Rovers that formerly served as Polisario's favored attack vehicle have even been put to use as taxis, ferrying people to schools, the administration center in Rabouni, Tindouf, and even Zouerate or the liberated zones. Indeed, a major problem facing Polisario is the fact that some refugees use their cars in trans-Saharan clandestine trade, such as cigarettes and migrants. With the Algerian, Malian, Nigerien, and Mauritanian governments "concerned" about illegal activities along their shared borders, including alleged terrorists such as the Groupe salafiste pour la Prédication et le Combat (Salafi Group for Preaching and Combat, now al-Qaida in the Islamic Maghrib), Polisario has had to increase its own monitoring of the population in the camps. Since 2004, uniformed RASD officials have "professionalized" the once lax checkpoints into the camps, so that identification cards are now checked and license plates recorded.

Education in the camps is as rigorous as can be expected, with the lack of supplies being the most debilitating problem. The goals that RASD has set for itself—and achieved—in education are a point of pride for those in the camps. Primary schooling is free, compulsory, and coeducational. Adult literacy classes in Arabic and European languages are offered, with day-care service available for attending parents. As a result, the Sahrawi refugees claim one of the highest literacy rates in Africa. Spanish is taught as a second language from the primary grades up, and other European languages are taught at higher levels if teachers are available. Secondary students complain about the low educational standards, which make it difficult for them when they transfer to schools abroad, as well as about the lack of French-language training in the camps, which is very important for those seeking to transfer to Algerian schools (see Chatty and Crivello 2005). Some refugee students move on to the two national boarding schools and can then transfer to schools or universities in Algeria. Some of the refugees have gone on to attain university degrees in various other countries, including Libya, Syria, Cuba, and Spain. Many of these students who leave the camps on scholarship return to apply the knowledge and skills they have acquired, if possible, in their various specializations, such as engineering and medicine. In the refugee schools, there is no obvious program for ideological orientation, although the national narrative is known among the youngest of children. In the mid-1980s, one local informant claimed that the political leadership is reluctant to indoctrinate young people for fear that they will be less able to think for themselves and participate in daily affairs (Zunes, interview with Brahim Mohammed Arbi, Dakhla camp, Algeria, June 19, 1987). Nonetheless, the names of schools are principal dates in the independence movement, and pictures of the late Polisario founder El-Ouali Mustapha Sayed feature prominently in some classrooms.

International aid workers in the camps, with comparative experience elsewhere in the world, feel that the Sahrawi refugees are one of the most politically aware refugee populations in the world—from the political leadership down to mothers collecting their monthly rations. In the camps, the overall ideological features are no greater or lesser than in any other society that is attempting to create, reinforce, and naturalize a national consciousness. Remarking on the imagined use of Algerian dinars as "Sahrawi currency," scholar Pablo San Martin recently highlighted the way in which even this banal, quotidian practice suggests that "because circumstances do not permit the construction of a 'normal' state, it is built more explicitly at the symbolic level" (2005, 573–74).

At a more concrete level, the use of money in the camps, ever increasing since the 1991 cease-fire, is a sign of the recent growth of independent markets. In the early days of the camps, there was little for families to trade, except for the small herds of goats and camels (Zunes, interview with Mohammed Abdel Khadeh, Dakhla camp, Algeria, June 21, 1987). Since the cease-fire, with greater numbers of ELPS fighters demobilized and with some outside sources of income (e.g., immigrant remittances, tourist dollars, Spanish pensions), the camps now have thriving markets where all sorts of goods are available for purchase. These goods originate from the town of Tindouf, Mauritania, and as far abroad as central Sahara. Trade is greatly facilitated by numbers of privately owned trucks now put to personal rather than collective military needs.

Long before the growth of the open markets in the 1990s, which have made a wider variety of food choices available, the Wilayah Popular Assemblies decided in 1979 to attempt growing vegetables. Each *wilayah* has several experimental gardens ranging from five to fifteen hectares for growing carrots, parsnips, onions, tomatoes, beets, melons, and other fruits and vegetables. Most of the produce is reserved for patients in the hospitals and other health facilities. These gardens are irrigated with water from deep wells, some of which are brought to the surface through solar-powered water pumps. Such agricultural experiments provide training in practical skills but were never meant to make the camps self-sufficient. Chronic protein shortages were reduced somewhat by the construction of four large climate-controlled chicken houses for egg and meat production, built by the refugees in conjunction with several European NGOs. Yet the availability of fresh meats and vegetables in the local markets now means that the families that can afford them can diversify their diet, although the starch-heavy aid food still forms the base of most families' diet. Levels of acute and severe malnutrition (7 and 2 percent, respectively) have declined, but stunting related to malnutrition and chronic micronutrient deficiencies remains around 40 percent. The rate of anemia among children (six to fifty-nine months old) is greater than 60 percent and almost as high among women age fifteen to forty-nine (UN Standing Committee on Nutrition 2005).

Nevertheless, health care has progressed remarkably since the initial days of the exodus. The epidemics of 1975 and 1976 that ravaged the camps and killed thousands of children were met with a delayed medical response due to the lack of refrigeration for vaccines. The first months of the camps also saw widespread outbreaks of tuberculosis, bronchitis, and dysentery (Harrel-Bond 1981, III:3). Since that time, vaccination programs have virtually eliminated many communicable diseases, but RASD health authorities today are still battling diseases associated with the harsh conditions, in particular bronchitis in the winter and various intestinal disorders in the summer. Because of the financial constraints, there is an emphasis on preventative medicine, similar to the Cuban example, and education campaigns to encourage breast-feeding and to discourage smoking. The health committees ensure that families get clean water and that a sick or pregnant individual gets care. When children show signs of malnutrition, they are sent to nearby prevention centers, where they are put on special diets. Mothers are encouraged to stay with their children as part of the education process to see what it takes to improve the children's health (Harrel-Bond 1981, III:3–5). The hospital system is adequate, although there are often shortages of some drugs and medical equipment. The health facilities have been praised for keeping excellent medical records, which bodes well for future epidemiological studies. Yet, as mentioned earlier, there continue to be major problems related to nutrition. It is estimated that between 40 and 50 percent of pregnancies end in miscarriage because of malnutrition (UN Development Fund for Women 2005).

Although the camps themselves remain socially cohesive, participation in the committees has somewhat declined since the 1991 cease-fire and the demobilization of the ELPS (which created a greater number of men in the camps). The committees still exist on paper, and several are still required for the basic functioning of the camps (e.g., food-aid distribution), yet the growth of male-dominated markets and the reassertion of male power in the homes has reduced the need for some of these previously female-driven institutions. There is also a simple lack of work to be done in the camps, which has engendered the postwar market economy in the camps as well as trans-Saharan smuggling among the refugees. With the population ever increasing and with highly educated young males now returning from universities abroad, finding the means of "employing" males is becoming a major problem in the camps. Staving off boredom is the primary motivation for many economic, social, and educational activities.

## SAHRAWI WOMEN IN THE NATIONALIST MOVEMENT

Observers and supporters of Polisario have frequently lauded the deployment of women in the nationalist struggle, in the administration of the camps, and in almost all levels of office in RASD. Since its inception in 1973, Polisario has made a conscious effort to incorporate women and women's issues in the struggle for independence.[4] Women played "a decisive role in the anticolonial struggle" against the Spanish occupation, including smuggling arms and documents, providing intelligence, using their homes as sanctuaries for activists, selling jewelry to finance the struggle, and encouraging their husbands to take up arms, which "led people to acknowledge the importance and strength of women in revolution" (Zunes, interview with Brahim Mohammed Arbi, Dakhla camp, June 20, 1987). In the war, women also played important roles in the armed resistance as radio operators, drivers, and medics, and some even received training in hand-held arms, such as AK-47s and rocket-propelled grenades. The ELPS, however, reserved combat responsibilities for men. According to one Polisario official, Mohammed Al-Wali, "The war of liberation is necessary for everyone. You divide up responsibilities according to their ability. Women's work is different, but not less important" (Zunes, interview, Saqiyah al-Hamra', Western Sahara, June 24, 1987). "Women's work," however, was dictated by necessity as much as by Polisario's acclaimed "progressive" attitudes toward women. Given the near-total mobilization of able-bodied men in the ELPS during the war, as much as 80 percent of the civilian population in the refugee camps consisted of women.

The diffusion of Sahrawi women into positions of responsibility in the government and the camps is also a sign of the general disposition of females in Saharan and various other Bedouin societies. For example, Sahrawi women have traditionally had equal rights to men in inheritance and divorce and keep their maiden names following marriage. As scholar H. T. Norris observed in 1964, "The *baydaniya* has always enjoyed an honorable status compared with her sister in many Arab countries. She grows up and marries in a monogamous society, and although divorce is common, it is very often she who wishes it to further her own interests. The influence she plays in affairs openly and behind the scenes is quite remarkable, and . . . there is plenty of evidence to show that in days past her scholastic achievements were comparable with the men's" (10–11). Such observations undermine Western perceptions of women in Arab societies as repressed. And contrary to another popular Western prejudice, some of the Sahrawi refugees argued in conversations with the authors that Islam justifies the responsibilities given to women in the camps.

Polisario activists have generally attempted to link their political and social organization with traditionalist notions, as if to say that their struggle is the expression of indigenous ideas rather than foreign revolutionary concepts grafted onto their society. As one elderly *qadi* (judge) in a refugee camp argued, "What Polisario is doing is not really new. Their programs derive from our historical traditions. The Constitution and programs have their source in Islamic law, but we also know that these are new and different times. Thus, we have new terminology and new issues, but it remains faithful. Conflicts between old and young in other countries are primarily due to differing ideologies. We don't have those sorts of conflicts: there may be different roles between the old and young, but we have the same objectives" (Zunes, interview with Mohammed Abdel Khadeh, Dakhla camp, Algeria, June 21, 1987).

However, one might make the mistake of minimizing the agency of Sahrawi women by relying too heavily on explanations drawn from overemphasized cultural premises. Some female Sahrawi refugee activists have seen their participation on a higher ideological plane than even some of Polisario's male leaders have seen it. According to Senniya, governor of the Smara camp in 1987, "As an integral part of Sahrawi society, women must play a major role. This role is a necessity, not just a slogan. Women have a national duty to work for liberation, and we will continue when the war is over. We will not return to the home because we have begun a revolution for justice and equal rights. For example, there will not be equal rights if there are not also equal duties. That is why women have taken on such a major role in Sahrawi society" (Zunes, interview, Smara camp, Western Sahara, June 18, 1987). Culture-dependent explanations also fail to clarify the motivation that is often drawn from examples set by women in the Algerian revolution and other Third World liberation struggles. The difference in Polisario's "revolution" is that some of the women participating in it do not see their work as temporary and pragmatic, but rather as a model that prefigures the social arrangements of an independent state. Unlike in other revolutions wherein women were resubordinated following triumph, in the Sahrawi revolution many female refugee activists do not plan on relenting after independence (*New Internationalist*, Dec. 1997). Women's strong leadership in the resistance movement inside the occupied territory testifies that this phenomenon is not just relegated to the Polisario-run camps (see chapter 6).

By numbers alone, women's participation in the RASD has been impressive, even if women have been excluded from the elite core of Polisario and the ELPS. During the war, the grassroots body of the RASD, the annual Base Congress, was almost 90 percent women. The overwhelming majority of the committees outlined earlier, particularly at the lower levels, were composed of women (Lippert 1991, 645). Women have held governorships at the *wilayah* level, and three members of the Political Bureau prior to its abolition were women. Throughout the national liberation struggle, women have also taken up diplomatic responsibilities, with some traveling alone or in small groups to international conferences and other functions around the world. Speaking in 1987, the secretary-general of the UNMS thought that women would eventually fill at least 50 percent of the posts at all levels (Zunes, interview, February 27 School, Algeria, June 22, 1987). More than twenty years later, this goal is still far from met.

The UNMS was founded as an arm of Polisario to unify and link all the women's groups working toward independence in Spanish Sahara. It has evolved into one of the RASD's three main "mass organizations"; the other two—labor and student groups—were also dominated by women until recently. The Women's Union is based at the February 27 School, a facility specifically created for women's education and organizing. The school has its own minicamp so that families can join their daughters, sisters, or mothers while they attend, teach, or manage the affairs there.

In the early days of the camps, the same women who were almost totally neglected by Spanish colonialism had to take on enormous responsibilities to protect the population and distribute emergency provisions. "We had to learn by doing," stated a refugee named Khadidja, who described how women took on the roles of teachers and medics during the early years: "Women's education under Polisario included not just formal education, but practical skills, such as issues of hygiene, child-rearing, etc., which are indeed revolutionary. This is not just a military and political revolution, but a revolution of the whole fabric of society. It is a total revolution to the very essentials of life" (Zunes, interview, February 27 School, Algeria, June 22, 1987). During the Spanish colonial period, the literacy rate for women was well under 10 percent, as much a result of underdevelopment of the territory as of "the colonial attitude" (Zunes, interview with Ein Beida *da'irah* council members, Dakhla camp, June 20, 1987). Today the refugees boast a near-universal literacy in Arabic among adult women, to such an extent that primary literacy classes for older women are no longer needed. The majority of today's women leaders in the camps received their education once each camp's overall system was in place (i.e., after three hard years of foundational work).

## THE POLITICAL ECONOMY OF "PEACE": THE CAMPS AFTER 1991

The goal-driven optimism of the war has more recently been dealt a serious blow by what many of the camps' residents see as years of false promises from the UN. Although the camps remain unified, it is difficult to find a single refugee who thinks that camp residents will be returning home anytime in the near future. Rather than despair, most refugees now focus on improving their daily situation. Many pin their hopes on the increasing militancy of the intifada inside Western Sahara rather than on the Polisario leadership.

Two factors helped feed the growth of the local economy in the camps and the subsequent reassertion of male power. The 1991 cease-fire saw the reintroduction of large numbers of men into the camps and small-scale independent economic activity, but the large market economy exploded after 2000, when the UN placed the referendum on indefinite hold. International aid workers familiar with the camps before and after 2000 describe the change as "night and day." The prospect of a referendum throughout the 1990s kept most families from investing too much in the camps. Now it is the opposite; most refugees focus on making and improving their lives as much as possible. Not only have shops and cafes proliferated, but dwellings have become much larger, with extra rooms being added as families can afford them. The demilitarization of males has radically transformed the landscape in the camps—a transformation motivated by economic advancement and boredom.

Fueling this transformation was the introduction of relatively large quantities of cash in the early 1990s. The first significant input was from pensions Spain granted to former Sahrawi soldiers in the colonial army. After a long legal battle, some Sahrawis won two-thirds of their promised Spanish pension, a significant income in the camps. Families receiving pensions started acting as banks, offering zero-interest loans to their neighbors. Once it became clear in the late 1990s and early 2000s that a referendum was unlikely, people invested in or borrowed for small enterprises (e.g., shops, cafes, taxis, goat herds, and pay-per-minute cell phone booths). Some families also benefit from remittances from family members living and working abroad, mostly in Spain. There are even reported cases of NGOs' refusing to work in the camps because they think there is now little need for outside help. The Sahrawi refugees are also aware of the fact that their standard of living is now far better than that of most people in Mauritania, Mali, or Niger.

Another significant economic input is the cash gifts given to refugee children participating in the summer vacation programs with Spanish families. Each summer around ten thousand refugee children visit Spanish host families and bring home an average gift of at least 50 euros each, but sometimes as much as 350 euros, so that a total of between half a million and one million euros is injected into the camps each year. In addition, Spanish host families often visit the camps, buying products or leaving similar cash gifts. For Sahrawi families with multiple children participating in the summer program, the effects are obvious, increasing the already visible class differences developing in the camps (Refugee Studies Center 2005, 20–21). The growth of "solidarity tourism" also accounts for a percentage of the local economy, with several shops now catering directly to foreigners.

Besides creating economic stratification, these changes have also affected the once dominant role of women in the camps. Not only have former soldiers encroached into women's social and political spheres, but the camps have seen a resurgence of *al-mahr* (bride-price) coinciding with the growth of the local economy. The same study reported an increased and likewise contested use of the *milhafah,* the traditional female full-body covering, which can also be used to cover the face. The *milhafah* was formerly reserved for married women, but the camps have seen its increasing use among girls as young as age eleven. The issue is particularly sensitive among women who have studied abroad, especially those returning from Cuba, who now find it difficult to readjust to the culture of the camps (Fiddian 2002, 39–41).

For many refugees, independence seems farther off because the international community has been unable or is unwilling to force the Moroccan government's hand. Although most Sahrawis express a preference for a peaceful settlement, most assume that only force of arms will bring them self-determination. Nevertheless, the overall single-minded effort to achieve independence during the war and referendum periods has given way to meeting quotidian needs through the new and growing avenues for economic advancement in the camps. The establishment of markets, which diversified the "jobs" available, has helped reduce some of the direct pressure on Polisario's leadership to come up with a solution to providing for the people in the camps. Markets and employment have also helped to offset some of the difficulties of earlier camp life. The proliferation of televisions and video-viewing rooms (powered by solar-recharged car batteries) has also diversified the uncensored information and entertainment options available. There are also Internet cafés in the camps and sporadic cell phone access, so most refugees have a clearer picture of the world around them, especially regarding the realities inside the Moroccan-controlled Sahara relayed from family members and proindependence activists there. As is the case all over North Africa, the young often express a strong desire to study and work in Europe or the United States, to earn money to support their families in the camps, perhaps to educate their own children in Europe, but also to return home if needed for war or independence.

The growing affluence in the camps also has ramifications for the peace process. The false assumption among many observers and mediators in the conflict is that the Western Saharan refugees live uncomfortably, and this belief is seen as a pressure point to leverage compromise from Polisario. However, it is not the case. As the camps have economically opened up in recent years, the refugees have become more entrenched, more focused on building a decent life in the camps, and thus more reticent to accept any peace plan that does not offer them full independence. The UN must now confront the fact that the refugees would rather live in an increasingly acceptable exile than return to an uncertain future in Western Sahara.

## FROM COLONIAL SUBJECTS TO CITIZENS

Anticolonial nationalism was a powerful idea that swept through the world like wildfire in the twentieth century. Following the end of the Cold War, nationalism as an idea, an identity, and a practiced political project has come under sustained attack. No sooner had Francis Fukuyama (1992) declared the end of history than Samuel Huntington (1993) predicted a new clash of civilizations, notably between the West and the Islamic world. Where the former saw the eventual eclipse of nation-states by the forces of neoliberalism, the latter saw the consolidation of rival epistemic boundaries between contending world-views. The sovereign state, if not the very idea of nationalism, stood against the hegemonic forces of the post–Cold War world—powers that would quickly erase borders and national identities. Evidence of these forces was seen in the initiation of broad multilateral trade agreements, such as the North American Free Trade Agreement and the founding of the World Trade Organization; political-economic integration projects, such as the EU; and the ability of transnational capital to flow in and out of borders, almost at will. Supporters of Huntington's thesis pointed not only to China's economic boom, but to the growth of militant Islamic organizations operating transnationally, manifesting themselves in insurgencies that grew out of U.S.-backed mujahideen in Afghanistan (e.g., in Algeria and Egypt). For obvious reasons, this thesis gained an even wider audience after September 11, 2001.

Counter to these two theses of globalization (the inexorable hegemony of liberal capitalism versus clashing civilizations), other theorists noted the proliferation of "ethnic" conflict in the 1990s, citing the bloody disintegration of Yugoslavia, the genocide in Rwanda, and a dozen other civil wars. So, the argument goes, the Cold War had kept the forces of Balkanization under control by overriding political realities in the postcolonial world, which was rife with ethnic fracture lines. Robert Kaplan's (1994, 2001) widely read prediction of a "coming anarchy" was one of the more popular versions of this pessimistic counterthesis. The nation-state was not under attack from above and beyond, but instead from below and within. Either way, the Westphalian project was coming to an end.

In addition to these liberal-utopian, civilizational, and pessimist critiques, liberation movements began to rethink the state as well. The failures of top-down socialism in the twentieth century engendered skepticism as to whether the state could ever become a vehicle for equality and justice. This fourth critique, however, did not come from U.S. intelligentsia as did the other three. It came from a most unexpected place: the Lacandon jungle of southwestern Mexico. On the same day as the inauguration of the North American Free Trade Agreement, the Zapatista Army of National Liberation, taking control of several key cities in the Mexican state of Chiapas for a short time, captured the postmodern world's imagination. The movement, led by indigenous Mexicans, did not call for independence but rather claimed that it sought to establish an autonomous "democratic space" within Mexico. The Zapatistas regularly deployed nationalist imagery, symbols, and devices from Mexican history, claiming that their project was one of dignity and autonomy, not secession and independence. Rather than create an identity that ran counter to—or sought to separate itself from—Mexican nationalism, the Zapatista project aimed at a reconceptualization of what it means to be Mexican. In the face of cleaving "civilizations," a new world order "after history," and violent "anarchies," the Zapatistas suggested an alternative.

For Polisario, its Saharan republic, and the refugees, the world today, unlike the world of 1975, seems largely at odds with movements seeking to create new and totally independent nation-states. An anticolonial struggle for national self-determination seems an anachronism. Yet the fact that Western Saharan nationalism continues to thrive in the face of such immense macrolevel forces suggests that the world is far more complicated than any totalizing theory can imagine. The project of liberating Western Sahara has not only lived in defiance of exile and the interests of the West, but also survived more than thirty years of brutal occupation, which we turn to next.

# 6

# The Sahrawi Intifada

*Western Saharan Nationalism under Moroccan Occupation*

May 2005 saw the opening of a new front in the Western Sahara conflict. On the streets of the occupied Western Sahara, a whole new generation of Sahrawi nationalists declared "enough," using their bodies, voices, and minds to confront the nearly thirty-year-old occupation of their land. Tired of UN promises, unwilling to wait for Polisario's long-promised diplomatic breakthrough, and frustrated with socioeconomic marginalization, the second-generation nationalists began staging demonstrations in increasing size and number in the early 2000s. Behind these impatient youths were an older generation of Sahrawi activists who had suffered the worst of Morocco's occupation—imprisonment, torture, and "disappearance." Together they would proclaim the Sahrawi intifada, or uprising.

From 1975 onward, the locus of Western Saharan nationalism was in exile, across the border in Algeria. From there, Polisario coordinated its war of liberation, launched its international diplomatic efforts, and created a kind of nation-in-exile. Since the turn of the millennium, though, Western Saharan nationalism's center of gravity has shifted, coinciding with the drawn-out death of the long-postponed referendum on independence (Shelley 2004, 108–9). Unprecedented Sahrawi demonstrations in the Moroccan-controlled cities of Western Sahara in September 1999 marked the beginning of this rebalancing of nationalist poles. By May 2005, which saw the largest wave of demonstration and repression ever, the nationalist movement was clearly operating on two fronts, internationally (Polisario/RASD) and internally (the intifada).

Before the eruptions of 1999 and 2005, most observers of the conflict had suspected that there was some nationalist sentiment in areas under Moroccan control, but the extent was unknown. Given Morocco's extraordinary expenditures to defend and develop the occupied territory, it was widely assumed that many Sahrawi hearts and minds had been won over. Yet for more than two decades life under Moroccan occupation—west of the berm—was largely obscure to the outside world. During the war, Morocco kept these areas under tight control. Any indigenous attempt to voice opposition to Moroccan policies or to show support for Western Saharan nationalism was met with harsh repression. The

140

arrival of UN peacekeepers in the early 1990s did little to alleviate the situation because Morocco constantly obsessed over controlling international perceptions.

The first sign that all was not well finally came in September 1999. Almost six years later, the May 2005 demonstrations testified to the fact that nationalist sentiment had only intensified under King Mohammed VI. Indeed, overt acts of Western Saharan nationalism had even spread to areas in southern Morocco heavily populated by ethnic Sahrawis, especially Tan Tan and Assa. The participation of Sahrawis from southern Morocco was a further indication that Western Saharan nationalism had become, in a sense, transnational.[1]

In this chapter, we examine the historical trajectory of Western Saharan nationalism under Moroccan occupation. The first step is to contextualize the situation in terms of international politics and show how internationalization helped feed the intifada. Among Western Saharan nationalists, the widespread feeling is that internationalizing the dispute—putting their fate in the hands of the UN—has failed. Second, we use a diachronic analysis to help explain Sahrawi mobilization, looking at the historical patterns of repression and resistance. Then we turn to the intifadas of 1999 and 2005, their naissance and trajectories, and follow with an examination of the synchronic conditions behind the uprisings. Last, we access the intifadas' strengths, weaknesses, and larger significance to the conflict.

## THE ROAD TO INTIFADA: THE FAILURE OF INTERNATIONALIZATION

From 1988 to 2000, the UN attempted to resolve the Western Sahara conflict by calling for a referendum to decide on either independence or integration with Morocco. Even though Polisario's stated goal is to achieve independence, it has always been amiable to holding a referendum, despite the uncertainty involved. The true opinions of all native Western Saharans are not known, but there is a firm belief among nationalists that an overwhelming majority would opt for independence if given the proper chance. This is exactly what the UN was offering in the late 1980s, which helped bring the war to an end. However, a new kind of war started. Given the high stakes involved in the UN referendum, Morocco and Polisario's behavior off the battlefield was just as antagonistic as it had been on the battlefield.

The Security Council adopted the secretary-general's peace proposal, the Settlement Plan, in April 1991. The plan called for a staged peace process, beginning with a cease-fire, which would be followed by a reduction and cantonment of troops and guerillas, a repatriation of the refugees, and, finally, a UN-organized vote for either independence or integration with Morocco. Although the Settlement Plan seemed like a good idea on paper, Polisario and Morocco maintained radically different interpretations of it, especially regarding the matter of who would vote in the referendum.

Polisario felt that it had agreed to a referendum of persons listed on the 1974 Spanish census and their direct descendants. This definition would limit the electorate to Sahrawis of unquestionable Western Saharan origin and thus, they believed, push the vote toward independence. Morocco, in contrast, wanted to expand the electorate to include persons who had either fled Western Sahara before 1974 or had not been counted in the census. Morocco hoped that additional voters, many then resident in southern Morocco, would be sympathetic to integration. (And with broader ways of establishing voter eligibility, Morocco also tried to enfranchise persons of Moroccan, or non-Sahrawi, ancestry.) Although the UN agreed with Morocco in principle, opening the electorate up to persons outside the 1974 census created a whole new problem. The UN mission had to find a way to certify that every applicant who wanted to vote in the referendum was actually an ethnic Sahrawi from Western Sahara.

As a major concession, Polisario agreed to broaden the criteria for voter enfranchisement, which allowed MINURSO to start voter identification in 1994. Yet Polisario still believed that Rabat was presenting native Moroccans and non-Sahrawis as Western Saharans in order to skew the vote toward integration. Indeed, this seems to have been the case. Leading Morocco's efforts to stack the vote in its favor was the king's right-hand man Driss Basri, then interior minister. Even former MINURSO officials sympathetic to Morocco joked about Basri's election-fixing reputation (Jensen 2005, 73), and Morocco's efforts apparently included Interior Ministry classes for Moroccan citizens on how to act Western Saharan (Dunbar 2000, n. 25).

Polisario's well-justified skepticism contributed to a lengthy identification process with numerous starts and stops. After the process came to a dead halt in 1996, the new UN secretary-general, Kofi Annan, assuming his post in 1997, asked former U.S. secretary of state James Baker to lead new negotiations. Baker found that both Morocco and Polisario still wanted a referendum, so he brokered a set of agreements in mid-1997 that put it back on track. When MINURSO finished voter identification in 1999, it arrived at a figure of 86,386 voting-age Western Saharans. For Polisario, this figure was a great victory because it corresponded closely to the 1974 Spanish census. In the late 1990s, many refugees prepared to return home for the vote, which they felt certain would lead to independence. Rabat, however, demanded a revetting of almost every rejected Moroccan-sponsored voter.

Following the death of King Hassan in July 1999, his son, Mohammed VI, succeeded him and quickly fired Basri, the architect of Morocco's referendum strategy. That August and September, the UN held a similar referendum in East Timor. The vote precipitated mass violence when Indonesian-backed militias went on a rampage after it became apparent that supporters of independence had won by a huge majority. In Western Sahara, the UN secretary-general and members of the Security Council, especially France and the United States, had always doubted that a referendum would actually take place. And if a vote did happen, the council knew it would not force Morocco to accept independence. As one former head of the mission noted, "The Security Council never so much as whispered the word *sanction*" (Jensen 2005, 75). Rather than push the young and inexperienced King Mohammed to hold a highly contentious plebiscite in Western Sahara, Annan decided to try a new approach toward resolution. Baker was put in charge of making it happen.

In late 2000, Morocco signaled its willingness to negotiate a final-status option with Polisario, something between independence and integration. This option became known as the "third way." In 2001, Baker presented a proposal for an autonomous Western Sahara, which would be submitted to some kind of referendum after a five-year trial period. The vote would include Moroccan settlers in Western Sahara along with native Sahrawis. King Mohammed liked the proposal, but Polisario, supported by Algeria, would only talk about the 1991 Settlement Plan.

After drafting a revised plan, Baker proposed a final-status referendum that would include the options of independence or integration or continued autonomy. The autonomy offered was wide ranging, granting Western Sahara significant freedom during a four-year trial period before the referendum. Baker believed that Morocco would accept this referendum because most of its settlers would be allowed to vote, giving Rabat a numerical advantage in the electorate. Surprisingly, Polisario and Algeria accepted Baker's 2003 proposal, but Morocco rejected it. The Moroccan government claimed that it would not have its "territorial integrity" put to a vote.

For almost a whole year, Baker tried to work with both sides, but in the end he felt that he could not reconcile their positions. Morocco presented three counteroffers, but none satisfied the right of self-determination or minimum standards of autonomous self-rule. Polisario continued to claim the right to a vote on independence, yet such a vote was the very thing that Morocco had categorically ruled out. In 2002, the Security Council had called on Baker to incorporate a vote for independence into his proposal, yet in 2003 and 2004 the veto-wielding French and American governments made it clear that they would not force Morocco to accept self-determination. Without Security Council leverage, Baker realized he could not move Morocco. He resigned his position in June 2004.

During the long war for Western Sahara, Polisario believed, perhaps naively, that given the strength of its position in terms of international law, internationalizing the conflict would work to its benefit. Although its military fortunes declined in the 1980s, its diplomatic efforts were paying off. In 1981, Morocco had committed to a referendum, and in 1988 the UN promised to organize it. Yet, as always, the major problem Polisario faced at the UN was the same interests that supported Rabat's war. Both of Morocco's major allies—France and the United States—have held immense influence on the Security Council and since 1991 have consistently protected Morocco throughout the peace process. Western Saharan nationalism continued to smash against the rock of Western security interests.

Even under the best conditions, Polisario has learned that these interests are difficult, if not impossible, to overcome. The Security Council debate on the Baker Plan in the summer of 2003 is a good example. When Polisario accepted the Peace Plan, it assumed that it had won the support of the United States, a potent counterbalance against France's steadfast position in support of Morocco. In addition, the Spanish government, then under the conservative, Polisario-sympathetic Partido Popular, was holding a Security Council seat. Yet owing to French intransigence and vociferous Moroccan lobbying, the Security Council failed to find sufficient backing for the Baker Plan. Although the United States offered some support to Baker, Morocco was able to erode that support in late 2003 by appealing to the longstanding pillars of U.S. support for the Moroccan regime: Morocco's stability and willingness to advance U.S. interests (detailed in chapter 3).

It is difficult to imagine conditions more favorable for Polisario than those obtained in 2003, and it is unlikely it will ever get as powerful and sympathetic a negotiator as Baker ever again. Furthermore, despite its willingness to compromise, and despite the international consensus backing Western Sahara's right to self-determination, Polisario's diplomatic efforts failed. These realities are as clear to Sahrawi nationalists living under Moroccan administration as they are to Polisario's leadership. The frustrations motivating the 1999 and, more so, the 2005 Sahrawi demonstrations in Western Sahara, although also rooted in local socioeconomic grievances, are as much a result of the failure of Polisario's diplomatic efforts and of the international community's betrayal. Nationalists working inside Western Sahara are keenly aware that Polisario has made a good-faith effort to liberate its country and are also aware that international politics have thwarted these efforts. Noting the failure to secure self-determination, first, by force of arms and, second, by diplomacy, a new generation of Western Saharan nationalists began trying a new tactic.

## EARLY REPRESSION OF SAHRAWI NATIONALISTS IN THE OCCUPIED WESTERN SAHARA

Sahrawi activism in the occupied Western Sahara has been motivated by a deep-seated antipathy toward the Moroccan occupation. This animosity has several interrelated and reinforcing causes, from cultural, social, economic, and political marginalization to the existential threat Morocco poses to Western Saharan nationalism. In terms of underlying factors, the most motivating is the years of Moroccan repression that nationalists have suffered from 1975 onward. Although most acts of the intifada appear to be carried out by Sahrawi youth, the key organizers and strategists tend to be Sahrawis who spent significant amounts of time in Moroccan prisons, often as multiyear victims of incommunicado detention or enforced "disappearance." Before 1999, the history of Western Saharan nationalism under the Moroccan occupation was largely a history of Moroccan repression in Western Sahara.

Not long after Spain signed away its colony in November 1975, Morocco initiated an antinationalist campaign in the occupied Western Sahara. The early waves of Moroccan state terror against Sahrawis focused primarily on the remaining Polisario activists and their families, those who could not or chose not to flee to Tindouf. Morocco's favored method for dealing with suspected proindependence militants, along with their associates and relatives, was simply to "disappear" them. Indeed, some Sahrawis claim that as soon as Moroccan forces crossed into the Spanish Sahara in late October 1975, the abductions started (Karmous and Decaster 2003, 5–6).

According to the most reliable figures, the number of political "disappearances" is several hundred. However, a precise number is difficult to attain for several reasons: the population is divided; sometimes entire families were disappeared, leaving no one behind; and the Moroccan regime's lack of transparency in general and its ongoing reticence to account for abuses against Sahrawis in particular. In terms of scale, Moroccan state-orchestrated disappearances of Sahrawis pale in comparison to the disappearances that occurred during dirty wars in Argentina and Chile in the 1970s and 1980s or even in Algeria in the 1990s. Yet given the small native population, it is difficult to find a Western Saharan who has not been touched by this practice. The "disappeared" have entered into the halls of the Western Saharan independence movement as martyrs, becoming an important aspect of the nationalist narrative. Indeed, a founding father of Western Saharan nationalism, Ibrahim Bassiri, given that his whereabouts have never been accounted for since Spanish colonial officials detained him in 1970, is considered the first Sahrawi "disappeared" in addition to being the first martyr (see chapter 4).

The International Federation of Human Rights Leagues has claimed that the number of Sahrawi "disappeared" may be as high as fifteen hundred (U.S. Department of State 2002). If this number is true, then it represents roughly one percent of the territory's 1974 population. The Asociación de Familiares de Presos y Desaparecidos Saharauis (Association of Families of Sahrawi Prisoners and Disappeared), based in the refugee camps, has registered roughly 890 total Sahrawi "disappearances" since 1975. In this group, 50 apparently died in custody, and 310 have been released, leaving 526 cases outstanding (Bureau International 2002). Amnesty International (1990) cites a slightly lower figure, 488 Sahrawi "disappearances" committed during the Moroccan occupation.

Beyond "disappearing" people, the Moroccan security forces also summarily executed known activists as well as their acquaintances and their family members. Sahrawi human rights activists in the occupied Western Sahara claim to have documented several cases where Sahrawis were flown out over the ocean in a helicopter and dropped from a high altitude, far from the shore (see Smith 1987, 145). In many cases, Sahrawi activists claim that they have obtained documents that identify the Moroccans responsible for these actions, including the military and security officers who gave the orders. In an interview, Omar Abdelsalem, president of the Association of Families of Sahrawi Prisoners and

Disappeared, claimed that there are sixty known cases—that is, with physical evidence—of entire families being buried alive in the desert (Mundy, interview, Rabouni, Algeria, Sept. 1, 2003). Over time, Sahrawi nomads have stumbled across some of these burial sites, now revealed by the desert's shifting sands.

Extralegal detention was also rampant during the first years of the occupation. In 1977, Amnesty International reported that King Hassan's forces were holding 100 to 150 POWs and suspected Polisario sympathizers in southern Morocco and the occupied Western Sahara. The same briefing noted, "The Moroccan authorities maintain great secrecy about the names and number of those detained; and in the Western Sahara there may be several hundred members of the local population held in army camps" (Amnesty International 1977, 10). Following arrest, Sahrawi political prisoners faced harsh conditions, torture, and execution. As one released prisoner recounted,

> Just before the Green March I was living in Tan Tan. The Moroccans took about 42 women, including me, and 70 Sahrawi men up to Agadir. They were all people known for their links with the Polisario Front. . . .
>
> We spent the first 24 hours blindfold with our hands tied in some flour silos in Tan Tan. Then we moved to Agadir, to a very small cell. We were a group of women and babies. We had to remain standing the whole time for a month . . . We were fed once every 24 hours—a bit of bread and dirty water.
>
> Every day there were interrogations. We were beaten and tortured with electricity and had [bleach] put up our noses. Some of the children died in the cells; others stayed alive but died later. Some women had their heads shaved. (quoted in Amnesty International 1990, 9)

Of the hundreds of Sahrawis detained, the majority either "disappeared" or was suddenly released without due process. Among those "disappeared" were the eleven family members of Polisario-leader Mohammed Lamine (Amnesty International 1991b).[2]

Like Moroccan political prisoners, Sahrawi detainees regularly suffered torture. Documented torture methods in Morocco include beatings all over the body, often with stones, whips, chains, and metal rods; beatings on the bottom of prisoners' feet, a method known as *falaqa;* partial suffocation by either forced near drowning or the stuffing of rags soaked in bleach into the mouth; suspension of prisoners by hands and feet tied behind their back and then the application of beatings or pressure to their backs (i.e., a method known as "the aeroplane"); the hanging of prisoners by their hands and feet tied together in front of them, followed by beatings or partial suffocation (i.e., called "the parrot" or "the roast chicken"); and the hanging of prisoners by the hands so that only their toes touch the ground, causing massive swelling of the hands and feet (Amnesty International 1991b, 23–25).

Moroccan and Sahrawi prisoners as well as the unacknowledged "disappeared" were often held in secret prisons. The most well-known secret prisons in postcolonial

Morocco were Derb Moulay Cherif in Casablanca, abandoned precolonial forts near Agdez and Qal'at M'gouna, and the infamous mountain prison of Tazmamart in the High Atlas near Errachidia. Some Sahrawis were also held in smaller prisons in southern Morocco (e.g., Agadir and Tan Tan) and in the occupied Western Sahara, notably the Cárcel Negra (Black Prison) or the Calobozo (Dungeon) of al-'Ayun. The Moroccan security services operated a number of detention centers outside major cities such as Fez and Rabat. The military also held prisoners in special camps throughout the country and the occupied territory.

Indeed, it was often as difficult to determine a prisoner's whereabouts because various arms of the Moroccan military/security apparatus conducted such "disappearances." According to witnesses, perpetrators were often in plainclothes and would detain suspects at all times of the day. It is suspected that several branches of the Moroccan government took part in "disappearances," including the Moroccan army, the FAR; the Gendarmerie royale, which acts as a rural police force and monitors the army; Renseignements généraux (General Intelligence, operating from police stations); the Direction générale des études et de la documentation (General Office of Research and Documentation, normally for external espionage), with one wing controlled by the royal palace and the other by the prime minister; the civil and judicial police; al-Makhazini (provincial authorities); the Interior Ministry's Direction de la surveillance du territoire (Directorate of Territorial Surveillance), now the Direction générale de la surveillance du territoire (General Directorate of Territorial Surveillance); and the clandestine Compagnies mobiles d'intervention (Mobile Intervention Companies), which transported and detained "disappeared" persons in secret villas and farms, often making arrests in civilian clothes (Amnesty International 1994, 71).

In the 1980s, Moroccan security agents often arrested Sahrawis en masse before royal visits or in the wake of demonstrations (a pattern that has continued under King Mohammed VI). A number of Sahrawis were arrested as a prelude to King Hassan's 1985 visit to the Western Sahara. The same happened in November 1987 shortly before a visit by a UN technical mission, a mass arrest that ensnared three hundred Sahrawis in al-'Ayun alone. Although the Moroccan government eventually released most of the latter, fifty cases remained outstanding more than three years later, Aminatou Haidar being the most famous. Moroccan security agents also arrested some seventy Sahrawis and held them without charge or trial between 1987 and 1990, although most were eventually released. Why the Moroccan government freed certain prisoners but detained others has never been explained (Amnesty International 1990, 40–41).

Even with the noticed decrease in long-term "disappearances" in the 1990s, the continued practice of random and arbitrary arrests, detentions, and releases only added to the state of fear in Western Sahara. Furthermore, King Hassan's regime continued to deny that the Moroccan state had committed any of the gross abuses claimed by domestic dissidents, Sahrawis, and international organizations. In 1990, Interior Minister Driss Basri dismissively referred to such accounts as a "pack of lies." A year before that, King Hassan boldly told French television, "[If] one percent of the human rights violations signalled by Amnesty International were true, I wouldn't get a wink of sleep" (quoted in *The Guardian,* Dec. 16, 1990).

In 1990, Human Rights Watch reported, "None of Morocco's best-known human rights cases was resolved during 1990" (1991, 496), even though Hassan had established the CCDH, a human rights council, ostensibly to "put an end to allegations . . . to close this dossier" (2004, 11). Yet in mid-1991, King Hassan startled his critics when he released hundreds of political prisoners from secret detention centers, including many "disappeared" detainees long considered dead. It was also reported that the ultrasecret detention center Tazmamart had been razed, its prisoners released or moved to new locations. Roughly three hundred "disappeared" Sahrawis were among those arbitrarily freed, including whole families and some persons missing since 1975 (U.S. Department of State 1994).

Emboldened by the reappearance of some of the "disappeared," Sahrawi and Moroccan families petitioned the Moroccan government to disclose information on prisoners who had not been released. Local and international civil society groups also pressed the government to be more forthcoming and to hold state actors accountable. Although welcoming the positive steps taken in 1991, Human Rights Watch commented, "Morocco's penchant for stone-walling and lying about human rights matters continues to astonish" (1992). For most of the 1990s, the Moroccan regime refused to discuss the "disappeared," whether the case was outstanding or involved compensation for those released in 1991. Because the Moroccan regime had long denied the existence of any "disappeared" Sahrawis, political prisoners or secret detention centers such as Tazmamart, Rabat refused to justify its actions or clarify the fate of other prisoners. Indeed, the same month that Tazmamart's prisoners were released, Basri opined, "Tazmamart only existed in the minds of evildoers" (Amnesty International 1994, 70).

Nor was life easy for the formerly "disappeared." Freed Sahrawis claimed that they faced harsh restrictions on their movement and intimidation from security forces. Some also showed obvious signs of past torture and maltreatment, not to mention psychological scars, yet the communities to which they returned often shunned them. In several cases, the Moroccan government rearrested numerous Sahrawis after their release, holding them for indefinite and prolonged periods in secret detention centers. After being released, one Sahrawi woman told Amnesty International,

> I was very ill when I was released and I could not get any treatment; others . . . were in even worse condition. . . . Other women who were "disappeared" with me and who were released at the same time have been rearrested and again "disappeared" for months. . . . I think about those who died while we were "disappeared"; I so much want to console their

families, but I can't because it is dangerous; surveillance is heavy, especially for us former "disappeared," for the families of the dead "disappeared" and for the families of those who are still "disappeared." . . . I am watched all the time and can't even go to the nearby village without a special permission, which is often impossible to get. (1996, 9)

Human Rights Watch reported similar stories and noted that the Moroccan government claimed it had resolved 60 cases from a list of 285 "disappeared" Sahrawis provided by the UN Working Group on Enforced and Involuntary Disappearances (1995, 12). The Moroccan government also claimed that it was working on the other cases, sorting the dead from the unaccounted. Amnesty International pointed out, "Of the hundreds of people arrested in Western Sahara in the past five years, the vast majority were never charged or afforded due legal process." Furthermore, the Moroccan regime replaced long-term "disappearances" with shorter stays. Amnesty International claimed that most of those detained in the Western Sahara "were held in unacknowledged detention for weeks and months without access to their families or to the outside world and were subsequently released without charge" (1996, 14).

The arrival of UN peacekeepers and referendum supervisors in 1992 did little to mitigate the human rights situation in Western Sahara. The UN soldiers, officials, and employees, who found themselves under intense surveillance by Moroccan security agents, reported witnessing Moroccan acts of intimidation and repression against the indigenous population (Ziai 1995, 30–32). Former U.S. ambassador Frank Ruddy, who headed the UN voter-identification effort in 1994, later testified to the U.S. House Appropriations Committee that

[s]ome Sahrawis who reported what the Moroccans were doing to them asked that our U.N. people keep an eye out for them after they left, in case they disappeared. Many said they were scared for their lives if the Moroccans saw them talking to U.N. people. Others asked not to be recognized outside the U.N. center. Terrorized may be too strong a word, but they were afraid. Their comments reminded me of nothing so much as South Africa in the early 70's when blacks would talk to you freely in the safety of the U.S. embassy then pretend they didn't know you as soon as they left. (Ruddy 1995b)

Despite several years of disturbing accounts from MINURSO officials, the UN Secretariat and Security Council repeatedly failed to take action. In 1996, Amnesty International charged that MINURSO was a "silent witness to blatant human rights violations" (1996, 12).

In the name of diplomacy, secretaries-general Boutros-Ghali and Annan refrained from criticizing the most obvious acts of Moroccan repression. For example, in April 2003 three well-known Sahrawi human rights activists of the now disbanded Sahara Branch of the Forum vérité et justice (Truth and Justice Forum)—Sidi Mohammed Daddach,

Cheikh Khaya, and H'med Hammad—attended a meeting with MINURSO officials in al-'Ayun. After these Sahrawis left the UN compound, Moroccan security forces arrested them, interrogated them about the nature of the meeting, and detained them for several days. Much to the activists' disappointment, MINURSO officials took no action on the matter and the secretary-general failed to mention this episode in his subsequent report on the Western Sahara (see U.S. Department of State 2004). Virtually cloistered in their hotels and offices, MINURSO personnel have little direct access to the people on the street in Western Sahara. Because the mission's mandate contains no human rights provisions, it cannot report even the most blatant violations unless UN personnel are direct witness to such acts. Yet even when MINURSO personnel have witnessed Moroccan abuses in Western Sahara, UN officials in New York have removed the accounts from the secretary-general's regular reports.

The Moroccan government finally made its first serious steps toward dealing with all cases of "disappearance"—Sahrawi and Moroccan—in 1998. That year King Hassan accepted the findings of his CCDH, although it acknowledged only 112 cases of "disappearance." Of those, the CCDH found that 56 had died. With the publication of its final report, issued April 1999, the council claimed that it had "definitively closed" the dossier on "all cases" of "disappearance." International observers were quick to criticize the Moroccan regime for attempting to "close" the issue while hundreds of "disappearances"—mostly Sahrawis—went unaddressed. Amnesty International highlighted the 450 Sahrawis "whose fate remains unknown," the 70 "disappeared" Sahrawis "who died in the secret detention centers," and the 300 Sahrawi "disappeared" but released in 1991 who had not yet received compensation or rehabilitation. The same report also underscored the fact that none of the perpetrators of "disappearance" and summary executions had been brought to justice (Amnesty International 1999, 6–7).

It was not until August 1999—following the ascension of King Mohammed VI in July—that the regime formally acknowledged the government's hand in "disappearances." The new king established an independent Commission d'arbitrage (Arbitration Panel) within the CCDH to deal with compensating the survivors and relatives of forced "disappearances." By mid-2003, when its work came to an end, the panel had taken in five thousand applications and answered almost four thousand claims with roughly $80 million in compensation. However, Moroccan and Western Saharan human rights activists continued to press for more than mere compensation. In 2004, King Mohammed met this challenge by creating the Instance equité et réconciliation (Equity and Reconciliation Commission), a kind of a "truth commission." Under its mandate, the new commission set out to write a "general history of repression" under King Hassan's reign and to offer "specific details about the fate of the hundreds of "'disappeared' Moroccans" by April 2005. This history included naming the specific "state or other apparatuses in the violations," although, as Human Rights Watch lamented, "[t]he commission can not name perpetrators." By April 2004, the commission had received more than twenty thousand petitions for redress covering acts committed between 1956 and 1999 (Human Rights Watch 2004, 12–16).

Since the beginning of the occupation of Western Sahara, the Moroccan regime has maintained a near zero tolerance policy toward proindependence thought and action, even when it is nonviolent. This visceral reaction to Western Saharan resistance signals an uncompromising attitude that continues to bode ill for a peaceful resolution to the Western Sahara conflict. If the Moroccan government has been willing to take whatever measures it has deemed necessary to silence dissent in the Western Sahara, what steps will it take to make sure that the Western Sahara is never "severed" from the "motherland"? Although this question is impossible to answer definitively, the history of the Moroccan occupation in the Western Sahara indicates a strong propensity toward repression and violence. In its occupation of Western Sahara, the Moroccan regime has been willing to suffer diplomatic isolation, economic losses, and even international scorn. If shame will not move Rabat to address the issue, and if France and the United States will guarantee the protection of Morocco from UN intervention, then there is little to indicate that the Moroccan regime will refrain from continuing to use violence to hold on to the Western Sahara at all costs. This fact, however, does not seem to deter Sahrawi activists, who have become more and more emboldened by their own actions.

THE FIRST INTIFADA

There are two interesting features of the large-scale Sahrawi demonstrations of late 1999. First, they occurred after the death of King Hassan, amidst all of the promises of democracy and dramatic initial reforms in the early weeks of King Mohammed's reign. This timing suggested that Sahrawis remained unimpressed with the regime. Second, although Polisario cells had been active in Western Sahara from the late Spanish colonial period through the death of King Hassan, Sahrawi civil society in general and national-ist activists in particular had refrained from forming explicitly proindependence orga-nizations. Indeed, the 1999 demonstrations came almost in spite of a deliberate attempt by Sahrawi civil society to circumvent the discourse of self-determination in favor of charitable and civil rights organizations. This shift suggested not only that proindepen-dence sentiment was widespread (albeit latent), but also that it did not need activist elites to catalyze it.

Starting in early September 1999, dozens of Sahrawi students organized a sit-in dem-onstration for more scholarships and transportation subsidies to Moroccan universities far north. The students set up tents in al-Zamlah Square in al-'Ayun, where they held a constant vigil (similar in purpose to the "tent cities" that would play an important role in the subsequent nonviolent Ukrainian [2004] and Lebanese [2005] democracy movements).

Former Sahrawi political prisoners seeking compensation and accountability for state-sponsored "disappearances" soon joined the nonviolent vigil, along with Sahrawi workers from the phosphate mines at Bukra' and Sahrawi members of the most militant Moroccan union, the Association nationale des diplômés chômeurs au Maroc (National Association of Unemployed University Graduates in Morocco).

For twelve days, the protestors occupied the square in front of the Najir Hotel, home to a large proportion of UN personnel. Sahrawi activists also chose this location because of its historical importance to the nationalist movement: it is where Spanish troops massacred several Sahrawis demonstrating for independence in 1970. During the 1999 uprising, the Sahrawi organizers, although sympathetic to independence, deliberately avoided overt political slogans, deciding beforehand to limit their demands to social and economic claims.

Despite King Mohammed's early veneer of change, the Moroccan government's reaction to the demonstrations was consistent with the regime's previous patterns of behavior. The Moroccan authorities moved in to break up the tent camp after nearly two weeks of constant vigil. Police rushed in and began beating demonstrators—with what the U.S. State Department deemed "excessive violence." Dozens were arrested, and some were reportedly dumped in the desert miles out of town. Five days later, with the population increasingly radicalized as a result, a larger demonstration was staged, which included proreferendum and proindependence slogans. This time, however, the Moroccan authorities "encouraged gangs of local thugs to break into and vandalize the homes and places of businesses of some of the city's Sahrawi residents" (U.S. Department of State 2000). A later report by the State Department claimed that the Moroccan "police provoked the violence, and . . . unlawfully entered homes to arrest persons associated with the demonstrations" (2001a). Although only 150 were initially arrested, the Moroccan security forces arrested dozens more in early 2000 and continued to intimidate the families of known activists. The Moroccan government quickly released most of those detained, yet many indicated that they had been beaten and tortured while in custody (Amnesty International 2003a; Damis 2001, 38, 40–41).

Not all Moroccan settlers in Western Sahara opposed the Sahrawi-led demonstrations. Surprisingly, Moroccans from the shantytowns on the outskirts of al-'Ayun joined in the popular uprising. These neighborhoods were established after the so-called Second Green March in 1991, when Rabat moved thousands of its citizens into the territory to vote in the UN referendum scheduled for the following year. The economic thrust of the 1999 demonstrations had apparently attracted many poor and disenfranchised Moroccan settlers, especially those of Sahrawi origin in southern Morocco. These settlers, many of whom were relocated involuntarily and assumed they would simply vote and leave in 1992, faced a future as uncertain as the indigenous Sahrawi population. The joint non-violent resistance involving Western Saharan nationalists and Moroccan settlers was an especially interesting development. It also had a significant impact on the peace process. For the first time, the Security Council, as much as Rabat, saw that the proposed referendum would not favor Morocco. Not only had Morocco failed to win over the native Western Saharans, but it had also lost the hearts and minds of many of its own Sahrawis. Thus, in 2003, when Baker proposed a referendum roughly split between Moroccan settlers and native Western Saharans, Rabat chose to reject it.

In the wake of the 1999 demonstrations, the Moroccan government, to its credit, quickly removed the governor and local chief of police. It also announced new elections for the defunct Saharan affairs council, signaling the regime's desire to co-opt Sahrawi discontent as soon as possible. In addition, it singled out three activists to prosecute as alleged Polisario spies: Brahim Laghzal, Cheikh Khaya, and Laarbi Massaoud. A Moroccan court sentenced them to four-year terms in June 2000. King Mohammed, however, pardoned them in November 2001, along with twenty-five other Sahrawi political prisoners. Also released was Sidi Mohammed Daddach, one of Morocco's longest-held political prisoners (U.S. Department of State 2002). Daddach had joined the Polisario in 1973 but was detained and later forced to join the Moroccan military following the 1975 invasion. In 1980, he was sentenced to death for attempting to escape to the Polisario side, where most of his family had fled in 1976. Although his death sentence was commuted in 1994, his continued confinement made him the longest-held prisoner of conscience in Morocco (Amnesty International 1999, 13). Throughout his more than two decades of imprisonment, Daddach refused to renounce his support for Polisario.

In Morocco proper, the positive political space created by the death of King Hassan and the removal of Driss Basri, coupled with Mohammed VI's dramatic pledges, had allowed for the formation of unprecedented organizations. In November 1999, former prisoners and victims of "disappearance" created the Truth and Justice Forum, which pressed for more government action on past injustices (Slyomovics 2001, 20). In Western Sahara, Sahrawi human rights activists created a Sahara section of this organization in al-'Ayun on August 26, 2000, for the same purpose. (Before that, a small and informal group, the Coordinating Committee of Sahrawi Victims of Forced Disappearance, formed in 1998, had organized efforts around Daddach and other Sahrawi political prisoners.) The Moroccan state, however, kept the forum's Sahara Branch on a very short leash.[3] Finally, in November 2002, proceedings began in Moroccan courts to outlaw the Sahara Branch, which took effect in June 2003. The Moroccan government argued that the Sahara Branch had organized and agitated for an independent Western Sahara. Yet observers noted that the Sahara Branch's dissolution took place within the context of a broader Moroccan crackdown on civil society and human rights activists following the bombings in Casablanca on May 16, 2003 (Human Rights Watch 2004, 25). Under the cover of its own "war on terror," the Moroccan government succeeded in silencing numerous voices of dissent, Islamic and Sahrawi alike. Despite these setbacks, Sahrawi human rights activists regrouped in January 2004 under the informal Collectif des défenseurs sahraouis des droits de l'homme (Collective of Sahrawi Human Rights Defenders) and brazenly called for an international commission of inquiry into the history of abuses in the Western Sahara. That same month, King Mohammed pardoned twelve Sahrawi political prisoners, including several members of the dissolved Saharan Branch (Bureau International 2004).

THE 2005 INTIFADAH AL-ISTIQLAL

Impressions of a still simmering uprising were reinforced by several spontaneous stone-throwing episodes in February and March 2000, including some in southern Morocco. On one occasion, several Sahrawi youths used rocks to attack vehicles from the Moroccan security forces and the UN and allegedly attempted to set a police car on fire. The 2002 visit of King Mohammed notably elicited anti-Moroccan sentiment, which was met with a predictable degree of preemptive repression. As the UN-led peace process ground to a complete standstill following Baker's departure, tensions grew substantially from 2004 to the spring of 2005. In March 2004, coinciding with International Women's Day, several sit-ins became overtly political. The Moroccan authorities prohibited a May Day 2004 rally at which Sahrawi women planned to wear all black; similar demonstrations were not allowed the following year. World Human Rights Day rallies on December 10, 2004, also became overtly proindependence (Association marocaine des droits humains 2005).

The Sahrawi movement was somewhat tempered by the regular developments in the peace process between 2000 and 2004. However, the lack of a clear peace initiative from the UN following Baker's departure in June 2004 fueled nationalist frustrations. In May 2005, the situation exploded again. Unlike the protests of 1999 or the smaller events of 1987 and 1995, the 2005 uprising was not originally staged for international consumption. It involved raw displays of discontent and nationalist sentiment triggered by Morocco.

The second intifada began when Moroccan authorities were to transfer Sahrawi political prisoner Ahmed Mahmoud Haddi ("Al-Kainan"), known for his vocal support for Polisario, from al-'Ayun to a prison in southern Morocco. Kainan's family and a small group of Sahrawi human rights activists staged a small demonstration on May 21 and 22 outside the prison. Their complaint was that this transfer would make it nearly impossible for the family to visit their imprisoned son. Protests continued to grow for two days. When Moroccan authorities forcefully intervened on the evening of May 24, a larger demonstration came together later in the day. Sahrawis were soon shouting proindependence slogans and flying RASD flags; some burned tires and threw stones at the Moroccan security forces. A violent crackdown against the demonstrators provoked larger demonstrations in the Sahrawi neighborhoods near al-Zamlah Square and Ma'tallah or 'Askaykimah neighborhoods. Late on May 25, Moroccan soldiers and military police invaded and besieged the neighborhoods. Several homes were ransacked, the crowds were forcefully dispersed, and dozens of activists were arrested and imprisoned. Demonstrators took to the streets in even larger numbers the next day. Protests also erupted in the Western Saharan towns of Smara and Dakhla as well as in the southern Moroccan towns of Tan Tan and Assa. In the Moroccan universities in Agadir, Marrakech, Casablanca, Rabat, and Fez, Sahrawi students organized solidarity demonstrations and condemned the repression in the occupied Western Sahara. In Rabat, Spanish news video showed Moroccan police indiscriminately beating students in response to stone throwing. After days of clashes, more than eighty Sahrawis had been detained; this number would soon exceed one hundred. Solidarity demonstrations were soon staged in front of al-'Ayun's prison.

Waiting until international attention shifted away from the territory, Morocco started arresting key activists in the following weeks. Many of these Sahrawis soon went on a hunger strike to protest prison conditions and the grounds of their arrest. Yet even with all well-known nationalist activists behind bars, smaller demonstrations continued in the following months, including almost nightly clashes between Sahrawi youths and Moroccan police. Perhaps the most startling act of defiance was the unfurling of the RASD flag in the middle of a high school courtyard in al-'Ayun in mid-October.

The situation reached a low point at the end of October when Moroccan security agents beat a Sahrawi demonstrator to death in full public view. The killing of Hamdi Lembarki, the intifada's first martyr, put a pall over Western Sahara and the protest movement. Following the release of his body by Moroccan officials, Lembarki's funeral in early January 2006 became a silent, though massive, demonstration; RASD's flag draped his coffin. Then Aminatou Haidar was released from prison, an activist who had served seven months for her participation in the uprising. Haidar quickly became a leading figure in the new intifada. Her release was met with a massive display of RASD flags, pictures of RASD founders, and, provocatively, Palestinian-style headscarves (kufiya).

Demonstrations are theoretically legal under Moroccan law in Western Sahara, but Sahrawi activists have learned that their requests for a permit rarely go answered. Although the smaller quotidian protests are more difficult for Moroccan authorities to prevent, they nonetheless carry with them the risk of beatings, detainment, torture, and prison terms. Some of these demonstrations have been planned, whereas others have been spontaneous. A typical action starts on a street corner or a plaza when someone unfurls the RASD flag, women start ululating, and people start chanting proindependence slogans, but then—within a few minutes, when soldiers and police arrive—the crowd will quickly scatter. Other tactics have included leafleting, graffiti (including of "collaborators'" homes) and cultural celebrations with political overtones. Other events have also morphed into nationalist protests. In the course of a Human Rights Day demonstration in December 2006, marchers found their route blocked by military police. In response, they staged a sit-in in front of a hotel where UN personnel were headquartered. Inevitably, they were violently attacked, scores were arrested, and most received beatings and other abuse while in custody. Even court hearings have been used as a rare public forum to denounce the occupation; on several occasions, prisoners have engaged in total noncooperation at their hearings to protest beatings and other abuse while in custody. Others have taken to wearing camouflage military uniforms to signal solidarity with Polisario.

By 2007, at least one minor public act of protest was usually taking place somewhere in Western Sahara every day. Indeed, the resistance movement had spread to every inhabited part of the country, save for some neighborhoods made up exclusively of Moroccan settlers, as well as to southern Morocco and Moroccan university campuses. Although all protests start with a commitment to nonviolence, some demonstrators have fought back when attacked. Some resistance leaders have argued the importance of nonretaliation, but there appears to be little systematic stressing of a nonviolent discipline. Unlike some nonviolent resistance campaigns in other countries, there has been no formal training of participants prior to actions in Western Sahara. The de facto leadership of the intifadas carried out so far has acknowledged the lack of long-term coordinated planning, noting that actions were more a result of individual initiatives coming from autonomous, neighborhood-based cells of young Sahrawis. If there was any cohesive organizing, it appeared to be coming from Sahrawi prisoners in Moroccan jails, which have become political educational centers for new activists.

## SOURCES OF FRUSTRATION AND DISCONTENT

To some extent, nonviolent resistance is a calculated move on the part of Western Saharan nationalism. The twin failures of military and diplomatic means have left Western Saharan nationalists with few options to affect the deadlock. Around the first anniversary of the 2005 intifada, one Sahrawi living in the diaspora suggested that "the uprising was the continuation of the negotiation process by other means, broadening its scope to include people on the ground instead of keeping it confined to the negotiators alone" (Beirouk 2006). Yet collective strategic thinking does not sufficiently explain why people are in the streets, why Sahrawi women and youth are so eager to risk their physical well-being, or why Sahrawi political prisoners are willing to endure death-defying hunger strikes. Although there is a guiding logic to the intifada, there is also an ensemble of political, social, economic, and cultural reasons also motivating Sahrawis to take to the streets and put their bodies on the line. Beirouk (2006) summarized these conditions as simply "the intolerable situation prevailing on the ground."

The Moroccan government has never attempted to enter into a dialog with Sahrawis who favor independence. During the reign of King Hassan, vocal Polisario supporters often "disappeared" for years at a time, as detailed earlier in this chapter. Any mass expression of nationalism was met with violent repression. It should come as no surprise that most of the leaders of the intifada and Sahrawi human rights organizations are such former "disappeared" prisoners of conscience. Sahrawi leaders in the occupied territory, in contrast, were always handpicked for their outspoken fidelity to the Crown.

King Mohammed's new regime has acted with more restraint toward overt acts of "separatism," yet there is still no indication that Rabat is willing to engage in a constructive dialog with any of the intifada leaders. Indeed, the tendency to silence nationalists still dominates Moroccan state policy. In December 2005 and January 2006, the intifada leaders received one- to three-year sentences for their alleged participation in the previous summer's demonstrations. Although most were later pardoned, some were rearrested in mid-2006. That the Moroccan government would rather imprison these activists and suffer the consequential international embarrassment is a strong indicator of Rabat's unwillingness to offer any kind of political accommodation to Western Saharan nationalism.

Under Moroccan administration, political life in Western Saharan does allow for some Sahrawi input. However, this input is very limited in scope. Those allowed to rise to prominence must swear allegiance to the king. For many years, the main body for Sahrawi representation outside of elected officials was the Conseil royal consultatif pour les affaires sahariennes (CORCAS, Royal Consultative Council for Saharan Affairs). Created by the monarchy under King Hassan, CORCAS was largely filled with tribal elders favoring integration. Defunct for a time, it was revived in early 2006. With former PUNS leader— and one-time advocate for independence— Khalihenna Ould Rachid at the helm, CORCAS became the centerpiece in Morocco's international campaign to earn support for autonomy under Moroccan sovereignty as the optimal final status for Western Sahara. Also claiming to represent Sahrawis inside the territory and in the camps are Polisario defectors. Through promises of money and power, Morocco has enticed a number of former Polisario members to defect, offering them well-paid positions in government, especially if they are willing to denounce their former comrades internationally. Rabat also on a regular basis organizes public displays of Sahrawi fidelity to the monarchy for domestic and international consumption, although the sincerity of these demonstrations is questionable.

For independence activists, economic complaints do not top the typical litany of grievances, yet there are visible divisions between ethnic Sahrawis and Moroccan settlers in the occupied Western Sahara. Morocco's limited political engagement with Western Saharans has translated into limited economic enfranchisement. Indeed, far more emphasis has been placed on accommodating settlers in the territory than on helping the native population. Unemployment is officially 25 percent in the region, although some sources think it is perhaps twice as high. Likewise, economic activity in Western Sahara is worse than in Morocco (Shelley 2005, 2006). Morocco itself already is a dangerous mix of authoritarianism and economic inopportunity. With the political and economic environment much worse in Western Sahara, and with the added dimension of a fully realized nationalist identity at play, an intifada—or something like it—seems inevitable. Furthermore, Sahrawis living both under occupation and in the camps know that Moroccans attempt illegal immigration to Spain every day, although these individuals are only a small portion of the three-quarters of Moroccans who want to emigrate. This point raises the question, Why do Sahrawis want to be a part of a country that so many Moroccans would like to leave?

Nationalist Sahrawis firmly believe that Morocco has taken far more from Western Sahara than it has given. They assert that fisheries and phosphates provide the Moroccan government with billions in revenue every year, monies that are not necessarily reinvested into the territory. As in Morocco proper, corruption is rampant in Western Sahara and most visible among the elites in Morocco's military stationed there. The confluence of military and economic interests in Western Sahara not only fuels nationalist discontent, but also should be a cause for concern when it comes to international peacemaking efforts.

There is even a sense among some Sahrawis that they are being robbed at the microlevel as well as at the macrolevel. Activists note that much of Morocco's settler population is there for personal economic gain and not for the good of the Western Saharan community. For example, Tashilhit-speaking Imazighen from the Sus and the Anti-Atlas—one of Morocco's strongest merchant groups—own and operate numerous cafes, hotels, and shops in Western Sahara. Their permanent residence, however, is in their place of origin, where they send remittances and build their houses. Another segment of the population consists of military personnel, sometimes accompanied by their families, who leave as soon as their duties are finished.

Another major complaint made by Western Saharan nationalists is that Morocco and its settlers are eradicating their culture. From education to architecture, the territory has undergone a process of "Moroccanization" in order to create a feeling of seamless integration with the rest of Morocco. For many years, the largest population in Western Sahara has been Moroccan settlers, who have controlled most of the local economy and political bodies. Approximately one-third of the Moroccan population in Western Sahara consists of soldiers, to which must be added an unknown number of military police, gendarmes, regular police, agents of the Interior Ministry, royal secret services, plainclothes security agents, and civilian informants.

This attempt to make Western Sahara more like Morocco has left many Sahrawis feeling marginalized, particularly in terms of language. On the streets of Western Sahara, the traditionally sedentary cultures of Moroccan Arabs and Berbers stand in perceptible contrast to the traditionally nomadic Sahrawis. Hassaniyyah Arabic and Spanish, which nationalists favor over Moroccan Arabic and French, are not official languages in Western Sahara. Sahrawi political prisoners made a point of this at their trials in al-'Ayun in December 2005. They refused to speak in any other language than Hassaniyyah. In a similar assertion of their distinct culture, males in the Moroccan-controlled Western Sahara make more effort to wear traditional clothing than do their counterparts in the refugee camps, who tend to favor modern Western clothing donated from other countries.

Despite massive Moroccan outlays to develop and encourage settlement, the patterns of corruption, mismanagement, and authoritarianism are as acute in Western Sahara as they are in Morocco, if not more so. For these reasons, it is not inconceivable that many Moroccans end up siding with Western Saharan nationalists in a referendum. In fact, Polisario was counting on this factor when it accepted the UN's 2003 Peace Plan, which called for a referendum for both Western Saharans and Moroccan settlers. Western Saharan nationalism has so far been ethnically homogenous, limited to Sahrawis, yet the Peace Plan would have established four years of autonomous Sahrawi-led rule in the territory before the referendum. This period might have convinced many Moroccans that they would be better off in an independent Western Sahara than in Morocco. Rabat's rejection of the Peace Plan seems to indicate that Moroccan officials do not trust their own settlers—especially the thousands of ethnic Sahrawis from southern Morocco who were imported into the territory in the 1990s. Some of these settlers, transplanted there to vote for integration in favor of Morocco in the referendum, ended up participating in the 1999 intifada. Indeed, nationalist Sahrawis are not ethnically chauvinist and would gladly work with Moroccans for an independent Western Sahara. This fact alone is the only reasonable explanation for Rabat's otherwise inexplicable rejection of the 2003 Baker Plan.

## THE NEW FRONT IN THE WESTERN SAHARA CONFLICT

The greatest challenge facing nationalist activists in Western Sahara is their isolation from Moroccan civil society and the outside world. Although recent developments in telecommunications have helped overcome this barrier, it is still difficult for the activists to operate and even more difficult for foreigners to visit them or for Moroccans to challenge their government. The success of the most recent intifada will depend to a large degree on the Sahrawi activists' ability to overcome these barriers in order to "internationalize" their conflict in such a way as to embarrass Morocco out of Western Sahara.

There is so far no acknowledged official or clandestine Sahrawi organization behind the demonstrations. Daddach leads a group called Comité pour la défense du droit à l'autodétermination pour le peuple du Sahara Occidental (Committee for the Self-Determination of the Sahrawi People), which is one of the few explicitly political Sahrawi organizations, although it makes no pretension to leading the intifada. Most nationalists believe that they are acting on behalf of or in concert with Polisario, but few will publicly claim actual membership in that organization. Polisario membership, however, is loosely defined in the first place; any ethnic Sahrawi who supports independence probably can claim "membership." Some activists are more overt and provocative in their support for Polisario. Appearing in court in December 2005, one Sahrawi wore military fatigues to signal his solidarity with the exiled nationalist front. Polisario also acknowledges that it has several "representatives" from areas under Moroccan control in its National Secretariat. These activists would secretly travel to Tindouf for the RASD's General Congress, but with innovations in technology such secret travel might no longer be necessary. There are others in the resistance who are no less fervent in their nationalism, but who have serious political differences with the Polisario leadership and who—although acknowledging that Polisario is the external representative of the nationalist struggle—see the internal resistance as an autonomous movement distinct from the Polisario Front.

Most Sahrawi activism has been confined to the field of human rights. The only human rights organization ever to receive recognition from the Moroccan state was the Sahara Branch of the Truth and Justice Forum, yet that recognition was withdrawn in 2003. Since then, more radical activists have operated under two unofficial groups not recognized by the Moroccan government: the Collective of Sahrawi Human Rights Defenders, a long-standing informal group, and the provocatively titled Association sahraouie des victimes des violations graves des droits de l'homme commises par l'état du Maroc (Sahrawi Association of Victims of Grave Human Rights Violations Committed by the Moroccan State). There are also Association des familles des martyrs dans les commissariats de police marocains (Association of Families of Martyrs in Moroccan Police Stations), Comité d'action contre la torture (Committee of Action Against Torture), Comité des familles des disparus Sahraouis (Committee of Families of Disappeared Sahrawis), Comité pour la protection des prisonniers politiques sahraouis à la Prison Noire (Committee for the Protection of Sahrawi Political Prisoners in the Black Prison), Association des victimes de la torture de Smara (Association of Victims of Torture in Smara), and Comité sahraoui pour la défense des droits de l'homme (Sahrawi Committee of Defense of Human Rights in Smara).

Although many nationalist activists continue to work in the field of human rights, it is no longer the mask they hide behind. The recent intifada has allowed many Western Saharans to express their true beliefs, which is support for the cause of independence. The late February 2006 reconstitution of the Sahara Branch of the Truth and Justice Forum went largely unsupported by radical nationalists, who feel that the branch's time has come and gone. However, the human rights group Sahrawi Association of Victims of Grave Human Rights Violations has continually provided some of the most timely and detailed accounts of happenings on the ground.

Western Saharan nationalists receive little direct support from Polisario and international solidarity activists, so they have to make do with what they have at hand. Their greatest asset is the support provided by Sahrawi society—that is, the submerged networks of everyday life that make both overt and covert forms of resistance possible. These networks allow the nationalists to address a range of needs, whether by sewing RASD flags or by finding "safe houses" for activists hiding from the authorities (sometimes for years at a time). Officially recognized charitable Sahrawi organizations are not allowed to address political issues and, as with all sanctioned organizations, must claim that Western Sahara is Moroccan. These rules, however, do not stop them from providing indirect aid to the nationalist cause by strengthening the social connections and relations among them that support Sahrawi political activism.

Readily available new technologies are also an invaluable resource to Sahrawi nationalists. The Internet, first and foremost, has become the major channel for organization and the dissemination of propaganda. With connections in the refugee camps, the Internet has become a vital tool for communication and coordination across the berm. Text and digital-voice chat rooms allow for real-time communication between Sahrawis, including the diaspora. Cellular phones provide rapid international communication, helping some activists inside the territory gauge the global effects of their work and quickly correct their aim. Portable phones also put family and fellow nationalists in daily real-time contact. Digital video and photo cameras let activists distribute—easily and widely—images of protests, human rights violations, and day-to-day realities on the ground in Western Sahara.

There currently are no Moroccan organizations or sectors of civil society that support Western Saharan nationalism. Calling for the independence of Western Sahara is illegal and serves as grounds for imprisonment and the disbanding of an organization—Sahrawi or Moroccan. The far left Moroccan activist Abraham Serfaty served many years in prison in part because of his support for self-determination in Western Sahara. Some Moroccan groups, however, are willing to call for the respect of the "principle" of self-determination, and others support human rights work in Western Sahara, although they must do these things carefully so as not to provide direct support to nationalists.

The most respected independent human rights association in Morocco, the Association marocaine des droits humains (AMDH, Moroccan Association for Human Rights), which supports a "democratic solution" in Western Sahara, operates an office in al-'Ayun and works closely with Sahrawi human rights defenders. Although AMDH has to be very cautious, it nonetheless attempts to address human rights issues objectively, calling for the accountability of Moroccan government agents in Western Sahara. Critics charge that AMDH is a remnant of the Moroccan Marxist Left and is thus not objective. Likewise, the far left political party Annahj Addimocrati (Democratic Path), the successor to Morocco's old Marxist organizations, is the only political organization that breaks with the national consensus on Western Sahara. It vocally supports the right of self-determination as a solution to the conflict and has sent a delegate to Tindouf. However, it is one of Morocco's most electorally weak parties.

In recent years, there is clearly a growing space in Morocco for raising new questions about Western Sahara. Without lending direct support to Polisario, some Moroccan journalists have called into question the regime's policies and characterizations of the situation in Western Sahara. At the end of 2004, journalist Ali Lmrabet, well known for his political satires and critiques of the Moroccan government, visited the refugee camps. Although he continued to claim on the surface that Western Sahara is Moroccan in his reportage from Tindouf, Polisario allowed him to explore the camps freely, which resulted in articles that directly challenged his government's claims about the camps being prisons. For this act, Lmrabet was banned from working as a reporter in Morocco for ten years (Reporters sans frontères 2005). Aboubakr Jamai, managing editor of *Le Journal Hebdomadaire,* wrote a relatively critical editorial in response to the intifada in 2005, suggesting that Moroccan policies in Western Sahara had failed to win the population over (see Finan 2006). More surprising than that, however, was *Le Journal*'s charge that the controversial 2005 report on Polisario from the European Strategic Intelligence and Security Centre—widely denounced for being partisan, factually inaccurate, and intentionally defamatory—was "remote controlled" by the Moroccan regime (*Le Journal,* Dec. 9, 2005). Few papers, however, have followed suit, and none of the Moroccan press has yet questioned the legitimacy of Morocco's historical claim to Western Sahara. *Le Journal,* meanwhile, has since been persecuted out of existence by the Moroccan state.

Where once Moroccan academics were allowed to question everything but Western Sahara, some scholars have recently taken to criticizing that aspect of national master narrative as well. On the thirtieth anniversary of the Green March, the Moroccan weekly *Tel Quel* boldly published a revisionist account of the November 1975 events, challenging many nationalist myths. However, outside of Sahrawis, there is still no sector of Moroccan civil society that openly supports independence. The most likely candidate for support for Sahrawis, Amazigh activists in the Spanish-colonized North, have not as yet demonstrated any ties of solidarity, although groups in the Rif have recently called for "autonomy" (International Crisis Group 2007). Indeed, May 2007 saw bloody clashes between Amazigh and Sahrawi students on Moroccan campuses. The acknowledgment of such ties, however, would also support claims that the loss of Western Sahara will trigger the balkanization of Morocco and will thus work to Rabat's advantage.

Western Saharan nationalists working under Moroccan occupation receive little support regionally except from the camps and the European diaspora. Algeria, other than verbal praise from officials, has little to with the situation. The Western Sahara issue is not a popular issue for most Algerians, although they are aware of the conflict and are naturally sympathetic. The Comité national algérien de solidarité avec le peuple sahraoui (Algerian National Committee for Solidarity with the Sahrawi People) is the only civil society group in Algeria dedicated to supporting Western Saharan nationalism, yet most Algerians have not heard of it, and former military/government officials run it.

Spain is home to the largest number of grassroots organizations supporting Western Saharan nationalism. Hundreds of local community groups host Sahrawi refugee children during the summer. These personal connections help build natural bonds of solidarity, yet for most Spanish activists it is far easier to visit the refugee camps than the Moroccan-controlled Western Sahara. All foreigners are watched closely in the territory; Morocco regularly turns around Spanish solidarity groups at al-'Ayun's airport before they even leave the plane. Support for the Sahrawi cause is not limited to the Spanish Left, however; it can also be found among some aging former Falangist officers who served in Spanish Sahara and feel that their honor was compromised when civilian politicians in Madrid, under foreign pressure, took away the independence that these officers had promised.

Western Saharan nationalists receive long-distance support from activists in Australia, Great Britain, Norway, France, Belgium, and the United States. These foreign activists maintain a host of Web sites that help disseminate information, images, video, and breaking news. Various solidarity campaigns also attempt to affect government policy. Although the constant theme of foreign activism has been the right of self-determination, many activists have started working on the issue of natural-resource exploitation by Morocco in Western Sahara. The two major foci have been efforts to stop oil exploration in Western Saharan waters and the EU's fishing in the area.

ADVANTAGES AND CHALLENGES
OF A NONVIOLENT ESCALATION STRATEGY

The most important advantage of nonviolent resistance is that it has the potential to overcome the major hurdle facing Western Saharan nationalism: the Franco–American consensus that supports Morocco. When handled strategically and with some media savvy, nonviolent resistance can highlight the moral differences between a people claiming their rights and the government that denies them. The more this difference is highlighted and contrasted, the more transnational sympathy will flow to the former. Likewise, countries allied with the latter will inevitably draw to themselves international shame and scorn because of this association. The more Paris and Washington support repressive Moroccan control in Western Sahara, the more they will seem aligned with a repressive regime. Nonviolent resistance also provides Western Saharan nationalism with a tool to destabilize Morocco in a way that will force Morocco's backers to choose sides.

Some activists in the intifada liken their struggle to the "people power" revolutions in Nepal (2006), Lebanon (2005), Ukraine (2004), Serbia (2000), South Africa (1994), Czechoslovakia (1989), and the Philippines (1986), to name just a few (see Zunes, Asher, and Kurtz 1999). The advantages of this kind of strategy are most clearly demonstrated by the antiapartheid movement. As South African activists worked to expose the disparities and inequities in their country, international activists could increasingly make it into a pariah state. Thus, it was more and more embarrassing for other countries to continue their support for Pretoria, which eventually resulted in the worldwide divestment and boycott movement. Outside of RASD–Pretoria relations, South African and Sahrawi grass-roots activists have even created some lines of solidarity. In July 2006, Aminatou Haidar took part in a symbolic twinning of the Ma'tallah neighborhood of al-'Ayun and Soweto, home of a well-known antiapartheid uprising in South Africa in 1976.

Overcoming support for Morocco will be key for Western Saharan nationalism. For Polisario, the military option and UN-led internationalization could not overpower Morocco's backers in Paris and Washington. In the 1970s and 1980s, at the height of the Cold War, it was too easy for Western powers to justify arming Morocco in its war against a guerilla army with ties to Algeria, Libya, and Cuba. During the UN peace process, France and the United States protected Morocco from a referendum and the Baker Plan in the name of stability and realism. As the conflict moves into the streets of the contested Western Sahara, and as more images of bludgeon-wielding Moroccan police circulate globally, general impressions may radically change. And if perceptions change in Polisario's favor, it will become harder for Paris and Washington to justify their support for Rabat.

This argument also works against a resumption of conventional warfare, though, because Polisario might easily undermine the intifada. Sahrawi activists are aware of how parallel violent resistance can undermine nonviolent efforts. One of the failures of the Palestinian movement has been that its violent wings have overshadowed its nonviolent ones. The general perception in the United States, that Israel is the victim of Palestinian terrorism, helps justify Washington's unquestioned support for Israel's occupation of the territories seized in 1967.

The West's backing of the Moroccan monarchy is now also premised on the war on terror, so any violent acts on the side of Polisario might easily be portrayed as acts of terrorism. Indeed, Morocco has already tried to make this connection; since September 11, 2001, the Moroccan press has insinuated or linked Polisario with *jihadi,* Salafi, or Takfiri terrorist organizations and ideology.[4] Strangely, at the same time, Morocco continues to use Polisario's leftist rhetoric and its ties with Cuba as a way of trying to undermine support for Polisario in the U.S. Congress. Given Polisario's socialist-nationalist roots, the Sahrawis cultural disposition toward individual religious practice, and Algeria's desperate need for more U.S. military aid to fight alleged terrorist groups in the Sahara, it is conceptually and practically unlikely that Polisario will link up with armed transnational Islamic organizations.

The intifada faces two main challenges in changing the political dynamic in Western Sahara. One is internal and the other external to Morocco. On the external, international stage, the intifada will have to expand the scope of people who know and care about the conflict. Much of this work will fall on the shoulders of international solidarity activists, who will have to engage and educate larger numbers of people. Recent literature on transnational activist networks sheds light on the important role such groups can play in conflict resolution (e.g., Keck and Sikkink 1998). Likewise, the small Sahrawi diaspora outside of Spain, which is especially minimal in the United States, means that the intifada will ultimately have to link up with non-Sahrawi activists in key Western countries to affect their governments.

The Internet, digital video recorders, and cellular phones equipped with cameras have played a huge role in Western Saharan resistance since May 2005. Compared with the 1999 intifada, where few images escaped the territory, there is now a regular flow of pictures and videos of street melees, wounded Sahrawis, ransacked homes, and portraits of new political detainees. The power of new technology was most clearly on display in the posting of images from inside al-'Ayun's municipal prison, which nationalists call the Cárcel Negra (Black Prison). Taken from a camera phone during the height of repression in 2005, these images showed dozens of Sahrawi prisoners crammed into a tiny room, sleeping on the floor and even next to the toilet. The images were a huge embarrassment for Rabat, and they even drew criticism from the domestic Moroccan media. The Moroccan government denied the photos' authenticity, yet it quickly reduced the prison's population and repainted it. New technologies have thus allowed nationalist activists to circumvent what they have long described as Morocco's "media siege" on Western Sahara. These Sahrawis no longer have to rely on the small number of journalists coming to Western Sahara or on Polisario representatives to convey their story to the world.

The intifada faces a far greater challenge internally. In order to maintain a level of discord inside the territory, nationalists will have to continue to press for militant action and perhaps continually elevate the level of confrontation. Doing so will inevitably elicit a heavy Moroccan counterresponse, which will in turn only serve to inflame tensions. Continually increasing the levels of resistance and counterresistance is necessary to draw desperately needed international attention to the situation, but it comes at the cost of bodies and lives. It also develops the likelihood of terrorism—which the Polisario has scrupulously avoided thus far—if it seems that no other option is left for Sahrawi nationalism. Extensive Moroccan repression might also trigger a Polisario counterresponse, thereby plunging Western Sahara back into all-out war.

The one thing that Sahrawi activists need more than anything else is sympathy from the general Moroccan public. For the time being, Moroccans seem indifferent to, if not supportive of their government's heavy-handed measures in Western Sahara. However, it might be in Moroccan democrats' interests to open a dialog with Sahrawi activists. With the unchallenged popularity of Islamic movements in Morocco, Moroccan secularists might find that they agree with many principles held by Western Saharan nationalists. Assuming they can find some common ground, a Moroccan–Sahrawi nonviolent movement may also help the cause of democracy in Morocco. As a 2005 study by the human rights organization Freedom House concluded, broad-based, nonviolent, antiauthoritarian revolutions have the greatest chance of actually instituting lasting change in a political system. Examining sixty-seven cases, the report concluded that "'people power' movements matter, because nonviolent civic forces are a major source of pressure for decisive change in most transitions," whereas "there is comparatively little positive effect for freedom in 'top-down' transitions that were launched and led by elites" (2005, 8–9). Although democracy in Morocco and Western Sahara is currently seemingly unthinkable, its future prospects may rest on unlikely allies.

For the first time in a long while, the Western Sahara conflict seemed at a crossroads in the first decade of the new millennium. The international community's blasé attitude had allowed the situation to deteriorate, forcing Western Saharan nationalists to pursue the one means of resistance left to them short of terrorism. Yet direct confrontation in any form is deliberately provocative and likely to produce an escalation of violence and eventually counterviolence. Thus, once again the international community's response remains key. But the UN Security Council's recent track record in dealing with obscure African crises is a significant source of skepticism. One need only cite the genocides in Rwanda and the Darfur region of Sudan or the millions of dead in the Congo war as examples of gross, immoral inaction in the face of unspeakable atrocity.

# PART THREE
# Irresolution

"Peace" is nothing more than a change in the form of the conflict.
—MAX WEBER, *The Methodology of the Social Sciences*

# 7

# Searching for a Solution

*The United Nations and the Organization of African Unity*

Since 1963, a broad international consensus has treated the issue of Western Sahara as a matter of decolonization. In 1975, the ICJ added to this consensus in the strongest language possible. Yet only weeks after The Hague released its opinion, Western Sahara became a rare aberration in the history of decolonization. Thomas Franck, the late scholar of international law, highlights this perversity:

> To the very limited extent that a colony was permitted to become independent either by dividing into two states . . . or by joining another nation . . . it was only after the indigenous population concerned had been consulted in a democratic electoral process under supervision or observation of the United Nations.
>
> In the entire four-decade history of the decolonization of a billion people, there were only three exceptions to this rule of decency, reason and good order: Western New Guinea and [East] Timor—colonies, respectively, of The Netherlands and Portugal, which were seized by Indonesia without the democratic consent of the inhabitants—and the Western Sahara—a Spanish colony which was occupied by Morocco against the clearly evident wishes of its inhabitants. (1987, 11)

Following East Timor's independence through an internationally supervised referendum in 1999, Western Sahara has become all the more exceptional.

Standing against this "rule of decency" with regard to Western Sahara has been the Franco–American consensus, which has supported Morocco's rejection of self-determination. Efforts to bring a lasting solution to the Western Sahara dispute have so far failed to overcome the Franco–American consensus or to find a bridge between it and the international consensus for self-determination.

In this study, part three deals with the long war between these two opposing forces. In this chapter, our focus is the early years of the peace process, starting when Western Sahara was still a Spanish colony. As mentioned, the OAU took the lead in the peace process following Spain's withdrawal from and the Moroccan–Mauritanian takeover of Western Sahara in 1976. The OAU guided the peace process until the mid-1980s, when Morocco left the organization in protest of the RASD's ascension. The UN took over the process in the late 1980s and put forth a plan to end the war and hold a referendum. In concluding this chapter, we note that the sustainable intractability of the war in Western Sahara lent itself to a similar peace process. Morocco and Polisario, facing a military situation they could neither win nor lose in the late 1980s, came to the UN peace process unwilling to make fundamental concessions. Given the winner-take-all nature of the 1991 UN-OAU Settlement Plan, the peace process simply became war by other means. Tension between the Franco–American consensus and the international consensus has only fueled both sides' intransigence.

Chapter 8 picks up right where this chapter ends. Although a cease-fire was enacted in 1991, the UN was never able to implement the UN-OAU Settlement Plan and hold a referendum on independence. Chapter 9 then examines the peace process after the Security Council abandoned the referendum in 2000, including the 2001 and 2003 Baker Plans and the subsequent push toward "autonomy." The book's conclusion is thus largely dedicated to charting the failure of either the international consensus or the Franco–American consensus to prevail in Western Sahara.

DECOLONIZATION AND RECOLONIZATION: 1963 TO 1976

In 1963, the UN-designated Spanish Sahara—along with Spain's Ifni enclave—a non-self-governing territory. The UN litany of colonies was established under General Assembly Resolution 1514 (XV) of 1960, known as the Declaration on the Granting of Independence to Colonial Countries and Peoples. The resolution also set up a Special Committee of Twenty-Four, known as the Fourth Committee, to deal with the decolonization agenda. In 1965, the General Assembly passed, almost unanimously, Resolution 2072 (XX), which "urgently" requested that "the Government of Spain . . . take immediately all necessary measures for the liberation of the Territory of Ifni and Spanish Sahara from colonial domination." Morocco, Mauritania, and Algeria voted for the resolution; Spain and Portugal were the only two nations to vote against it; France, South Africa, the United Kingdom, and the United States abstained (UN 1967, 585). Spain had attempted to dodge this UN pressure by first relabeling Western Sahara as an offshore province of Spain, like the Canary Islands. When that approach failed to convince, Spain expanded the role of the council of notable Sahrawis, the Jama'a, portraying the expansion as a sign of Spanish commitment to gradual self-determination. But the majority of UN countries still remained unconvinced.

Spain finally conceded in 1966, voicing a willingness to enter into discussions with the secretary-general to facilitate self-determination. At the same time, Morocco and Mauritania were asserting their interests, as evidenced in the General Assembly's 1966 resolution. Resolution 2229 (XXI) reaffirmed "the inalienable right of the peoples of Ifni and Spanish Sahara to self-determination," but it also requested Madrid to consult with Morocco and

Mauritania, albeit "with a view to enabling the indigenous population of the Territory to exercise freely its right to self-determination." Morocco, Mauritania, and Algeria again voted in support of Resolution 2229; the governments of Portugal and Spain continued their lonely dissent; and the governments of Belgium and of several Madrid clients joined France, the United States, and South Africa in abstention (UN 1969, 588–92). Although this development seemed positive, one prescient journalist, Rene Pelissier, predicted,

> If Spain decides one day to divest itself of this expensive sandbox, sovereignty is likely to be transferred to one or both of the interested parties [i.e., Morocco and Mauritania], perhaps by a partition along arbitrary lines. The surgery could be painful, given the complexity of the Saharan nomads' tribal attachments and the foreseeable resistance of the settled tribes to incorporation in either Morocco or Mauritania. But if Spain should lose the initiative, partition or swallowing by force of arms would almost certainly follow. (*Africa Report*, Feb. 1966)

The Spanish government attempted to keep the initiative on its side in 1967 by formally accepting the idea of a UN visiting mission to the Spanish Sahara, a return of Sahrawi refugees, and a referendum in the territory; Madrid also entered into negotiations with the Moroccan government on the question of reincorporating the tiny enclave of Ifni into Morocco, which happened in 1969.

Returning to the issue of Spanish Sahara in 1972, the General Assembly's Resolution 2983 (XXVII) was the strongest yet, supporting the territory's right to independence. Spain convinced several Latin American dictatorships, along with fascist Portugal and apartheid South Africa, to vote against the resolution. The United States abstained, along with a number of other countries, including Morocco. The Algerian government, which had voted in favor of the resolution, informed the General Assembly that it had joined with the Moroccan and Mauritanian governments in January 1972 "to coordinate actions to speed up the liberation of the territory," which followed a 1970 agreement in Nouadhibou among King Hassan, Mauritanian president Ould Daddah, and Algerian president Boumedienne to call for the Spanish Sahara's decolonization (UN 1975, 569–70, 579–80). Despite what appeared to be a united Maghribi front against Spain, Morocco's abstention was an indication of Rabat's discomfort with the emphasis placed on independence. Indeed, the General Assembly's clarification of a right to independence, reiterated in 1973, coincided with signs that the Western Saharans were developing a national consciousness.

Yet the situation became even worse for King Hassan when in July 1974 Spain announced that it intended to hold a self-determination referendum in early 1975. In response, Morocco asserted that "decolonization of the two provinces of the Sahara, Rio de Oro and Sakiet El-Hamra, had always implied their reintegration into the Moroccan State." With support from Algeria, King Hassan then requested a ruling from the ICJ on Morocco's claim. Because Spain would not submit to binding arbitration, the General

Assembly, in its Resolution 3292 (XXIX), passed December 14, 1974, simply asked for an ICJ advisory opinion. The ICJ would consider whether the claims of Morocco and Mauritania trumped the Western Saharans' right to self-determination or not. It also called for a special visiting mission to assess the realities on the ground (UN 1977, 794, 805–6). In the meantime, Spain agreed to postpone the referendum.

The ICJ held hearings on the question of Western Sahara from late June to late July 1975, a month after the UN visiting mission toured the region in May. The latter's findings, which confirmed broad indigenous support for both independence and Polisario, were released on October 15. The ICJ's ruling, issued the following day, October 16, was another clear defeat for Morocco's position (see chapter 4). Yet it is doubtful that the court could have said anything that would have changed Hassan's mind. Hours later Morocco issued a statement that declared, "The Opinion of the Court can only mean one thing . . . [t]he so-called Western Sahara was a part of Moroccan territory." Hassan quickly announced that he would personally lead 350,000 Moroccan civilians on a peaceful march to seize Western Sahara from Spain at the end of October.

While the Spanish cabinet was formulating its strategy on October 17, Franco's health failed him, and he soon thereafter suffered two heart attacks and later lapsed into a coma (he died on November 20). Amidst this turmoil, Spain's UN representative, Jaime de Piniés, invoking Article 35 of the UN Charter, presented a letter to the Security Council on October 18, claiming that the Green March "threatened international peace and security." The Security Council opened debate two days later, in which the Costa Rican representative presented a draft resolution calling on the Moroccan government to "desist from the proposed march on Western Sahara" (quoted in Mundy 2006, 286). Instead, on October 22, the Security Council, under pressure from the United States and France, adopted Resolution 377, which appealed for "restraint" on all sides and requested the secretary-general to enter into consultations with the parties. Getting only this weak response from the UN, Spain was forced to pursue direct negotiations with Morocco simultaneously, which resulted in a postponement of the march until November. As ordered by the Security Council, Secretary-General Kurt Waldheim toured the region between October 25 and 28 but obtained little cooperation from King Hassan, who favored keeping up the pressure until Spain relented.

On October 31, the same day that Moroccan military forces secretly penetrated Spanish Sahara, Secretary-General Waldheim issued a report following his visit to Madrid, Rabat, Algiers, and Nouakchott. In order to obtain an audience with Hassan during his tour, Waldheim offered him a UN peace medal and later joined him on his royal train while the king was out drumming up support for the Green March. In his memoirs, Waldheim's biases are clearly laid out. He generally found Algeria's Boumedienne "not an easy man to deal with," although Boumedienne and Hassan were "equally intransigent" regarding Western Sahara. Waldheim had the most sympathy for Mauritania's president,

Ould Daddah, whom he felt had bitten off more than he could chew. Regarding the fate of the Western Saharans, Waldheim argued, in an echo of U.S. secretary of state Henry Kissinger's sentiments, "it would have been almost impossible to conduct a referendum to determine their political future" because they were "predominantly nomads [*sic*]" (Waldheim 1986, 128–29). If the secretary-general had bothered to consult with Spanish officials, he would have learned that the 1974 Spanish census had recorded 80 percent of the population as living in urban areas. Not surprisingly, Waldheim's shuttling made little headway on the issue, which the United States had reportedly intended (Moynihan 1978, 247).

Following an apparent breakdown in Rabat–Madrid talks in late October 1975, the Security Council answered, on November 2, a second Spanish request for an emergency meeting "to oblige the Government of Morocco to desist from the march it has announced" (quoted in Mundy 2006, 288). Spain's UN representation insisted that halting the march was sine qua non for a peaceful solution; if not, force would be used to block the march. In its Resolution 379, the Security Council urged all parties to avoid any actions that might escalate tensions and requested the secretary-general to intensify his mediation efforts. Waldheim's spokesman, André Lewin, visited the region between November 3 and 6, where he simply gathered opinions on Waldheim's proposal to place Western Sahara under temporary UN administration so that a referendum, respecting all concerned interests, could be held. Whereas the Spanish and Algerian governments might have found this proposal pleasing, Rabat would have found it anathema to Moroccan interests unless a vote for integration was guaranteed. Besides, as Hassan informed Lewin on November 4, a deal was almost finalized, and the Green March would be a symbolic, nonconfrontational gesture. Whether this was the case or not, both Spain and Morocco continued to act publicly as if they were playing a real game of brinksmanship.

Once Moroccan civilians started to approach the border on November 5, Spain once again pressed the Security Council for action. The council president quickly sent an "urgent request to put an end forthwith to the declared march on Western Sahara" to King Hassan (UN 1978, 187), who replied that the Green March would continue until Spain agreed to "undertake urgent bilateral negotiations." The Security Council finally passed a more strongly worded resolution (380) late on November 6, which "deplored" the Green March and called on Morocco to withdraw immediately, to respect self-determination, and to cooperate with the secretary-general's mediation efforts. But Resolution 380 was passed under Chapter VI powers and thus came with no enforcement mechanism. It was the last Security Council action on Western Sahara for ten years.

Unable to obtain any meaningful UN response to stop Hassan's invasion, Spain decided to cut a secret deal with Morocco and Mauritania, which was finalized between November 12 and 14 in Madrid. Meanwhile, Waldheim issued three subsequent reports; the final, issued November 19, informed the Security Council that a tripartite agreement had been reached in Madrid five days earlier. At the same time, the UN Fourth Committee was holding its annual hearings between November 14 and December 4, at which Western Sahara would be a hot agenda item. The committee forwarded two resolutions to the General Assembly. One resolution (3458 A), adopted on December 10 by a vote of eighty-eight to zero (with forty-one abstentions, including the United States), called on Spain, with the help of the secretary-general, to hold a popular referendum on self-determination in Western Sahara. The other resolution (3458 B), passed by a vote of fifty-six to forty-two (with thirty-four abstentions), took note of the Madrid Agreement and requested that the parties to the agreement "ensure" that all persons originating from the territory "exercise their inalienable right to self-determination" (UN 1978, 188–90). Morocco, France, and the United States supported the latter resolution.

With the outbreak of a war and the massive refugee exodus triggered by the Moroccan–Mauritanian invasion, a special envoy of the secretary-general, visiting the territory in February 1976, found that the prevailing conditions in Western Sahara were not suitable for a referendum. Nor was the UN convinced that the endorsement of the Madrid Agreement by the defunct Jama'a constituted an act of self-determination. The same body had in fact endorsed Polisario in November and so dissolved itself. Thus, when the General Assembly passed Resolution 31/45 in December 1976, it decided to wait for the results of a scheduled extraordinary OAU session on the Western Sahara (UN 1979, 756–57). General Assembly resolutions adopted over the next three years—32/22 (1977), 33/31 (1978), and 34/37 (1979)—show that the UN had deferred the matter totally to the OAU.

## THE ORGANIZATION OF AFRICAN UNITY
## AND THE WESTERN SAHARA CONFLICT

In the years immediately following Spain's abandonment of Western Sahara, the OAU took the lead and pressed the issue in international forums. Some OAU officials believed that were it not for their organization's role, the UN would have simply let the Western Sahara conflict take its own course (Zunes, interview, OAU official, New York, Jan. 1991). By comparison, the failure of the Association of Southeast Asian Nations and other Asian/Pacific states to raise the issue of Indonesia's occupation of East Timor abetted high-level UN indifference to that issue. In the case of Western Sahara, the OAU provided ample groundwork for the UN to build upon. On its own, the Security Council, led by France and the United States, would never have taken up Western Sahara unless Morocco requested mediation. It was the OAU that first obtained King Hassan's consent to a referendum, and thus the OAU's work on the conflict between 1976 and 1984 laid the foundation for the subsequent UN approach.

The Moroccan–Mauritanian takeover of Western Sahara in 1975, a gross violation of the OAU Charter's prohibition of altering colonial boundaries by force, was of particular concern to the OAU. In early 1976, the OAU Council of Ministers decided against admitting the RASD government as a full member, but it left the door open for African states to establish bilateral relations with the RASD (Damis 1984, 274–75). Yet support for Polisario as a liberation movement was strong; in June 1976, the OAU Council of Ministers adopted a resolution offering "unconditional support for the just struggle of the Saharan people for the recovery of their national rights." The OAU summit, however, under threat of a Moroccan and Mauritanian withdrawal from the organization, refused to consider the resolution. As a compromise, the OAU agreed to an Algerian request for an "extraordinary summit" on Western Sahara, but the summit repeatedly failed to take shape (Sesay, Ojo, and Fasehun 1984, 53–54).

It took the 1978 coup in Mauritania to draw attention to the gravity of the situation. At the July OAU summit in Khartoum, Sudan, the idea of an extraordinary summit was abandoned in favor of an OAU Committee of Wisemen. Led by the heads of state of Mali, Nigeria, Sudan, Tanzania, and Ivory Coast, this ad hoc committee would study the conflict and present possible solutions at the 1979 OAU summit in Monrovia (Layachi 1994, 33). Although the OAU was officially under the leadership of Sudanese president Jaafar Numeiri, its chair from 1978 to 1979, Mali's president General Moussa Traoré and Nigeria's president Lieutenant-General Olusegun Obasanjo did most of the work on the committee. Hassan appreciated inclusion of Numeiri, a strong ally, but knew that Traoré, Obasanjo, and Tanzania's president, Julius Nyerere, were in Polisario's camp. In contrast, Ivory Coast, which has never recognized the RASD, was the committee's most unengaged member (Damis 1984, 276). Traoré and Obasanjo held a series of meetings with high-level officials in Morocco, Mauritania, and Algeria late in 1978 and early 1979. Behind the scenes, Traoré had organized a secret Morocco–Polisario meeting in Bamako, Mali, on October 20 and 21, 1978, although nothing reportedly came out of it.

The Wisemen finally presented their report at the OAU's sixteenth summit in Monrovia, Liberia, in July 1979, which outlined a settlement plan based on a cease-fire, a withdrawal of armed forces, and, finally, a referendum. The summit leaders adopted the report by a vast majority and asked the Wisemen to push the plan forward. Moroccan foreign minister M'hamed Boucetta angrily accused the OAU of "sabotage orchestrated by Algeria and its clients" and walked out, joined by Senegal, a staunch ally (Sesay, Ojo, and Fasehun 1984, 54–55). King Hassan also personally boycotted a meeting arranged by the Wisemen to bring all the parties together, including Algeria's new president, Chadli Bendjedid. Polisario accepted the proposals in principle yet ruled out a unilateral cease-fire until Morocco accepted the idea of a referendum (Damis 1984, 277).

By the next OAU summit, July 1980, in Freetown, Sierra Leone, Morocco's intransigence was wearing thin with several member states pressing for the RASD's admittance. A requisite majority of states then backed the RASD's admission, but a Moroccan-led boycott—backed by Senegal, Ivory Coast, Guinea, Cameroon, Zaire, Egypt, Sudan, Somalia, and Tunisia—threatened to break up the organization.

With support from Sierra Leone, the new chair of the Committee of Wisemen, and from Kenya, Morocco attended the next Wisemen meeting, also held in Freetown, that September. Having voted down an Algerian proposal to mandate a full Moroccan military withdrawal, the Wisemen simply recommended that both sides confine their troops to quarters. In its final act, the committee ambitiously proposed that the parties enter into a cease-fire in December 1980. The Wisemen believed the OAU and the UN could organize a referendum in the territory once their forces were demobilized. With that, the Wisemen said that their work was finished. But the date of the cease-fire passed virtually unnoticed, and the situation on the ground remained unchanged.

To much astonishment, King Hassan consented to an OAU-UN-organized referendum in Western Sahara at the 1981 OAU summit in Nairobi, Kenya. The OAU gladly welcomed Morocco's new cooperative spirit, although Hassan's obvious short-term goal was to delay the RASD's admittance into the organization. Whether for the same cynical reasons or not, there was also likely some pressure on Hassan from France, the United States, and Saudi Arabia to cooperate (Damis 2000, 23). Following the July announcement, the *New York Times* reported from Rabat that despite the referendum offer, "few well-placed Moroccan or Western diplomats here believe that the King has any intention of allowing a referendum that would challenge Morocco's long-standing claim to the phosphate-rich desert" (July 7, 1981). In fact, Hassan quickly reassured his subjects that the referendum would be "an act of confirmation." He added, "Moroccan citizens of the Sahara will not go back on all the manifestations of loyalty they have shown" (quoted in *Africa Confidential,* July 15, 1981). Hassan later told a press conference that the Western Saharan refugees could vote in the referendum, but "if they are against us," they should not participate "because we have no need of troublemakers." He also said that allowing any campaigning for independence "would be asking too much of us." The referendum, according to Hassan, should pose one question: "Do you confirm the act of allegiance that ties you with His Majesty the King of Morocco and which indicated that you are a part of the Kingdom of Morocco?" (quoted in Parker 1987, 122). But then Hassan also suggested that a referendum was inapplicable because "the people do not want one" (quoted in *Africa Report,* May 1986, 57).

For the OAU, it did not matter whether King Hassan was sincere or not because both sides were finally speaking somewhat the same language. The 1981 OAU summit created an Implementation Committee to work out the modalities of the referendum, assigning Kenyan president Daniel arap Moi, Sierra Leonean president Siaka Probyn Stevens, and the former Wisemen from Guinea, Nigeria, Mali, and Tanzania. Yet Morocco's concessions did not elicit modesty from either Polisario or Algeria. Both continued to demand a full withdrawal of Moroccan forces and civilian administrators from the territory during the voting period. Polisario also wanted direct negotiations with Morocco before a cease-fire (which would imply Moroccan recognition of Polisario's legitimacy); that Moroccan settlers be confined to specific areas during the actual voting; the establishment of a provisional OAU–UN administration in cooperation with the RASD; international peace-keeping forces along the Moroccan–Western Sahara border; repatriation of all Sahrawis; three months between the cease-fire and the vote; and the liberation of all Sahrawi detainees. Outside of the Implementation Committee, Polisario and Algeria did tone down their demands for RASD's admittance into the OAU. But on the battlefield, Polisario smashed the Moroccan garrison at Galtah Zammur and downed several planes in the process in mid-October 1981.

The Implementation Committee met again in Nairobi in early February 1982, hearing from petitioners on all sides. It prepared afterward a more detailed outline of the settlement proposals and suggested the appointment of a commission, with Morocco and Polisario's agreement, to carry the plan forward.[1] Although the OAU itself was never able to put any aspect of this plan into effect, the plan itself became the framework for the subsequent UN effort.

Following the Implementation Committee meeting, OAU secretary-general Edem Kodjo unilaterally admitted RASD as the OAU's fifty-second member state on February 22, 1982, at a Council of Ministers sessions in Addis Ababa, Ethiopia. Kodjo argued that his move was consistent with Article 28 of the OAU's charter, given that a majority of member states had come to recognize RASD formally (King 1996, 166). Morocco and some other member states strongly criticized this move, charging that the OAU could not recognize a government not yet in full control of its territory, as stipulated under Article 27. Supporters of Kodjo's decision, however, noted how Guinea-Bissau was granted full membership a full year before the withdrawal of Portugal in 1974 (Hodges and Pazzanita 1994, 320). The Moroccan government's response was particularly fierce. Foreign Minister Boucetta declared that "[f]or us the Polisario does not exist either legally or internationally. We will never recognize the Polisario. There will be no withdrawal of Moroccan troops from our Saharan province, and there is no way that the Moroccan administration will leave the Western Sahara territory" (quoted in *New York Times,* Feb. 10, 1982). The Moroccans led a successful eighteen-member walkout that broke quorum and ended the February meeting early.

The OAU attempted to hold its 1982 summit in Tripoli, Lebanon, that August, but Morocco and its eighteen allies continued their boycott, again blocking quorum. The seriousness of the crisis, unrivaled in OAU history, threatened to tear it apart. Although the OAU had successfully weathered other storms, such as the dispute over recognition of the Angolan government in 1975 and 1976, certain elements of the Western Sahara controversy were unprecedented. It was the first time ever that the OAU had failed to convene, and the controversy included the accusation that a fellow African state was engaged in occupation and colonization.

The Algerian regime, recognizing the extent of the crisis, persuaded the RASD to withdraw "voluntarily and temporarily" from the OAU shortly before a second attempt was made to reconvene in Tripoli. The November summit failed as well, but this time because of a dispute between two sides claiming to represent the Chadian government. Egypt, Somalia, and Sudan did not want the meeting to take place either, as a means of denying Mu'ammar Qadhdhafi the OAU chairmanship. The Moroccan-led group was equally obstinate. Rather than face RASD on equal footing, King Hassan seemed perfectly willing to split apart the OAU. Following the collapse of the second Tripoli summit, Polisario no longer considered itself bound by its earlier agreement to stay out of the organization (Hodges and Pazzanita 1994, 322–23).

At an OAU-sponsored conference in December 1982, Senegal, the pro-Moroccan host government, refused to admit an RASD delegation, resulting in a walkout by Polisario's supporters. A subsequent OAU-sponsored conference in Zimbabwe, with the RASD in attendance, resulted in a boycott by the pro-Moroccan bloc (Mortimer 1982, 143). The RASD also tried to attend the June 1983 summit in Addis Ababa, Ethiopia, as a member state, yet the threat of another Moroccan-led boycott brought enough pressure on Polisario to sit out.

In order to keep up the pressure on King Hassan, the OAU passed Resolution 104. Most important, the resolution called on "the parties to the conflict, the Kingdom of Morocco and the Polisario Front, to undertake direct negotiations with a view to bringing about a cease-fire to create the necessary conditions for a peaceful and fair referendum for self-determination of the people of Western Sahara, a referendum without any administrative or military constraints, under the auspices of the Organization of African Unity and the United Nations" (OAU 1983). Widely seen as a consolation prize for Polisario, Resolution 104 not only named the independence movement as the other party to the dispute, but explicitly called for direct talks. The OAU also set up a second Wisemen Committee, including six of Africa's most respected heads of states from across the ideological and geographic spectrum (Sudan, Guinea, Senegal, Tanzania, Mali, and Sierra Leone) to facilitate face-to-face negotiations between Morocco and Polisario. Yet Hassan still refused to negotiate with Polisario.

As a result of the Moroccan government's noncooperation and with no more options available, the OAU resigned itself to seating the RASD at its next summit, held in Ethiopia in November 1984. Its support dwindling within the OAU, the Moroccan government did not attempt to organize another walkout but simply withdrew from the organization, the first and only country to do so. In a brief show of solidarity, Zaire joined Morocco's boycott for six months.

Since then, the RASD's membership has been a nonissue in the OAU and its successor organization, the African Union. RASD president Mohammed Abdelaziz was elected vice president of the OAU in 1985 and again in 1990 (Lippert 1991, 13), indicative of the support the RASD has received in the OAU. The RASD has more recently participated at the highest levels of the African Union and joined with a multicountry North African peacekeeping force. Morocco, meanwhile, has maintained its boycott and continued to call on the African Union to derecognize the RASD.

The OAU's efforts were laudable, but Western Sahara had stretched its limited political and material resources. Unlike the UN Charter, the OAU Charter lacked provisions allowing for it to compel cooperation or enforce resolutions. The Western Sahara episode demonstrated that the OAU had few carrots and weak sticks; the one threat it did have—recognition of the RASD—simply resulted in the Moroccan government's departure from the organization rather than its cooperation. Given the OAU's limited financial means to administer a referendum and dispatch a peacekeeping force, it had always expected the UN to provide the financial and human resources to implement such a project. Even if the OAU had been more successful and received Moroccan cooperation, it eventually would have had to partner with the UN anyway (Zunes, interview with OAU officials, New York, Jan. 1991).

## BACK TO THE UNITED NATIONS

Although the OAU had more direct involvement with the parties between 1976 and 1984, the Fourth Committee continued to follow the issue closely, and the General Assembly supported the OAU with encouraging resolutions. For example, Resolution 35/19, adopted in November 1980 by eighty-eight votes to eight, with forty-three abstentions, named "Morocco and the Frente Popular para la Liberación de Saguia el-Hamra y Río de Oro, representative of the people of Western Sahara" as the parties to the dispute (UN 1983, 1100). As one observer later noted, by 1981 "[s]ome states (including Nigeria) [had] lost patience with Rabat's familiar tactic of shifting the Sahara problem from the UN back to the OAU and then ignoring OAU decisions and mediation attempts" (Damis 1984, 278). Resolution 35/19 was a firm reminder to Morocco that it would have to confront reality in one venue or another.

A year after Morocco quit the OAU, UN secretary-general Javier Pérez de Cuéllar took on the issue, visiting Morocco and attending the OAU summit in Addis Ababa in 1985. He followed these acts with an attempt to hold proximity talks in New York in April 1986, but Morocco refused to attend with the OAU present. So Pérez de Cuéllar visited Morocco in July, alone. It was there that King Hassan reportedly recommitted himself to a UN-organized referendum "without administrative or military constraints" (Pérez de Cuéllar 1997, 338). Polisario, however, remained recalcitrant, demanding direct negotiations. When Pérez de Cuéllar proposed sending a UN technical mission to Western Sahara to explore the feasibility of a referendum, Polisario withheld its commitment to a cease-fire in order to make sure that the mission's composition was neutral, thus forcing the secretary-general to meet with Polisario's leader, Mohammed Abdelaziz, in Geneva to secure support.

The technical mission finally visited Western Sahara at the end of November 1987. Although the UN never released its report, the mission reportedly noted "the almost total lack of facilities in the territory, the wide dispersal of the population and the severe problems that were likely to be encountered in monitoring a cease-fire" (Pérez de Cuéllar 1997, 339). The report informed the subsequent "Proposals of a Settlement of the Question of the Western Sahara," drafted in secret by a special assistant to Pérez de Cuéllar, Issa Diallo from Guinea. The proposals outlined a settlement plan based on the OAU Implementation Committee's framework. First, the secretary-general would declare a cease-fire once the Moroccan government had significantly reduced its troops in the territory; remaining Moroccan and Polisario forces would be cantoned and monitored by UN military observers; a special representative appointed by the secretary-general, vested with authority over all matters relating to the referendum, would be aided by a police unit; the 1974 Spanish census and a UNHCR census in the Tindouf refugee camps would be used as the basis for establishing the electorate; the UNHCR would also facilitate the eventual return of Sahrawi refugees from Algeria to Western Sahara; finally, the vote would offer all Western Saharans, eighteen years of age and older, the choice of either independence or formal integration with Morocco (Goulding 2002, 200).

Morocco and Polisario officially saw the finalized proposals in August 1988, although King Hassan and Algeria's president Bendjedid had been privy to a draft version months earlier, brought to them by Pérez de Cuéllar personally. Among his many concerns, King Hassan portentously emphasized was that it would be difficult to determine who should be allowed to vote. The secretary-general suggested that King Hassan should consider a third option for the referendum: the Western Saharans could choose to live under Moroccan sovereignty with significant autonomy. The king seemingly rejected this idea outright, claiming that it would inspire other regions in Morocco to press for autonomy as well. In Algiers, Bendjedid had expressed fears that the Moroccan government would find a way to "win" the referendum and so apparently agreed that autonomy might be a good compromise. Although autonomy was not included in the finalized proposals, Pérez de Cuéllar's memoirs reveal a growing premonition that the referendum's winner-take-all approach—independence or integration—would not elicit the most cooperative and compromising behavior from either side. He even recognized that King Hassan had warned him about the voter-identification issue, "perhaps on the basis of his own intentions" (1997, 341–42). The secretary-general had set September 1, 1988, as his deadline for Morocco and Polisario to accept the proposals, which both did "in principle."

As one prominent theorist of conflict resolution notes, "A combination of several changes is generally needed to bring about the transition into a de-escalation movement, particularly for protracted conflicts" (Kriesberg 1998, 198). In the case of Western Sahara, a number of new conditions contributed to deescalation, however belated. First, with the decline of the Cold War, there was an increasing international consensus to put these regional fires out finally. Another factor was the process of reconciliation in the Maghrib, later codified in the UMA, which was as much influenced by the end of the Cold War as by the concurrent economic crisis following the global hydrocarbon price collapse in 1985–86, which hit Algeria particularly hard. Finally, there was the OAU's perseverance, followed by Pérez de Cuéllar's efforts. For Polisario, which bore in mind that it could no longer force a Moroccan withdrawal militarily, a UN referendum on independence was a second-best option, despite reservations about Morocco's and the Security Council's willingness to bring about the referendum. For King Hassan, any further diplomatic isolation would raise the possibility of the UN's adopting the referendum proposal anyway. A cessation of hostilities would also lower the costs of the occupation. By cooperating with the UN, Morocco could also rebuild its international credibility and retard recognition of RASD by more states. However, both Morocco's and Polisario's reticence to endorse the plan wholeheartedly hinted at the toxic atmosphere of mistrust hanging over the peace process. As one prominent African diplomat put it at the time, "Both parties are serious about this agreement since they are tired of war, but both have a hidden agenda if the referendum doesn't go their way" (Zunes, notes on UN briefing, New York, Jan. 1991).

In September 1988, the secretary-general informed the Security Council that both sides had accepted the proposals "in principle" with minimal "remarks and comments" (Goulding 2002, 201). In reality, both sides had presented the secretary-general with a litany of concerns that were kept secret. Although the proposals' specifics were not presented to the Security Council until 1990, the council approved of the progress and allowed for the appointment of the first special representative to Western Sahara, Hector Gros Espiell, a Uruguayan lawyer. Unlike for any other UN mission, the special representative for Western Sahara worked directly with the secretary-general, cutting the two key UN departments—political affairs and peacekeeping—out of the loop. Not only was Pérez de Cuéllar keeping his cards close to his chest, but he was also withholding vital information from some of the UN officials designing the referendum mission. His attitude toward the conflict was also largely at odds with the international community's attitude. Where the OAU and UN resolutions had named Morocco and Polisario the parties to the conflict, Pérez de Cuéllar personally considered the Algerian government a much more important player than Polisario. Over the course of his four-year effort to settle the Western Sahara conflict, he held 132 talks with Moroccan officials: 128 with Algerian officials, yet only 33 with Polisario representatives. "I repeatedly found," he later claimed, "that the best way to obtain greater flexibility from POLISARIO was through President Chadli [Bendjedid of Algeria] or members of his government." King Hassan, Pérez de Cuéllar felt, was "extremely shrewd," "highly cultivated with a quick intelligence," and "of elegant expression and great courtesy." President Bendjedid was "reasonable and helpful," "genuinely committed to the concept of a peaceful community of Maghreb states," and "clearly not motivated by personal hostility towards King Hassan." In contrast, Polisario head Mohammed Abdelaziz "was a very different sort" whose apparent inability to speak Spanish, for a "man who pretends to be the leader of what was formerly the Spanish Sahara," perturbed Pérez de Cuéllar (1997, 338–43). In his heart, the secretary-general was already convinced that independence was not in Western Sahara's best interests, a revelation that later came as a shock to Polisario officials who had worked with him (Jensen 2005, 42). Although the UN Secretariat's influence rested in its claim to neutrality, this was far from the case in Western Sahara, as demonstrated by both Waldheim's and Pérez de Cuéllar's activities. And there was more to come.

In the UN Secretariat, the Task Force for Western Sahara, charged with planning the referendum, soon became aware of the irreconcilable caveats Pérez de Cuéllar had hidden. During further technical discussions with the parties on the 1988 proposals, UN Peacekeeping Department head Marrack Goulding wondered whether "the two sides had been shown the same document" or not (2002, 202). Desiring progress above all else, Diallo carefully controlled what the taskforce knew, never allowing its members to contact either Morocco or Polisario for clarification (Jensen 2005, 39). This control of information, in turn, led the taskforce to create excessively optimistic proposals and timelines. Without the two parties' commitment to the same uniform document, it was impossible to hold either party accountable, so either side could interpret the proposals to its advantage and hold up the process when it felt things were not going its way. Pérez de Cuéllar, however, described the proposals as "a delicate balance of essential elements and a compromise aimed at promoting a just and definitive solution to the question of the Western Sahara" (*UN Chronicle,* Mar. 1989). Yet by sacrificing transparency and consent in the name of expediency, the UN would soon find that the "delicate balance" of the settlement proposals would have to be constantly modified.

The peace process received a small boost in early 1989 when King Hassan, under increasing pressure from Saudi Arabia and some other allies, met Polisario face to face. In the course of the brief January meeting in Marrakech, King Hassan sat down with key members of Polisario's historical leadership, Bachir Mustapha Sayed, Mahfoud Ali Beiba, and Ibrahim Ghali. By all accounts, the talks were brief, and subsequent statements ruined prospects for future meetings. The Sahrawi delegation, however, declared that the meeting constituted official Moroccan recognition of Polisario as the legitimate representative of the Western Saharans. King Hassan insisted that these talks were discussions only, not negotiations, with no more than renegade Moroccans (Zoubir 1996, 200–201). Despite Algerian hopes, it appeared that the restoration of formal diplomatic relations between Algiers and Rabat in May 1988 had not lent to a speedy settlement of the Western Sahara issue. Just prior to a trip to Spain in September 1989, Hassan reneged on a promise to Algeria to resume talks with Polisario, saying "there is nothing to negotiate because Western Sahara is Moroccan territory" (quoted in Zoubir 1990a, 29).

The failure of high-level direct negotiations also led Polisario to abandon its unilateral cease-fire. Polisario had warned that its commitment to cantoning its forces for the referendum was conditioned on the Moroccan regime's willingness to talk face to face. Following the January meeting, Polisario forces launched a series of attacks against Moroccan forces along the defensive barrier. These attacks not only served as a reminder that Polisario could still fight, but were an implicit Algerian message to Morocco. Between September and November 1989, Polisario continued to mount intense assaults against Moroccan positions in the regions of Galtah Zammur, Hawzah, and Amgala, reportedly inflicting serious casualties and material losses on FAR. In response, the Moroccan government attempted to obtain additional weaponry from the United States. In February 1989, the George H. W. Bush administration announced that it was considering a Moroccan request for the sale of twenty-four (two full squadrons) of advanced F-16 fighter-bombers. In addition, in March 1990 the White House indicated that it might sell Morocco some of the M-60 tanks it planned to remove from western Europe as part of agreed force reductions between NATO and the Warsaw Pact (*Washington Post,* Mar. 1, 1990). With the war heating up again, there was increased pressure on the UN Secretariat to achieve results.

THE SETTLEMENT PLAN

Several months after the failed Morocco–Polisario talks of January 1989, Pérez de Cuéllar visited Algeria, Mauritania, Morocco, and Mali (then chairing the OAU) in June 1989. With the track-one negotiations in shambles, the secretary-general tried to stoke the behind-the-scenes efforts. The UN Secretariat established a technical commission to work out the "terms, ways and means of carrying out the peace proposals" that had been agreed to "in principle" in 1988 (*UN Chronicle,* Sept. 1989, 25). The technical commission first met on July 12, 1989, and included representatives from Polisario and Morocco. While the proposals were being hammered out, two issues surfaced as the most contentious: the number of Moroccan troops to be withdrawn and the process of voter identification for the referendum. Work and discussion at the technical level proceeded over the course of the year, primed by Pérez de Cuéllar's March 1990 visit to North Africa with his new special representative to Western Sahara, Johannes Manz, a respected Swiss diplomat.

The secretary-general finally unveiled his revised settlement proposals to the Security Council on June 13, 1990. The plan detailed the role of the UN special representative, the arrangements for a cease-fire, the guidelines for the referendum (including voter-identification procedures), the exchange of political prisoners and POWs, and the return of the refugees to the territory. It confidently estimated that the entire process would take only thirty-five weeks. An Identification Commission would handle voter applications and screening process. The "Identification Commission," the secretary-general explained, "will implement the agreed position of the parties that all Western Saharans counted in the 1974 census undertaken by the Spanish authorities and aged 18 years or over will have the right to vote" (UN Secretary-General 1975–2007, doc. S/21360, para. 61). The Security Council approved the Secretariat's work and unanimously passed Resolution 658 that June. The council called for a more detailed report, asked for the parties' continuing cooperation, and welcomed the secretary-general's plans to send a technical mission to the region in the near future. The council had no idea that it was being kept in the dark.

With the publication of the secretary-general's June 1990 report, the UN settlement proposals were finally in the public domain. Both Morocco and Polisario launched vehement critiques. King Hassan sent a personal letter to the secretary-general enumerating Morocco's reservations, specifically the issues of voter enfranchisement and the question of independence. The Moroccan regime had long argued that the last Spanish census had failed to take into account the Western Saharan diaspora (e.g., the significant number of Western Saharans who had sought refuge inside Moroccan territory during the joint Franco–Spanish counterinsurgency operations of 1957–58). Furthermore, Hassan still wanted the question of independence to be suppressed. He proposed that voters could either accept or reject Moroccan nationality.

Although UN Peacekeeping Department head Goulding had helped brief both sides on the plan, he was never made privy to Hassan's letter, nor was the taskforce. The Secretariat's Peacekeeping Department had already moved forward on a finalized plan, meeting with representatives of the Moroccan government and Polisario met in Geneva in early July. At the same time in Geneva, respected Sahrawi leaders and elders (shaykhs) worked with the UN to revise the 1974 Spanish census and bring it up to date. A UN technical mission, called for in the 1990 Security Council resolution, visited the region later that month.

To the surprise of many in the Secretariat, Hassan's letter was published in the Moroccan press in October 1990 (Jensen 2005, 40). Polisario had also raised numerous issues and concerns, yet only Diallo and the secretary-general knew about them (Goulding 2002, 203–4; Jensen 2005, 40). For example, Polisario sent a private letter to the secretary-general in August 1990 in which it reiterated its demand for a total Moroccan withdrawal so that Western Sahara could be placed under UN trusteeship for the referendum. Polisario also presciently requested that the UN seal off Western Sahara to prevent Morocco from creating any additional facts on the ground by bringing in new settlers.

Having been sidetracked by the Iraqi occupation of Kuwait and the U.S.-led war that followed, the UN Secretariat could pay little attention to Western Sahara until the spring of 1991. A finalized plan was presented to the Security Council prematurely on April 19, 1991. Yet it continued to use, against Morocco's expressed concerns, the 1974 Spanish census as the sole criteria for voter enfranchisement and called for substantial Moroccan troop reductions, although not a total withdrawal and no UN trusteeship as Polisario had requested. Indeed, it seemed that Polisario's forces would face tougher restrictions than

Moroccan troops. The Moroccans had stated a need to maintain a military presence to protect the referendum process from Polisario attacks. This claim had apparently found a sympathetic audience, underscored by the South West Africa People's Organization's attempted military infiltration on the eve of Namibia's referendum. Whether unaware of or indifferent to the objections presented by Morocco and Polisario, the Security Council in its Resolution 690 called into being on April 29, 1991, the UN Mission for the Referendum in Western Sahara, given the pronounceable acronym MINURSO from the French name Mission des Nations Unies pour l'organisation d'un référendum au Sahara Occidental. The Security Council, grappling with a host of higher-priority issues, believed that it had both parties' full consent to the finalized plan, but this was not the case, and Pérez de Cuéllar apparently did nothing to assuage this misconception (see *Middle East International*, June 28, 1991).

The Security Council's major concern, especially for the five permanent members (China, Russia, France, Great Britain, and the United States), was not so much consent but cost. The Task Force for Western Sahara constantly worked to reduce MINURSO's price tag, mostly by shortening the operation's expected life span. The council's concern largely stemmed from escalating UN peacekeeping costs in Namibia, Central America, Afghanistan, and Cambodia, as well as UN involvement in the Middle East after the Gulf War. Some suspected that the United States, traditionally the largest donor to such operations, was dragging its feet on the budget in order to help Morocco, although other observers thought it was just the normal U.S. recalcitrance regarding a UN operation it did not control. Originally budgeted at $260 million for the thirty-six-week operation, MINURSO was whittled down to a final budget of $177 million, mostly by outsourcing the refugee aspects to the UNHCR (Durch 1993b, 419).

When the Security Council authorized the creation of MINURSO, the original blueprint described a process set to conclude within forty-six weeks. According to the overly optimistic, cash-starved timetable, the secretary-general, with the parties' consent, would set a "D-Day"—the date of the cease-fire and the beginning of the "transitional period"—twelve weeks before the referendum. On D-Day, MINURSO's special representative would assume authority over all matters relating to the referendum in the territory and control of a full complement of military observers, police, and administrative personnel at her disposal. Shortly after the commencement of the transitional period, Morocco and Polisario would exchange POWs and political prisoners. Within eleven weeks after D-Day, Morocco would reduce its occupation forces from one hundred thousand to sixty-five thousand, including the neutralization of "paramilitary units in the existing [Moroccan] police forces." Voter identification would be completed by this time, and a UNHCR-supervised refugee repatriation program would commence, to be completed by the beginning of the referendum campaign, seventeen weeks after D-Day. The referendum itself would take place on D-Day plus twenty weeks. After the announcement of results, within seventy-two hours of voting, MINURSO would begin a six-week phase-out. If the vote favored independence, Morocco would withdraw, and if the vote favored integration, Polisario would disband (see UN Secretary-General 1975–2007, doc. S/22464).

In order to cut costs, the Secretariat's taskforce planned to have MINURSO complete several preliminary aspects before the official implementation of the cease-fire and transitional period, especially the drafting of the voter list by MINURSO's Identification Commission. Before D-Day, the UN Identification Commission would finish updating the 1974 Spanish census, Morocco would collect voter applications for the occupied Western Sahara, and Polisario would collect them for the refugee camps. The Identification Commission would then announce the rules for the voter vetting process, including the grounds for appeals. Following D-Day, it would publish the list of persons that MINURSO had predetermined were eligible to vote and who would then be personally interviewed to assure their authenticity. The new plan also noted that persons not on the initial list of eligible voters could petition for inclusion on the grounds that they were omitted from the 1974 census. Although this clarification of the identification process obviously sought to accommodate the Moroccan concerns, it did not offer any way for a petitioner to prove Western Saharan ancestry outside of the 1974 census. Indeed, defining and identifying native Western Saharans would consume MINURSO's energy for the next nine years.

Still unhappy with the plan, Polisario officials felt that, relative to prior decolonization plebiscites, this proposal clearly favored the occupier. They were extremely concerned about security arrangements during the vote, given that only around seventeen hundred UN peacekeepers would be tasked to keep sixty-five thousand Moroccan soldiers in check. Although most of the voting would take place in a few population centers, making monitoring easier, this setup would also make it easier for Morocco to target nationalist Sahrawis returning from the camps. By contrasting Namibian referendum, for example, South African troops had been withdrawn prior to the vote. However, unlike Namibia, where the colonizing party had already consented to independence, much more was at stake in Western Sahara, and so there was even more need for a drastic Moroccan withdrawal and a stronger UN force. The UN learned this lesson the hard way in 1999, when it allowed Indonesian occupation forces to remain in East Timor during that country's 1999 referendum, which made possible the series of massacres and widespread destruction of that island's national infrastructure by Indonesian-backed anti-independence militias.

Furthermore, important logistical roles were given to Morocco (e.g., access to ports and mission supplies), which Polisario had hoped to be under the control of Spain, the UN, or another more neutral body. Moroccan administrators would stay in place, however, leaving open the possibility of the continued presence of secret police. Indeed, never before had the UN given an occupier's armed forces such freedom prior to and during a plebiscite. The UN plan called for the release of political prisoners, detainees, and POWs, although no provision was made to try to locate the hundreds of "disappeared" Sahrawis. Nor did the UN plan guarantee independent observers or press coverage. The UN indicated that only a limited number of independent observers should be allowed in the territory. It seemed highly irregular that the people monitoring the vote would be the same people organizing it.[2]

Citing the elections during the transition period from white minority rule in Rhodesia to an independent Zimbabwe, which involved a brief return to British colonial administration, Polisario suggested that Western Sahara temporarily revert to Spanish administration during this period, given the illegality of the 1975 Madrid Agreement. Although a strong legal and practical case could be made for the establishment of a neutral transitional administration, obtaining the Moroccan government's consent would have been impossible. There was little support within the regime and domestically throughout the country for the referendum. Indeed, all the major political parties condemned the proposed referendum as "meaningless" (Foreign Broadcasting and Information Service, Aug. 14, 1991).

Knowing that France and the United States would prevent the Security Council from forcing anything on Morocco, Pérez de Cuéllar surmised that a referendum on independence in Western Sahara would have to be on terms that Morocco would accept. So there was some surprise that Hassan had accepted such a plan, even "in principle." Speculation regarding this decision centered on his need to put the conflict behind him because he was more and more concerned about succession, the scale of popular discontent from the deterioration of the social and economic situation in the country, and the desire to take advantage of Polisario's recent internal problems and high-level defections. In addition, King Hassan was sensitive to pressure from the international community and was concerned about Morocco's declining usefulness to the West (the lessening need for proxies after the Cold War), Rabat's decreasing role as an intermediary in Israeli–Arab negotiations, and the reduced support from Morocco's financial supporters. However, Hassan did not walk blindly into the vote. He and Interior Minister Driss Basri had a clear strategy to win the referendum.

As the weaker party, Polisario recognized that it would have to compromise in order for the referendum to take place at all. Nonetheless, it easily adapted guerilla warfare tactics to politics. Again and again using timing and tactical concessions, it would turn apparent diplomatic defeat into political gain. Although some elements of the Western Saharan independence movement were skeptical about Morocco's intentions and thus reticent to lay down arms, others believed that the 1991 Settlement Plan represented an international intervention on their behalf. There were widespread celebrations in the refugee camps upon the creation of MINURSO, and Polisario officials worldwide were feeling upbeat and very optimistic. Many nationalists believed it was only a matter of months before a new flag would be flying in al-'Ayun. Unfortunately, this naïveté, fueled by the secretary-general's false promises, had humanitarian implications. Polisario, assuming that the camps would be largely empty by 1992, planned and allocated its resources for moving the refugees for the vote. Only a little more than half the normal annual food requirement was thus assured, and the camps' supplementary gardens were not replanted. After a few months of hardship, when it was clear that the referendum was on hold, these shortfalls were corrected in mid-1992 (Bunch, Chandrani, and Smith 1992).

BEGINNING OF THE ENDGAME?

The end of armed hostilities in Western Sahara did not result from a peace agreement, but ironically from the lack of one. Although the Security Council had backed the Settlement Plan and inaugurated MINURSO in April 1991, these moves were made without formal agreement between the parties. Indeed, during the summer of 1991, as the UN Secretariat pushed toward implementation, military tensions between Morocco and Polisario escalated. The Moroccan government had demanded a full withdrawal of Polisario forces to Tindouf, yet the ELPS refused to abandon its bases in the areas of Western Sahara east of the defensive wall. Furthermore, Polisario began setting up more visible bases in the major settlements on its side of Western Sahara. In August 1991, Morocco's forces launched attacks beyond the berms, notably at Polisario/RASD facilities at Bir Lahlu and Tifariti, mainly former colonial buildings that Polisario had set aside for UN peacekeepers (Hodges and Pazzanita 1994, 617–18). With military tensions increasing, the situation was getting out of control.

Instead of determining a D-Day with the consent of the parties trilaterally, as called for by the Security Council under the Settlement Plan, Pérez de Cuéllar brokered a bilateral deal with the Moroccan government. Without consulting Polisario, the Secretariat announced that a cease-fire would come into effect on September 6, 1991, immediately followed by the deployment of 240 "blue helmets" to monitor the cessation of hostilities. However, Pérez de Cuéllar had separated the cease-fire from the rest of Settlement Plan, which had yet to receive full backing from either Morocco or Polisario. Likewise, the secretary-general had single-handedly thrown the Security Council–approved timetable out the window. For Polisario, the choices were to reject the armistice and appear the spoiler or to respect it. Polisario chose the latter. But what little leverage the Secretariat had over the parties was spent because it had been based on incentives offered against a mutually frustrating military stalemate. Decoupling the cease-fire from the Settlement Plan was Pérez de Cuéllar's last and most costly mistake.

Although changed global, regional, and local conditions had resulted in deescalation, the intractability of the military situation had not engendered a willingness to make the concessions necessary for peace. Such willingness—clearly absent from Western Sahara in 1991—would have resulted from a situation that is both intractable and unsustainable. As we argued in chapter 1, by the late 1980s the war in Western Sahara had become indefinitely sustainable yet forever unwinnable for both sides. Polisario could not wage a war of a successful attrition. Still, there was a widespread belief within the Western Sahara independence movement that the war had worn down Morocco and finally brought it to the table. In truth, the war ended with Morocco holding the dominant military position. Yet the war was sustainable for Polisario as long as there were Sahrawis willing to fight it. To its credit, the UN intervention had induced "constructive de-escalation strategies" (Kriesberg 1998, 215) but in doing so had simply shifted the terrain of struggle by offering a settlement proposal that would exacerbate, rather than address, the fundamental causes of the conflict.

Although the war was not easy for Morocco in the beginning, outside financial and military support from France, the United States, and Saudi Arabia made it easier to prosecute by the mid-1980s. Yet even if Moroccan forces had expanded the berms to encompass all of the territory or been willing to strike into Algeria to smash Polisario (triggering a war with Algeria), neither action would do anything to vanquish the specter of Western Saharan nationalism. Morocco had erased Polisario's military gains in the late 1970s and put an advantageous stalemate into effect, so the only thing it lacked was international recognition of its attempted annexation. With backing from France and the United States, among other allies, it easily weathered diplomatic isolation in Africa and the UN. Although the prospect of an eternal thorn stuck in its side by its regional rival seemed unpleasant, it would be a small price to pay for de facto control. Because neither Morocco nor Polisario faced an existential threat to its interests, the situation was one of sustainable intractability.

Pérez de Cuéllar had not offered Polisario and Morocco an agreement that forced them to compromise their mutually exclusive objectives. On the table was an alternative approach to winning Western Sahara, one that did not require military losses. For members of the Western Saharan independence movement, the UN was finally offering them their right to self-determination, which they firmly believed would lead to victory. For the Moroccan regime, the UN was offering a way to receive the international imprimatur on its annexation of Western Sahara. Although the conflict had induced—and would continue to induce—Morocco and Polisario to make minor concessions, these concessions were the diplomatic equivalent of tactical retreats. Neither side was motivated to sacrifice its maximal goals.

The 1991 Settlement Plan was not a plan for peace, but simply war by other means. Pérez de Cuéllar justified his approach—which critics within and outside the UN have seen as secretive, manipulative, and deceptive—on the grounds that talking was better than fighting. Yet in the course of the UN peace process since 1991, including the abandonment of the original referendum in 2000 and Baker's resignation in 2004, the parties' mutual mistrust and animosity have only increased. The UN's credibility with those who matter most, the people of Western Sahara, has been severely compromised. In 1992, most Western Saharans greeted MINURSO as liberators. Before long, however, they began to see it as an accessory to occupation.

# 8

# The Abandoned Referendum

In the 1990s, the war for Western Sahara became a demographic struggle. Ballots, not bullets, would determine the victor. Controlling the composition of the UN referendum's electorate—qualitatively and quantitatively—was key. Polisario originally wanted only Western Saharans listed on the 1974 Spanish census and their direct descendants to vote. A vote limited to persons of indubitable Western Saharan origin, Polisario has always believed, would favor independence. Polisario also feared, however, that Morocco would exploit any attempt to go beyond the 1974 census and rig the vote by enfranchising voters with little or no ties, whether ethnic or territorial, to Western Sahara. Morocco indeed argued that relying on the 1974 census would disenfranchise native Western Saharans who had escaped repression and economic hardship during late Spanish colonialism. The biographies of several founding members of Polisario backed Morocco's claim. Rabat's motivation, however, was far from principled. As Polisario expected, Morocco flooded the voter-identification process with thousands of unexpected applicants. King Hassan's right-hand man, Interior Minister Driss Basri, had been put in charge of managing Morocco's effort to win the Western Saharan referendum. Indeed, fixing elections and referenda in Morocco was Basri's main job (see chapter 2).

The 1974 census registered 73,497 Sahrawis in the Spanish colony.[1] Several former Spanish colonial officials disputed the Moroccan claim that tens of thousands of Western Saharans fled to southern Morocco during the late colonial period, whereas others felt the 1974 count was far from comprehensive. Spain's most intensive demographic studies in 1942 and 1967, which measured the population before and after the 1957–58 conflict, revealed an insignificant change in the native population of Western Sahara (Chopra 1994, 78). Official documents show the demographic trends from 1955 to 1974:

1955: 24,563
1957: 17,525
1959: 18,912
1960: 18,489
1961: 16,929
1962: 16,353
1963: 33,439

1964: 37,356

1966: 33,512

1967: 46,558

1970: 59,777

1972: 68,697

1974: 73,497 / 74,902 (Aguirre, 1988: 603)

Assuming that all these figures are somewhat accurate, we can see a discernable drop in the population between 1955 and 1957, nearly 30 percent. This drop might support Morocco's thesis. However, the doubling of the population from 1962 to 1963 suggests that either many refugees returned or there was a more accurate count. This period saw increasing amounts of enticed and forced sedentarization by the colonial administration, which—combined with prolonged drought conditions—motivated many nomadic Sahrawis to move to the cities, where they were much easier to count. This startling increase might also explain why the 1942 and 1967 census did not support an exodus on the order claimed by the Moroccan government. It is also possible that Spain's methodologies were seriously flawed. Critics charged that the Spaniards focused on Western Saharans in or near the major cities, as revealed in the incredibly high level of recorded sedentarization (Pazzanita 2006, 350). A 1954 survey used a count of tents rather than a headcount (Damis 1983, 8).

One of the goals of a 1975 UN General Assembly Visiting Mission was to arrive at a reliable figure of native Western Saharans residing outside the territory. Spanish authorities believed that 3,000 to 4,000 native Western Saharans were then living in southern Morocco, and another 4,000 to 5,000 were living in Mauritania, but no more than 9,000 total. The Moroccan government, however, claimed that upward of 30,000 to 35,000 Sahrawi refugees from Spanish Sahara lived in southern Morocco. Algeria claimed that no more than 7,000 native Western Saharans resided on its soil. Ironically, Polisario gave the highest figure, claiming there were at least 50,000 "political refugees and exiles" living in neighboring states in 1975. Early in its history, Polisario often exaggerated Western Sahara's potential population. In 1975, the two-year-old liberation movement told the General Assembly Visiting Mission that there were 750,000 Western Saharans by "historical association with the Territory" (UN General Assembly 1977, par. 156).

By the end of this effort, it became apparent that Polisario's fears were well founded. Morocco, under false pretenses, presented thousands of its own citizens as native Western Saharans—both Arabs and Berbers in addition to ethnic Sahrawis of non–Western Saharan origin. In late 1999, MINURSO arrived at an electorate of 86,386 voters for Western Sahara's long overdue shot at self-determination. Out of the 244,643 applications the UN mission received, the vast majority was either fielded from Morocco proper (99,225) or from the Moroccan-occupied Western Sahara (83,971). Together, this majority was more than double the 72,370 names on MINURSO's updated version of the 1974 Spanish census and more than four times the number of applications sponsored by Polisario from the refugee camps (42,337). Out of the candidates from Morocco proper, only 5 percent qualified to vote, and a little less than half of Moroccan-sponsored candidates from the occupied Western Sahara qualified to vote. Surprisingly, the UN mission arrived at this result despite the fact that the criteria and procedures for vetting applicants were crafted—and recrafted—to obtain Morocco's cooperation.

Critics of Polisario often claimed that the liberation movement repeatedly held up the identification process for little or no reason (e.g., Theofilopoulou 2006, 4). In retrospect, however, it is clear that Morocco was the party that undermined the spirit of the vote. Polisario's "obstructionism" was warranted from the perspective of international law, even if it seemed obstinate from a "realist" perspective. Derision should have been aimed at the UN Secretariat and Security Council for being so indifferent to Morocco's efforts to pollute the electorate.

As much as elements of the UN leadership tolerated Morocco's behavior, they expected it. Neither the three secretaries-general during the referendum process nor Baker believed that Morocco would actually allow an honest vote on independence, so hopes were placed on the instrumental value of referendum *as a threat* rather than on the referendum itself. It was thus doubly sad, from both a realist perspective and a liberal-idealist perspective, when the UN Secretariat and Security Council abandoned the referendum in early 2000 without even exploiting the UN's coercive potential. At that time, in the shadow of East Timor's referendum massacres and the recent death of King Hassan, the veto-wielding French and American governments were convinced that Morocco should not be forced to accept self-determination in Western Sahara—a vote Rabat would not win. How and why the proposed UN referendum in Western Sahara was never allowed to take place is the subject of this chapter.

BLUE HELMETS IN WESTERN SAHARA

The UN was created to "save succeeding generations from the scourge of war." In an effort to meet this challenge, the UN has developed and continues to refine a set of practices for the prevention and resolution of conflict. As early as 1947, it sent military observers to Greece, and then in June 1948 it dispatched the Truce Supervision Organization to Palestine. In subsequent years, the UN engaged in several other operations, including missions to Kashmir (1949), Sinai (1956), Congo (1960), West New Guinea (1962), Cyprus (1964), the Golan Heights (1973), southern Lebanon (1978), Iran–Iraq (1988), Afghanistan (1988), Angola (1989), and Namibia (1989).

The UN's overall performance in preventing wars in the second half of the twentieth century and even in the early twenty-first has been checkered, through little fault of its own. Blame clearly falls on the shoulders of its constituent member states, especially the

Security Council's five permanent members, who wield—and sheath—its coercive powers, often hypocritically. During the Cold War, the U.S.–Soviet rivalry greatly limited the UN's capacity. That global political battle, so visible in the jungles of Vietnam and the mountains of Afghanistan, was also waged in the chambers of the Security Council. Western Sahara is an acknowledged victim. However, with the easing of Cold War tensions in the 1980s, the UN became involved in an increasing number of peacekeeping missions. Naive observers foretold a new era when the UN would become a true force for peace. The success of the 1991 UN-authorized coalition's liberation of Kuwait from Iraqi occupation helped fuel this newfound optimism. A peace agreement in Central America and the referendum polling hundreds of thousands of Namibians made Western Sahara seem simple by comparison.[2]

However, by the end of 1991 almost every aspect of the new UN mission in Western Sahara was politicized. Even the initial, partial deployment of UN personnel was more difficult than anticipated. Shortly after the cease-fire, the Moroccan government began to create roadblocks in front of MINURSO's deployment, literally and metaphorically. At the port of Agadir, Morocco refused to allow UN-chartered supply ships to unload vehicles, prefabricated dwellings, and other material for the peacekeepers (*Christian Science Monitor,* Aug. 26, 1991; *Los Angeles Times,* Mar. 7, 1992). The Identification Commission did not have free access to Western Sahara, and a number of foreign visitors—including journalists, the president of the European Parliament's Commission on Development and Cooperation, and representatives of the International Committee of the Red Cross and the UNHCR—were denied entry. There were widespread reports of harassment of journalists and MINURSO personnel by Moroccan authorities, including threats to fire on peacekeeping patrols and the physical obstruction of UN vehicles. Morocco refused to reduce or canton its forces or even to provide MINURSO with force size and location information, prompting Polisario to do the same (see Durch 1993b, 427–29).

Soon after the cease-fire, Moroccan authorities informed the population of Western Sahara that they were forbidden from making contact with any foreigners, including journalists or members of MINURSO (*Washington Report on Middle East Affairs,* Aug. 1992). As a *New York Times* reporter wrote from al-'Ayun, "In truth, surveillance is so intense that it is hard to know what the 100,000 or so people in this desert outpost really think about the referendum" (Feb. 23, 1992). One MINURSO observer force member, who had also served in Latin America and Asia, claimed that Moroccan-occupied Western Sahara was "the worst police state I have ever seen" (*Washington Post,* Mar. 14, 1992).

The initial UN peacekeeping force, with personnel from all five permanent members of the Security Council, reported poor living conditions, shortages of food, water, and medicine, and an absence of accurate maps of minefields. The result was that UN forces put the bulk of their time into addressing logistical and infrastructure needs rather than into monitoring Morocco and Polisario forces. On its side of the berm, Morocco monitored the monitors, restricting their movements, flying over UN posts, withholding vital supplies at the ports, and even threatening MINURSO personnel at gunpoint. According to a field report commissioned by the U.S. Senate Committee on Foreign Relations, "When asked to explain their difficult situation, the U.N. soldiers respond that they see two sources of their problems: the government of Morocco and the UN hierarchy in New York," which seemed unwilling "to pressure the government of Morocco to cooperate more fully with the peacekeeping operation" (U.S. Senate 1992b, 9). Conversely, UN forces on the other side of the berm were generally satisfied with Polisario's level of cooperation in assisting with logistical matters, providing basic shelters for the first of the UN troops, and providing them with maps of mined areas. Canadian general Armand Roy, the original commander of MINURSO's military unit, praised Polisario's cooperation, saying that it had enabled MINURSO to "establish a climate of trust" (quoted in De Froberville 1992, 13). The same U.S. Senate field report had reached a similar conclusion: UN peacekeepers in Western Sahara reported "Moroccan interference in nearly every sphere of MINURSO's activities. In contrast, the soldiers in the field until recently received a great deal of cooperation and assistance from Polisario" (U.S. Senate 1992b, 9).

BLOOD AND LAND

Following the Security Council's creation of MINURSO in April 1991, Morocco presented a list, compiled by its Interior Ministry, of more than 120,000 additional "Western Saharans" to be added to the updated 1974 Spanish census. The Moroccan government demanded that the UN add all these voters to its revised list without prejudice. Polisario rejected this demand outright, arguing that it had agreed only to allow *individuals* to petition for inclusion. If the Identification Commission took all 120,000 applicants seriously, it would add months, if not years, to MINURSO's timetable. The Identification Commission had budgeted for, at most, 10,000 additional petitioners outside of the revised 1974 census (Bolton 1998; Jensen 2005, 74; Zoubir and Pazzanita 1995, 618). The absurdity of Morocco's demand was even apparent to Morocco's allies. Under vigorous questioning at a congressional subcommittee hearing, the U.S. deputy assistant secretary of state for Africa acknowledged that this Moroccan demand was a "violation" of the Settlement Plan (U.S. Senate 1992a). Yet because there was no formal Morocco–Polisario agreement, nothing had been formally violated with the demand.

As a sign of Morocco's seriousness on this issue, Hassan organized what would be called the Second Green March. On September 15, 1991, a little more than a week after the cease-fire, he informed Secretary-General Pérez de Cuéllar that 170,000 additional Moroccan citizens would move into Western Sahara for the referendum. Although these citizens were ostensibly Western Saharan refugees from the time of Spanish colonialism, the vast majority were ethnic Sahrawis of Moroccan territorial origin. To most observers,

Morocco's intentions were obvious. James Baker, U.S. secretary of state at the time, considered the move a "very thin disguise for rigging the results of the election," as paraphrased by Pérez de Cuéllar (1997, 349). The UN undersecretary-general for peacekeeping intended to dispatch a cable to MINURSO's special representative, Johannes Manz, describing the Moroccan regime's move as "a major departure from the plan," but Pérez de Cuéllar struck this line from the communiqué. UN Peacekeeping Department head Marrack Goulding also advised the secretary-general to inform the Security Council of these negative developments, which posed a grave threat to the complete implementation of the Settlement Plan. Pérez de Cuéllar, as always, kept the Security Council out of the loop (Goulding 2002, 211). By the end of 1991, Manz had had enough. Following his resignation, born out of frustration with the process, Manz wrote in a "confidential letter" to his former boss, "Concerning the non-military violations, the movement of unidentified persons into the Territory, the so-called 'Second Green March,' constitutes, in my view, a breach of the spirit, if not the letter, of the Peace Plan" (quoted in Chopra 1999, 198). This brave act of dissent, however, had little impact on Pérez de Cuéllar, who was about to retire from his post.

The 1991 Settlement Plan had stipulated that MINURSO's Identification Commission could consider "applications from persons who claim the right to participate in the referendum on the grounds that they are Western Saharans and were omitted from the 1974 census" (UN doc. S/22464, par. 20).[3] Although this consideration was a nod to Moroccan concerns (i.e., Hassan's letter of June 1990), the Identification Commission still had no means to evaluate the claims of Rabat's tens of thousands of applicants. Since 1990, MINURSO's Identification Commission had been updating the 1974 Spanish census with the help of Sahrawi shaykhs (shuyukh). Out of the 74,343 on the final Spanish census, 1,498 had died, and 484 had been duplicates. High fidelity to this new list, from Morocco's point of view, would disenfranchise the majority of its applicants.

In order to accommodate these "applications from persons who claim the right to participate in the referendum on the grounds that they are Western Saharans and were omitted from the 1974 census" and thereby to keep Morocco engaged in the peace process, MINURSO needed other grounds for voter enfranchisement. On December 19, 1991, in his last report to the Security Council, Pérez de Cuéllar proposed three new identification criteria, in addition to the claims of blood (jus sanguini) of persons listed on the 1974 census or their direct descendents: (1) persons "born of a Saharan father born in the territory" (restricted to one generation only); (2) persons who resided in the territory for a period of six consecutive years before December 1, 1974; and (3) persons who resided in the territory intermittently for a total period of twelve years prior to December 1, 1974 (UN doc. S/23299, Annex I, par. 23, 29–31). The latter two criteria, which favored Morocco, would help enfranchise applicants with ties to the land (jus soli) but without direct blood ties to anyone counted in 1974. But just as Pérez de Cuéllar had misrepresented the parties' level of agreement, this proposed expansion of the identification criteria also caught the Security Council off guard. In an unprecedented move, the Security Council simply "welcomed" Pérez de Cuéllar's final report without approving the criteria, thereby deferring the issue to the next secretary-generalship.

As a former foreign minister in Egypt, Boutros Boutros-Ghali had extensive experience—and thus political baggage—in the Western Sahara issue. He had represented Egypt at the OAU in the late 1970s and early 1980s, vigorously defending Morocco's position. Polisario was therefore very guarded when he entered the scene in January 1992. Morocco, in contrast, was doubly pleased, having the advantage of a sympathetic secretary-general and a newly acquired two-year stint on the Security Council. Indeed, Boutros-Ghali initially pushed behind the scenes to abandon the 1991 Settlement Plan, arguing that Morocco would not accept any outcome except annexation.

The first step was to appoint a new special representative of the secretary-general to serve as mediator. Events in the previous months had so discredited the process that the secretary-general had difficulty finding any credible diplomat willing to take on the assignment. Boutros-Ghali initially put forward Vernon Walters for the position. Although Polisario had lobbied for an American who could put pressure on Morocco, Walters's close personal ties with King Hassan, his secret role in the 1975 Madrid Agreement, and his efforts to ship arms to Morocco to bypass Carter administration restrictions, made him totally unacceptable. Boutros-Ghali eventually chose Sahabzda Yaqub-Khan, Pakistan's former foreign minister under the U.S.-backed dictatorship of Zia al-Haq and with close ties to Boutros-Ghali and King Hassan. He was thus not well received by Polisario. Indeed, it soon became apparent that Yaqub-Khan shared the secretary-general's proannexation sentiments.

In the secretary-general's January 1993 report, it was noted that Yaqub-Khan's efforts to build confidence through track-one and track-two negotiations had failed to make headway in 1992, even on minor technical issues. Boutros-Ghali proposed three options to move forward: (a) further negotiations, which the secretary-general felt were unlikely to work; (b) implementation of the Settlement Plan with Pérez de Cuéllar's expanded identification criteria; or (c) "an alternative approach not based on the settlement plan" (UN doc. S/25170, par. 32). Fearing that the Security Council might seriously entertain the second option, Polisario head and RASD president Mohammed Abdelaziz initiated some predictable Kalashnikov rattling: "I see no other way out but a return to war" (quoted in *The Guardian,* Feb. 22, 1993). The Security Council opted in its Resolution 809 for "intensified" negotiations based on proposals offered by New Zealand and Spain, but also added a deadline of May 1993 to nudge the parties toward consensus. Otherwise, as the Security Council threatened Polisario, it might go with the second option at the next juncture. It also invited Boutros-Ghali to "make the necessary preparations of the referendum" and "to consult accordingly with the parties for the purposes of commencing voter registration on a prompt basis," which put some pressure on Morocco (UN doc. S/Res/809). By taking these steps, the Security Council hoped to create some momentum on the ground.

May 1993 came and went with no breakthrough, so Boutros-Ghali toured the region and presented a "compromise" identification formula (Smith de Cherif 1993, 103). The new formula accepted Pérez de Cuéllar's proposals, but it kept the 1974 census as a touchstone. Boutros-Ghali listed the five criteria to be eligible to vote (for persons eighteen years of age or older at a date set by the special representative):

> 1. Persons whose names are included in the revised 1974 census list;
> 2. Persons who were living in the Territory as members of a Saharan tribe at the time of the 1974 census but who could not be counted;
> 3. Members of the immediate family of the first two groups;
> 4. Persons born of a Saharan father born in the Territory;
> 5. Persons who are members of a Saharan tribe belonging to the Territory and who have resided in the Territory for six consecutive years or intermittently for 12 years prior to 1 December 1974. (UN doc. S/26185, Annex I: par. 2)

For Polisario, this compromise meant that the 1974 census would remain central. All applicants would have to demonstrate some link to a Western Saharan "tribal subfraction" listed in the 1974 census, thereby decreasing the possibility that persons with no ethnic ties would be allowed to vote. For Morocco, persons not listed on the revised register could apply to vote, although they would later have to provide evidence for their inclusion in person before the Identification Commission.

This solution, however, led to another problem: the number of persons who could register under a specific "tribal subfraction." This problem was acute for groups whose majority had resided outside the territory in 1974, if not during the whole of Spanish colonialism (Adebajo 2002, 15–16). Polisario was concerned that a significant percentage of Morocco's applicants claimed tribal affiliation in groups that traditionally inhabited southern Morocco, not Western Sahara. These groups were "Western Saharan" to the extent that a small number—less than 3,000—were residing in Spanish Sahara in 1974.

There was also disagreement on the process of vetting applicants, especially for those lacking textual evidence. Although Polisario opposed a system based on personal testimony, Morocco successfully claimed that Sahrawi culture was oral and that Sahrawi refugees and migrants from Spanish Sahara, especially their children, would likely lack colonial documents or identification. To accommodate these concerns, Boutros-Ghali's compromise also proposed that Sahrawi shaykhs "of the Saharan sub-fractions included in the 1974 census" play an essential role in the vetting process, whereby they would "testify on every application" presented to MINURSO (UN doc. S/26185, Annex I: par. 20). The proposal was a political compromise in that for every individual's identification session, two shaykhs, one nominated by Morocco and one nominated by Polisario, would give their opinion as to the veracity of applicants' testimonies in cases lacking documents. Although this compromise proposal opened the door to all of Morocco's applicants, the UN Secretariat tried to convince Polisario that these measures would only authenticate native Western Saharans. The shaykh breakthrough had come from Erik Jensen, who had taken the helm of the Identification Commission in the spring of 1993 and later rose to the position of deputy special representative in March 1994.[4]

For as long as possible, Polisario resisted pressure to accept Boutros-Ghali's proposals. Yet by early 1994 it seemed as if Polisario, rather than Morocco, was the party least interested in a free and fair referendum. When Polisario agreed to the procedures, it was in part to test Morocco's willingness to go forward as well; at the same time, Polisario maintained its objections to the large number of Moroccan applicants from the "contested tribes." With Polisario's partial acquiescence in April, followed quickly by Morocco's assent, the secretary-general reported in July 1994 that MINURSO would soon begin processing applicants from noncontested tribal subfractions (UN doc. S/1994/819).

Before the vetting process could begin, MINURSO had to jump one more hurdle. Under the Settlement Plan, the OAU was still a partner to the process; OAU observers were expected to take part in the identification sessions to help ensure transparency. However, the Moroccan government objected to the OAU's presence because the latter had recognized the RASD. Although the identification process had been set to start on June 8, 1994, the Moroccan government, questioning the neutrality of the OAU's observers, refused to participate as long as the RASD remained an OAU member state. If the RASD left the OAU, then Morocco would allow the observers. To resolve the row, the OAU simply made its observers "personal envoys" of the Tunisian president Zinedine Ben Ali, who was serving as chair of the OAU that year. The Moroccan government acquiesced, and so the identification process commenced (Seddon 1996, 103; Zoubir and Pazzanita 1995, 625).

IDENTIFICATION, ROUND ONE

The UN's deadline for receipt of all voter applications was October 25, 1994. On that night, MINURSO received roughly 130,000 last-minute applications from Morocco, bringing Rabat's official total to more than 180,000 (83,971 from Western Sahara and 99,225 from Morocco). Polisario submitted 42,337. The number of applications, initially 233,487 (later revised to 244,643), exceeded all predictions at three times the size of the updated Spanish census. By the end of 1994, it was clear that a referendum would not be feasible until at least October 1995 (UN doc. S/1994/1420, par. 22). Adding to this problem was the fact that other highly explosive issues—Moroccan troop withdrawal, a code of conduct for the campaign period, and postreferendum arrangements—had yet to be broached.

The UN process maintained no prejudice against applying, except that an applicant had to be at least eighteen years of age by December 31, 1993, and a member of one of the

Sahrawi tribal subfractions listed in the 1974 Spanish census. The 1974 Spanish census listed the following confederations, assigning each one a letter (A though J):

A. Rgaybat al-Sharq (Erguibat Charg)

B. Rgaybat al-Sahil (Erguibat Sahel)

C. Izargiyyn (Izarguien)

D. Ait al-Hasan (Ait Lahsen)

E. Al-'Arusiyyn (Arosien)

F. Awlad Dulaym (Ulad Delim)

G. Awlad Tidrarin (Ulad Tidrarin)

H. Tribes of the North (Tribus del Norte)

I. Shurafa' (Tribus Chorfa)

J. Tribes of the Coast and South (Tribus Costeras y del Sur)

Groupings A through G listed the seven major confederations or "tribes" found in and around Spanish Sahara; these confederations were further divided into fractions and sub-fractions. Groups H through J, just 14 percent of the 1974 census, were minor tribes in Spanish Sahara or tribes predominantly alien to it. Spanish authorities also had a category K for persons of sub-Saharan origin (Residentes de Origin Africano, see Aguirre 1988, 611) that MINURSO did not use.

During the UN identification process, the most problematic of these subgroups came from the H and J categories: H41 (Ait Baamaran), H61 ("Varias del norte"), and J51/52 ("Idegob y otras del sur"); Spain registered only 609, 536, and 1,387 Sahrawis from these groups (2,532 total), respectively. Rabat, however, presented nearly 60,000 candidates under these three groupings, three-fourths resident in Morocco. Although Polisario was suspicious about the implausible number of candidates Morocco presented in the H, I, and J groups in general, it absolutely rejected applicants from H41, H61, and J51/52—the "contested tribes"—as being categorically non–Western Saharan (Dunbar 2000, 528–30).

The identification process got under way on August 28, 1994, with the uncontested groupings. On paper, the Identification Commission convoked all the members of a given subfraction on the same day and at specific identification centers, which were initially located in the major cities of Western Sahara, the refugee camps in Algeria, and, later, Mauritania (Zouerate and Nouadhibou) and Morocco (Rabat, Casablanca, Meknes, Sidi Kacem, El-Klaa, Zagora, Taroudant, Tata, Goulemine, Assa, and Tan Tan). Applicants were fingerprinted, photographed, and questioned in front of the commission. Within twenty-four hours of the hearing, the commission determined each applicant's eligibility, although the outcome was not to be officially released to the parties or applicants until all potential voters had been vetted.

Each UN team consisted of one member of MINURSO's Identification Commission and a member of MINURSO's technical staff. Also present were the two shaykhs, translators if necessary, observers from Morocco and Polisario, and the OAU chair's "personal envoys." The ideal shaykh was an elected member of the Spanish Sahara's 1973 consultative assembly, the Jama'a (Adebajo 2002, 17–18). The shaykhs, who swore oaths on the Qur'an, were there to help verify the familial claims of applicants lacking colonial documents. Although the shaykhs' opinions were important, the MINURSO officials made the final decision on each applicant. Even with the shaykhs' presence, the process was still problematic. Mission head Charles Dunbar later noted that "the most serious problem facing the referendum process . . . [was] the failure of most applicants lacking clear, often documentary, ties to the Western Sahara to convince MINURSO's Identification Commission that they [were] eligible to vote under one or more of the five criteria" (2000, 531). Given that most of Morocco's candidates were not native Western Saharan or even ethnically Sahrawi, it is easy to see why so many applicants failed to pass the screening process. Another major problem was that the two shaykhs' political biases often canceled each other out, so the Identification Commission had to fall back on the very documents that the shaykhs' presence was supposed to circumvent.

The secretary-general informed the Security Council in his first report of 1995 that roughly 21,300 persons had been processed. With seven centers running at full pace, an overall rate of more than 20,000 identifications per month was achievable. Yet there was still reason for pessimism. Boutros-Ghali also noted that a troublesome ethic of "strict reciprocity" had developed, whereby one identification center would operate if and only if its counterpart on the other side of the berm was operating as well. If on any given day the observer from Polisario or Morocco felt uncomfortable with the identification process in a particular center, as they often did, the withdrawal or absence of one observer would halt identification at both that site and the corresponding site. For example, identification in the Smara camp would halt if identification in Smara city stopped and vice versa. This norm of reciprocity thus created significant drag on the rate of identification. The secretary-general also noted that there was a lack of shaykhs for about one-third of the tribes (UN doc. S/1995/240, par. 4 and 8). Identification had commenced on subfractions with available shaykhs, but MINURSO had to find some way to find proper substitutes for tribal subfractions without shaykhs or the son of a shaykh. This was especially problematic for Polisario because there were few shaykhs in the camps for the H, I, and J groups (Jensen 2005, 66).

Near the end of 1995, Boutros-Ghali informed the Security Council that the identification process had "virtually come to a halt" owing to "certain tribal groups and . . . persons not resident in the Territory [in 1974]" (UN doc. S/1995/986, par. 2). Polisario had withdrawn its participation from the process, refusing to cooperate with the vetting of Moroccan-sponsored applicants from the H41, H61, and J51/52 groups. Polisario was equally grieved by Morocco's sentencing of eight Sahrawi activists to more than fifteen years in prison following an antioccupation demonstration in al-'Ayun that May. To restart the identification process, Boutros-Ghali made several proposals. As a threat to Polisario, he suggested implementing a fixed schedule, one that would not require the presence of the shaykhs, representatives from the parties (i.e., Polisario or Morocco), or the OAU envoys. As a threat to Morocco, he proposed to allow, in the absence of one shaykh or both, only documentary evidence. And as a threat to both sides, he suggested that only one shaykh would be necessary for the identification of the three contested groupings and in identification centers outside the territory (i.e., Morocco, Mauritania, and the refugee camps). To head off concerns, he reminded everyone that the Identification Commission still intended to accept appeals, which would make up for any mistakes made during the initial round (UN doc. S/1995/779, par. 7, 15–17).

Although the secretary-general clearly wanted to overcome the debilitating norm of strict reciprocity, the third proposal was not much of a threat to Moroccan interests, given the relatively low number of applicants in the camps and Mauritania. It would in fact reward Moroccan efforts to block Polisario shaykhs and observers in the occupied territory and Morocco proper, where the vast majority of Moroccan-sponsored candidates had registered.

On Polisario's behalf, two sympathetic nonpermanent Security Council members, Germany and Argentina, raised serious questions about the identification process, which precipitated some doubts in the council as to the transparency and neutrality of the process. On behalf of Morocco, France attempted to amend the draft September 1995 resolution, countered by pro-Polisario amendments from Argentina. Pressure from the United States forced a more neutral resolution that simply extended MINURSO's mandate. However, the council expressed displeasure with Polisario's noncooperation and Rabat's refusal to prescreen the 100,000 applicants from Morocco proper (UN doc. S/Res/1017). Basri quickly flew to New York, where he told the Security Council on October 9, 1995, that Morocco would not prejudice any of its applicants by prescreening them.

Regardless of the Security Council's opinion, Boutros-Ghali wanted full implementation of these proposals without approval from the parties, arguing that the proposals were merely technical modifications at the secretary-general's discretion. While the United Kingdom, France, and the United States worked on a set of bridging proposals, behind their back Boutros-Ghali sent a secret "nonpaper" to the parties in early November setting out his revised proposals. Polisario's reaction was to inform the Security Council that if Boutros-Ghali's proposals were adopted, Polisario "would have no other option than reconsidering its obligations under the [1991] Settlement Plan" (Bukhari 1995). To make matters worse, Boutros-Ghali bluntly told the Security Council that he did not really expect the referendum to take place. Rather, once identification was completed, Morocco would realize it would never win via the ballot box. It would then offer Polisario generous autonomy (Chopra 1997, 54; Jensen 2005, 74–75, 83). This announcement did not sit well with the Security Council. In its December 19, 1995, resolution on Western Sahara, it simply called for continued cooperation from the parties and requested Boutros-Ghali to "intensify" his efforts (UN doc. S/Res/1033; *UN Chronicle*, Dec. 1995).

MINURSO UNDER THE MICROSCOPE

External criticism of the UN effort in Western Sahara increased as soon as the voter-identification process faltered in 1995. Most of the blame centered on the UN failure to denounce Moroccan abuse of the mission's personnel. Former U.S. military representative to MINURSO Douglas K. Dryden described this abuse before the UN Fourth Committee: "The atmosphere at the MINURSO Force Headquarters in Laayoune [al-'Ayun] is practically a siege mentality. The mission is not allowed to function independently, but as a creature of the Moroccans. . . . It is the only UN mission that I am aware of where the flag of one of the parties [i.e., Morocco] is required to fly alongside that of the UN. Telephones were tapped. Mail was tampered with. Rooms of MINURSO personnel were searched" (Dryden 1996). Reports from foreign journalists during this period reported similar problems, including a *New York Times* article published on March 1, 1995, in which reporter Chris Hedges echoed these accusations.

Frank Ruddy (1995b), the former deputy chair of the Identification Commission, spoke to a U.S. congressional subcommittee about MINURSO's operations and the Moroccan government's efforts to control the process. A conservative Republican with extensive diplomatic experience in Africa under the George H. W. Bush administration, Ruddy likened Moroccan-occupied Western Sahara to apartheid South Africa. Like Dryden, Ruddy claimed that the Moroccan government had exerted an inappropriate level of control over UN functions in Western Sahara. More startling were Ruddy's claims that Moroccan forces had either blocked or intimidated many Sahrawis—who had what Rabat considered questionable political allegiances—from registering to vote. Ruddy stated that in the face of these Moroccan excesses, the UN leadership in the mission and New York had been silent and even almost deferential to Moroccan interests.

During the same period, Human Rights Watch investigated MINURSO's operations and came to the conclusion that "Morocco, which is the stronger of the two parties both militarily and diplomatically, has regularly engaged in conduct that has obstructed and compromised the fairness of the referendum process" (Ziai 1995, 3). This conclusion was backed up by numerous interviews, both on and off the record, with UN officials involved in the process. The report noted that some Moroccan-sponsored candidates were obviously posing as Western Saharans: "Testimony from members of MINURSO's identification commission indicates that many of the applicants proposed by Morocco and identified so far have no documents proving links to the Western Sahara, do not speak the Hassaniya dialect of the region, are not familiar with the tribal structure of the region and have clearly memorized answers to the factual and biographical questions posed by the identification commission" (quoted in Ziai 1995, 18).[5] The report also found a growing awareness that the shaykhs were succumbing to political influence. One MINURSO official told Human Rights Watch that "a couple of times, I saw a Moroccan observer take one of the Moroccan sheikhs aside during the break and yell at him, because he was deciding the wrong way. But usually it was more subtle: we would identify people from a subfraction in one of the identification centers and we were supposed to continue with the same subfraction in the other identification centers [on subsequent days]. But a certain [Moroccan] sheikh, who had been voting the wrong way, would suddenly not appear again the next day" (quoted in Ziai 1995, 21).

According to one former MINURSO official, "The sad case of the missing sheikhs became an almost farcical part of MINURSO folklore" (quoted in Adebajo 2002, 18). In 2000, a former head of the UN mission wrote, "The Moroccan Government apparently went to some lengths to ensure that as many of its applicants as possible were found eligible to vote. A document published in the March 24–30 1998 edition (No. 1941) of the French-language magazine, *Jeune afrique,* was purported to be an official Moroccan Interior Ministry instruction to provincial officials to see to it that referendum voter applicants were enrolled in a Ministry-run crash-course on MINURSO voter identification procedures" (Dunbar 2000, n. 25). Polisario officials widely believed that Rabat had even bribed members of the Identification Commission, especially those who had final say on an applicant's authenticity. The fact that MINURSO's Legal Review Unit would later overturn 4,000 Moroccan-sponsored candidates accepted by the Identification Commission suggested Polisario's accusations had some merit.

From near and far, the credibility of the identification process was under attack. The UN Secretariat and Security Council, however, ignored or dismissed most the criticism. The only effort to investigate MINURSO was a Security Council mission, dispatched from June 3 to June 9, 1995, to Morocco, Western Sahara, and Algeria, only the sixth such mission in the council's history. The informal Group of Friends for Western Sahara—France, Spain, the United Kingdom, the United States, and Russia—headed planning efforts (for background, see Whitfield 2007, chapter 6). Led by Botswana, the actual visiting mission was "balanced" between pro-Moroccan (France and Oman), pro-Polisario (Argentina), and self-proclaimed neutral (United States and Honduras) permanent and nonpermanent Security Council members. The team's findings, in line with its mandate, focused on technical aspects impeding the implementation of the Settlement Plan and the difficulties blocking the voter-identification process. The report also asked both parties to refrain from inhibiting "access to the identification centers" and called upon the Moroccan government to "conduct preliminary vetting of the 100,000 applicants currently not residing in the Territory" itself (UN Security Council 1995, par. 5; see also Seddon 1996, 104, and Zoubir and Pazzanita 1995, 626). Behind the scenes, the Security Council mission had asked both sides to consider direct talks. Morocco, quite comfortable in its position, felt that there was nothing to discuss unless Polisario wanted to talk about what would happen following integration. Polisario withdrew from the identification process later in June. From there, the climate further deteriorated until by the end of 1995 the secretary-general was being pressured to consider a withdrawal of the mission.

THE ROAD TO HOUSTON

The opening months of 1996 were one of the bleakest periods for MINURSO. By May, the secretary-general could report no progress and recommended a total suspension of the identification process, to which the Security Council agreed (see UN doc. S/1996/343 and S/Res/1056). By September, all of the identification centers had been closed, and both Moroccan and Polisario forces resumed live-fire exercises. In his last report on MINURSO (UN doc. S/1996/913), Boutros-Ghali indicated that the mission's military observer force had been drawn down by 26 percent, its police presence reduced from 91 to 9 officers, nonmilitary personnel had been reduced from 410 to 170, and all but one political office had been closed. The military observer force, meanwhile, had been reduced by 20 percent. He also noted the release of 66 Sahrawi POWs by Morocco and of 185 elderly and infirm Moroccan POWs by Polisario. Although Polisario had released the POWs in 1989, Morocco had refused to accept them because Rabat would not recognize Polisario. Upon learning of the Moroccan POWs' plight, diplomats from the United States and Argentina bravely and forcibly repatriated them.

Behind the scenes, there had been growing pressure on Morocco to meet with Polisario. Although identification was far from finished, and the provisional voter list had been kept from the parties, both sides could tell that Polisario had performed far better than expected, even with constant and multiple attempts by the Moroccan Interior Ministry to distort the outcome. With the likelihood that a free and fair referendum would result in independence, Polisario finally had some leverage in direct negotiations. Morocco still hoped the scarcity of shaykhs and documentation surrounding the contested tribes would help it recoup its electoral losses. Yet the very real threat of MINURSO's withdrawal created a new source of pressure on both sides in mid-1996.

The problem facing Polisario–Morocco talks was not a paucity of mediators. Early in 1996, South Africa—recently liberated from white minority rule and now under the leadership of President Nelson Mandela—indicated some interest in mediating. Yet the fact that South African leaders were openly discussing formal recognition of the RASD precluded Moroccan acceptance of this proposal. Later that spring the United States tried to arrange secret talks, which both Morocco and Polisario favored. The State Department, however, was reluctant to be seen as deviating from the Settlement Plan. The United States, with backing from the Group of Friends, briefed the Security Council in April 1996 on this initiative. Washington, however, had demanded a high price for its help: Polisario could not raise issues related to independence, and the initiative had to be kept secret. To sweeten the deal, Washington proposed a meeting in Algiers with then U.S. assistant secretary of state for Near Eastern affairs Robert H. Pelletreau and Polisario head Mohammed Abdelaziz. Polisario, however, refused to meet these last two conditions, so Washington quickly backed off.

That summer, following withdrawal warnings from the Security Council in May, Jensen, then head of MINURSO, made his own secret attempt to start talks. With quiet Algerian support, Jensen wanted to open a dialog between Basri and Polisario's Bachir Mustapha Sayed. The only precondition was that neither side could talk about full integration or total independence. Secrecy was also a condition, and only Boutros-Ghali knew about this initiative. The two key Moroccan and Polisario interlocutors met in early August in Geneva, where they made plans for a high-level meeting in Rabat. Although not present for the meeting in Morocco, Jensen reports that five top Polisario members (Bachir Mustapha Sayed, Brahim Ghali, Mahfoud Ali Beiba, Emhamed Khadad, and Ayoub Ould Lahbib) met with the Crown Prince Mohammed (later King Mohammed VI) and Basri. The expected meeting with King Hassan, however, did not happen at these encounters. After the Geneva meeting, there were differing interpretations of what had transpired and thus what went wrong. Subsequent meetings failed to materialize, particularly after news of the meeting was leaked. The Moroccan side claimed that Polisario had broken the rules by discussing independence (Bachir Mustapha Sayed had uttered the ambiguous phrase "independence within interdependence"). Polisario, however, would later claim that Basri's autonomy proposal was simply a copy of Morocco's Constitution (Jensen 2005, 87–89; *Le Journal Hebdomadaire*, Mar. 11–17, 2006). Boutros-Ghali's waning influence was another factor; the Security Council refused to terminate MINURSO in anticipation of a new secretary-general.

Although Jensen's initiative failed, it did have one major effect: the UN Secretariat falsely concluded that the situation was finally ripe for a compromise solution outside the 1991 Settlement Plan. Under this premise, Kofi Annan, the recently inaugurated secretary-general, wasted no time in pursuing an alternative to the UN-OAU referendum project. Annan had previously served as head of the UN Peacekeeping Department, but he had had little direct involvement with MINURSO. There were indications, quickly proved wrong, that Algeria would push Polisario toward autonomy. The problem was that the secretary-general could not be seen as abandoning self-determination; such an outcome would be acceptable only if the parties—especially Polisario—did it themselves.

In his first report on Western Sahara in February 1997, Annan raised three fundamental questions:

> (*a*) Can the settlement plan be implemented in its present form?
>
> (*b*) If not, are there adjustments to the settlement plan, acceptable to both parties, which would make it implementable?

*(c)* If not, are there other ways by which the international community could help the parties resolve their conflict? (UN doc. S/1997/166, par. 17)

Annan believed that the UN would need a strong negotiator to get Morocco and Polisario to move quickly from A to B to C. For that to happen, Annan needed someone with leverage on both sides.

On February 19, Annan sent his undersecretary for peacekeeping, Marrack Goulding, to ask former U.S. secretary of state James Baker to become the lead UN negotiator for Western Sahara. In his official letter to Baker that March, Annan posed the same three questions so that it would not appear that the Secretariat had abandoned the Settlement Plan (Annan 1997). However, as Goulding recalls, he was sent to tell Baker that Baker would be negotiating outside the independence/integration referendum framework (Goulding 2002, 214; *El País,* May 1, 2003). Most experts had advised Baker that a referendum would never work (Bolton 1998). Indeed, after resigning his UN appointment in 2004, Baker admitted, "When I first took the job on I was led to believe that the conflict was ripe for some sort of autonomy-based solution where the Moroccans would give self-government to the Sahrawis, the conflict would be resolved, the people from the camps would move back into the territory itself, and they would be given a liberal degree of self-government" (interview in Husain 2004). News of Baker's appointment leaked early. Polisario was ecstatic, whereas Morocco quietly tried to oppose it. Polisario's optimism was also rooted in the more neutral U.S. position adopted since the 1991 cease-fire. Because Morocco could not easily impede or dismiss Baker, Polisario saw a U.S. negotiator of Baker's stature as a blessing. Polisario also emphasized Baker's lead role in rallying the international community to support the liberation of Kuwait six years earlier and never failed to draw comparisons between that occupation and the occupation of Western Sahara. Familiar with Baker's negotiating style from the Gulf War, Morocco knew that Baker would have the will and, with Washington's backing, the power to twist arms. When press reports indicated that Baker was pursuing an alternative approach, the most vehement rejections of autonomy came from the Moroccan side (e.g., *Financial Times* [London], May 16, 1997).

On March 17, 1997, the UN officially announced the appointment of Baker as Annan's new personal envoy to the Western Sahara. Baker, who would report directly to the secretary-general, also had the explicit endorsement of the Clinton administration (Annan 1997). In many ways, this appointment was better than direct State Department mediation because U.S. influence was being exercised through an independent agent of the UN secretary-general rather than directly by Washington. Baker's appointment also had the virtue of "rescu[ing] a forgotten conflict" by bringing desperately needed government and media attention to it (Crocker, Hampson, and Aall 2004, 66). Why Baker, one of the most influential conservative elites in the United States, agreed to get involved with a backburner African dispute such as the one over Western Sahara was unclear. For expertise, Baker also brought along two of his former deputies: former U.S. assistant secretary of state for African affairs Chester Crocker and former U.S. assistant secretary of state for international organizations John Bolton. Both were more familiar with the issue than Baker and thus became his key consultants.

Starting in late April 1997, Baker traveled to Northwest Africa, visiting leaders in Rabat, Algiers, Nouakchott, and Tindouf in order "to make a fresh assessment of the situation and to discuss with all concerned ways of breaking the current stalemate" (UN doc. S/1997/358, par. 22). It was during these discussions that all of the principals—Polisario head Abdelaziz, Morocco's king Hassan, and Algeria's president Liamine Zeroual (1994–99)—reportedly recommitted themselves to the original 1991 Settlement Plan. After making this initial assessment and with further Security Council backing in May, Baker quickly pushed for high-level direct talks. Meeting separately with delegations from Morocco, Mauritania, Algeria, and Polisario on June 10 and 11 in preparation for "consultations" in London, Baker told Polisario and Morocco that they would have to engage in negotiations to fix the Settlement Plan. To Morocco, Baker stipulated that he would not deal with Interior Minister Basri, instead demanding legitimate representation from the Moroccan Foreign Ministry. Algeria and Mauritania would be present and consulted on relevant decisions. Hoping to remove all the interrelated roadblocks, Baker offered a holistic approach: "no issue would be considered as finally agreed until all outstanding issues were agreed" (UN doc. S/1997/742, par. 6). Both Polisario and Morocco offered positive gestures, with the former agreeing to resume identification and the latter agreeing to delay the identification of the 60,000 contested applicants.

The first direct talks were held in Lisbon on June 23, 1997, where Baker presented a compromise plan of his own design for the parties to take home for consultations. At the next round, July 19 and 20 in London, both sides agreed to Baker's compromise on voter identification, whereby each side would neither help nor hinder convoked applicants, although all applicants could present themselves, including those from contested groups. This first agreement was followed by talks on provisions for troop withdrawal and confinement during the voting period. The third round of talks took place back in Lisbon on August 29 and 30; issues of troop withdrawal, confinement, political prisoners, POWs, and a code of conduct for the referendum were further decided. The final round of talks took place from September 14 to September 16 at the Baker Institute for Public Policy at Rice University in Houston. In the end, the two sides signed a final document on all outstanding issues, which became known as the Houston Accords (see UN doc. S/1997/742, par. 4–13). For the first time in the entire Western Sahara peace process, both Morocco and Polisario had committed their signatures to paper. Baker's skill and U.S. backing were obviously key to this breakthrough. According to Bolton, Baker's power was "his ability, in effect, to blow the whistle on the party that might have caused the negotiations to come to a halt" (Bolton 1998).

Besides resolving the vexing issue of the contested tribes, the Houston Accords also made it clear that the results of identification would be provided to each side in numbers but not "in name." The accords also reaffirmed oral testimony as legitimate evidence. On the other substantive issues relating to troop confinement, troop withdrawal, refugee repatriation, political prisoners, and POWs, Morocco and Polisario agreed to provisions already set forth in the original Settlement Plan, but the Houston Accords also put forth a "Declaration of the Parties," a "Code of Conduct for the Referendum Campaign," and a set of "practical measures for the resumption of identification," all of which aimed at creating a free, fair, and transparent referendum as soon as possible (see UN doc. S/1997/742, Annexes I, II, and III). Some reports indicated that Baker told the parties to expect a final voter pool representing the 1974 Spanish census plus 15 percent, roughly 80,000 to 86,000 voters (Seddon 2000, 338).

For the first time in the history of MINURSO, the UN not only had a bona fide agreement, but also had the diplomatic muscle to make it work. In March 1998, Bolton claimed that the lesson of the Houston Accords was that the UN had to avoid a "culture of negotiations" and instead take the position that when an agreement is signed, the parties must be held to it. Bolton seemed quite optimistic that the referendum would actually take place. Contradicting this view, however, Baker's assistant in the UN Secretariat, Anna Theofilopoulou, would later write, "Nobody on the Baker team really believed that the UN would sail towards the implementation of the settlement plan. After the parties had locked themselves in, it was a question of who would back away from their commitments first" (2006, 7; see also Jensen 2005, 96).

IDENTIFICATION, ROUND TWO

In November 1997, the secretary-general put forth a timetable forecasting a referendum in Western Sahara on December 7, 1998. To make this happen, a preliminary technical mission had visited the area in October, allowing MINURSO to resume the identification process on December 3 in al-'Ayun (Western Sahara) and in the Smara camp (Algeria). These centers were soon joined by identification centers in Smara, Western Sahara; Dakhla camp, Algeria; and Tan Tan, Morocco. In the first nine days of resumed identification, MINURSO screened 2,386 persons (UN doc. S/1997/974, par. 6–7). Adding further muscle to MINURSO, Annan announced in late December that former U.S. ambassador Charles Dunbar would officially become the new special representative in February 1998, taking over from Jensen. Dunbar's presence meant that when the proposed transitional period began, there would be a former U.S. diplomat watching over Morocco.

Yet no sooner had the identification process commenced than new problems arose. On a day when MINURSO had convoked only 830 individuals listed on the 1974 Spanish census to al-'Ayun, some 3,927 applicants claiming the same tribal subfraction managed to present themselves, followed by 8,613 more in subsequent days. As reported by Annan in January 1998, these 12,540 "unconvoked" individuals from the contested tribal groupings had presented themselves for identification in al-'Ayun in December, with, in the words of mission head Dunbar, "the apparent active encouragement and logistical support of the Moroccan Government" (Dunbar 2000, 531). The new director of the Identification Commission, Robin Kinloch, reported this violation of the Houston Accords to UN headquarters in New York, and Baker and Bolton were informed in early January. Polisario sought to have these individuals disqualified owing to the obvious help they received from Morocco. MINURSO's own estimates indicated that more than 95 percent of the 65,000 applicants from the contested tribes would fail in their applications, so Baker recommended using this information to convince Polisario that it had nothing to lose by processing the first 3,927. However, Morocco's attitude, as always, was to oppose any differential treatment. Feeling that the time was not yet ripe to abandon the Houston Accords, Baker advised MINURSO to push forward with identification of noncontested groups while a new solution to "unconvoked" applicants was worked out (Jensen 2005, 96; Theofilopoulou 2006, 7).

The Identification Commission was so accommodating to Morocco that in January 1998 the secretary-general announced plans for identification centers "where the number of resident applicants exceeds 10,000, that is, at El Klaa des Sraghna [near Marrakech] and at Sidi Kacem [near Fez]" (UN doc. S/1998/35, par. 10–11, 29–30).[6] By February, MINURSO had opened three new centers in Western Sahara, two in the refugee camps in Algeria, two in southern Morocco, and one at Zouerate in Mauritania. Out of 42,484 persons convoked since December 3, 1997, MINURSO had vetted 30,425 applicants, making the total 90,537 processed since identification started in August 1994. However, with no agreement on the issue of nonconvoked applicants by April, it was clear that the target date for completion of the identification process, May 31, 1998, could not be achieved.

By September 1998, MINURSO had screened all 147,350 noncontested applicants (UN doc. S/1998/849). The Security Council decided to keep MINURSO on a short leash, extending its mandate just to October 31. For several months, Dunbar and Kinloch had consulted with internal and external legal advisors and with members of the UN Secretariat on a set of proposals to solve the latter problem. In secret, Baker had gone to visit King Hassan to see if he could convince him to change his mind on the referendum. Baker pointed to the autonomy negotiations in East Timor, and King Hassan seemed interested (Theofilopoulou 2006, 7). Basri, though, had too much personally invested in winning the referendum project. In addition, the dispute over the contested groups was delaying the process, just as Rabat wanted. This delay gave the Moroccan Interior Ministry more time to coach its last applicants before their hearings, which Rabat hoped would make up for its losses in the noncontested groups. Renewing MINURSO's mandate at the end of October, the Security Council pushed the referendum to December 1999 in the face of waning Polisario–Moroccan agreement.

To solve the final impasse stalling identification, it had been proposed that the simultaneous vetting of all remaining applicants would commence with the beginning of the appeals process for all others. The "key" aspect presented to the parties was a procedure "developed by MINURSO in the summer of 1998, under which, with the addition of several more Shaykhs, all members of the three [contested] groupings could be identified in three months" (Dunbar 2000, 531). The package also contained provisions for establishing UNHCR refugee repatriation capacities and clarifications related to other aspects of the transitional period (UN doc. S/1998/997). Baker wanted this package accepted on a take-it-or-leave-it basis. His aim was "to press Morocco to see the mistake of continuing with the identification" and "accept the inevitability of a political solution" (Theofilopoulou 2006, 8). Annan personally toured the region in November to get responses from Morocco and Polisario, but his trip was cut short by renewed U.S. air strikes on Iraq. Dunbar ended up going to Tindouf for the secretary-general. Polisario agreed to the proposals, but "the Government of Morocco expressed concerns[,] . . . sought clarifications" (UN doc. S/1999/88, par. 2; see also Seddon 1999, 497), and continued to withhold cooperation. As one Polisario official noted, "Now that we are saying 'yes,' the Moroccans have been left without any excuses" (quoted in *The Guardian*, Feb. 1, 1999).

However, the issue of the contested tribes was not really Morocco's central concern. Since the Houston Accords, both sides had received confidential reports on the identification process from MINURSO. These reports indicated that the Moroccan-sponsored candidates were failing at an alarming rate, especially persons outside the 1974 Spanish census. What Morocco really wanted was a revision to the appeals process that would allow a formal hearing for every appeal—in essence, a replay of the entire vetting process (Dunbar 2000, 532; UN doc. S/1999/307).

Around this time, in March 1999, Dunbar refused to extend his contract, apparently as a result of his frustration with the international community's lack of commitment to resolving the Western Sahara conflict (Seddon 1999, 498). In late 1998, he had told UN headquarters that it was time to abandon the Houston Accords and had taken issue with the way the Secretariat was letting the Moroccan press smear the Identification Commission's work. Baker and Annan, however, were not yet willing to abandon the referendum before Morocco saw the light. But Polisario's position was so strong and Morocco's so weakened that new negotiations were deemed inopportune. Another factor allegedly influencing Dunbar's resignation was a meeting in France between the UN undersecretary for peacekeeping and Basri, where the two discussed identification problems without Dunbar's knowledge. Kinloch, whom the Moroccans personally blamed and assailed for their poor performance in the identification process, temporarily took over Dunbar's post.

Finally, in April 1999, the secretary-general reported that the Moroccan government had accepted a redesigned version of the package, albeit "in principle" and with "the understanding that certain amendments would be incorporated into the identification and appeals protocols" (UN doc. S/1999/483, par. 4). Stalling for time, France and Morocco pushed for a six-month extension of MINURSO, whereas the United States and most other members wanted a shorter three-month period, so the compromise was four months. With formal acceptance of the "Appeals Procedures and Operational Directives" in May, identification resumed on June 15 under the leadership of the newly appointed special representative, another respected former U.S. ambassador, William Eagleton.

With identification centers in Western Sahara, Algeria, Morocco, and Mauritania screening the final applicants, the appeals process began on July 15, 1999. By August 11, nearly 19,000 persons had presented themselves for appeals and submitted 22,159 requests to review their files, even though only 2,000 actual appeals had been filed (UN doc. S/1999/875, par. 8). If it seemed that Morocco would launch a manageable amount of appeals, that assumption should have been thrown out the window following the public release of the provisional voter list on July 15. Out of the initial 147,249 applicants personally interviewed by MINURSO, only 84,251 had been found eligible to vote. Moroccan-sponsored candidates totaled little more than half: 46,255: 5,569 from Morocco and 40,686 from the Moroccan-occupied Western Sahara. From the Tindouf area and the refugee camps, 33,786 applicants had qualified, and a further 4,210 applicants from Mauritania had made it onto the list (UN doc. S/1999/875). In response to these numbers, the Moroccan government flooded MINURSO with appeals. By September, the total number rose to 47,796: 40,440 appeals against "noninclusion" and 7,356 against someone else's inclusion (UN doc. S/1999/854, par. 5).

The unexpected death of King Hassan on July 23, 1999, brought a sudden end to his nearly forty years of rule. The UN waited to see if there would be any change in Morocco's attitude toward the referendum under Mohammed IV, but for a time Basri remained firmly in charge of the effort. As Annan noted in August, "In his Throne speech on 30 July, His Majesty King Mohammed VI renewed his commitment to Morocco's territorial integrity through the holding of a 'confirmative' referendum under the auspices of the United Nations" (UN doc. S/1999/875, par. 3).

MINURSO resumed identification of the contested tribes on September 6 after a suspension during Morocco's mourning period. Toward the end of MINURSO's mandate in December 1999, the UN Secretariat reported that screening of the contested tribes was almost complete. MINURSO reported that it had received appeals from "almost all the applicants who, on the basis of their interviews [with MINURSO's Identification Commission], did not meet the criteria for voter eligibility" (UN doc. S/1999/1219, par. 9). Polisario, of course, denounced these appellants, asserting "that a large number of appeals could be eliminated by adhering strictly to the provisions concerning their admissibility."

The Moroccan government, in contrast, maintained "that every prospective voter [has] the right to appeal." The crux of the impasse, according to the secretary-general, was "the parties' radically opposed interpretations of articles 9, paragraph 1 (iii) and 12 of the appeals procedures" (UN doc. S/1999/1219, par. 4, 6, 9).[7] Polisario asserted that an appeal should not be entertained unless new documentary evidence could be produced, whereas Morocco argued that oral testimony from corroborating witnesses should suffice to establish eligibility during the appeals process. Indeed, almost all of Moroccan-sponsored appeals came with the intent to produce two or three witnesses in support, suggesting a scenario in which rejected Moroccan applicants would be vouched by other rejected applicants and vice versa, thus creating a self-authenticating network of "Western Saharans." Other appeals filed by October 1999 included 925 persons in Mauritania (who had submitted an original application but were never convoked) and 14,053 appeals against someone else's inclusion. This latter category of appeals had been brought forward by 1,199 persons, 96 percent from areas under Morocco's jurisdiction.

In his December 1999 report, Annan also reminded the Security Council that more appeals might be coming. Given that only a "small percentage of applicants from the [contested] tribal-groupings [have] been found eligible by the Identification Commission," he warned that if "all those who may be found ineligible were to file an appeal, the number of appeals to be processed could almost double" (UN doc. S/1999/1219, par. 8). Indeed, by the end of December, the Identification Commission had interviewed all applicants from the contested tribes. Of the 64,188 convoked applicants from subfractions H41, H61, and J51/52 (51,220 personally interviewed since June 15, 1999), only 2,135, or 3 percent, had qualified to vote. Altogether, nearly 70 percent of these applicants came from Morocco proper, and 22 percent were Moroccan-sponsored candidates from the occupied Western Sahara. Of those found eligible, 1,306 were from Morocco, the rest from Western Sahara (464), Tindouf (212), and Mauritania (179). The UN mission began collecting appeals from these groups on January 17, 2000. By May 2000, 54,889 appeals had been filed for the contested tribal groupings, 96 percent of them from Moroccan-sponsored candidates, the vast majority "against exclusion" under Article 9, based on the promise of corroborating witnesses (UN doc. S/2000/131, par. 6) (see table 2).

A "SOBERING ASSESSMENT"

On January 17, 2000, the UN published a preliminary list of all eligible voters for the long overdue referendum in Western Sahara. Of the 244,643 applications MINURSO had received and the 198,469 prospective voters interviewed in person, a total of 86,386 were found eligible to vote (UN doc. S/2000/131, par. 6). For members of the Western Sahara independence movement, this provisional voter list was a total victory. The outcome could be nothing but independence. The list vindicated their participation, their

TABLE 2. DISTRIBUTION OF VOTER APPLICANTS, ELIGIBLE VOTERS, AND APPEALS FILED FOR THE REFERENDUM IN WESTERN SAHARA AS OF FEBRUARY 2000

| | Moroccan-Occupied Western Sahara* | Morocco* | Tindouf and Refugee Camps** | Mauritania*** | Total |
|---|---|---|---|---|---|
| Voter Applications Received, Nov. 1994 (18 yrs. and older) | 83,971 | 99,225 | 42,337 | 10,070 | 244,643 (revised total) |
| First Round of Applicant Processing, Aug. 1994–Dec. 1995, Dec. 1997–Sept. 1998 (i.e., noncontested tribal subfractions) | | | | | |
|   Convoked | 68,308 | 60,946 | 39,749 | 15,366 | 184,369 |
|   Interviewed ("identified") | 61,189 | 45,858 | 34,764 | 5,438 | 147,249 |
|   Qualified (provisional voter list) | 40,686 | 5,569 | 33,786 | 4,210 | 84,251 |
| Second Round of Applicant Processing, June 1999–Dec. 1999 (including "contested" tribal subfractions) | | | | | |
|   Convoked | 14,645 | 44,740 | 1,125 | 3,678 | 64,188 |
|   Interviewed | 12,447 | 37,372 | 667 | 734 | 51,220 |
|   Qualified | 464 | 1,306 | 212 | 179 | 2,135 |
| Provisional Voter List | | | | | |
|   Total Convoked | | | | | 248,557 |
|   Total Interviewed | | | | | 198,469 |
| | 41,150 | 6,875 | 33,998 | 4,389 | 86,386 (revised) |
| Appeals | | | | | |
|   First Round | 39,920 | 41,270 | 3,571 | 914 | 79,125 |
|   Second Round (contested groups) | 12,922 | 41,319 | 499 | 149 | 54,889 |
|   Total Appeals | 52,842 | 82,589 | 4,070 | 1,063 | 134,014 |

Source: UN secretary-general reports on MINURSO (UN docs. S/1999/1098, S/2000/131, S/2000/461, S/2001/148, S/2002/467), from UN Secretary-General 1975–2007.

Notes: Mathematical discrepancies result from later decisions made by MINURSO's Identification Commission.

The 1974 Spanish census (all ages) indicated a total of 74,373, whereas the 1993 MINURSO revision of the 1974 Spanish census indicated a total of 72,370.

* Applications and appeals handled by Morocco.

** Applications and appeals handled by Polisario.

*** Applications and appeals handled by MINURSO.

stubbornness, and their tactical concessions. From Morocco's point of view, the numbers indicated total defeat. Of particular embarrassment for Basri was the performance of Moroccan applicants under the contested tribal groupings. For all of the time, money, and energy spent facilitating the inclusion of these applicants, only seven out of every two hundred qualified.[8]

By late 1999, shortly after MINURSO received the first avalanche of appeals from the Moroccan government, Annan publicly questioned the feasibility of a referendum before 2002. UN officials had originally expected to face, at most, 15,000 appeals (Canadian Lawyers Association 1997, 43). When the true number of appeals came to light in late 1999, one of MINURSO's worst fears had come to fruition: Morocco was appealing every rejected voter—and even opposing other voters' inclusion. The final onslaught of Moroccan-sponsored appeals from the contested tribal groupings in early 2000 only made the situation seem more hopeless.

Using these developments as the excuse Baker and others had been looking for, the secretary-general began to question the feasibility of the UN-OAU referendum effort. In his report announcing the final outcome of the identification process, Annan enumerated a host of reasons to abandon the Settlement Plan and the Houston Accords, starting with the potentially explosive issue of the (in)admissibility of Morocco's tens of thousands of appeals. The secretary-general had already noted that Morocco and Polisario maintained "radically opposed interpretations" (UN doc. S/1999/1219, par. 9) of the criteria for submitting appeals, even though both sides had ostensibly agreed to the criteria just ten months earlier in Houston. Harkening to the onerous eight years it had taken just to accomplish a *preliminary* aspect of the Settlement Plan (i.e., establishing the voter roll), Annan argued that, given the two parties' mutually exclusive interests, MINURSO could not afford to continue with the original Settlement Plan. "The respective positions of the two parties," Annan argued, "do not augur well for an early resolution of the issue of admissibility of appeals"—not to mention, Annan noted, the equally contentious issues of "a protocol for the repatriation of Saharan refugees" and the "appropriate security conditions" for the actual vote. Most important of all, the secretary-general admitted that there was no realistic mechanism—military or otherwise—to force either party to accept the results of the referendum. Given this "sobering assessment," he concluded that it was high time to seek an alternative solution. With that, he informed the Security Council in early 2000 that he had invited Baker to reengage the parties in talks to "explore ways and means to achieve an early, durable and agreed resolution" (UN doc. S/2000/131, par. 32–37).

The Security Council largely agreed with Annan's "sobering assessment," passing Resolution 1291 on February 29, 2000, in which the council called for an "early, durable and agreed" solution (UN doc. S/Res/1291). The only notable dissent came from the representative from Namibia, the first ever abstention on a Western Sahara resolution. The Netherlands, Canada, and Argentina were also reticent to back away from the Houston Accords so quickly. France, however, wanted to scrap the Houston Accords completely. Contrary to Bolton's assessment in 1998, the "culture of negotiations" was clearly alive and well in the Security Council when it came to Western Sahara.[9]

A full explanation of the Security Council's abandonment of the Houston Accords in 2000 is still lacking. The official reasons, of course, are presented in Annan's "sobering assessment." However, in the years since, as we detail in chapter 9, the UN has not been able to overcome the same problems that undermined the Houston Accords. More than a decade later, the goal of an "early, agreed and durable" peace is still far off. In retrospect, the secretary-general's reasons for dropping the Houston Accords do not hold. His complaint in February 2000, for example, that the referendum was at least two years away seem particularly incredulous. A similar sense of urgency for Western Sahara was completely absent in his final six years as secretary-general. In early 2000, Western Sahara had become a crisis because it was close to resolution rather than because it was a crisis stemming from irresolution. Lacking a reasonable explanation, one is forced to consider other possible rationales behind the desire to abandon the referendum.

Within the historical context, there are three interesting contingencies: Bouteflika's election in Algeria, Hassan's death, and the referendum in East Timor. For various reasons (see chapters 2 and 9), President Bouteflika's election in April 1999 brought with it the hope of a Morocco–Algerian détente. In early 2000, it seemed that the time was ripe to rethink the referendum, largely based on misinterpreted signals from Algiers, although those hopes soon turned out to be misplaced. Not only has Bouteflika proven unwilling to compromise on Western Sahara during his first two terms as president, but he has been more and more willing to damage Moroccan–Algerian relations for the sake of Western Sahara.

Another important contingency was Mohammed VI's ascension to the throne, just as MINURSO was finishing up the identification process. As noted earlier, Baker and the UN Secretariat were skeptical that the Houston Accords would actually lead to a vote. The "referendum" was a threat, a game of chicken, and they were waiting for Hassan and Basri to balk. Yet when Hassan died, an old dynamic came into play. The governments of France and the United States realized that it was not the time to threaten Mohammed VI during the early years of his consolidation of rule. With a reformist and democratizing facade, yet lacking his father's three decades of hard-won credibility, Mohammed was not in a position to suffer any disgrace on an issue as vital as Western Sahara. He had assumed the same throne but did not assume the same absolute power. He would have to manipulate skillfully the networks of elite clients that had enabled his father's authoritarian rule, many of whom had vested interests in Western Sahara.

Moreover, in a startling move Mohammed VI dismissed Basri in November 1999. Naive observers saw this dismissal as a sign of the new king's commitment to reform. Years later, however, it is clear that Basri was the sacrificial lamb, allowing for a reconfiguration—not a revolution—of power. His removal also eliminated one of the major impediments to a political solution. Whereas Baker tried to push Hassan away from a referendum process he could not win, Basri, whose credibility had been on the line, convinced Hassan otherwise. With Basri out of the way (happily, for most Moroccans), Mohammed could slowly back away from his government's signature on the Houston Accords. France and the United States eagerly encouraged this process by simultaneously backing the Security Council away from the referendum as well.

Yet Annan's "sobering assessment" is not completely misleading. There is at least one interesting admission related to the demise of the Houston Accords. In his February 2000 report, Annan had noted that the Security Council would never enforce the outcome of the referendum. In other words, if Morocco lost the vote and Polisario won it, the Security Council would still not force Morocco to leave Western Sahara. As one Western diplomat explained in 2000, "We must accept that the referendum is not the right answer. What happened in East Timor last year made this only too clear. No one will play the game. If Morocco lost the referendum, it would be a national disaster. It [Morocco] would not leave the Sahara and [Morocco's] position under international law would be untenable" (quoted in Ramonet 2000). Not only would a vote for independence forever vindicate Western Saharan nationalism, but it would also make Morocco's occupation all the more egregious. Likewise, the Security Council would have been even more legally obligated than ever to act against Morocco's occupation.

The problem, however, was more than mere Moroccan reluctance to withdraw. The parallels to East Timor go further: had the Western Sahara vote gone forward, the Moroccan government would have found itself in a position similar to the Indonesian regime in East Timor in 1999. A vote for independence would have inevitably triggered widespread calls for a full Moroccan withdrawal, leading to demonstrations, government repression, and an escalating cycle of violence. If atrocities followed, France and the United States would have been as morally obligated to act as they are legally obligated to oppose the Moroccan occupation right now. The lesson many international officials took from East Timor was sadly not that referendums should be carried out with sufficient safety guarantees for the voting population, but that contentious plebiscites should be avoided.

The UN secretariat and the Security Council's Group of Friends for Western Sahara were never comfortable with a winner-take-all vote. The referendum had only functional value, as an empty threat designed to extract a final political solution out of Morocco. The right of the Western Saharans to take part in a plebiscite to determine their political self is an idealistic and legally sound principle, yet it appears that no one besides Polisario and a handful of supporters actually took it seriously. The referendum process was further justified on the grounds that the parties were at least fighting with words and not guns. Going through the motions of a referendum was better than letting the war simmer throughout the 1990s and beyond. All along, however, the French and U.S. governments knew that they would eventually have to stop the process if it came too close to threatening their interests vis-à-vis Morocco. The inherent danger posed by the referendum to their interests finally crystallized in 1999. The explosive referendum in East Timor and the seating of the untested King Mohammed only hastened the inevitable end of the Settlement Plan and the Houston Accords. From the moment MINURSO was created, abandoning the referendum was never a question of if, but of when.

# 9

# The Baker Plan and the End
# of the Peace Process

On February 29, 2000, the UN Security Council stated its support for "an early, durable and agreed resolution" to the Western Sahara conflict. The language of "early, durable and agreed" was UN-speak for a political—as in not necessarily legal—solution outside the framework of self-determination. The approach that appeared to have the most support within the UN Secretariat and among the major powers on the Security Council was an autonomy agreement, to be negotiated by Morocco and Polisario directly. Autonomy's proponents underscored its positive-sum (win-win) outcome rather than the referendum's zero-sum (win-lose/lose-win) approach. Under autonomy, Morocco and Polisario would at least get "something" (sovereignty and self-rule, respectively). Otherwise, they would get nothing (status quo) or, worse, face a negative-sum (lose-lose) situation (i.e., a return to armed conflict). The 1991 Settlement Plan, its detractors argued, had engendered competition, not cooperation, with its win-lose (independence-or-integration) approach.

Autonomy as a solution to the Western Sahara dispute was not an idea hatched in 2000. Since the beginning of the conflict, numerous mediators had attempted to broker an asymmetric power-sharing compromise, and King Hassan seemingly indicated support for the idea on several occasions. In the early 1980s, he reportedly said that besides "the stamp and the flag . . . everything else is negotiable," which spurred a fruitless Algerian peace initiative between 1983 and 1985. In 1988, Hassan again expressed interest in autonomy (Zoubir 1994, 20–23). In the 1990s, during the early stages of MINURSO's voter-identification process, the Moroccan government began to open up to the idea of autonomy. Because neither Polisario nor Morocco could yet tell how the electorate was shaping up, there apparently was some motivation to talk about alternatives. Former head of the UN mission Erik Jensen, who set up these discussions in 1996, noted that high-level Moroccan officials had been examining the German *länder* and Spain's autonomous regions. In the final years of his life, King Hassan reportedly formed a secret think tank that examined the feasibility of transforming Morocco from a unitary state into a federalist one. Such a model would simultaneously settle the Western Sahara dispute and also preempt Amazigh

(Berber) demands for autonomy. Under King Mohammed VI, Morocco has wholeheartedly embraced the idea of autonomy as much as it has come to reject the notion of self-determination. In 2005, Rabat announced plans to begin implementing a kind of autonomy unilaterally. Then, in mid-2007, after several years in anticipation, Morocco submitted an autonomy proposal to the UN.

The Western Saharan independence movement, in contrast, has shown little interest in autonomy. For thirty years, Polisario has cultivated its base constituency on the principle of "all the homeland or martyrdom." This nationalist absolutism is increasingly supported by segments of Sahrawi society in the occupied Western Sahara, as evidenced by the uprisings of 1999 and 2005. However, Polisario's diplomatic corps have often shown much more flexibility in their thinking off record than their public statements imply. Given their close contact with Western diplomats, who have long demanded compromise, Polisario envoys have been continually pressed on the idea of autonomy. Yet the 1996 meetings are the only known occasion where Polisario has entered into discussions with Morocco on a solution between independence and integration. Once Baker became involved in the peace process in early 1997, and as the referendum's electorate began to favor independence, Polisario's position hardened. By late 1999, Polisario refused to show interest in autonomy (Theofilopoulou 2006, 9). Although Polisario accepted Baker's 2003 Peace Plan, which provided for four years of autonomy, its support for the proposal was based on the final-status referendum, which offered the option of independence. In the years since Baker's resignation in 2004, Polisario's rejection of autonomy has been proportional to Morocco's embrace of the idea.[1]

The idea of autonomy has come to dominate the discourse surrounding Western Sahara since 2000, but an "early, durable and agreed resolution" seems farther away than ever. How the peace process came to this dismal state of affairs is the topic of this chapter. Here we describe the disintegration of the peace process, from 2000 to Baker's resignation in 2004 and afterward. We focus on the processes behind the development of Baker's two alternative proposals, the first presented in 2001 (the Framework Agreement) and the second in 2003 (the Peace Plan). Whereas the UN referendum effort in the 1990s was conditioned by the immediate post–Cold War world, the search for a third way in Western Sahara was affected and ultimately undermined by the U.S. global war on terror after September 11, 2001. As the peace process ground to a halt in 2004, Sahrawis in the occupied Western Sahara again rose up the following year to confront Moroccan brutality and intransigence. All the while, Morocco conferred with its allies in Washington, Madrid, and Paris, who seemed more and more amenable to the idea of endorsing autonomy and explicitly rejecting self-determination. After eight years spent organizing a referendum and eight more years searching for a compromise, no one could claim that the conflict was any closer to a resolution than when the Security Council abruptly abandoned the Houston Accords in 2000.

THE FRAMEWORK AGREEMENT

Following the Security Council's decision in February 2000 to distance itself from the Houston Accords, Baker resumed his duties as the secretary-general's personal envoy on a full-time basis. His first move was to gauge the parties' attitudes, especially those of the new Mohammed VI and Bouteflika regimes. Along with Bolton, UN mission chief William Eagleton, and UN staff from New York, Baker toured the region from April 8 to April 11, 2000. The UN claimed officially that it had not abandoned the Houston Accords, but the thrust of the April talks was to move the parties away from the accords—especially Polisario. Baker presented a draft of the UN East Timor autonomy proposal as modified for Western Sahara. (The proposal was ironically one that the East Timorese had overwhelmingly rejected in favor of independence.) As a reality check, Baker highlighted the Security Council's increasingly negative attitude toward the Houston Accords. Furthermore, he presented a list to Polisario of parties that had failed to recognize ripe moments in negotiations and claimed that Algeria's position would soon change under Bouteflika.

A month later in London Baker and his team convened the first direct talks since Houston. The ground rules were the same as in 1997, and the parties were invited to provide their own proposals to move the Houston Accords forward. The secretary-general later admitted in his May 22 report that the talks had been unproductive (UN doc. S/2000/404).[2] Annan's suggestion that the parties should discuss "other ways" to resolve the conflict further infuriated Polisario, whose key supporters on the council at that time—Mali, Jamaica, and Namibia—tried to block this language in the resolution. The United States, the United Kingdom, and France, in contrast, wanted to push the parties away from the Houston Accords. Other states—Argentina, Tunisia, Netherlands, Bangladesh, and Canada—were, however, still uncomfortable with a drastic move away from the referendum. Although the council reiterated its "full support" for the Houston Accords in its Resolution 1301, the council also asked Baker to "explore all ways and means to achieve an early, durable and agreed resolution" (UN doc. S/Res/1301).[3] This directive drew a "no" vote from Namibia, abstentions from Mali and Jamaica, and instant protest from Polisario. However, MINURSO's mandate was given an extremely short extension of only two months.

The second round of Polisario–Morocco talks ended even more acrimoniously than the first. Although Morocco and Polisario still backed the Houston Accords, neither side offered suggestions or concessions in advance or at the meetings on June 28. Annan later reported that Baker felt that "the meeting, instead of resolving the problems, had moved things backwards" (UN doc. S/2000/683, par. 7). With little progress made, the Security Council decided to extend MINURSO until the end of October (UN doc. S/Res/1309). At the same time, the council's permanent members rejected an effort, led by Namibia, to make the Houston Accords viable. This proposal would have obliged the Security Council to impose the outcome of the referendum.

From the point of view of those favoring a political settlement, the next meeting was more successful. During talks on September 28, 2000, the Moroccan delegation signaled its willingness to consider an alternative to the Houston Accords. For Baker's team, this was the "breakthrough" they had been waiting for. In order to gauge Morocco's flexibility, Baker requested a draft proposal from Rabat. To add incentive, he warned that unless Morocco put forward an offer, he would set the rules for appeals and push the Houston Accords forward (Theofilopoulou 2006, 9). Adding his voice, Annan also warned Morocco that "further meetings of the parties to seek a political solution cannot succeed, and indeed could be counterproductive, unless the Government of Morocco as administrative Power in the Western Sahara is prepared to offer or support some devolution of governmental authority, for all inhabitants and former inhabitants of the Territory that is genuine and in keeping with international norms" (UN doc. S/2000/1029, par. 30). Baker promised Polisario that the Houston Accords were still on the table, but he ominously suggested that "there [are] many ways to achieve self-determination" (UN doc. S/2000/1029, par. 30). In fact, the September 2000 negotiations were the end of the road for the Houston Accords. They would also be the final face-to-face meetings under Baker and the last Morocco–Polisario talks for almost seven years. Showing obvious frustration and perhaps wanting to fire a shot across the Security Council's bow, Polisario almost initiated a new war in January 2001 when Moroccan forces crossed the berm to prepare for the Paris–Dakar Rally. High-level international pressure on Polisario, via Algiers, averted a new armed conflict (see chapter 1).

Baker returned to the peace process in early 2001, yet in his February 2001 and April 2001 reports, the secretary-general lamented that no progress had been made. Although Polisario expectedly showed no interest in a solution outside the Houston Accords, Morocco also seemed uninterested in any real devolution of its power in Western Sahara. On two occasions, Rabat had presented outlines for power sharing that Baker and the UN Secretariat internally dismissed as neither serious nor credible. Even under pressure from France, the United States, and the United Kingdom, Morocco refused to offer Baker a realistic proposal. As promised, pressure was ratcheted up in March 2001 when the UN mission began preparing to hear appeals for persons barred from voting in the referendum. In response, Rabat, with backing from France, asked for more time, which eventually ran into MINURSO's renewal on April 27. The following month Morocco's prime minister, Abderrahmane Youssoufi, publicly hinted that his government was finally beginning to take autonomy seriously (*Africa Confidential*, May 18, 2001). Although the Moroccan Foreign Ministry understood the need to offer a serious "devolution of governmental authority," the Interior Ministry rejected the idea in the name of national unity. It was, after all, the entrenched clientelist networks radiating from the Interior

Ministry and the military who would have to make all the sacrifices in any devolution of power in Western Sahara.

Baker was left with no option but to devise his own proposal. The first Baker Plan, the "draft Framework agreement on the status of the Western Sahara," arrived in June 2001, although Polisario, Algeria, and Morocco had seen copies in May. It was first shown to Morocco, where it received Mohammed VI's approval. In Algiers, Baker met with civilian and military leaders, where he presented, along with the Framework Agreement, a supplemental proposal for a passage from Tindouf to the Atlantic via Western Sahara. If Algiers wanted the passage, Baker claimed, it could be annexed to the plan. In Tindouf, Baker received a cool welcome. Polisario's leader, Mohammed Abdelaziz, would not even take his copy of the draft proposal from Baker's hand. Polisario had obviously received advanced warning from Algiers (Theofilopoulou, 2006, 9).

At one page in length, the first Baker Plan was short on details. Its main goal, though unsuccessful, was to spur dialog. For Polisario, the Framework Agreement was a radical departure from the Houston Accords in one key respect. It did not explicitly offer a referendum on independence, the *conditio sine qua non* of self-determination. Under the Framework Agreement's proposed autonomy, the Moroccan government would have control over foreign relations, defense, and some internal-security issues. Most internal matters would fall under the control of the Western Saharan autonomous government, consisting of an executive, an assembly, and courts. The proposal addressed the issue of self-determination through an ambiguous "final-status" referendum within five years of the plan's implementation. The first autonomous government of Western Sahara would be a balance of native Western Saharans and Moroccan settlers, but the electorate for the final-status vote was very favorable to Morocco. According to the plan, "To be able to vote in such a [final-status] referendum a voter must have been *a full time resident of the Western Sahara for the preceding one year*" (UN doc. S/2001/613, Annex I: par. 5, emphasis added). With this opening, the Moroccan government would have been able to move any number of its citizens into the territory in the year prior to the referendum and thus fix the vote.

The Moroccan government's enthusiasm for the plan was hardly disguised. On September 4, King Mohammed boasted in *Le Figaro* that he had "settled" the Sahara issue. Polisario, in contrast, reacted negatively—rejecting it from the start. The liberation front refused to provide comments on Baker's proposal and only offered additional suggestions on the Houston Accords. The Algerian critique of the Framework Agreement claimed that the plan was biased toward integration, was short on details, and was in violation of the longstanding legal principle of self-determination. Algeria further charged that Baker was not following his own mandate by neglecting the Houston Accords. The UN Secretariat, however, largely dismissed these concerns in a biting critique (see UN doc. S/2001/613, Annexes I–V). Baker's plan drew further criticism when the press reported that it grew out of the formerly secret proposals Rabat had submitted earlier in the year. On the Security Council, Jamaica, backed by Mauritius and Ireland, tried to get stronger support for Polisario's proposals for the Houston Accords. As always, France and the United States, along with Great Britain, blocked these efforts, hoping to build a new consensus around a political solution. This time the Security Council gave Baker five months to work. Although Resolution 1359 was careful to support a simultaneous—Houston Accords and Framework Agreement—approach, its language was clearly pushing the latter. This reality was further underlined when the size of MINURSO's Identification Commission was reduced from 120 to 36 personnel.

Baker convened a meeting in late August 2001 at his ranch near Pinedale, Wyoming, but with Algeria, Polisario, and Mauritania only. The Algerian regime had sent Baker some signals that it was willing to discuss the Framework Agreement more seriously. To that end, it sent then minister of justice Ahmed Ouyahia, who had also been a part of Algeria's team in Houston in 1997, as well as several members of the military to the meeting. Likewise, Polisario's contingent was the same as in 1997. Morocco was not invited because it had implicitly accepted the Framework Agreement, and Baker wanted to avoid any Moroccan provocation so that Polisario would not have a reason to walk out. The meetings wisely began with discussions of Polisario's proposals to revive the Houston Accords and then moved to separate discussions on the Framework Agreement. Mauritania reiterated its support for Baker's efforts, and Polisario and Algeria agreed to offer substantive responses in the near future (UN doc. S/2002/41, par. 3–8; *BBC News and World Service Online,* Aug. 28, 2001).

The attacks of September 11, 2001, in the United States occurred shortly thereafter. Algeria was one of the first countries to offer support to the George W. Bush administration in Washington's new war on terror. This and other signals from President Bouteflika had given Baker and the UN Secretariat optimism that Algiers was willing to compromise with Morocco. However, when Algeria and Polisario submitted their comments on the Framework Agreement in early October, their positions remained the same. Indeed, Algiers's response was an even more thoroughgoing critique than previously, and Polisario rejected the agreement prima facie. However, President Bouteflika, who had been invited to speak at the Baker Institute in Houston on November 2, told Baker on the sidelines that Algeria and Polisario were willing to discuss a territorial division of Western Sahara. When Baker personally presented this idea in Rabat, King Mohammed and his advisors rejected it (Theofilopoulou 2006, 10). Underscoring his regime's attachment to Western Sahara, Mohammed VI made his first royal visit there in November, which brought with it the release of fifty-six political prisoners, including Sidi Mohammed Daddach, the longest-held Sahrawi prisoner of conscience in Morocco, captive since 1979. Yet even with this gesture, King Mohammed was unable to visit the city of Smara owing to ongoing demonstrations against him (BBC Monitoring Service, Nov. 18, 2001; Reporters sans frontères 2001). In light of all these developments, although with no actual progress toward peace at the end of 2001, the Security Council renewed MINURSO's mandate for another three months.

In February 2002, the Security Council was presented with what the Secretary-General considered a "bleak" assessment. Both Algeria and Polisario reiterated more vehemently their rejections of the Framework Agreement. In order to move forward, Baker demanded a strong mandate from the Security Council based on one of four nonnegotiable choices: the Houston Accords, the Framework Agreement, territorial division, or MINURSO withdrawal (UN doc. S/2002/178, par. 48–51). Given that option four still felt premature, the council was clearly being asked to take a harder line with one side or the other. Options one and three would require putting more pressure on Morocco; option two would require getting tough with Algeria and Polisario; yet the Security Council also recognized that forcing options two (no self-determination) and three (territorial division) would constitute dangerous precedents under international law.

Baker's four options, which he delivered in person on February 27, were intended as a wake-up call. The Security Council was still operating as if Baker could produce another Houston Accords without the council's having to lift a finger. Baker, however, knew that the council's partiality for a self-implementing, self-enforcing agreement between Morocco and Polisario was a pipe dream. The context in 2002 was far different than it was in 1997, most important because Morocco and Polisario were no longer on the same page regarding acceptable outcomes. For Western Sahara to see peace, Baker knew that arms would have to be twisted by a higher authority. Without the Security Council's Chapter VI and VII powers, Baker's peacemaking toolkit was actually quite limited (Theofilopoulou 2006, 11). For the Security Council, the status quo was far more attractive than the unexpected consequences of radically altering the equation. Already overburdened with far bloodier, more devastating conflicts, the Security Council never wanted to take a chance for peace in Western Sahara. Giving itself two months to decide, it followed the already well-established patterns of global interests and alliances. France and the United Kingdom tried to build a new consensus toward option two, with support from Guinea, Norway, Cameroon, and Bulgaria. Although Mexico favored option one and Colombia option three, the Russian Federation wanted to continue simultaneous refinement of the Houston Accords and the Framework Agreement. Partial to option one, the U.S. government also wanted to give Baker a clear mandate. It even threatened to veto a renewal of MINURSO if consensus could not be obtained—in effect, option four (Jensen 2005, 109). Rather than force the issue to a contentious vote, the Security Council gave itself two months. Near the end of April, Baker intimated that he was ready to resign unless given a "clear path forward" (*Financial Times* [London], Apr. 26, 2002). Baker and Annan warned the Security Council against modifying any of the options to require consent because doing so "would simply encourage a continuation of the conflict and the current stalemate" (UN doc. S/2002467, par. 22). Needing more time, the council pushed the deadline to the end of July.

In the end, the Security Council chose "none of the above." Its members had seen the need for a clear path forward but could not agree on which way to go. The normally cohesive core of the Group of Friends for Western Sahara—the United States, France, Russia, and the United Kingdom—was itself internally divided. In Resolution 1429 on July 30, 2002, the Security Council stated its desire to "secure a just, lasting and mutually acceptable political solution which will provide for the self-determination of the people of the Western Sahara." More important, in the operative paragraph one, the council expressed "its readiness to consider any approach which provides for self-determination that may be proposed by the Secretary-General and the Personal Envoy" (UN doc. S/Res/1429). The resolution was neither an endorsement of the Houston Accords, favored by Russia, nor backing for the Framework Agreement, favored by France, the United States, and the United Kingdom. It was a compromise between the personal envoy, who requested strong language in favor of self-determination, and the Security Council, which was not willing to press Morocco. The resolution's primary purpose was to send a positive signal to Polisario by offering strong support of self-determination, which had been missing from the Framework Agreement. The Security Council thus gave Baker six more months, until the end of January 2003, to come up with a solution.

## THE QUESTION OF RESOURCE EXPLOITATION

The peace process was further complicated in late 2001 when Morocco announced efforts to look for oil and gas in Western Sahara, both onshore and offshore. That September Morocco's Office national de recherches et d'exploitations pétrolières (National Office for Petroleum Exploration and Exploitation) signed contracts with France-based Total and the smaller U.S. firm Kerr-McGee. As president of the Security Council in November 2001, Jamaica requested an official opinion from the UN Legal Affairs Department. On February 5, 2002, Hans Corell, the UN legal counsel, issued a response that was well received by Polisario and its supporters. First of all, the opinion highlighted Morocco's precarious legal position in the territory, having obtained the territory through an illegal invasion in 1975. The opinion also clearly reiterated that Western Sahara is a non-self-governing territory—a colony—requiring self-determination. His conclusion was that Morocco's current resource-exploration contracts would not be illegal under international law, but that it would be illegal for the Moroccan government, as the de facto colonizing power in a non-self-governing territory, to extract Western Sahara's resources without adequate approval from the population. Although not explicit on Western Sahara's two main exports, fisheries and phosphates, the opinion clearly implied that profits gained from those industries by Rabat were in contravention of international law. In the Security Council, the opinion provoked a debate on the ambiguities of Morocco's illegal status in Western Sahara, but some members of the council dismissed such talk as unproductive.

In a provocative countermove, RASD signed a 2003 exploration contract with the Anglo-Australian oil company Fusion to access the entire acreage off the coast of the Western Sahara (*PESA News,* Apr.–May 2003). Then, in 2005, RASD signed contracts with seven different companies covering areas onshore and offshore, mostly British and Australian. Knowing their favorable position under international law, Polisario officials hoped these concessions might force some kind of international legal battle on the RASD's sovereignty in Western Sahara. Yet the prospects that there might be significant deposits on or offshore Western Sahara continued to receive significant skepticism, even with global oil prices at all time highs. Just south of Western Sahara, for example, Mauritania had already signed agreements to begin oil and gas production at seventy-five thousand barrels a day from its first offshore wells by the year 2005. However, when production finally began in 2006, output was revised significantly downward several times, eventually to less than 50 percent of the original assessment. Although this situation suggested that Western Saharan reserves might be equally meager, ever-increasing oil and gas prices continued to provide incentive for even the most miniscule finds.

In fact, a powerful confluence of economic and strategic interests had started bearing down on Northwest African energy reserves by 2002. Despite the numerous conflicts that have plagued West Africa, the Gulf of Guinea increasingly became seen as a "stable" source of oil for the United States over the more volatile Middle East and Central Asia. Vice President Dick Cheney's National Energy Policy report noted that West Africa had become "one of the fastest-growing sources of oil and gas for the American market" (quoted in *Time,* Oct. 28, 2002). Some estimates have predicted that by 2015, West African hydrocarbons could provide up to 25 percent of U.S. petroleum imports. The Institute for Advanced Strategic and Political Studies (2002), a Jerusalem-based think tank, convened a working group composed of U.S. business and policy leaders and called the African Oil Policy Initiative Group. Among its list of recommendations, it advised the U.S. government to declare the Gulf of Guinea an area of "Vital Interest." Meanwhile, China—increasingly considered the leading rival of the United States for dwindling global hydrocarbon reserves—impressively expanded its own stake in African oil and gas production (Klare and Volman 2006, 621–24). In 2007, the U.S. Department of Defense finally created a separate military command for Africa, called Africom, suggesting that the continent's strategic significance had finally caught up with its climbing economic importance.

Selectively parsing the 2002 UN legal opinion, Morocco and the companies associated with the hydrocarbon deals seized on the distinction between exploration and exploitation. As an oil-importing country, Morocco had good reason to secure any potential oil reserves in its grasp. The 2000 U.S. Geological Survey of World Energy thought that reserves could be "substantial" offshore Western Sahara, whereas sources in Morocco proper were "low and insecure" (quoted in *BBC News and World Service Online,* Mar. 4, 2003). The Moroccan regime's moves toward exploration and exploitation in late 2001 focused primarily on the waters off the coast of Western Sahara. The firm conducting the exploration for Kerr-Mc-Gee and Total, TGS-Nopec, however, came under intense grassroots pressure from European activists, charging that the company's activities were complicit with the Moroccan occupation. These efforts led TGS-Nopec to withdraw hastily from the affair under threat of Norwegian government divestment, but only after the company had completed most of its survey. The Norwegian government then divested $52 million in Kerr-McGee stock, citing the company's activities in Western Sahara as the cause.

With all of this talk of oil in Western Sahara, Baker's own interests began to be called into question, especially his connections with Kerr-McGee and the notoriously oil-friendly Bush–Cheney administration. Indeed, the Bush administration's first ambassador to Morocco, Margaret Tutwiler—a personal friend of Baker who had served as his spokesperson in the State Department—was reportedly placed in Rabat to expedite oil deals, among other things (Madsen 2003). With the Total and Kerr-McGee deals unfolding in the context of Baker's pro-Moroccan Framework Agreement, it was difficult for observers not to think that Western Sahara was being sold out to U.S. energy interests. Baker, however, would prove an honest broker.

Polisario's supporters in the U.S. Congress made sure later that Western Sahara was specifically exempt from provisions of a free-trade agreement with Morocco. As U.S. trade representative (and future World Bank president) Robert Zoellick was forced to emphasize, "The United States and many other countries do not recognize Moroccan sovereignty over Western Sahara" (quoted in Mundy 2005). By then, 2004, Total had dropped out of Western Sahara ostensibly for business reasons. Isolated, Kerr-McGee came under increasing pressure, even in its home state of Oklahoma; Christian activists who had built up humanitarian relations with the Sahrawi refugees helped put pressure on the company and on the state's political leaders. Kerr-McGee finally withdrew in 2006, although other companies from around the world soon stepped in to take its place.

Polisario's case for sovereignty—or at least the claim that Morocco has no right to exploit Western Saharan resources—suffered a huge setback in early 2006. The EU signed a heavily contested fisheries accord with Morocco. Estimates vary, but in 2002 Moroccan-licensed ships harvested roughly one million tons. Rabat has made investments totaling $325 million to upgrade the industry's infrastructure between 1997 and 2001, including new fishing ports in Dakhla, Boujdour, and al-'Ayun in Western Sahara. The port at Dakhla, which cost Morocco $42 million to build, opened in August 2001, becoming Morocco's largest fishing port south of Agadir (Economist Intelligence Unit 2003b, 34–35; Reuters, Aug. 27, 2001). As with oil and phosphates, the world's escalating demand for fish was leaving legal and political considerations by the wayside in Western Sahara. Yet there were political effects. In late 2006, Annan warned Polisario, in an effort to jump-start negotiations, that the EU fisheries accord was a sign that the international community was beginning to accept the Moroccan occupation.

THE ULTIMATE COMPROMISE: BAKER'S PEACE PLAN

The second Baker Plan, the Peace Plan for the Self-Determination for the People of West-ern Sahara ("Baker Two" or the Peace Plan), was presented to the parties in early 2003 and unveiled publicly in May. Work on the plan had started in September 2002 with Baker, members of the UN Secretariat, and Professor Hurst Hannum, a legal expert from Tufts University who had helped draft the UN autonomy agreement for East Timor. The final version was completed in late November 2002 and shown to the secretary-general the following month. Baker's goal was to make an offer that neither side could reason-ably reject (Theofilopoulou 2006, 11). Yet under the constraints of the Security Council's recent mandate, Baker would have to offer Western Sahara what Morocco had explicitly rejected: a shot at independence. Although the small UN team had worked on the docu-ment in total secrecy, there were indications it had been leaked to Morocco. For example, on November 5, 2002, the twenty-seventh anniversary of the Green March, Mohammed VI declared that a referendum in Western Sahara was simply "not applicable" any longer (Jensen 2005, 110).

Baker visited North Africa between January 14 and 17, 2003, presenting the Peace Plan to King Mohammed, President Bouteflika, Polisario's leadership, and President Maaouiya Ould Taya (1984–2005) of Mauritania. Secretary-General Annan had called the parties beforehand to encourage their receptivity and had asked France to use its influ-ence on Rabat. All sides reportedly accepted the document; Algeria, sensing Morocco's discomfort, was the most positive, whereas Morocco's cool reaction was further indication that Rabat's officials had somehow already seen it. Although Baker had asked for Polisa-rio to wait for Morocco's reaction to the plan, Polisario stated the following day that it would likely reject it (*afrol News,* Jan. 18, 2003; Theofilopoulou 2006, 11). By March 2003, Morocco, Polisario, and Algeria had submitted their formal reactions.

Like the Framework Agreement, the Peace Plan offered a short period of autonomy followed by a "final-status" referendum within five years. However, the Peace Plan's refer-endum was initially a clear choice between independence and integration. Furthermore, the voter pool was decidedly more balanced than under the Framework Agreement. The electorate would consist of persons of voting age either on MINURSO's December 30, 1999, list (without addressing appeals), the UNHCR repatriation list as of October 31, 2000, and persons "who have resided continuously in Western Sahara since December 30, 1999" (UN doc. S/2003/565, Annex II: par. 5). The Framework Agreement, in contrast, had proposed a final-status referendum with no explicit options and would have been a plebi-scite of persons resident in Western Sahara a year before the vote, thus giving Morocco more control over the outcome. The Peace Plan limited the size of the electorate, making it more balanced between Sahrawis and Moroccans and thus explicitly offering Polisario a shot at independence.

Another major difference was the amount of detail, which offered a very robust autonomy under the direct control of native Western Saharans. Following a transitional period allowing for the repatriation of the refugees, indigenous Western Saharans from the MINURSO and UNHCR lists would elect the first autonomous government, the Western Sahara Authority (WSA). This body would consist of an executive and a legislative body, with a judicial branch being appointed later. During the four-year period before the referendum, the WSA would be solely responsible for "local government, law enforcement, social welfare, cultural affairs, education, commerce, transportation, agriculture, mining, fisheries, industry, environment, housing and urban development, water and electricity, roads and other basic infrastructure." Unlike under the Framework Agreement, under the Peace Plan the Saharan judiciary would be totally independent of Morocco. The Moroccan government would have exclusive control "over foreign relations . . . , national security and external defense," including control over firearms (except for WSA law enforcement needs) and the "preservation of territorial integrity against secessionist attempts." The flag, the stamp, customs, currency, and telecommunications would also remain Moroccan. The majority of the population—Moroccan settlers—would have no voice in the WSA itself, although they would be able to vote in the final-status referendum (UN doc. S/2003/565, Annex II: par. 8–16).

If Moroccan settlers could not participate in the autonomous government, as they would have under the Framework Agreement, the Peace Plan raised the very real possibility that Polisario officials and their supporters would dominate the WSA. The idea of Mohammed Abdelaziz as the WSA executive must have sent chills down the spine of Moroccan Interior Ministry officials. Furthermore, Western Sahara's most important economic aspects would come under WSA control, including future petroleum prospects, fisheries, and raw phosphate exports. Given the networks connecting Moroccan military and political elites to these key industries, handing all of this over to the WSA would definitely pose a threat to important interest groups within the Moroccan regime. The WSA would theoretically have enough autonomy to override these interests and perhaps enough to influence the opinion of Moroccan settlers regarding the final vote. Some settlers might even opt for independence if the WSA demonstrated enough competence and provided a better future than under continued Moroccan rule. Indeed, Baker tried to sell the Peace Plan to Polisario leaders on the idea that it gave them the opportunity to win Moroccan settlers' support for independence.

The linchpin of the Peace Plan was, of course, its final-status vote. Like the 1991 Settlement Plan, the composition of the electorate was key. Yet instead of weeding out the non–Western Saharans, as MINURSO had attempted to do in the 1990s, Baker proposed pitting native Western Saharans against the majority nonnative settlers of Moroccan origin. Baker reasoned that this was the only way Morocco would ever participate in an act of self-determination—if the vote seemed in Rabat's favor. From the Moroccan government's perspective, one disadvantage of the Peace Plan, unlike the Framework Agreement, was that it cut off the date for voter enfranchisement at 1999, so Rabat could not flood the territory with voters before the final-status referendum. In fact, Baker and his team engineered an electorate that was almost evenly split, though slightly in Morocco's favor.

Native Western Saharan voters for the Peace Plan's final-status referendum would be drawn from MINURSO's 1999 list (totaling 86,386, all voting age) and UNHCR's 2000 repatriation list (totaling 129,863, all ages). Between these two groups, there would be significant overlap, and, as noted in chapters 5 and 8, the UNHCR list is imprecise and very likely an overestimate. The third voter group in the Peace Plan's final-status referendum would be residents of Western Sahara since 1999, both indigenous Western Saharans (overlapping significantly with MINURSO's list) and Moroccan settlers—Arabs, Berbers, and the thousands of ethnic Sahrawis from southern Morocco transplanted in the early 1990s for the referendum. Numbers vary, but a 1994 Moroccan census counted a total Western Saharan population of 252,118 (Thobhani 2002, 104), yet the 2004 census recorded a significant increase to 415,945 in the areas of Morocco's "southern provinces" that rest within or overlap Western Sahara (Haut Commissariat au Plan 2005). Assuming a steady rate of growth between 1994 and 2004, the total population in the Moroccan-occupied Western Sahara could reasonably be estimated at roughly 334,000 in 1999. Then assuming approximately half of these persons (i.e., 167,000) were of voting age at that time, and subtracting the number of native Western Saharans listed on MINURSO's 1999 voter list from the territory itself (41,150), we come up with some 126,000 voting-age Moroccan settlers (Arabs, Berbers, and ethnic Sahrawis) being pitted against 86,386 native Western Saharans (plus any additional Sahrawi voters from the flawed UNHCR list).

According to these very rough numbers, the final-status electorate under Baker's Peace Plan would clearly be in Rabat's favor if all native Moroccans voted for integration. All parties involved in negotiations over the years—Polisario, Morocco, MINURSO, and Baker—have assumed at one time or another that among native Western Saharans, an overwhelming majority favors independence. So Polisario would have to win over at least 40,000 voting-age Moroccan settlers. It is assumed that Western Saharan nationalists would have a hard time changing the minds of Arab and Berber settlers from northern Morocco, but the fidelity of ethnic Sahrawis from southern Morocco has become increasingly contested since many joined the 1999 uprising in al-'Ayun. Because Moroccan census figures do not record ethnolinguistic differences, it is difficult to know the exact size of the nonnative Sahrawi population in the occupied Western Sahara. The Second Green March of mainly ethnic Sahrawis in 1992 was reportedly 120,000 strong, suggesting that Polisario might indeed have the Sahrawi numbers to swing an independence vote in its favor. For non-Sahrawi Moroccan settlers, there might even be deterrents against voting for Rabat. An integration vote might put an end to all the incentives that come with living in Western Sahara, such as tax breaks and double salaries (*Middle East International,* July

11, 2003). Polisario officials have long maintained that their state will be viable only with the continued presence of Moroccan settlers as a part of the labor force, especially the Tashilhit-speaking Imazighen (Berbers) who dominate small commerce and are native to regions just north of Western Sahara. These settlers, who are far more economically than ideologically motivated, might go either way in a vote so long as they can maintain their Moroccan citizenship and thus their real homes in the Sus and Anti-Atlas regions. With the right promises, just enough Moroccan Arab and Berber settlers might switch sides. However, some Moroccan settlers might violently oppose independence. A small number of Moroccans attacked Sahrawi demonstrators in the 1999 uprising, though similar attacks were not reported following the outbreak of the 2005 intifada.

On May 23, 2003, the UN secretary-general finally publicly released the Peace Plan and the parties' responses to the public. Even down to the title, the second Baker Plan made obvious overtures to Security Council Resolution 1429's call for self-determination. Annan argued that it satisfied self-determination by "providing the bona fide residents of the Western Sahara . . . the opportunity to determine their own future" (UN doc. S/2003/565, par. 50). Although without qualifying "bona fide residents," Annan took a step toward erasing the lines between Moroccan settlers, ethnic Sahrawis, and indigenous Western Saharans. The Moroccan regime had tried to blur those categories in the 1990s, and now the secretary-general was doing it for Rabat in 2003. As Africa's last official colony, Western Sahara was exceptional enough, yet Baker and Annan appeared to be ready to give it the distinction of being the only colony whose self-determination vote would be dominated by the occupier's settlers. In this way, the plan showed an almost blatant disregard for the Fourth Geneva Convention, which clearly prohibits the transfer by an occupying power, such as Morocco, of its citizens into a territory seized by force.

All parties except Mauritania submitted numerous pages of critique. The secretary-general took issue with the copious amount of "ostensibly technical" points in the feedback provided by Morocco and Polisario. Taken together, Annan claimed, "these objections suggest that the parties still lack the genuine will required to achieve a political solution to the conflict" (UN doc. S/2003/565, par. 55).

As always, Rabat started from the premise that Western Sahara is Moroccan. The Moroccan government was obviously uncomfortable with the idea of not being able to tightly control Western Saharan affairs during the autonomy period. More important, Morocco objected to the independence option on the final-status referendum. Responding to this objection, Annan argued, "It is difficult to envision a political solution that, as required by Security Council resolution 1429 (2002), provides for self-determination but that nevertheless precludes the possibility of independence as one of several ballot questions" (UN doc. S/2003/565, par. 54). Annan suggested that, to address Morocco's concern constructively, the Peace Plan should contain a third ballot option: "continuation of the division of authority set forth in article III of the peace plan"—that is, "self-government or autonomy." He justified this option on the grounds that "Morocco has for some time supported the concept of self-government or autonomy as the solution to the conflict over Western Sahara" (UN doc. S/2003/565, par. 53). Morocco, however, liked this compromise even less, believing that it could split the final-status vote three ways, taking away prointegrationist votes from Rabat (Theofilopoulou 2006, 12).

Polisario's fundamental objection to the Peace Plan was, in the secretary-general's words, "that it is not the [1991] settlement plan." Among the twenty-four points and additional subpoints raised by Polisario, the most serious had to do with the Peace Plan's final-status electorate, which Polisario deemed "unfair and fatal to the Saharan people." With this objection, Polisario was expressing concerns about Moroccan participation in the vote and about Morocco's use of its position as the dominant power under the Peace Plan to keep Western Sahara as its territory even if the final-status vote was for independence. Again reverting to the Houston Accords, Polisario proposed several concessions to motivate a return to the referendum. However, its proposal required that the Security Council consent to enforcing the outcome of the referendum under Chapter VII of the UN Charter (i.e., by coercive means). Yet the secretary-general argued that Morocco would never agree to Polisario's conditions on a nonnegotiable basis. Nor would the Security Council likely ever be willing to enforce the outcome of a referendum, as evidenced by its refusal to take firm action in 2002 when Baker demanded it (UN doc. S/2003/565, par. 54).

Annan ironically admitted two paragraphs later that Baker was placing the Security Council in a situation where it would have to make some hard choices. The contradiction was glaring: Baker and Annan were asking the Security Council to do for the Peace Plan what the council had deemed impossible for the Houston Accords. Summing up his May 2003 report, the secretary-general warned, "After more than 11 years and an amount of assessed contributions close to $500 million, it should be acknowledged that the Security Council is not going to solve the problem of Western Sahara without asking that one or both of the parties do something they are not otherwise prepared to do" (UN doc. S/2003/565, par. 57). Indeed, during a briefing with the Security Council in early May 2003, Baker had insisted that the parties should be forced to accept the Peace Plan. A Security Council request for further negotiations, Baker reasoned, would undermine his work. Facing a rather difficult decision, the Security Council again gave itself two months to decide (Resolution 1485).

The May 16 attacks by Moroccan terrorists in Casablanca, which took the lives of thirty-three civilians and the twelve bombers, had already cast a shadow over the Western Sahara peace process. The Moroccan state remained firmly in control following the attacks, but the bombings provided the regime with an opportunity to remind the West of its important role in their global interests after September 11, 2001. The effects of May 16 on Western Sahara would be felt farther down the road, during and after the contentious Security Council vote of July 2003.

END OF THE ENDGAME

At the UN, the United States tried to rally a consensus behind Baker's Peace Plan. This effort generated support from the United Kingdom, Spain, Germany, and Chile. France, taking Morocco's position, wanted more negotiations before endorsing the Peace Plan and found support from Guinea and Cameroon (two governments dependent on French foreign aid) as well as Bulgaria. The other states on the Security Council—China, Russia, Syria, Mexico, Pakistan, and Angola—were divided (Theofilopoulou 2006, 12). Morocco's opposition to the Baker Plan was well known, and Rabat lobbied the Security Council for more time to negotiate. Polisario, toning down its own denunciations, perhaps under pressure from Algiers, watched as Morocco's protests grew louder.

On July 11, Spain, holding the Security Council presidency, announced that Polisario had accepted the Peace Plan. Shortly after this breakthrough, the U.S. representative on the council, John Negroponte, told reporters, "I wouldn't want to guess at this point how the other Council members are going to react to this, but we have put forward a resolution that would . . . endorse . . . Baker's plan and urge the parties to the conflict to implement it." In no uncertain terms, Moroccan foreign minister Mohamed Benaissa responded, "Morocco's position is clear: we refuse that any decision pertaining to the sovereignty of the kingdom be imposed on us" (quoted by Reuters, July 16, 2003). King Mohammed even made personal phone calls to U.K. prime minister Tony Blair and U.S. president George W. Bush to press his country's position against the Peace Plan. French president Jacques Chirac also lobbied for Morocco behind the scenes (*Washington Report on Middle East Affairs,* Oct. 2003).

Although Algeria had rejected the 2001 Framework Agreement and supported dividing Western Sahara in 2002, its early embrace of the 2003 Peace Plan was widely read as a sign of diminishing support for Polisario.[4] It was assumed that Algeria's new "pragmatism" on Western Sahara came from its special relationship with the Bush administration, especially after September 11, 2001 (see Quandt 2002). By 2005, the United States was Algeria's largest investor and the largest recipient of Algeria's exports, both predominantly related to hydrocarbons (Zoubir 2006, 5–6). With U.S.–Algerian relations at their best at this moment in the postcolonial period, there was reason to believe that Algiers backed the Baker Plan and pushed Polisario just to further its own interests vis-à-vis the United States and possibly in relation to Bouteflika's reelection bid in 2004.

However, Algeria's support for the Baker Plan and its convincing Polisario to do likewise were actually a carefully calculated move to turn the tables on Morocco and undermine its support in the United States. If there was any Algerian pressure on Polisario, it was not to sell out self-determination. Rather, Algiers pressed Polisario to understand that Morocco was not comfortable with the Peace Plan. With agreement to Baker's proposal, the major benefits to Algeria and Polisario were to place the burden of rejection on Morocco and to earn the Bush administration's favor through Baker. Rather than sell out Polisario, Algeria was attempting to incorporate Polisario into its renewed relations with the United States. Yet when the Bush administration later opted to back Morocco's rejection of the Baker Plan, it was clear Algeria had underestimated Rabat's "tenacity" (discussed later) as much as Morocco's importance to Washington.

At the Security Council, the debate boiled down to UN semantics: whether to "endorse" or merely to "support" the Peace Plan. As always, it was never a question of moving to Chapter VII—to impose the plan against Morocco's will. "Endorsing" the Peace Plan would have signaled the Security Council's strongest possible backing under Chapter VI, which the United States championed for Baker's sake. France, with backing from China and Russia, demanded a consensus resolution on the grounds that obtaining consensus was the tradition on Western Sahara, even though Paris had been more than happy to violate this rule of etiquette in Morocco's favor in 2000, when the Houston Accords were on the chopping block. As one analysis of the resolution noted, this "'tradition' developed in response to constant French and American attempts to railroad a pro-Moroccan position past the other Security Council members in defiance of all previous decisions" (Williams and Zunes 2003). Nevertheless, "consensus" won.

In Resolution 1495 of July 31, 2003, the Security Council tepidly offered to continue to "support strongly the efforts of the Secretary-General and his Personal Envoy and similarly supports [i.e., does not *endorse*] their Peace plan for self-determination of the people of Western Sahara." Russia, normally more favorable to Polisario, demanded the addition of an ambiguous qualification—"as an optimum political solution on the basis of agreement between the two parties." Although not clear at the time, this phrase, which acknowledged the Peace Plan's virtues, would be used by the Moroccans to demand further negotiations (i.e., through the phrase "on the basis of agreement").

Quick to call the resolution a victory, Polisario and Algeria had at least put Morocco on the defensive for the first time since 2000. From then on, they refused further negotiations until Rabat accepted the Baker Plan. Morocco, in contrast, argued that the resolution did not force anything on it. As France's UN representative Michel Duclos explained, "[T]he resolution did not impose a solution on the parties, which would have likely 'tipped the dynamic process' of dialogue and the peace process. Rather, it prompted a resumption of sustained discussion." Negroponte was just as quick to point out that nothing had been "imposed," but he also stated that "the resolution responded to the Secretary-General's recommendations on the way ahead in Western Sahara" (quoted in *Beirut Daily Star*, Aug. 12, 2003). In an obvious warning to Rabat, the Spanish representative, who had backed the United States, said, "If Morocco moves away and doesn't do anything to comply . . . the matter will come back to the Security Council" (*Financial Times* [London], July 31, 2003). The council gave Baker and Morocco until the end of October 2003 to work things out.

On September 17 in Houston, Morocco's foreign minister Mohamed Benaissa, interior minister delegate Fouad Ali El-Himma, and permanent representative to the UN Mohammed Bennouna met with Baker to request more time to respond to Resolution 1495. Six days after the meeting in Houston, Mohammed VI pleaded his case to President Bush on the sidelines of the General Assembly. According to reports, Bush let it be known that he wanted King Mohammed to "address this constructively and see if a solution acceptable to Morocco can be found," although he assured the monarch "that the UN and the U.S. would not impose a settlement on Morocco" (Agence France Presse, Sept. 24, 2003). The following month President Chirac stated France's "steadfast position . . . consists in supporting the position of Morocco." He reiterated, "[A] solution cannot be imposed by the international community against the will of one of the parties" (quoted in Jensen 2005, 113). U.S. assistant secretary for Near Eastern affairs William Burns visited Rabat soon thereafter and reaffirmed U.S. opposition to a take-it-or-leave-it approach (Jensen 2005, 113).

At the same time, Morocco's Foreign Ministry opened up an attack on the secretary-general by calling his neutrality into question. In a letter from Bennouna, the Moroccan government said the UN Secretariat had "deviated from its neutrality and its objectivity by deliberately giving an erroneous interpretation of Resolution 1495." He then asserted, "All the members of the Council clearly rejected the option of imposing the plan" because the resolution had called for "the approval of the parties" (quoted by Agence France Presse, Oct. 22, 2003), in reference to the phrase Russia had inserted into the resolution. Nevertheless, in his October 16 report Annan tried to apply as much pressure as possible. He hoped that by the end of 2003, "the Kingdom of Morocco will be in position to engage positively in the implementation of the plan" (UN doc. S/2003/1016, par. 28). The Security Council honored Morocco's request for more time and extended MINURSO to the end of January 2004. In reality, this extension just gave Morocco more time to undermine Baker.

Instead of offering revisions to the Peace Plan, Rabat drafted a new counterproposal, which it first showed to the U.S. government in early December. Baker finally received a copy on December 23, even though France and Spain were also privy to early copies as well. The Moroccan government called its proposal a "draft Autonomy status," but it in reality offered even less self-governance than Baker's 2001 Framework Agreement (e.g., all judicial and security duties were Moroccan). Although this "nonpaper" offered a final-status referendum, independence would not be an option, and Morocco—not MINURSO— would manage the vote (Theofilopoulou 2006, 13). To develop the proposal into a viable counteroffer, the UN Secretariat again enlisted the help of Hurst Hannum, who worked with a Moroccan team to refine it. Baker, who had at this time also taken on a large assignment for the White House rescheduling Iraq's debt, needed more time to examine Morocco's "final response to the Peace Plan" (UN doc. S/2004/39, par. 28). The Security Council gave Baker three months.

Arriving on April 2, 2004, Morocco's second counterproposal was almost identical to the first. Rejecting it as inadequate, Baker demanded a more serious effort by the end of the month. Two weeks later the Moroccan government presented the exact same plan. In his report to the Security Council four days later, Annan noted the meetings between Morocco and Baker but did not disclose Morocco's secret counterproposals or the fact that Rabat's attitude had grown increasingly uncooperative. What the report did disclose was that Morocco had finally submitted its formal rejection of the 2003 Peace Plan: "as far as the Kingdom is concerned, the final nature of the autonomy solution is not negotiable. . . . It is, therefore, out of the question for Morocco to engage in negotiations with anyone over its sovereignty and territorial integrity" (UN doc. S/2004/325, Annex I). In light of this response and Morocco's secret counterproposals, Baker and Annan presented the Security Council with two options: (1) admit failure and terminate MINURSO or (2) "try once again to get the parties to work towards acceptance and implementation of the Peace Plan." Calling the Peace Plan "the best political solution to the conflict," the secretary-general hoped "the Security Council will reaffirm its recent unanimous support for the Peace Plan" and "call upon the parties to work with the United Nations and each other towards acceptance and implementation" (UN doc. S/2004/325, par. 37–38). Baker had obviously come to the conclusion that in order for the Western Sahara conflict to reach resolution, pressure would have to be brought to bear on Morocco. Clearly frustrated with a lack of support, Baker confronted the Security Council with a choice it would never make. Its response would determine Baker's continued participation.

As in 2002, the Security Council opted for evasion rather than action. It neither terminated MINURSO nor endorsed the Peace Plan, but instead offered to "support" Baker's work and his efforts to "to achieve a mutually acceptable political solution." Resolution 1541's weak language was the result of a new consensus. The new Socialist government of Spain, led by José Luis Rodríguez Zapatero, elected in March 2004, quickly sought to repair Hispano–Moroccan relations damaged by the previous government's strong support for the Peace Plan. Because of its "war on terror," the United States had also prioritized good relations with Morocco over Baker's peace efforts in Western Sahara. If not for Algeria, which was then also on the council, Resolution 1541 could have been much worse for Polisario (Theofilopoulou 2006, 13). Annan and his personal envoy were given another six months to achieve the impossible.

Baker's failure to complete his breakthrough in 2003 confirms what several leading experts on conflict resolution have concluded: "Intractable conflicts are no place for mediation initiatives undertaken as a substitute for clear policy or designed to conceal inaction or disarray in the ranks" (Crocker, Hampson, and Aall 2004, 113). Calls from the Security Council and the Secretariat asking simultaneously for self-determination and compromise revealed an incoherent approach to Western Sahara.

Always the consummate diplomat, Baker waited several weeks, until June 1, to submit his resignation. When he had taken the position in 1997, he had brought with him the explicit backing of the U.S. government. When he resigned seven years later, it was because he had lost that support. In his first public interview after leaving Western Sahara behind, Baker offered the following appraisal:

> Well I think any dispute like this is solvable given goodwill on the part of both parties but you haven't had that. If you don't have that, if they're not willing to exercise the political will necessary to reach a solution and the Security Council is not willing to move from Chapter 6, that is consensus, to Chapter 7 where they can ask the parties, force the parties, one or both of them, to do something they don't want to do. Then I don't know where the solution comes from. This issue is really not unlike the Arab–Israeli dispute: two different peoples claiming the same land. One is very strong, one has won the war, one is in occupation and the other is very weak. (in Husain 2004)

The loss of Baker was a huge setback for the Western Saharan independence movement. For a short period, just before and after the July 2003 showdown, Polisario had achieved a diplomatic coup—winning the support of the United States. That victory was short-lived, however. Over the course of the following three years, Polisario's foreign policy came under a sustained attack from a reinvigorated Morocco, backed by a new consensus in Washington, Paris, and Madrid favoring autonomy. Algiers, however, did not forget the favor it had done for the United States in convincing Polisario to accept the Baker Plan. As U.S.–Moroccan relations climbed, U.S.–Algerian relations cooled off.

In Rabat, there was little love lost for the departed personal envoy. Morocco's foreign minister boasted that Baker's resignation was the "outcome of the tenacity of Moroccan diplomacy." The Moroccan press was less kind, charging that Baker had "flagrantly sided with Algeria" and, as an Agence France Presse dispatch noted, his resignation "was greeted with thinly veiled satisfaction" in Rabat (June 13, 2004). Using the "war on terror" as an excuse, Morocco had found a way to accomplish what had once seemed impossible: divide Baker—a close Bush family friend who had played a key role in bringing the president to office—from the White House and the State Department. Where Moroccan diplomats once described 2003 as a crisis period in their relations with the United States, two years later they were claiming that their relations then had never been better. Indeed, the same month as Baker's resignation, the Bush administration designated Morocco a "major non-NATO ally," a coveted status given to only a handful of nations, which, among other things, allows designees to receive the most advanced U.S. military equipment. The White House awarded this prestigious—albeit nonobligatory—status because of what a senior administration spokesman described as "the close US–Morocco relationship, our appreciation for Morocco's steadfast support in the global war on terror, and for King Mohamed's role as a visionary leader in the Arab world" (*BBC News and World Service*

*Online,* June 4, 2004). Officials involved in the decision stressed that the designation was a show of solidarity with the Moroccan regime after the May 16, 2003, attacks, a warning that the United States would not tolerate any destabilization of Morocco. Likewise, that same month, the Senate ratified a free-trade agreement with Morocco by an eighty-five to thirteen margin, making the kingdom one of only a half-dozen countries outside of the Western Hemisphere to enjoy such a close economic relationship with the United States. Under the administration of George W. Bush, U.S. aid to Morocco increased almost fivefold from 2001 to 2006.[5] Several months after Baker's resignation, on November 19, 2004, Deputy Secretary of State Richard Armitage told Aljazeera, the Qatar-based Arabic television network, that the United States supported what he called "the territorial integrity of Morocco," with respect to Western Sahara. Although this description was not yet the administration's explicit policy, Armitage had articulated the essence of U.S. policy since 1975.

AUTONOMY OR INTIFADA?

In the years following Baker's June 2004 departure, the Western Saharan peace process drifted dangerously toward total collapse. Digging in its heels, Polisario refused for three years to participate in further talks—either direct or indirect—until Morocco accepted the Peace Plan. Algeria, echoing Polisario's attitude, increased its vocal support for Western Saharan independence, not just self-determination. More comfortable with its standing in Washington, Rabat increased its efforts to delegitimize Polisario and to "bilateralize" the dispute with Algiers. The French presidency of Jacques Chirac supported this effort and encouraged Morocco's unilateralist approach to autonomy. The United States decided, after seven years of high-level involvement behind Baker, to back off.

The only member of the Group of Friends to make an effort in the immediate post-Baker period was Spain. Yet Madrid's effort was clouded by mixed messages—one that seemed tailored for Rabat and one for Algiers. During the brief period when MINURSO lacked both a special representative and a personal envoy, and in the midst of the largest proindependence demonstrations in Western Sahara's history, from May to July 2005, Spain quietly approached Morocco, Algeria, and Polisario about holding direct talks without preconditions. For Algeria and Polisario, trilateral negotiations were as repugnant as the previously suggested bilateral Algeria–Morocco talks. In addition, both Polisario and Algeria had adopted the posture that there was nothing to talk about until Morocco accepted the Peace Plan. Having failed to spur either a Moroccan–Polisario or a Moroccan–Algerian dialog, Spain pressed the UN for a new personal envoy.

Late in Baker's tenure, Alvaro De Soto, a Peruvian diplomat with extensive peacekeeping experience in Cyprus and Central American, was appointed to head MINURSO in August 2003. After June 2004, he assumed additional duties as acting personal envoy.

Before De Soto, former U.S. diplomats had led the mission since the Houston Accords of late 1997. After Ambassador Charles Dunbar resigned in early 1999 (see chapter 8), Ambassador William Eagleton, a career "Arabist" in the U.S. foreign service, headed MINURSO until late 2001. His replacement, Ambassador William Lacy Swing, having served as a U.S. diplomat in Africa, held the special representative post until mid-2003. With De Soto's appointment, shortly after the Security Council's unenthusiastic show of support for the Peace Plan in July 2003, the U.S. presence in the mission was already more diminished. Although the United States had been one of the main contributors to MINURSO's military monitors in 1994 (thirty) and 1997 (fifteen), by 2004 it was contributing zero. French, Russian, and Chinese contributions, however, remained consistent and high.

Desperate to keep pressure on Morocco, Polisario approached the U.S. government in search of another high-level mediator, brazenly floating names such as Bill Clinton and Colin Powell. The response from Washington was a categorical "no." The logic was simple: If Baker could not find agreement, who else could? The State Department even learned how counterproductive low-level engagement could be. In early 2005, Polisario approached the United States to see if Washington wanted to help mediate the release of the last 404 Moroccan POWs held near Tindouf. Careful to play it safe, Washington demanded ground rules that would force Polisario to take a back seat to Algiers and Rabat. Senator Richard Lugar, then chair of the Senate Foreign Relations Committee, was appointed as an emissary of the White House to oversee the POW transfer. On August 18, 2004, speaking from the city of Tindouf (not in the camps), Senator Lugar thanked Polisario for this gesture but added, "Although our mission is purely humanitarian, I am hopeful that Algeria and Morocco can seize on this occasion to create a climate conducive to the settlement of the Western Sahara issue." This language, clearly crafted for Rabat, did not go over well in Algiers or in the camps. Furthermore, Morocco failed to reciprocate in any meaningful way; Moroccan repression related to the ongoing Sahrawi intifada actually increased. Smarting from the experience, Washington retreated farther from the frontlines of Western Sahara diplomacy.

Washington was also not happy with the fact that Polisario and Algeria refused to meet with De Soto, even to talk about the Peace Plan, although this important fact was not reported in any of the secretary-general's reports. To his credit, De Soto was able to get Morocco and Polisario to sign an agreement on one of several UNHCR "confidence-building measures" related to the refugees, allowing brief family visits from the camps to the occupied Western Sahara and vice versa. For many families, this opportunity allowed them to see close relatives for the first time in almost thirty years. Indicative of the parties' mutual mistrust, this ostensibly humanitarian measure took three years to negotiate. Once off the ground in mid-2004, the program suffered repeated setbacks, starts, and shutdowns through 2007. For MINURSO and UNHCR, their confidence-building measures had become as contentious as the broken track-one process. For any would-be mediator, they were further proof that the situation was "rotten" for resolution.

Approaching the final year of his tenure, Secretary-General Annan appointed a new personal envoy to Western Sahara on July 25, 2005, former Dutch diplomat Peter Van Walsum. This appointment came two months after De Soto's reassignment to the Middle East and the eruption of widespread Sahrawi demonstrations for independence in the occupied Western Sahara. (A new special representative, Francesco Bastagli, an Italian UN officer, took the mission's helm several weeks later.) Following his first tour of the region from October 11 to 17, Van Walsum, in an attempt to sound both diplomatic and realistic, summed up Morocco and Polisario's attitudes as "quasi-irreconcilable." His first briefing to the Security Council was on January 18, 2006, when he stated his belief that a solution was at least a year away. Regarding Baker's Peace Plan, he noted that recent Security Council resolutions had shown no renewed support for the plan. Likewise, little pressure had been put on Morocco by its allies—France and the United States—to reconsider its stance toward a referendum. The Western Sahara paradox, as the secretary-general and his personal envoy described it, remained the same: "A new plan would be doomed from the outset because Morocco would reject it again, unless it did not provide for a referendum with independence as an option. . . . [T]he United Nations could not endorse a plan that excluded a genuine referendum while claiming to provide for the self-determination of the people of Western Sahara." In light of this assessment, Van Walsum asserted that there were two realistic options. The UN could wait for either a "different political reality" or "direct negotiations between the parties." Because the former was deemed a "recipe for violence," the latter was seen as the only reasonable option. Direct negotiations without preconditions, it was argued, should "work out a compromise between international legality and political reality . . . which would provide for the self-determination of the people of Western Sahara." Van Walsum stated that, according to Annan, "the question of Western Sahara can only be achieved if the parties work to seek a mutually acceptable compromise with each other based upon relevant principles of international law as well as current political realities" (UN doc. S/2006/249, par. 31–39). Having again admitted that Morocco's position constituted a rejection of international legal norms and that, despite this fact, the Security Council would never take action against Rabat, Annan's recommendations and observations were becoming more and more paradoxical. In typical fashion, the Security Council simply deferred the issue for another six months, to October 2006.

In his November 2005 speech marking the thirtieth anniversary of the Green March, King Mohammed announced that he would enter into a national dialog with Morocco's political parties on the subject of autonomy for Western Sahara. Once this internal process was complete, the Moroccan regime promised that it would present its own autonomy proposal to the UN in early 2006. By MINURSO's April 2006 deadline, however, Morocco was reportedly still working on its proposal. A month later it was revealed that Morocco's "autonomy" initiative mainly involved the revival of CORCAS, the royal Saharan advisory council, with Khalihenna Ould Rachid as its head. First groomed by Madrid as a part of a neocolonial elite, but having defected to King Hassan in May 1975 in the face of near unanimous Sahrawi support for Polisario, Ould Rachid had served several positions in the Moroccan government and had earned a small fortune from various enterprises and corrupt practices in Western Sahara. As the new face of Western Saharan "autonomy," Ould Rachid toured several important global capitals to tout the virtues of Morocco's approach to settling the conflict. The major effect on most Sahrawi nationalists was to undermine the concept of autonomy by equating it with an old client (Ould Rachid) and an old institution (CORCAS) of the Moroccan monarchy.

For the Security Council to take Rabat's autonomy project seriously as a legitimate peace offer, Morocco would first have to present Van Walsum with a detailed proposal. Yet in the three years after Baker's resignation, Morocco stalled, knowing that once its ideas were made public, it would be formally committing itself to something less than full integration. There were two clear disincentives for presenting a proposal. First, the Security Council would likely hold Morocco to its commitment to autonomy. Although the council had let Mohammed VI back away from his father's commitments to self-determination, regional autonomy would be impossible to retract. Second, the Moroccan government's autonomy proposal would have to find a delicate balance between domestic and international interests. Whereas the former would call for the weakest autonomy possible (to ensure continuity of political and economic interests), the latter expected something that both Polisario and the Security Council would have to take seriously. Although it was understood that Mohammed VI had accepted the 2001 Framework Agreement, Rabat's secret autonomy proposals of late 2003 and 2004 indicated that Morocco's own conception of "autonomy" still needed to mature. The problem for Mohammed VI's patron states—France, Spain, and the United States—was that Morocco had yet to provide a serious rejoinder to the peace process. Given that Paris, Madrid, and Washington had helped scrap Baker's Houston Accords and the Peace Plan for Morocco's sake, the onus was on Rabat to provide a credible counteroffer.

Whereas Spain and France tended toward continued quiet encouragement of Morocco, the temporary appointment of John Bolton to the post of U.S. ambassador to the UN in August 2005 created a new dynamic in U.S. policy toward Western Sahara. Having served as Baker's assistant during the Houston Accords and afterward, Bolton was intimately familiar with the conflict and made it one of his priorities during his one-year mandate at the UN. Polisario officials were ecstatic following his appointment, suggesting that Bolton, like Baker, had been won over to their side. Although Bolton did not press for a revival of the Baker Plan, he did question the utility of UN missions that could not fulfill their mandate (e.g., MINURSO following Morocco's rejection of a referendum). Behind this "principled" stance against UN inertia, however, was Bolton's longstanding belief that the UN should be an instrument of U.S. policy rather than a forum where weaker nations could openly defy Washington.

Bolton knew quite well that France would block any pro-Polisario initiative on the Security Council. Thus, his only means of asserting effective pressure on the peace process was to threaten a veto of MINURSO's mandate—well within the right of any of the five permanent Security Council members. Minimally, as Bolton argued, a threatened withdrawal of MINURSO might entice the parties to reconsider their positions. Maximally, it might be used to force Morocco to accept the Baker Plan. For Polisario, a U.S. veto of MINURSO, based on right-wing claims of Moroccan intransigence, would at least cast a bright light on the occupation of Western Sahara.

The real aim of Bolton's strategy, however, was never very clear. In his memoirs (2007), he claims that he simply wanted MINURSO to complete its mission or be done with it. Yet a threatened withdrawal of MINURSO was hardly enough leverage to overcome French support for Moroccan intransigence or the culture of consensus that had governed Security Council decisions on Western Sahara since 1988. Self-determination in Western Sahara, as Baker had made clear following his resignation, would require the Security Council to commit the unthinkable: move to Chapter VII against Morocco. For obvious reasons, Bolton's arguments did not sit well with his colleagues in the State Department bureaucracy or the White House. The presence of MINURSO was still widely seen in Washington as a force for North African stability, an argument with even more traction in the post–September 11 mindset. Bolton's greatest opponent, however, sat even closer to the president. Elliot Abrams, head of Near East Affairs on the White House's National Security Council, argued in favor of Morocco's long-awaited autonomy proposal (Bolton 2007, 246–47, 367–69). In October 2006, Abrams even met with CORCAS's Ould Rachid. When Bolton's short tenure expired at the end of 2006, having accomplished nothing in Western Sahara's favor, Abrams was left the strongest voice backing Morocco, largely on the grounds that Moroccan cooperation in the war on terror (e.g., extraordinary renditions and proxy torture) had become indispensable to the United States (Amnesty International 2004; *London Observer*, Dec. 11, 2005). By early 2007, Abrams had implemented what one U.S. analyst considered "a major U.S. policy shift . . . backing Morocco's unilateral imposition of its so-called Western Sahara Initiative, or autonomy plan" (Swisher 2007).[6]

With French, U.S., and Spanish support, Rabat finally submitted its long-anticipated autonomy proposal to the new UN secretary-general, Ban Ki-moon, on April 11, 2007. It came a day after Polisario submitted—without warning to the UN Secretariat—several dramatic bridging proposals for the Peace Plan. Yet the long-anticipated Moroccan proposal received far more attention than Polisario's desperate attempt to steal the spotlight.

In many ways, Morocco's autonomy statute was far more detailed than either the 2001 Framework Agreement or the 2003 Peace Plan. Where it differed most significantly with the Peace Plan's autonomy was the lack of any actual autonomy. On the one hand, Morocco proposed a "Saharan Autonomous Region" with a locally elected government (executive, judicial, and legislative) granted significant competences. On the other hand, the Moroccan monarch (retaining his far-reaching powers) and a representative of the Moroccan government (charged with capacities granted the Moroccan state) would ultimately rule over the proposed autonomous region. Under Morocco's conception of "autonomy," Western Sahara would remain firmly subordinated to the powers of the central Moroccan state. The minimal international standard for an autonomous regime is to have a locally elected government that cannot be abolished by the central state. An autonomous regime in Western Sahara, to be worthy of the name, would have to be free to manage its affairs without any interference from the Moroccan state. Yet Rabat put forward a system whereby the executive would be "invested" by the Moroccan king and beholden to him. Of greater significance, Morocco's autonomy statute was particularly silent on the fundamental issue of whether royal investment would come with the royal power to disinvest and thereby override the democratic wishes of an autonomous Western Sahara (see Ruiz Miguel 2007).

As far as the Western Sahara peace process was concerned, the details of autonomy were far less important than Morocco's approach to the question of self-determination. Rabat's Western Sahara initiative simply called for a referendum that would ratify the statute determined in negotiations. As Morocco had argued in its response to Baker in April 2004, "the autonomy solution, as agreed to by the parties and approved by the population, rules out, by definition, the possibility for the independence option." Three years later Morocco did not provide a legal argument for such a deduction. Equally vague were the proposed electorate for such a referendum ("the populations concerned") and the body that would conduct the vote (a "Transitional Council" of the "the parties"), which appeared to eschew a role for MINURSO. The actual proposal was likewise vague concerning the geography of the Saharan Autonomous Region (Western Sahara or Morocco's larger set of "Saharan provinces"?) and regarding those who would negotiate the statute's final draft ("the parties"). Continuing Morocco's efforts to divide and rule Western Saharans through the manipulation of ethnicity, Rabat proposed a vaguely structured and democratic parliament partially elected by "various Sahrawi tribes." Yet the proposal refused to use the name "Western Sahara" and tried to avoid acknowledging a Sahrawi people (instead using the Moroccan diminutive for Hassaniyyah speakers, *Hassani*). And it ostentatiously proposed a "blanket amnesty" clearly targeted at Polisario. Yet Morocco offered no mechanisms for either monitoring or enforcing the agreement, thus leaving the door open for massive repression and a unilateral reneging of the statute (e.g., in the name of stymieing threats against Morocco's "territorial integrity").

The Moroccan government and its supporters rejected specific criticisms of the statute on the grounds that it represented a basis for negotiations rather than a finalized proposal. Yet there were larger reasons that warranted skepticism. First, there is a poor history of centralized authoritarian states' respect for regional autonomy. Instead of creating peace, regional autonomy has often led to violent conflict. In 1952, the UN granted the British protectorate (and former Italian colony) of Eritrea autonomous, federated status within Ethiopia. In 1961, however, the Ethiopian emperor unilaterally revoked this status, annexing Eritrea as his country's fourteenth province. The result was a bloody thirty-year struggle for independence and subsequent border wars between the two countries. Similarly, Serbian leader Slobodan Milosevic's decision to revoke the autonomous status of Kosovo in 1989 helped precipitate armed conflict, eventually resulting in NATO intervention ten years later. Based on Rabat's pattern of breaking promises during the UN and OAU peace processes and on the Security Council's willingness to tolerate such behavior, the autonomy statute should thus have inspired widespread concern as to its durability.

Despite all of these serious problems with the Moroccan proposal, the Bush administration and some congressional leaders rushed to legitimize it. In June 2007, the State Department's undersecretary for political affairs Nicolas Burns called it "a serious and credible proposal to provide real autonomy for the Western Sahara" (Agence France Press, Apr. 11, 2007), a point underscored before the House Foreign Relations Committee by Assistant Secretary of state for Near Eastern affairs David Welch (2007). Welch even warned in the course of his testimony that the conflict needed quick resolution because the Polisario-administered refugee camps presented "a potentially attractive safe haven for terrorist planning or activity" (Welch 2007). Nor was there any change in French policy following the election of Nicholas Sarkozy in May 2007. In a speech before the Moroccan Parliament several months later, Sarkozy, like Washington, described Morocco's proposal as a "serious and credible" basis for a "political solution, negotiated and agreed by the two parties." The new president added that when it came to negotiations with Polisario, "France will stand shoulder to shoulder with you" (Sarkozy 2007).

The Security Council's April 30, 2007, response to the Moroccan proposal, Resolution 1754, was equally welcoming, borrowing the language —"serious and credible"—used by Washington and Paris. Although the response also took note of Polisario's concessions and reiterated the council's support for a "mutually acceptable political solution" that "will provide for the self-determination of the people of Western Sahara," its most important aspect was its call for negotiations (UN doc. S/Res/1754). For the most part, the Security Council's language was on the same page as Rabat's rhetoric, especially the UN call for "negotiations without preconditions" and a "mutually acceptable political solution." Yet the mandate for self-determination was clearly an implicit precondition even if Rabat chose to ignore it. Indeed, with the Security Council ostensibly promising self-determination, Polisario had nothing to lose by going to the negotiations.

This call for direct talks was also a victory for Van Walsum's slow and steady approach. Possessing few carrots and no sticks, the personal envoy had to use time, encouragement, and preexisting power relations to his advantage. Following his dire assessment in early 2006, he slowly maneuvered the parties—first Morocco and then Polisario—into positions where their rejection of negotiations would be patently unreasonable. In the wake of Baker's efforts and the Security Council's demand that a solution would have to come from the parties, the first step was to convince Morocco and its allies that Rabat, as the more powerful party, had to put a credible offer on the table. At the same time, the Security Council and the Secretariat would have to distance themselves from Baker's Peace Plan and convince Polisario that its right to a referendum on independence was still guaranteed. Once a proposal was on the table from Morocco and with sufficient UN assurances for self-determination, Polisario would have much credibility to lose and none to gain by rejecting face-to-face talks. The problem was that these negotiations would be in bad faith. Morocco had no intention of discussing self-determination, and Polisario had no intention of discussing autonomy. Although Van Walsum had set the stage for the first direct talks in almost seven years, that stage was dangerously unstable and might collapse at any moment.

The reason for this instability was that the Security Council, the Secretariat, and Van Walsum were just as guilty of bad faith as the two main parties involved. The clear subtext of UN thinking since 2004, if not 2000, had been how to get Polisario to abandon a vote on independence. Doing so was technically impossible under international law because only the Western Saharans can, through a referendum, give up their right to self-determination. Yet in his final report on the Western Sahara dispute, Annan was even bold enough to suggest that the right of self-determination for Western Sahara rests with the Security Council: "Polisario would be well advised to enter into negotiations now, while there is still consensus in the Council that a negotiated political solution must provide for the self-determination of the people of Western Sahara" (UN doc. S/2006/817, par. 20). Yet during such negotiations, it was inconceivable that Van Walsum would place the modalities of a referendum on the agenda, knowing full well that such a discussion would trigger a Moroccan boycott or walkout. Yet if Polisario openly discussed autonomy, even under the most noncommittal circumstances, that would be the point of no return.

The danger in these direct talks was clear to Polisario. Although the 2007 negotiations were ostensibly simultaneous talks on autonomy and self-determination, Polisario was already very familiar with this bait-and-switch game. From 2000 to 2003, the peace process was supposed to be based on concurrent discussions of both the 1997 Houston Accords and an alternative political solution. The real objective, though, was to get Polisario to talk about the advantages of the latter to the detriment of the former. By 2003, the Houston Accords had long been dead, and Polisario's self-determination referendum on independence had been severely compromised. The danger in 2007 was that as soon as Polisario showed any willingness to discuss the modalities of autonomy, the Security Council would either abandon or redefine self-determination to suit new "political realities."

Two months after the Security Council called for new talks, delegations from Morocco and Polisario met in Manhasset, New York, on June 18–19 and August 10–11, with Algerian and Mauritanian observers present. A second set of talks followed the Security Council's review of MINURSO in October, with parties again meeting on January 7–9 and March 16–18, 2008, in Manhasset. According to accounts and statements issued afterward, there was little substance to the meetings. This result was in part owing to the composition of the Moroccan delegation. The Polisario team—Mahfoud Ali Beiba, Brahim Ghali, Ahmed Boukhari, and Emhamed Khadad—was essentially the same as in 1997 and 2000, underscoring the continuity and consistency of Polisario's position. The Moroccan side was almost entirely new, formed of Mohammed VI's most trusted advisors, including Minister of the Interior Chakib Benmoussa, Minister Delegate for Foreign Affairs Taieb Fassi Fihri, Minister Delegate for the Interior Fouad Ali El-Himma, Counterintelligence Chief Yassine Mansouri, and Morocco's UN representative Mostafa Sahel. Rabat had also provocatively dispatched members of CORCAS, including Ould Rachid. This delegation underscored Rabat's commitment to its autonomy statute as much as the negotiating team's heavy bias toward Morocco's perception of the conflict as an "internal" matter rather than a foreign-policy one (Theofilopoulou 2007). Because Polisario's side was not used to these new Moroccan faces and Rabat's team had yet to become acclimatized to dealing with Polisario, the first two meetings in 2007 were little more than introductions, and the second set in 2008 were perfunctory (re)statements of position.

Briefing the Security Council at the end of April 2008, Van Walsum decided it was time to call the council's bluff. He bluntly said Western Saharan independence was unrealistic and that the Security Council should say so. Although this view was quickly leaked to and widely circulated in the Moroccan press, the Security Council opted not to take such a bold step. Instead of the normal six-month extension, MINURSO was given a full-year mandate, and more negotiations were demanded. Polisario's response to Van Walsum's assessment came quickly: a May 4 statement from Tindouf declared no confidence in the secretary-general's personal envoy. Yet the Secretariat remained eerily silent on the matter. Showing obvious frustration with the lack of support from Secretary-General Ban Ki-moon and the Security Council's trepidation, Van Walsum gave his first interview since becoming UN envoy to Western Sahara in 2005. He told the Dutch paper *NRC Handelsblad* what he had told the Security Council: Western Sahara will not achieve independence if the United States and France do not support it (May 24, 2008). Again, the UN secretariat did not respond either to Van Walsum's public statements or to Polisario's declaration of no confidence. Aiming for a wider and more engaged audience, Van Walsum granted an interview with the leading Spanish daily *El País* on August 8. He bluntly acknowledged that "international law is on [Polisario's] side," but he reasserted his belief that it was in the best interests of Western Saharan nationalism to accept "reality" and give up its right to independence. Three weeks later, at the end of August, the UN Secretariat unceremoniously fired Van Walsum by simply letting his contract expire.

Already waiting in the wings to replace Van Walsum was retired U.S. ambassador Christopher Ross, a highly competent Arabic-speaking diplomat with extensive background in the Middle East and, more important, North Africa. Ross had attended the first four Manhasset rounds as an observer for the U.S. government, suggesting either a keen interest in the issue or a preexisting effort by the State Department to insert Ross into the process (or perhaps both). Indeed, after his nomination was leaked to the press, it seemed that Ross was an envoy of the United States rather than of the secretary-general. Secretary of State Condoleezza Rice welcomed Ross's selection even before the UN had secured Morocco and Polisario's consent to his appointment (*Alhurra*, Sept. 9, 2008). Although Polisario would have normally welcomed increased attention from the United States, recent statements by the Bush administration had reversed long-standing U.S. rhetorical support for self-determination. Recent U.S. statements went far beyond earlier affirmations of support for Morocco's autonomy proposal, instead openly declaring autonomy as the only feasible solution. Following a year-long extension of MINURSO in April 2008, a State Department official said in no uncertain terms, "An independent Sahrawi state is not a realistic option. In our view, some form of autonomy under Moroccan sovereignty is the only realistic way forward to resolve this longstanding conflict." A personal letter from President Bush, celebrating the ninth anniversary of the ascension of Mohammed VI on July 23, 2008, reiterated U.S. opposition to Western Saharan independence. Secretary of State Rice further underscored this new policy when she prematurely announced Ross's appointment as the new personal envoy: "There are proposals on the table. We don't need to go back to square one. Obviously, this is going to involve some kind of autonomy" (all quotes from *Alhurra*, Sept. 9, 2008).

By the end of 2008, the parties had accepted Ross's appointment but were unsure whether the recently elected Barack Obama administration in the United States would take a different direction than its predecessor or not. During the campaign, Obama had not articulated an explicit Western Sahara policy, though his convincing electoral victory was fueled in part by a promise to correct the foreign-policy wrongs of the previous administration, especially in the Middle East. Polisario had reason to welcome the Obama presidency (e.g., Obama's close relations with Senator Edward Kennedy, a longtime supporter of Western Saharan self-determination). Indeed, two weeks after Obama's election, Aminatou Haidar, one of the most prominent Sahrawi independence activists, received the Robert F. Kennedy prize for human rights, further raising Western Sahara's profile among key figures close to the new administration. Yet if the analysis we have put forward in this book holds true, then reasons of state will force Obama, like all his predecessors since 1975, to prioritize Morocco's needs over Western Sahara's rights.

Polisario faced serious choices as 2008 drew to a close. Although the May 2005 intifada, still simmering in the streets of the occupied territory, had given Western Saharan nationalists some hopes, Morocco's selective yet persistent use of torture, intimidation, and detainment kept protests to a minimum. Moroccan repression only convinced the refugees in Algeria that they are still better off in exile. On the international stage, Polisario's successful rejection of Van Walsum suggested that in the short term it did not have to fear an imposed solution. In the long term, Polisario would have to choose either to continue working under UN auspices in the face of Morocco's continued rejection of self-determination or to pursue independence through other means. Toward the end of 2007, it seemed that Polisario's leaders were taking the military option more and more seriously or being forced to by their constituents in the camps. The December 2007 triennial Polisario General Congress in Tifariti, postponed from 2006, resolved to increase the readiness of its armed wing, the ELPS, in case the talks failed. Independent accounts from the congress—which was subtitled "The Struggle to Impose Sovereignty and Full Independence"—indicated widespread support for war among the two thousand delegates and attendees, although Polisario's diplomatic core pressed for more time. On December 20, the congress stated its opposition to endless negotiations, but, as had been the case since 1991, Western Saharan nationalism lacked a sufficient casus belli that would pass muster with Algeria or the international community. The Franco–American consensus had once again backed Western Saharan nationalism into a corner, robbing it of hope and leaving it few alternatives.

## AN AUTOPSY OF THE WESTERN SAHARAN PEACE PROCESS

The Western Sahara peace process has been guided by four faulty assumptions. The first two assumptions have been the most potent in the minds of mediators and have consistently engendered false hopes. First was the belief that sooner or later Algeria would sell out Polisario. As we argued in chapter 2 and as has been evident throughout the peace process, Polisario remains a part of Algiers's greater interests, not to mention a reflection of Algeria's self-image. The hollowness of this assumption was revealed in the trajectory of President Bouteflika's support for Western Saharan independence. For example, when Baker first approached Polisario in 2000 following the Security Council's abandonment of the Houston Accords, he claimed that Algerian support for independence would not last forever. Bouteflika's 2002 visit to Polisario in Tindouf, the first for an Algerian head of state, should have been the first sign that Algeria's position was not changing. It was with Washington's active support that Algeria pressed Polisario to accept Baker's 2003 Peace Plan. Yet Washington did not reciprocate by pressing Morocco; the White House did an about-face and backed Moroccan rejectionism. Neither Polisario nor Algiers would forget or forgive the Bush administration's betrayal in between the summer of 2003 and April

2004. With Algeria's internal conflict receding and oil and gas revenues skyrocketing, Algiers's support for Western Saharan nationalism has become only more hardened, especially after Bouteflika's successful—and largely legitimate—reelection in 2004. Although this vote finally gave the presidency decisive leverage over the military (e.g., chief of staff General Mohamed Lamari's subsequent "retirement" and General Larbi Belkhir's reassignment to Morocco), Bouteflika did not lessen his support for Polisario. This steadfastness refuted longstanding assertions that Polisario has simply been a pet project of the Algerian military or of any single "clan" within the Algerian power structure. As Algeria's regional dominance has grown in recent years, so has Polisario's strategic importance to Algiers. Polisario, feeling that it was aligned with the emerging regional hegemon, decided time was ultimately on its side. During the final years of the Bush administration, both Algiers and Polisario were placing their hopes on significant change in Washington in 2008.

Second, the Western Sahara peace process has also been repeatedly undermined by the assumption that Polisario, as the weakest party, could and should make the most concessions. Participants, mediators, and observers of the conflict have often and falsely assumed that Polisario was driving the cart of Sahrawi nationalism. The picture is indeed the opposite; Polisario's elites are able to rule because they serve the people, not vice versa. The tail does not wag the dog. The intifadas of 1999 and 2005 revealed that Western Saharan nationalism now transcends Polisario's founding fathers in Tindouf, as part two of this work details. Western Saharan nationalism has only grown in breadth and depth, and so its demands for independence, grounded in international law, have grown all the more unyielding. Any backroom deal—like the PLO's 1993 signing of the Oslo Agreement—would undermine Polisario's credibility with the people and feed factionalism, as evidenced in the emergence of Khatt al-Shahid. Giving up self-determination would be the moral equivalent of physically defecting to Morocco—that is, political suicide.

The third and fourth assumptions guiding the search for a political solution have been more deeply implicit than the first two, yet they have had equally devastating effects on the possibility of peace for Western Sahara. The third assumption is the idea that the Moroccan regime has been willing and capable of making compromises. This claim, however, ignores the most salient political reality in the conflict. The intersection of Morocco's military interests and its economic interests in the occupied Western Sahara has presented the greatest challenge to a pacific and legal resolution of the Western Sahara conflict. This problem is rarely even acknowledged, although in July 2004, shortly after Baker's resignation, Spanish foreign minister Miguel Moratinos was candid enough to admit it. "A referendum at this time," he claimed, "without a political solution could lead us to a generalized crisis in North Africa." For Moratinos, the major reason was clear, as he posed in this simple question: "Would the Moroccan armed forces accept being defeated in a referendum?" (quoted by Agence France Presse, July 11, 2004). In 1994, former MINURSO head Erik Jensen realized that the key to Western Sahara was not just Driss Basri, but also

General Abdelhak Khadiri, one of King Hassan's key advisors on the matter (see Jensen 2005, 55).

Since 1975, the Moroccan military has been a presence in the Western Sahara, yet its influence there has gone beyond security interests. Besides commanding tens of thousands of troops, high-level Moroccan officers in the Sahara have been given control over many aspects of the Western Saharan economy, especially in fisheries. In order to make the war in Western Sahara worthwhile for Hassan's notoriously mutinous officers, the spoils of the Sahara have gone to veteran generals (*Africa Confidential*, Aug. 6, 1992). In 2002, one scholar noted that "King Hassan combined his tight control over military activities with a deeply entrenched patronage system that enriched senior officers. Hassan also turned a blind eye to corruption and drug trafficking within the military. As a result, many senior officers accumulated substantial wealth in real estate, agriculture, and industry. They are opposed, therefore, to any change in the status quo" (Layachi 2002, 53). One of Hassan's legacies was to leave his heir a country in which fifty of the one hundred richest Moroccans were either military or police officers—their fortunes amassed through legal, parallel, and black-market activities (e.g., contraband and drugs). Around the time of Hassan's death, it was reported that the twenty wealthiest army officers were worth more than $15 billion (Ramonet 2000). These men included the four officers who held the most influence over Western Sahara: Generals Abdelhak Khadiri, Abdelaziz Bennani, Hosni Benslimane, and Hamidou Laanigri (Karmous and Decaster 2003).[7] Although this connection between wealth and military leadership in Western Sahara is one of many open secrets that the UN peace process has ignored, these generals are well known to Moroccans on the street. In 2001, the Moroccan press named six generals who were earning millions of dollars every year from fisheries licenses. Among them were key members of the Moroccan security apparatus in Western Sahara: the heads of the gendarmerie, intelligence, and military (Reuters, Sept. 12, 2001). During the reign of Mohammed VI, members of Hassan's old guard have become even more entrenched and are arguably the greatest impediments to democracy. The removal of Basri in 1999 was a welcomed change, but it only signaled a reconfiguration of power rather than an inversion of it. Basri's top protégées remained (Jamaï 2006). Not only do some of these Moroccan security-military-intelligence interests have the most invested in Western Sahara politically and economically, but they are also the best placed to use deception, coercion, and even violence if they feel those interests are threatened.

Even after fifteen years of UN on-the-ground monitoring of the Moroccan military, this crucial component of the Western Sahara deadlock has still not found its way into the secretary-general's reports, although Polisario attempted to raise this sensitive issue in its 2003 response to the Baker Plan. In discussing the transitional or autonomy period proposed by the 2003 Peace Plan, Polisario noted that this confluence of political and military interests, coupled with Morocco's sole competence over firearms during the autonomy and referendum periods, could become "a *'legal'* basis which would be established in favor of the occupying Power, which it could use to arm 'death squads.'" For these reasons, the Polisario reminded the secretary-general, "Without adequate protection from the UN, through, inter alia, the engagement of its own authority in the occupied Territory, many previous experiences (such as Rwanda and Timor) confirm in advance that the above mentioned one-year period [between the beginning of the autonomy period and the election of the independent Western Saharan Authority] will be the occasion [of] a mass repression of Saharans and a blemish on the name of the United Nations itself" (UN doc. S/2003/565, Annex III: par. 33–39, emphasis in original). Polisario based its point on well-founded fears that the Moroccan military might overreact and that the international community would underreact if a crisis were to develop. In the case of East Timor, the arrival of the UN mission also saw an increase in violence by pro-Indonesian militias. By the time of the vote in August 1999, the mission had failed to institute any of the UN security guarantees, which allowed looting and massacres to go forward uninhibited that September. The Indonesian military's reluctance to give up East Timor was as much ideological commitment to "territorial integrity" as desire for the material benefits reaped from the brutal occupation. In Western Sahara, key Moroccan generals likewise have a great deal to lose financially if the Western Sahara ever became independent or even genuinely autonomous.

This brings us to the fourth and most important false assumption that has been guiding the Western Saharan peace process since 2000: the claim that the Security Council has been willing to do what it takes to bring about a durable solution to the conflict. Although the Security Council has categorically ruled out any move to Chapter VII powers, such steps will be necessary for any solution that does not first require a full withdrawal of Moroccan civilians and military personnel. To create an environment where Polisario and the Sahrawi refugees feel safe to return, the UN would have to make a strong and substantial security commitment to Western Sahara. For autonomy to work, Western Sahara must revert to being Sahrawi, not Moroccan, in both the majority of its citizens and the visible elements of its regional security presence. Both Morocco's military-security apparatus and the numbers of Moroccan settlers will have to decrease. However, in any autonomy scheme, Rabat will constantly fear separatist moves, so it will demand a sizable military presence to guarantee its "territorial integrity." No matter how good the negotiated agreement, the conditions on the ground will be explosive. Yet given the international failure to mobilize against what has widely been seen as genocide in Sudan's Darfur Province since 2004, what hope is there for such support to implement autonomy in Western Sahara?

The real question is whether the international community, especially the Security Council, is willing to invest in the kind of multinational peace-building project that such an autonomy agreement would warrant. For any compromise political solution based on power sharing to work in Western Sahara, there has to be a tripartite willingness. But such willingness has been historically lacking—not just from Polisario and Morocco, but, more important, from the Security Council itself. Will France and the United States suddenly find the will to use coercion against Morocco in support of autonomy in Western Sahara? If so, this point begs the question: Why reject self-determination because it requires coercion when autonomy will need the same? Autonomy is, after all, a far more complicated solution to implement than an independent Western Sahara. The latter simply requires nonviolent international pressure on Morocco to withdraw. In their calls for self-determination, Polisario and its supporters have been accused of naive idealism. Yet charges of unrealistic optimism should have been leveled at the Security Council and its impossible pursuit of a self-implementing, self-enforcing agreement for Western Sahara.

# Conclusion

Our modest goals in this work have been twofold: first, to provide the reader with a self-contained narrative of the Western Sahara conflict; and, second, to elucidate and dissect the conditions that have made the conflict possible, highly resilient, and so far decidedly irresolvable. We explored the origins of the conflict in several chapters, ultimately identifying two key ideational forces at the heart of the dispute: Moroccan irredentism and Western Saharan nationalism. We charted the growth of the former in chapter 2 and the development of the latter in part two. The simultaneity of the outgrowth of Western Saharan nationalism and Moroccan irredentism in the late 1950s owes as much to the late colonial experience. In the case of Western Saharan nationalism, the self-determination consensus championed by the UN in the 1960s, which we outlined in chapter 7, also fanned the flames of Sahrawi nationalism.

With irredentism and nationalism already in place by 1970, this volatile admixture exploded upon being catalyzed by King Hassan's invasion in November 1975. The motivation for launching this aggressive bid for territorial expansion—against a powerful Western state such as Spain—came from two sources. There was, of course, the powerful idea of a Moroccan *terra irredenta,* and then there was the crisis of government that had plagued the Moroccan regime since independence. In chapter 2, we argued against the view that economic motivations (i.e., Western Sahara's phosphates) are a sufficient reason for Hassan's decision to invade. However, phosphates as well as Western Sahara's other major resource, fisheries, have become a significant disincentive for Morocco to quit Western Sahara—especially so now, given the skyrocketing global demand for both. If Morocco were to find hydrocarbon resources in Western Sahara, an issue we explored in chapter 9, it is even less likely that Rabat—an oil and gas importer—will heed the international consensus behind self-determination.

A far more important factor behind Morocco's invasion was the unstable political situation there in the early 1970s. Having narrowly avoided two coups, and facing popular disenchantment across the social spectrum, the Moroccan monarch was in desperate need of a fix. As we argued in chapter 2, the campaign to "recover" Western Sahara—and to hold on to it after 1976—has become central in Moroccan politics. Although the success of Hassan's invasion provided the monarchy with some political breathing room, obtaining

Western Sahara did nothing to address the conditions underlying Morocco's faltering political and economic development. Indeed, the key factor stunting Morocco—authoritarian government—was only reinforced by the seizure of Spanish Sahara. The subsequent war for Western Sahara thus exacerbated the bleak domestic situation with its high economic costs for Morocco (analyzed in chapters 1 and 2). Ironically, Western Sahara has become both the monarchy's crowning achievement and its greatest mistake since independence. The costs of occupying Western Sahara continued to undermine Morocco's development into the reign of Mohammed VI (following the death of Hassan II in 1999). It has also created a class of vested political-security interests whose material ties to Western Sahara are as powerful as the nation's ideological claim. At the end of chapter 9, we argued that these interests have disabled the Moroccan regime's willingness to make fundamental compromises in Western Sahara.

The other primary factor behind the Western Sahara conflict is, of course, the growth of indigenous nationalism. Indeed, one of the central corrective theses of this work is not just that Western Saharan nationalism exists, but that it has become only stronger as the conflict has progressed. In chapter 4, we backtracked to the Arabization of Western Sahara and the interplay of regional powers in that area, from the eleventh century to the Spanish conquest. However, we attempted to reevaluate critically previous, teleological accounts of Sahrawi nationalism, which have tended to see it as primordial or nascent within precolonial Saharan society. For us, the determinant factor in the middle of the twentieth century was colonialism. Just as colonialism had produced nationalisms around the world, the idea of a Sahrawi people was born out of a territorial bounding called "Spanish Sahara." However, as the ICJ determined in 1975, the people who would become known as the Sahrawis were politically independent and competent before colonialism. Their right to their land is not only internally justified by Western Saharan nationalism, but also externally grounded in international law.

In chapters 5 and 6, we looked at the evolution of Western Saharan nationalism. In the former chapter, we looked at this phenomenon at three levels: the international level (the diplomatic efforts of Polisario to earn political legitimacy through war and peace); the national level (the RASD's "domestic" politics in exile); and the grassroots level (the lived nationalism of the Sahrawi refugee camps). In the latter chapter, we looked at Sahrawi nationalism inside the area of Western Sahara under Moroccan control since 1975. This examination included an analysis of the formation of a dissident Sahrawi elite from the pressures of Moroccan repression and of the structural dynamics that have enabled the recent Sahrawi uprisings—intifadas—of 1999 and 2005. Taken together, these three chapters suggest two important facts for the Western Saharan peace process. First, Morocco has failed to win the hearts and minds of a significant number of Sahrawis under its administration. Second, against Morocco's assertion of a fait accompli, Western Saharan nationalism is still as much, if not more so, an accomplished fact. These two observations explain why Polisario is confident it will win a referendum and why Polisario and its constituents have been unwilling to consider compromise in recent years.

The Western Sahara conflict also has two main secondary factors: French and U.S. support for Morocco and Algerian support for Polisario. Along with our emphasis on Western Saharan nationalism, we believe that any understanding of the conflict must appreciate the decisive role played by Washington and Paris but must also avoid the pitfalls of overweighting Algerian influence. As analyzed in chapter 2, the Franco–American consensus is a pattern of behavior on the part of those two states in Morocco's favor in Western Sahara. This consensus is not based on the idea that Western Sahara is a part of Morocco's territory. Rather, it is grounded in the belief that the stability of Morocco, a key African and Middle Eastern state, is tied to its successful occupation of Western Sahara. Neither France nor the United States officially recognize Moroccan sovereignty over Western Sahara, yet the majority of their actions in relations to the conflict have betrayed their juridical neutrality. Throughout this work, we have argued that the Franco–American consensus has had two dominant effects: on the one hand, it has allowed and strengthened the Moroccan occupation; on the other hand, it has convinced Morocco that its occupation will never be legally and forcefully challenged by the only body legally allowed to do so, the UN Security Council.

Although we see the Franco–American consensus as a permissive condition, the United States also played a large role in triggering the war for Western Sahara. As detailed in chapter 3, the United States intervened diplomatically on Morocco's behalf during the Green March crisis. Were it not for U.S. support at the UN (and a likely French veto threat as well), it is possible the international community could have taken a stronger stance against Morocco's provocations. Counterfactuals aside, the United States, along with France, continued to back Morocco with diplomacy and arms well beyond the November 1975 crisis. In chapter 1, we argued that it was unsparing military aid from France and the United States, coupled with generous financing from Saudi Arabia, in the early 1980s that allowed the Moroccan military to undermine Polisario's early success on the battlefield.

During the peace process, detailed in part three, the Franco–American consensus backed plans for a UN referendum in Western Sahara, but only to the extent that Morocco had conceded to one. However, as we argued at the end of chapter 8, even before the UN referendum effort could pose a serious threat to Moroccan stability, the Security Council abandoned that project in 2000 on behalf of Morocco's new king, Mohammed VI, even before he himself rejected it. Likewise, the Franco–American consensus undermined the work of James Baker, the lead UN negotiator in the peace process from 1997 to 2004. As we explored in chapter 9, the ultimate test of the Franco–American consensus came in 2003, when the George W. Bush administration attempted to offer support for Baker's effort to impose a solution on Morocco. Baker was, after all, a close ally of the Bush family. For a brief period in mid-2003, it seemed that the old alliance between

Washington and Paris had come to an end, producing a state of panic in Moroccan foreign affairs. However, the U.S. government began a slow retreat in late 2003, and by April 2004 France and the United States had come back into alignment, triggering Baker's resignation. Since then, both of these countries have offered significant moral support for Morocco's plans to offer and implement autonomy as a solution to the Western Sahara dispute. For now, the historical record of this period remains a hidden transcript, so we have no way of knowing why the Bush administration chose Mohammed VI over Baker. There is, of course, the war on terror, in which Morocco has become a faithful ally. However, that reason ignores the previous thirty years, in which every U.S. administration, to one degree or another has made possible, in concert with French interests, the Moroccan occupation of Western Sahara.

The role of Algeria in the conflict is easily overstated and often misunderstood. We start from the basic claim, justified by the historical record, that Algeria created neither Western Saharan nationalism nor Polisario whole cloth, as is sometimes claimed by obtuse observers and Moroccan partisans. Similarly, Algerian motivations are often misunderstood. In chapter 2, we examined Algeria's position within the conflict, first arguing against the idea that Algeria's interest in an independent Western Sahara is about access to the Atlantic. Rather, Algerian support for Western Sahara has deep ideational roots yet serves Algiers' very real regional strategic interests. Moroccan–Algerian enmity predates the Western Sahara conflict by more than ten years, when King Hassan launched a failed invasion of the Algerian Sahara in 1963. This event, followed twelve years later by Morocco's invasion of Western Sahara and Algiers' resulting support for Polisario, totally undermined North African, not to mention African, political and economic cooperation. Although there are other factors behind the UMA's dysfunctionality, which chapter 2 delved into, the Western Sahara conflict is first and foremost among the reasons behind the lack of regional cooperation.

Algeria's self-image, especially the generation of leaders still in power, rests upon an ideal of radical, anticolonial nationalism, which they see reflected in Polisario. It is easy to become cynical toward a regime that is perhaps one of world's most opaque, militarized, and authoritarian, but one must keep in mind that Morocco holds no monopoly over ideological motivations. Nevertheless, the Western Sahara serves Algeria's perceived short-term strategic interests, which is to keep Morocco in check as a regional adversary for hegemony. As far as long-term interests go, a friendly and grateful Saharan state would serve Algeria's regional—North African and sub-Saharan—interests.

However, the true test is to consider whether a withdrawal of Algerian support would hasten or prolong the Western Sahara endgame or not. In this book, we have argued that Western Saharan nationalism would not collapse if Algeria withdrew support. Life would indeed become more difficult for Polisario's exiled leadership, yet East Timor's independence movement survived and succeeded under such circumstances. Indeed, a withdrawal of Algerian support for Polisario would bring the conflict into sharp focus; Morocco could no longer use Algeria as a scapegoat to deny the existence of Western Saharan nationalism. The international community would also lose a powerful player in the peace process, one that has repeatedly brought pressure upon Polisario to compromise (e.g., the Baker Plan; see chapter 9) or maintain the cease-fire (e.g., in January 2001; see chapter 1).

Now if we consider a withdrawal of French and U.S. support for Morocco, it is easy to understand why we argue that their role in the conflict is more important. Not only have France and the United States provided Morocco with ample material support, but they have also dominated the Security Council's approach to the conflict. On a moral level, the end of the Franco–American consensus would at the very least see Washington and Paris joining the international consensus in favor of self-determination. On a practical level, France and the United States would be obliged, as they are now, to oppose the Moroccan occupation of Western Sahara, which is a clear violation of the UN Charter (which we discuss more fully later). In terms of explaining the resiliency of the Western Sahara conflict, these two thought experiments justify our assigning the Franco–American consensus greater weight than Algerian support for Western Saharan nationalism. Although one must understand both factors, Franco–American consensus is the bigger roadblock to a just resolution.

In addition, the war in Western Sahara and the structure of the UN-OAU peace plan had a significant impact on prolongation of the conflict. With generous foreign aid, Morocco was able to construct the defensive walls that now cordon off most of Western Sahara in Rabat's favor. However, this success came at the cost of being able to defeat Polisario in a direct war of attrition. Indeed, Polisario's refuge in Algeria—and de facto refuge in northern Mauritania—precluded Morocco's ever decisively defeating the Sahrawi insurgency. Yet the berms also prevented Polisario from ever pushing Morocco out of Western Sahara by force. By the mid-1980s, the war was no longer totally winnable for either side, yet it was also difficult for either side to lose. In fact, we argued that both sides can wage war seemingly forever. Under these conditions, which we called "sustainable intractability," the only incentive toward a peace process was this intractability. Indeed, it was enough incentive to get Morocco and Polisario to lay down their arms, but not enough for either to make fundamental concessions. In other words, the war's sustainable intractability was important because there was no internal mechanism to apply pressure toward compromise. Of course, we are not suggesting that the right of self-determination should be compromised. We merely want to offer one factor that helps explain why the UN peace process has been so contentious.

The 1991 Settlement Plan essentially became war by other means, with Morocco and Polisario carrying their fight into the voter-identification process conducted from 1994 to 2000 (see chapter 8). The only internal pressures were Morocco's lack of legitimate occupation and Polisario's exile, and both parties have shown infinite tolerance for their positions. For there to be a political peace process, pressure would have to come from outside, primarily from the UN Security Council, which has underwritten the secretary-general's efforts since 1987. Given the Franco–American consensus, it is easy to see why the Security Council has been unwilling to use force where it is needed most: against the Moroccan occupation. Furthermore, as we described in chapter 8, Morocco's belligerent attitude toward the referendum, demonstrated in its desperate attempt to flood the polls with non-Sahrawi Moroccan citizens, was enabled by its supporters on the Security Council. Why else would Hassan think that he could get away with such behavior?

The steady disintegration of the Western Sahara peace process since 2000 owes much to these preconditions, which were set in place at the time of the 1991 cease-fire. Moreover, as we sketched at the end of chapter 9, we believe four faulty premises have undermined the Western Sahara peace process. The first is a belief that Algeria would and will sell out Polisario, which seems more and more unlikely as time passes. The second false premise is a backward conception about the relationship between Polisario and Western Saharan nationalism. Rather than the former dominating the latter, as is often supposed, the reverse is true. Polisario exists to serve Western Saharan nationalism, not its own needs. The third faulty premise is the idea that the Moroccan regime was and is capable of extracting itself either partially (for viable autonomy) or totally (for independence) from Western Sahara. Under King Hassan, either might have been possible; yet under Mohammed VI, it seems that the nexus of Moroccan political, economic, and security interests in Western Sahara has become too powerful. Fourth, we identified the faulty belief that the Security Council was and is willing to do what it takes to make peace in Western Sahara. The council's record in Western Sahara over the past twenty years suggests otherwise. In this work, we have challenged these assumptions, exposing their deficits. For the Western Sahara conflict to reach a pacific, durable, and just solution, policymakers will have to rethink their approach.

## WHY WESTERN SAHARA MATTERS

For more than three decades, the Western Sahara conflict has helped destabilize Northwest Africa and fundamentally challenged the basic norms of international order. Despite this pedigree, Western Sahara holds a marginal position in world affairs. Indeed, it has become a textbook case of a "forgotten conflict." Officials and observers offer many reasons as to why Western Sahara is and ought to remain on the backburner. There are, however, several compelling reasons, both "realist" and "idealist," as to why Western Sahara deserves attention.

One reason offered for the maintenance of the status quo is that the conflict affects very few people outside of Western Sahara and Morocco. However, as we demonstrated in chapter 2, the Western Sahara conflict has become a major impediment to North African and African cooperation. It affects not only the two hundred thousand Sahrawis of the territory and thirty-five million Moroccans, but also the ninety million Maghribis who would benefit from the revival of the UMA. The longer a settlement in Western Sahara is deferred, the more disconnected and unstable North Africa becomes—threatening not only the stability of security interests in the western wing of the Islamic world, but also interests in a stable trans-Saharan-Sahel region, which is ostensibly a strategic locus in the U.S. war on terror. One might extend that threat to the nearly billion inhabitants of Africa, given Western Sahara's role in Morocco's absence from the African Union and the impediment to African development that this absence presents.

There is also a counterintuitive reason why Western Sahara should receive more attention. The status quo in Western Sahara is often justified by recourse to a utilitarian argument: aggressive diplomacy would divert precious time, attention, and resources from more pressing matters. With violent conflicts in Iraq, Sudan, Somalia, and Afghanistan claiming hundreds of thousands dead, not to mention the million killed in Africa's "world war" in the Congo (to name just a few), why should the Security Council go out of its way to help two hundred thousand Sahrawis? It is likely that there will always be more important and far bloodier conflicts on the UN agenda. Set in that context, the status quo in Western Sahara is very attractive and seems to be a powerful argument, but it is easy to see why the inverse is even more powerful. If the Security Council will not raise a finger to help the world's least-populated country, what hope is there for the rest of the globe?

In terms of international law, there is more at stake in Western Sahara than just self-determination and decolonization. The case of Western Sahara goes to the heart of the international order established after World War II. The ongoing Moroccan occupation of Western Sahara is one of the most egregious yet most underchallenged affronts to the international system in existence today. The ramifications of the international community's failure to counter this basic violation of the prohibition against aggression are of far greater consequence than just the denial of self-determination.

The UN was founded, in part, to prevent the unilateral expansion of territory by force, the kinds of acts that had plunged the world into the worst mass-organized slaughter ever witnessed. Yet with regard to Western Sahara, the Security Council has largely turned a blind eye to Morocco's blatant contravention of the UN Charter, especially the laws governing the use of force in international relations *(jus ad bellum)* and laws governing war itself *(jus in bello),* including international humanitarian law. As described in chapter 1, Morocco's military invasion of Spanish/Western Sahara commenced on October 30–31, 1975. Days after armed Moroccan forces penetrated Spanish Sahara, thousands of Moroccan civilians, with the active encouragement and logistical support of the Moroccan government, crossed the frontier on November 5–6 in what was called the "Green March." Their expressed intent was to march to al-'Ayun and seize the territory from Spain. On November 6, 1975, the UN Security Council deplored the Green March and called for its immediate withdrawal in Resolution 380, which Morocco completely ignored. At that time, the Security Council was unaware of Morocco's military invasion, although Spain had brought the Green March to the Security Council's attention as early as October 17, 1975. At that time, Madrid had called it an invasion—a direct violation of the UN Charter.

Morocco's flagrant disregard of Security Council Resolution 380, its armed invasion, and its use of thousands of civilians to coerce Spain to negotiate amounted to a direct violation of the UN Charter's most fundamental constraints against the use of force in international affairs. These violations of *jus ad bellum* are unambiguous when we consider Article 2 of the UN Charter (1945):

> 3. All Members shall settle their international disputes by peaceful means in such a manner that international peace and security, and justice, are not endangered.
>
> 4. All Members shall refrain in their international relations from the threat or use of force against the territorial integrity or political independence of any state, or in any other manner inconsistent with the Purposes of the United Nations. (UN 1945)

Furthermore, the General Assembly's 1974 Definition of Aggression (Resolution 3314) stipulates that only the Security Council can determine whether an act, such as Morocco's invasion of Spanish/Western Sahara, is justified. Such a judgment was not rendered in Western Sahara, so Morocco is guilty of aggression under *jus ad bellum*.

Chapter VII of the UN Charter, "Threats to the Peace, Breaches of the Peace and Acts of Aggression," applied to Morocco's actions in Western Sahara in 1975 and still do now. Yet Resolution 380 and all Security Council resolutions since 1988 (when the Security Council again became "seized of the matter") have fallen under Chapter VI, "Pacific Settlements of Disputes." The reason for this distinction is political: two of Morocco's strongest Western allies, France and the United States, have effectively been able to limit the UN's management of the conflict. Though the UN Security Council should be commended for not recognizing Morocco's attempted annexation, its limitations in enforcing its mandate as a result of the power exercised by two of its veto-wielding members should be recognized.

Likewise, Morocco is clearly guilty of violating the laws governing the conduct of war and military occupation (*jus in bello*). There is some dispute as to whether Morocco is the occupying power in Western Sahara or not. Yet without Security Council authorization (indeed, the Security Council asked Morocco not to march forth), Rabat's presence in Western Sahara is therefore an occupation. Even though the UN has recently described Morocco as a de facto administering power (see chapter 9), in 1979 the UN General Assembly (Resolution 34/37) deplored what it called Morocco's occupation of Western Sahara. Yet an occupation does not require an international imprimatur. The International

Committee of the Red Cross stipulates that "it makes no difference whether an occupation has received Security Council approval, what its aim is, or indeed whether it is called an 'invasion,' 'liberation,' 'administration' or 'occupation'" (2004). Because Morocco is able competently and fully to discharge the duties and obligations of an occupying power, its presence in Western Sahara is an occupation. Not only does this definition of its acts pose the moral obligation to oppose its annexation, but the issue of war crimes (the Sahrawis "disappeared"; see chapter 6) and violations of the Geneva Conventions (Morocco's settler population) also come into play (see Clark 2007 for further legal analysis).

## THE MISSING DIMENSION: TRANSNATIONAL SOLIDARITY

The largest antiwar demonstration in the history of the world took place on February 15, 2003, voicing opposition to the upcoming U.S. invasion of Iraq. Two days later an article in the *New York Times* announced the birth of a new global superpower: world public opinion. Although the new superpower failed to stop the George W. Bush administration's invasion of Iraq, its credibility has only increased as Iraq turned into a military and humanitarian disaster for the United States. In terms of conflict prevention and resolution, the importance of international—and increasingly transnational—civil society had an effect long before 2003.

The end of apartheid in South Africa owes much to the work of activists all over the world, who campaigned for sanctions against the white regime. Audie Klotz has argued that although many international relations theorists "emphasize the difficulties of coordinating multilateral policies and the primacy of material interests," normative values manifested on a global scale were what led to South Africa's diplomatic, cultural, and economic isolation. "The loose coalition of governments, nongovernmental organizations, and individuals that made up the transnational anti-apartheid movement" successfully "globalized" their concerns as an influential political force, which could be replicated elsewhere. Most realist perspectives see little chance of a Moroccan compromise on these territorial issues, but Klotz notes how "norms constrain states' behavior through reputation and group membership, and that norms constitute states' definitions of their own identities and interests." She reminds readers of how the history of decolonization "demonstrates the power of weak and non-state actors to transform both global norms and the distribution of social power in the international system" (1994, 4, 6, 166, 173). For example, the greatest pressure in support of East Timor's right to self-determination came from nongovernmental actors. They eventually influenced the policies of major Western powers and the UN, which in turn helped force the Indonesian government into serious negotiations and offered some protection to the East Timorese against abuses.

Nongovernmental actors are more and more playing an important role in mobilizing global civil society to force foreign governments and international organizations to increase their efforts to resolve conflicts (see Moser-Puangsuwan and Weber 2000). According to Eileen Babbitt (2006) in her study of mediating rights-based conflicts, the first criteria in such situations should be to establish the view that international norms are at stake. Although such norms in relation to Western Sahara have long been reiterated through UN General Assembly resolutions and the 1975 ICJ decision, these norms have become increasingly marginalized in the peace process. Babbitt also notes, however, that human rights norms have more potency than they did several decades ago and have played a major role in the resolution of longstanding conflicts. Resolution to these conflicts came not simply from the parties' greater willingness to compromise, but from increased internal and international pressure on the more powerful of the parties to negotiate a settlement based on international norms.

Given the political deadlock in Western Sahara, a new factor must enter into the equation if things are to change. The Western Sahara conflict's intractability, as we have extensively argued, is reinforced by outside support to Morocco, so the withdrawal of French and American backing may play a critical role in making resolution of the conflict attainable. For the conflict to attain a just and peaceful end (i.e., one that meets with international law and does not involve violent means), the "second superpower" will have to be mobilized.

The strategy for such an objective is quite clear: an interlocking and mutually reinforcing effort to delegitimize Morocco's occupation and the Franco–American support it receives. Morocco will have to face increasing levels of international humiliation, scorn, and isolation. Because authoritarian rulers always offset punitive costs onto the general population, these measures should focus on symbolic rather than material targets outside of Western Sahara so as to avoid hurting the Moroccan population as much as possible. Inside Western Sahara, targeted boycotts and sanctions should find ways of highlighting the illegality of the occupation and Western support for it. At the same time, pressure has to increase on the U.S. and French governments to change their rejectionist policies. Supporting Morocco has to become embarrassing, as did supporting apartheid South Africa and Indonesia in East Timor.

Such efforts can be built upon the years of work transnational activists have already put into helping Western Sahara. Since the outbreak of the Morocco–Polisario war in 1975, grassroots organizations have worked toward a just and peaceful end of the conflict. Not surprisingly, the largest numbers of activists have come from Spain, although other European countries have their own networks and organizations. Whether confronting Morocco's human rights abuses or Franco–American support for the war and occupation, transnational civil society has clearly impacted the conflict. The release of the longest-held Sahrawi political prisoner, Sidi Mohammed Daddach, in 2001 came after years of campaigning. More recently, energy companies have come under pressure for signing illegal deals with the Moroccan government to explore and exploit possible Western Saharan hydrocarbon reserves. Likewise, groups have pressed the EU states to revoke the recent fisheries agreements with Morocco, which includes the waters off Western Sahara.

Even as actors in key Western states seek to change the immoral and illegal stances of their governments, nonviolent Sahrawi initiatives should be supported and protected in the occupied territory. The Sahrawi intifada has not yet evolved into a large-scale and sustainable movement like those that ended occupations or toppled dictatorships in recent decades. A major factor inhibiting Sahrawis from turning the occupied Western Sahara into an ungovernable space for Morocco is demographics. Not only is the Moroccan-occupied Western Sahara under intense security control, but there are now at least two to three Moroccan settlers for every Sahrawi. For every Western Saharan in the world, there are one hundred Moroccans. Part of the challenge to building a nonviolent movement for self-determination in Western Sahara is the double minority status of Sahrawi nationalists in their own country, both politically and ethnically. This factor is partly offset by the growth of proindependence sentiments among settlers from southern Morocco, who are also ethnically Sahrawi as well, but it does little to erase the sheer numbers Morocco has on its side. In other nonviolent struggles attempting to throw off foreign domination—such as the Baltic republics, East Timor, the West Bank, and Kosovo—the overwhelming majority of the resident population has favored independence. Sahrawis, in contrast, have to contend with a far different demographic situation. Thus, the greatest challenge for Sahrawi nationalists and transnational civil society is to build lines of solidarity between Moroccans and Western Saharans where few exist now.

In all the talk of a "third way" for Western Sahara, one alternative possibility has received scant attention. As we mentioned in our introduction, conflicts involving settler colonialism have tended to conclude in one of three ways: total independence for the natives, total subjugation of the natives by the colonizer, or independence based on an alliance between natives and renegade settlers. A Western Saharan independence movement with substantial support from Moroccan settlers has the significant advantage of creating the conditions for a nonviolent settlement of the dispute. In short, it would lay the groundwork for rapid postconflict reconciliation between Morocco and Western Sahara, whereas internationally forced independence or integration might extend the dispute far into the future. A Moroccan–Sahrawi alliance for self-determination would also allay fears that an independent Western Sahara will become an unstable "microstate" that threatens Moroccan and Western interests. On the contrary, by retaining Moroccan settlers, an independent Western Sahara would have a more feasible population. With a significant Moroccan population, an independent Western Sahara would naturally have robust economic ties with Morocco, thus warranting close Moroccan–Saharan cooperation in the areas of trade and security. A just settlement to the Western Sahara conflict would leave Algeria with little excuse not to reinstate full diplomatic relations and cooperation with Morocco, thus reopening the UMA's doors, which we saw closed in chapter 2.

Although this possibility might not seem realistic, Baker implicitly suggested it in his 2003 Peace Plan, and Polisario more recently put it forward in its April 10, 2007, proposal to the UN. The failed 2003 Peace Plan, which we detailed in chapter 9, recommended holding a referendum in which native Western Saharans and Moroccan settlers would together vote on a referendum that would include the option of independence. Morocco's steadfast refusal to accept the Peace Plan led most observers to make the inference that Morocco does not trust its own settlers to vote for integration. Certainly it is frightening for the Moroccan regime to imagine the Western Saharans voting for independence, yet it is even more terrifying to imagine Moroccans joining with them. But such an alliance will be necessary for a durable and lasting peace in Western Sahara. Indeed, Polisario's enthusiasm for the 2003 Peace Plan came from the recognition that retaining Moroccan settlers while jettisoning the Moroccan state will be key for a viable independence. It is for this reason that in April 2007 Polisario proposed political and economic guarantees and even citizenship to any Moroccan settler who wished to join the Sahrawis in an independent Western Sahara. Once enough Moroccan citizens come to realize that they share a common, mutually beneficial destiny with Sahrawi nationalists, Western Sahara will finally have the foundations for a just and lasting peace.

GLOSSARY

NOTES

REFERENCES

INDEX

# Glossary

Terms are given with diacritical marks, although these marks do not appear in the main text. Alternate and widely used transliterations found in other texts are given in parenthesis. Words appear alphabetically according to the English alphabet.

'Abd al-Ḥafīẓ, Mawlāy: Moroccan monarch who ruled from 1908 to 1912.

'abīd: Slave. See also harātīn.

Adrār: Northern region of Mauritania.

afkhādh: "Tribal fractions." Described as *fracciones nómadas* in the Spanish colonial ethnography. Singular: *fakhidh/fakhdh/fikhdh*.

Ahl al-Sāḥil (Ahel as-Sahel/es-Sahel): "People of the Shore or Littoral" (Atlantic), often used as a synonym for or description of Ṣaḥrāwīs.

Ait/Ayt al-Ḥasan (Ait Lahsen): One of the notable Ṣaḥrāwī social groupings found in the south of Morocco and the northern Western Sahara, considered a subgrouping of the Taknah.

'Alawī: Morocco's ruling monarchy since the seventeenth century.

amīr al–mu'minīn: Commonly translated as "commander of the faithful," one of the Moroccan *sulṭān*'s titles.

al-'Arusiyyn (Arosien): A sizable Ṣaḥrāwī social grouping located in the central Western Sahara.

'Askaykīmah: Sahrawi neighborhood in al-'Uyūn, often the site of demonstrations against the Moroccan occupation.

Awdaghust: Major trading point in the southern Sahara and a Ghanaian stronghold conquered by the Murābiṭūn in the eleventh century.

Awlād Dulaym (Awlād Dalīm, Ulad/Ouled/Oulad Delim/Dlim): One of the major Ṣaḥrāwī social groupings found in southern Western Sahara; also the name of one of the original groups of the Banū Maʿqil.

Awlād Tidrārīn (Oulad Tidrarin): A large Ṣaḥrāwī social grouping in Western Sahara, found from southern Morocco to northern Mauritania.

al-'Ayun: See al-'Uyūn.

Banū Maʿqil (Awlād/Banū/Bani Ḥassān): Umbrella term for the Banū Ḥassān, "Sons of Hassan," the Yemeni Arabs that invaded North Africa in the twelfth century.

Banū Marīn (Merinids): Successor regime to the Muwaḥḥidūn, ruling from 1258 to 1420.

baya'ah: An Islamic oath of allegiance to a ruler, regularly performed in Morocco.

**Bīḍān (feminine: Bayḍānīyah):** Most often equated with the term *Moor,* generally meaning the dominant Arabic-speaking "whites" of Mauritania; contrasted with the al-Sūdān, "black" Africans.

**Bilād al-Makhzan (Blad Al-Makhzen):** "Lands of the Makhzan," lands under direct control or within the acknowledged (indirect) territorial authority of the Moroccan *sulṭān.*

**Bilād Shinqīṭī:** A precolonial political entity in Mauritania.

**Bilād al-Sibā:** "Land of Anarchy" or "Land of Dissidence," lands considered outside of or rebelling against the Moroccan *sulṭān*'s direct authority, but nonetheless as Moroccan as the Bilād al-Makhzan.

**Būkrāʿ (Bu Craa, Bou Kraa):** Site of a major phosphate deposit in Western Sahara, first developed and exploited by the Spanish, but now run by Morocco.

**dawāʾr/dāʾirāt (dairas):** In the Western Sahara refugee context, districts or camp subdivisions. Singular: *dāʾirah (daira).*

**Ghāna:** The name of the great sub-Saharan kingdom that was dominant shortly before the rise of the Murābitūn.

**al-ghazī (razzi, gazi):** A raid.

**ḥammādah (hamada):** Dry, flat, rocky plains found in Western Sahara and the area around the Polisario-administered refugee camps near Tindouf, Algeria.

**harātīn:** A slave. See also ʿabīd.

**Ḥassāniyyah:** Arabic dialect of the western Sahara, used by most Ṣaḥrāwīs and Mauritanians.

**ḥayy:** Refers to a subdivision of the *dāʾirah* (district) in Western Saharan refugee camps, meaning "neighborhood" or "barrio."

**Ismāʿīl, Mawlāy (1672–1726):** The most successful ʿAlawi leader, personally venturing as far as Mauritania.

**Istiqlāl:** Independence. In this work, refers to the anticolonial, promonarchy Moroccan nationalist party led by ʿAllāl al-Fāsī.

**Izargiyyn (Zarkiyyin, Izarguien):** A Ṣaḥrāwī subgrouping of the Tiknah.

**al-Jabhah al-Shaʿbīyah li-Taḥrīr Sāqiyah al-Ḥamrāʾ wa Wādī al-Dhahab:** The Frente Popular para la Liberación de Saguia el-Hamra y Río de Oro (Polisario, Popular Front for the Liberation of the Saguia el-Hamra and the Río de Oro).

**Jamaʿa (Djemmaa, Djemma, Yemmaʾa):** In this work, refers to the indigenous council of notables established and co-opted by Spanish colonial authorities to legitimize their rule. Later redesigned to lead Western Sahara into independence, the colonial Jamaʿa formally dissolved itself in late 1975 and backed the Polisario.

**Jaysh al-Taḥrīr:** The Moroccan-led "Army of Liberation" that initiated an anticolonial guerilla campaign in the western Sahara following Morocco's independence in 1956, only to be crushed by a joint Franco–Spanish counterinsurgency operation in 1958.

**al-Jumhūriyah al-ʿArabiyah al-Ṣaḥrāwiyah al-Dīmuqrāṭiyah:** The República Árabe Saharaui Democrática (Sahrawi Arab Democratic Republic), founded in 1976 by the Polisario as a government-in-exile of Western Sahara.

**khaliyah, khalāyā:** Twelve- to fifteen-person cells that formed autonomous units within the Polisario.

**Khaṭṭ al-Shahid:** Literally, Line or Way of the Martyr; faction within Polisario founded in 2003–4.

**khaymah, khiyam:** Tent; for Ṣaḥrāwīs, traditionally made from black goat hair.

**Laayoun:** See al-ʿUyūn.

**Māʾ al-ʿAynayn, Shaykh:** Key figure in Western Saharan history and leader of a failed anticolonial campaign in the early twentieth century.

**Maghrib:** An Arabic name generally referring to the countries of North Africa from Libya to Mauritania, but also the country name for Morocco.

**al-Maghrib al-Kabīr:** "Greater Morocco" is the postcolonial idea that Morocco's precolonial borders encompassed all of Mauritania, Western Sahara, and parts of Mali and the Algerian Sahara. In the generic Arabic sense, refers to all the countries of North Africa.

**al-mahr:** Bride-price.

**al-makhāzinī:** Moroccan paramilitary force under the control of the Ministry of the Interior, concentrated in rural areas.

**Makhzan (Makhzen):** The Moroccan pre- and postcolonial state apparatus; an ensemble of elites and clients deputized by the Moroccan monarch to extend and enforce rule over lands under the royal purview, from the national to street level.

**masʾūl(ah):** Head of a *ḥayy* in the Western Saharan refugee camps.

**Maʿṭāllah:** Predominantly Ṣaḥrāwī neighborhood in al-ʿUyūn, often the site of nationalist demonstrations.

**milḥafah:** Shroud worn by Ṣaḥrāwī women, covering their body and head.

**mujahhidīn (mujahideen):** Often rendered as "holy warriors" in an Islamic context.

**al-Murābiṭūn (Almoravids):** Political and religious movement from the western Sahara that came to dominate all of Northwest Africa and parts of Spain in the eleventh century, under the initial leadership of Ibn Yāsīn.

**al-Muwaḥḥidūn (Almohads):** Successor regime to the Murābiṭūn based in the Moroccan High Atlas (c. 1147–269).

**Nūn (Noun):** Major region in southern Morocco named after the river that flows from the Anti-Atlas to the Atlantic between the Draʿa and Māssah rivers.

**qāḍī (qadi):** Judge.

**qāʾid:** Leader.

**Rgaybāt (Erguibat, Reguibat):** The dominant Ṣaḥrāwī social group, taking its name from Sīdī Aḥmad Rgaybī. There are two confederations of Rgaybāt: Rgaybāt al-Sāḥil (coastal) and the Rgaybāt al-Sharq/Sharg (eastern [ech-Charq/Charg], also known as Rgaybāt al-Gwāsim [Lgwasm, Lgouacem], from al-Qawāsim).

**Ṣaḥrāwī (Sahrawi, Saharawi, Saharaoui):** Generally meaning "Saharan," this name has come to refer to the Ḥassāniyyah-speaking peoples of the area in and around the western Sahara and is often equated with the name "Western Saharan." Plural: Ṣaḥrāwā.

**Ṣanhājah:** Arabic for Zenāgah.

**Sāqiyah al-Ḥamrāʾ:** Red River, located in and referring to the northern region of the western Sahara.

**sharīf:** Person claiming lineage from the Prophet Muhammad. Plural: *shurafā'*.

**shaykh (cheikh, sheikh):** Elder, notable, respected person in Muslim society. The UN used Ṣaḥrāwī shaykhs as experts during the referendum voter identification process from 1994 to 1999. Plural: *shuyūkh*.

**Sijilmāsah:** Major trade center on the northern end of the trans-Saharan trade routes whose ruins are located near Rissani in modern Morocco.

**Sūdān:** Sub-Saharan Africa (Bilād al-Sūdān) in Arab geography, meaning literally "Land of the Blacks."

**sulṭān:** In this work, the title of Moroccan rulers before independence in 1956, then changed to "king" *(malik)*.

**Sūs (Souss):** Major river and agricultural region in southern Morocco located on the Atlantic plain between the High Atlas and the Anti-Atlas, north of the Māssah River.

**Tiknah (Tknah, Tekna):** A large aggregate grouping of Ṣaḥrāwī "tribes" found in southern Morocco and Western Sahara; an alternative name for roughly the same area as southern Spanish Morocco, the Tarfaya Strip, or the Zona del Draa (i.e., the Tekna Zone).

**Tīris al-Gharbiyah:** The name given to the southern third of Western Sahara illegally annexed and occupied by Mauritania after the Madrid Accords, 1975–79. Subsequently occupied by Morocco when Mauritania attempted to cede the territory to the Polisario under a peace treaty.

**al-'ulamā':** The Moroccan religious elite whose primary function is to bestow political and spiritual legitimacy on the throne.

**al-'Uyūn (El-Ayoun, El-Aaiún, El-Aiun, Laâyoune):** In this work, al-'Ayun (from the colloquial), the largest city in Western Sahara, which the nationalists consider the (occupied) capital. Also the name of one of the four major Western Saharan refugee camps near Tindouf, Algeria.

**Wādī Dra'a (Dara'ah, Drâa):** Major river running from the Moroccan High Atlas Mountains along the edge of the Sahara into the Atlantic. Often considered one of Morocco's natural borders.

**Wādī al-Dhahab (Oued Eddahab):** Río de Oro (River of Gold), in the southern region of Western Sahara.

**walī:** In this work, a governor in the Western Saharan refugee camps; generically, head of a *wilāyah*.

**wilāyah (wilaya):** A province. Referring to one of the four Western Saharan refugee camps near Tindouf, Algeria. Plural: *wilāyāt*.

**al-Zamlah Square:** Large square in al-'Ayun, site of the first proindependence demonstration in 1970 and frequently used for demonstrations by Ṣaḥrāwīs since protests began there in 1999.

**Zammūr Massif:** Region in central Western Sahara.

**Zawāyā (Zwāya):** Religious-scholarly class in Western Saharan societies.

**Zenāgah:** Social group of Western Sahara that formed the base of the Murābiṭūn movement. Also known as "al-Mulaththamūn" for the veiling practices among the men. The Zenāgah/Ṣanhājah language could be found in Mauritania into the twentieth century.

**Zenātah:** Social groups that dominated North Africa from Libya to eastern Morocco; formed the core of the Banū Marīn.

# Notes

1. The organization is named after the territory's northern (Saguia el Hamra) and southern (Río de Oro) regions. In Arabic, it is al-Jabhah al-Sha'biyah li-Tahrir Saqiyah al-Hamra' wa Wadi al-Dhahab. See "A Note on Translation" at the end of this introduction for an explanation of our choices in the presentation of Polisario-related names.

## 1. THE WAR FOR WESTERN SAHARA

1. See "A Note on Translation and Translation" at the end of the introduction for an explanation of our choices in the presentation of Moroccan government, organization, and company names.

2. See Nossiter 1986. Among this equipment was a $200 million "intrusion detection system" from Northrop Page Communications installed in the first section of the wall. Additional assistance came from Westinghouse and some French firms. Polisario repeatedly demonstrated the system's ineffectiveness by taking foreign journalists and other visitors quietly onto the wall after sunset. Stephen Zunes was able to travel at night with ELPS forces at close proximity to the wall during June 1987, but he declined an invitation to be accompanied up onto the wall itself. Jacob Mundy saw a section of the wall during daylight hours, near Tifariti, in September 2003, but because of the UN cease-fire program, a strict buffer is now enforced, and the wall cannot be approached.

3. The relatively few major battles in the years immediately prior to the cease-fire went largely unnoticed in the international community. Western attention to the increasingly obscure war occurred only rarely, such as in several incidents when the ELPS accidentally shot down civilian aircraft mistaken for Moroccan air force planes. One such incident occurred in 1985, when Polisario downed a West German plane carrying members of an Antarctic expedition; another occurred in November 1988, when the ELPS shot two planes (and destroyed one) leased by the U.S. Agency for International Development that were returning from a locust-spraying operation in Senegal. Polisario immediately apologized for the attacks.

4. Abdalhay Muy Mansour, ELPS deputy commander for the Tifariti region, claimed that the younger men under his command who joined after the cease-fire are very eager to prove themselves and are always ready to fight, with some hoping to avenge their martyred relatives. He also noted that many young male refugees choose military service over advanced studies abroad. Several interviewed soldiers and refugees in the camps echoed these sentiments (Mundy, interview with Abdalhay Muy Mansour, Sept. 2003).

## 2. ARAB MAGHRIB DISUNITY: ALGERIA AND MOROCCO

1. The only Moroccan dissent on Western Sahara has come from the political margins. In the 1970s, Ila al-'Amam, a persecuted Marxist group, opposed the invasion of Western Sahara and supported the territory's

right to self-determination. One of the group's most famous leaders, Abraham Serfaty, a pro-Palestinian, pro-Polisario Moroccan Jew, spent years in prison and exile for supporting Western Saharan self-determination. But when he returned to Morocco in 1999 after the ascension of Mohammed VI, he surprisingly came out in support of the Moroccan government's proposal to allow Western Sahara autonomy under Moroccan sovereignty. However, the Moroccan political party Annahj Addimocrati (La voie démocratique, Democratic Path), one of the direct descendents of Ila al-'Amam, continues to support Polisario's campaign for self-determination.

Another notable dissenter on the Sahara issue was Shaykh 'Abdessalam Yacine. In early 2000, Shaykh Yacine issued a memorandum to King Mohammed VI in which he stated, "A mortgaged Sahara is the legacy of a bygone reign and a policy of prestige disdainful of man. Our Sahrawi brothers are divided between two choices. . . . Will they vote in the near future for a united Morocco that is truly Muslim, a rethought and reconstructed Morocco, or will they decide, on the basis of their past humiliation and the savage repression they were subject to so recently [i.e., because of the 1999 intifada], to choose dignity and freedom under another banner?" (quoted in Association de soutien, *Weekly News,* Jan. 31, 2000). Shaykh Yacine's point was obviously rhetorical, helping bolster his uncorrupted outsider image among those who matter the most—the millions of poor, marginalized, and frustrated urban Moroccans who form the core of the contemporary Islamic movement. By expressing such a radically deviant viewpoint in a country where publishers are still jailed for printing interviews with Polisario leaders or criticizing the monarchy, Yacine reaffirmed his position on the political fringe. Among the legal parties, organizations, and other political insiders in Morocco, the Sahara issue remains one of national consensus. Indeed, when Mohammed VI announced in late 2005 that he was going to consult the parties on "autonomy" for Western Sahara, the PJD emerged as one of the plan's strongest supporters.

As for Algeria, there is very little dissent on the question of Western Sahara at the elite political level in recent years, whether expressed through political parties or national newspapers. The leader of Algeria's Parti des travailleurs (Workers Party) and frequent presidential candidate Louisa Hanoune has actually accused Polisario officials and followers of being "reactionary" leftists (i.e., not being radical enough in their politics). In terms of popular Algerian attitudes toward the question of Western Sahara, no data is available to suggest that there is or is not widespread support among Algerians for their government's Western Sahara policy. Much attention has been given to the ransacking of a Polisario office in Algiers during the 1988 riots, which was sometimes read as popular contempt toward Polisario among Algerians. Given the depth of Algeria's economic crisis during that period, it is easy to see why some Algerians might have been upset at a perceived diversion of state funds to a foreign war that had nothing to do with their daily lives. Yet it would be a mistake to assign too much significance to the acts of a few angry demonstrators two decades ago; indeed, it is not clear whether the Polisario office was singled out by the demonstrators or was merely another victim of the general vandalism that accompanied the riots in central Algiers.

2. Content to let Islamic activism counter leftism on Moroccan campuses in 1970s, King Hassan could hardly have imagined that this policy, which was then much applauded in the West, would lead some of his country's most dispossessed to adopt a radically violent reading of Islam. In the year before the May 2003 bombing, one estimate held that Islamic Takfiri activists—those who violently oppose all forms of apostasy, even among other Muslims—participated in more than 160 civilian executions, mostly against petty government officials. Although local leaders—self-styled "emirs"—had organized Takfiri groups without central coordination, in the two years prior to the events of September 11, 2001, "dozens" of Moroccans left for training in Afghanistan (Belaala 2004).

Relatively few Moroccans—an estimated 78—joined the CIA-backed "jihad" against the Soviet invasion of Afghanistan in the 1980s, especially in comparison to the 2,800 Algerians who joined that war (Stone 1997,

182–83). The turn of the millennium, however, saw an increase in the number of Moroccans implicated in violent transnational Islamic networks and operations. Two Moroccans, Zacarias Moussaoui and Abdelghani Mzoudi, were implicated in the September 11 attacks. A year before the Casablanca bombings, Moroccan intelligence services discovered an alleged al-Qaida plot, with domestic connections, to attack NATO warships crossing the Strait of Gibraltar. Several Moroccans with recent experience in Afghanistan participated in the Madrid train bombings of March 11, 2004. In mid-2006, *Jeune afrique* magazine reported that 150 Moroccans had volunteered as fighters for al-Qaida's war against the United States in Iraq, making them second only to Algerians as the most significant North African contingent in that war (Soudan 2006).

3. The major difference between the Moroccan and Algerian regimes is the level of diffusion of power among elite agents. In Morocco, the balance of power is asymmetrical in the monarchy's favor. The postcolonial monarchs—Mohammed V, Hassan II, and Mohammed VI—have successfully garnered for themselves an unrivaled status as the ultimate authority in the regime. Backing this rule has been the military, as is also the case in the Middle Eastern kingdoms of Saudi Arabia and Jordan, and the Makhzan, an ensemble of agents and institutions appointed and established to enable surveillance and control at all levels of society (see Layachi 1998, 30–31; Maghraoui 2001).

Even in recent years, the picture in Algeria appears far more complex owing in large part to the regime's antiexecutive tendencies. Power has been more diffuse within Algerian politics, a "military-technocratic oligarchy" (Roberts 2003, 358). After independence, the real power brokers in the military and intelligence apparatus hid behind the FLN's mantle until the aborted elections in January 1992 forced them out of the shadows. The presidencies of Boumedienne and Bouteflika are noteworthy given their ambitions, albeit contested, toward executive hegemony (see Werenfels 2007).

3. THE FRANCO–AMERICAN CONSENSUS

1. In this book in general and this chapter in particular, much more attention has been given to the role of the U.S. government than to the role of the French government, although the French role in Western Sahara has been equally influential. The reason for this bias is ethical rather than scholarly. This book is being written by two citizens of the United States primarily for popular consumption by fellow citizens, whom we feel obligated to inform under democratic imperatives because citizens of the United States are best placed to affect U.S. policy.

2. One source—the former Polisario representative in the United States—reports that U.S. officials were also attempting to aid Hassan via clandestine arms shipments to Morocco: "Henry Kissinger and Vernon Walters, who were given the job of finding new military connections for Morocco, managed in 1978 to supervise secret transfers of guns, ammunition and planes from Jordan, Iran, Taiwan, South Korea and South Africa. According to government documents and interviews with the principals, Mr. Walters received at least $300,000 in early 1980 from a company that specializes in selling sophisticated military technology to foreign governments for his work with Morocco barely one year after he left the C.I.A" (Kamil 1987, 31).

3. Some of the strongest U.S. supporters of Morocco during this period came from mainstream Jewish organizations, which lobbied for increased U.S. support of the "moderate" King Hassan. In addition to his relatively nonbelligerent attitude toward Israel, Hassan was also more tolerant than most Arab rulers toward his country's remaining Jewish community. David Ginsberg, a prominent liberal attorney with close ties to several Jewish members of the U.S. Congress, was particularly active in encouraging U.S. assistance. Representative Stephen Solarz, once a strong critic of King Hassan on Capitol Hill, reportedly toned down his efforts because of pressure from members of the sizable Sephardic Jewish community in his Brooklyn district.

4. As Polisario often noted, U.S. policy toward destabilizing rebellions and insurgencies during the Cold War was inconsistent. In the 1980s, Polisario frequently asked U.S. officials and visitors to the refugee camps why they referred positively to the CIA-funded Afghani mujahideen as "freedom fighters" in their fight against the Soviets, but negatively to Polisario's soldiers. Another obvious example is the case of the Nicaraguan Contras, which were created, supported, and publicly endorsed by the Reagan administration despite committing gross human rights violations. Yet even without the Soviet menace and before the war on terror, this pattern of selective endorsement in U.S. policy remained basically unchanged. The George H. W. Bush administration's principled talk of protecting weak nations from predatory states as one of the prime justifications for the first Gulf War rang hollow among Western Saharan nationalists. The Sahrawi refugees in Algeria would later point out this contradiction to the key architect of the first Gulf War coalition, James Baker, who visited the refugee camps during his tenure as the UN envoy to Western Sahara. Baker bluntly told Polisario that Western Sahara is not Kuwait.

5. Most notable is France Libertés, former first lady Danielle Mitterrand's humanitarian foundation, which operates relief efforts in the refugee camps and has published reports critical of the Moroccan regime's human rights record in Western Sahara. Toward the end of François Mitterrand's presidency, there was a public row between the Moroccan royal palace and Mrs. Mitterrand. To placate the Moroccans, she cancelled a scheduled visit to the Polisario refugee camps. However, in 2003, the foundation published a scathing report on human rights practices in the Moroccan-occupied Western Sahara (Karmous and Decaster 2003). To balance things out, though, the foundation published a subsequent report dealing with Moroccan POWs' held by Polisario in Algeria. The report contained several serious accusations against Polisario and the Algerian government, including claims of forced labor by the POWs and, startlingly, a large number of summary executions of Moroccan POWs at the hands of Polisario and Algerian military agents. The number of claimed executions provided, however, exceeded any estimate of the number of the Moroccan POWs ever given by either of the combatants, any human rights group, or the International Red Cross, which had unfettered access to the Moroccan POWs. This discrepancy raised questions as to the foundation's methodological approach to gathering information on human rights abuses as well as to its overall political motive.

### 4. THE HISTORICAL FORMATION OF WESTERN SAHARAN NATIONALISM

1. Take, for example, the definition provided by Tony Hodges and Anthony Pazzanita in their dictionary of the Western Sahara: Sahrawis are "the Ahel es-Sahel ['People of the Littoral'], the inhabitants of the Atlantic coastal belt of the desert *roughly* encompassed by the borders of what is now known as Western Sahara." For these two scholars, defining the term *Sahrawi* is problematic in only two respects: "The term has thus come to be synonymous with 'Western Saharan,' though the tribes that composed the Ahel es-Sahel nomadized over a wide area, crossing the 'frontiers' imposed by the colonial powers in the 20th century. Moreover, during the process of sedentation in the second half of the 20th century, many Sahrawis settled in the neighboring territories" (1994, 395, emphasis added).

The problem with Hodges and Pazzanita's definition is that they seem to want to have it both ways. They recognize that the Sahrawis roamed a much greater expanse than the area that would become Spanish Sahara, yet there is a big difference between "crossing" and "inhabiting." And although it is true that many Sahrawis "settled in neighboring territories," this statement erroneously asserts that Sahrawis never permanently inhabited those lands previously. Furthermore, without making any reference to Spanish Sahara, an impossible feat when it comes to defining the Sahrawis, this definition becomes circular: Who are the Sahrawis? They are the Ahel as-Sahel. Who are the Ahel as-Sahel? They are the Sahrawis. These ideas are further explored in Mundy 2007a.

2. Based on our personal and professional correspondences with historians and anthropologists, especially those familiar with local and colonial texts, we find this to be the consensus. Other evidence is readily available. For example, in a 1960 study of the Awlad Tidrarin, a Saharan "tribe" ranging from northern Mauritania through Western Sahara and into southern Morocco, anthropologist Lloyd Briggs never once used the term *Sahrawi*. He instead described the entire native population of Spanish Sahara as "Moors," "the basically white and mainly pastoral nomadic population of the Spanish Sahara and of the French Saharan territory which adjoins it [i.e., Mauritania]" (211).

3. Despite the brevity of the Murabitun Empire, John Mercer contentiously argues that its effects on Maghribi society should not be overlooked: "The Almoravids' influence included the implantation of the Malikite rite, now a part of orthodox Islam, and the founding of Marrakesh. In fact, the Saharaoui influence on Morocco appears greater than that of the subsequent dynasties on the desert; one might feel that, had the nomads been allowed to put their case at the International Court of Justice in 1975, this would have given them as good a claim on Morocco as King Hassan was able to make out to the desert" (1976a, 500).

5. EXPRESSIONS OF NATIONALISM: THE POLISARIO FRONT, THE SAHRAWI
ARAB DEMOCRATIC REPUBLIC, AND THE SAHRAWI REFUGEE CAMPS

1. Moroccan officials complained that Polisario would not allow complete families to participate in the exchange program and would thus hold one family member "hostage" in order to deter defection during an exchange to Western Sahara. Off the record, officials with the UNHCR and MINURSO felt this supposed tactic had little to do with the low rate of defections, however. Rabat's official story was dealt another blow when dissident Moroccan journalist Ali Lmrabet visited the camps in 2005 and reported that they were indeed not prisons. Additionally, families in the camps and the occupied territory have been holding improvised reunions in Mauritania for years. The recent explosion of cellular phone use and Internet access has also increased communication across the berm. Far from separated, the Western Saharans are more in touch with each other than at any other time in the history of the conflict.

2. The Frente de Libertação and the Partido Africano were initially based on an indigenous African socialism mixed with certain applied Marxist concepts. Just prior to independence and subsequently as ruling parties, they evolved into a more traditional Third World Marxist-Leninist orientation.

3. Anne Lippert (1992), who traveled to the camps on many occasions during the war, notes that the base level in 1976 was the *friq*, a group of *khiyam* (tents) that anthropologist David Hart (1962, 1998) identifies as the base unit of the Sahrawi "tribe." The term *hayy*, however, refers specifically to a subdivision of a city, like a "quarter" or, as the refugees call it, a "barrio," which fits into the RASD's attempt to mimic the political geography of a modern state. Some refugees refer to their organizational system as *tuwiza*, which has meanings close to "self-help" and "solidarity."

Conservatively assuming four persons to a tent, the rough figure of two hundred tents per *hayy* and four *hayy* to a *da'irah* produces a population of roughly twenty thousand persons in each camp *(wilayah)*, or eighty thousand refugees total.

4. This point was emphasized repeatedly in our interviews and conversations with Sahrawi activists and officials, both male and female. Interestingly enough, these sentiments stood in direct contrast to remarks made in similar interviews that Stephen Zunes conducted with PLO leaders in 1981 in Beirut, Lebanon, including one with Lina Haba of the General Union of Palestinian Women. She emphasized the widespread attitude within the PLO that the national question must be resolved before the question of women's liberation can be adequately addressed, a perspective that is not uncommon in many national liberation struggles.

6. THE SAHRAWI INTIFADA: WESTERN SAHARAN NATIONALISM
UNDER MOROCCAN OCCUPATION

1. One of the most prominent second-generation nationalists—infamous, from a Moroccan perspective—is Ali-Salem Tamek, an ethnic Sahrawi from Assa and a labor union organizer. In spite of his origin in Moroccan territory, he publicly shares Polisario's ambition of an independent Western Sahara. As noted, Polisario supporters from southern Morocco are—for now—*Western Saharan* nationalists and not Sahrawi nationalists broadly. Many activists assert that many ethnic Sahrawis will move to Western Sahara when it gains independence. Although rare, some nationalists voice a counterirredentist claim on former southern Spanish Morocco (the Tekna or Dra'a Zone), saying "First al-'Ayun, then Tan Tan."

2. The one exception to the lack of judicial process during the years of war in the Sahara was the "Meknes Group." The twenty-six Sahrawi students in this group were arrested between April and December 1977. The Moroccan government held them in preventative detention until they faced trial in 1980. Each received four- to five-year sentences, but they were held in regular Moroccan prison, where they could smuggle secret letters to the outside world. In those letters, they wrote that all Sahrawi prisoners suffered "psychological and physical torture" while under secret detention (Amnesty International 1990, 14).

3. From the forum's inception, its leaders faced almost continuous harassment from the occupation authorities. Ali-Salem Tamek, an outspoken union organizer and Sahara Branch member, was given a two-year sentence in September 2002 for "undermining the internal security of the state." His conviction was based on allegations that he had received funds from the Polisario provided by Brahim Laghzal, Cheikh Khaya, and Laarbi Massaoud. Following their release in 2001, Laghzal, Khaya, and Massaoud claimed that their indictment of Tamek was forced under torture (Amnesty International 2002). In November 2002, Ahmed Nassiri of the Sahara Branch was given an eighteen-month sentence for allegedly organizing anti-government activities. A Moroccan court convicted Nassiri based on an unsigned statement that the police had attempted to force him to sign (Amnesty International 2003b). In March 2003, Bazid Salek, another Sahara Branch activist, received a ten-year sentence for allegedly organizing violent clashes that erupted in occupied Smara in November 2002. Following the November uprising, Moroccan courts handed down brief sentences to fourteen other Sahrawis based on confessions apparently extracted under torture (Amnesty International 2003a, 7–8).

4. See, for example, this Agence France Presse dispatch: "And if the fears of the Moroccan press are anything to go by, then the initiative should certainly include the north African kingdom, where newspapers have accused the Polisario Front of having ties with Al Qaeda. Polisario wants independence for Western Sahara, which was annexed by Morocco in 1975 and over which the two sides have fought a war. 'Polisario flogged weapons and explosives (to Al Qaeda),' the weekly *Gazette du Maroc* has accused, alleging that the secessionist group obtained in exchange the backing of Bin Laden's group for the creation of an Islamic state in Western Sahara. Newspaper *Al Ahdath al Maghribia* took the Western Sahara link further, saying that the bomb attacks in Madrid on March 11 were planned in the desert region, which lies in southern Morocco, bordering Mauritania" (June 15, 2004).

See also "Laâyoune: Man Hiding Hawn Rockets Arrested South Morocco," *Morocco Times,* Dec. 23, 2005; "Man Arrested in Southern Morocco in Possession of 13 Rockets 'Hawn'," *Maghreb Arab Presse,* Dec. 23, 2005; "13 vieilles bombes saisies à Laâyoune: Un 'terroriste' devant le tribunal militaire," *Al-Bayane,* Dec. 23, 2005; "Collusion entre le Polisario et Al Qaïda," *Aujourd'hui le Maroc,* Dec. 29, 2005; and "Deux éléments du POLISARIO et deux Algériens soupçonnés de terrorisme arrêtés par l'armée mauritanienne," *L'Opinion,* Oct. 26, 2005.

## 7. SEARCHING FOR A SOLUTION: THE UNITED NATIONS AND THE ORGANIZATION OF AFRICAN UNITY

1. The 1982 OAU's program for a referendum in Western Sahara states:

- Following consultations with the parties, the Chairman will advise the Implementation Committee on a suitable date for a comprehensive cease-fire including the cessation of "tactical moves, cross-border movements and all acts of violence and intimidation," as well as the reinforcement of forces with arms or soldiers;
- "A peace-keeping force and/or a military observer group," to monitor the cease-fire and to act as a civilian police force, will arrive shortly before the cease-fire.
- A week before the cease-fire, both the Moroccan government and Polisario will inform the monitors [of] the size of their respective forces and the monitors will fix their positions in locations in areas where they will not "constitute a psychological or any other hindrance to the conduct of a free and fair referendum."
- Prisoners of war will be released.
- The OAU Implementation Commission will appoint an Interim Administration with the legislative and administrative powers necessary to carry out the referendum and, with the consent of the parties one month before the cease-fire, a Commissioner to head the effort and to utilize, with the full cooperation of the two sides, their administrative apparatuses to maintain security required for the staging of a free and fair referendum.
- The referendum vote will determine whether or not the Western Sahara will become independent or will be integrated into Morocco. The electorate will be based on, but not limited to, the 1974 Spanish census with provisions for "claims and challenges" to the voter list.

The OAU Implementation Committee proposed that it would verify and ratify the results of the referendum, which would later receive the endorsement of the OAU Assembly of Heads of State and the UN General Assembly (see Damis 1984, 288–94, 279–80).

2. The proposed Western Sahara referendum fell well short of other standards as well. The International Human Rights Law Group, an NGO, published a 1984 manual entitled *Guidelines for International Election Observing,* which sets minimum standards for conducting free and fair plebiscites and provides a methodology for election monitoring. The continued presence of Moroccan administrators, the limited campaign time, and the lack of provisions for international observers raised serious concerns over whether MINURSO's referendum would meet basic minimal standards for a free and fair vote.

## 8. THE ABANDONED REFERENDUM

1. According to the 1974 census, the most populous groups were the two Rgaybat confederations. The Rgaybat al-Sahil numbered 18,374 and the eastern Rgaybat al-Sharq numbered 19,625. Far behind them, the two major subgroups of the Tiknah, the Ait al-Hasan and Izargiyyn, respectively totaled 3,540 and 7,984. The al-'Arusiyyn numbered only 2,858. In the southern part of the territory, the Awlad Dulaym numbered 5,382, and the Awlad Tidrarin totaled 4,842. The Spanish authorities placed the remainder in three categories: Tribes of the North (3,374), Shurafa' tribes (4,632), and Tribes of the Coast and South (2,362). See Gobierno General del Sáhara 1975, cited in Instituto Europea de la Mediterránea 2005. See also Aguirre 1988, 603, and Hodges and Pazzanita 1994, 356.

2. Most UN missions to conflict areas have been called "peacekeeping." The other kind of mission is called "peace enforcement." The major difference between the two is an issue of consent, which is critical in terms of the UN. In cases where the Security Council feels that a country's sovereignty should be respected or council members are unwilling to challenge a country's sovereignty (e.g., Morocco in Western Sahara), the consent of the parties to the

conflict is typically required. In these situations, peacekeepers tend to play a passive role as monitors. In peace enforcement, which the Security Council has been loathe to use except in rare cases, the UN actively uses force, military or otherwise, to put into effect a UN Security Council Chapter VII resolution (e.g., Iraq and Kuwait in 1990–91).

Although there are countless studies of UN operations, few have devoted significant attention to Western Sahara. Marrack Goulding, undersecretary-general of the UN Peacekeeping Department from 1986 to 1992), whose memoirs (Goulding 2002) deal extensively with Western Sahara, defined peacekeeping as the following: "Field operations established by the UN, with the consent of the parties concerned to help control and resolve conflicts between them, under UN command and control, at the expense collectively of the member states, and with military and other personnel and equipment provided voluntarily by them, acting impartially between the parties and using force to the minimum extent necessary" (1993, 455).

Goulding identifies six types of peacekeeping missions: preventative operations, which aim to stop conflict before it starts; traditional operations, which support ongoing conflict-resolution efforts; comprehensive operations, which seek to implement settlement plans agreed to by all the parties involved from beginning to end; operations to protect humanitarian supplies (e.g., Somalia and Bosnia Herzegovina); "post-conflict peace-building" or *the deployment of a United Nations force in a country where the institutions of a state have largely collapsed* (e.g., Congo, 1960); and, finally, cease-fire enforcement, which Goulding calls a "forceful variant" of traditional peacekeeping. As Goulding notes, the latter two verge on peace enforcement rather than on peacekeeping because they call for the active use of force rather than the passive use of observers who can use force only in rare cases of self-defense (1993, 456–59, emphasis in original).

Taking issue with Goulding's definition, William J. Durch, who has devoted significant attention to UN peacekeeping generally (1993b) and Western Sahara specifically (1993a), argues that any definition should ultimately "describe why or when peacekeeping works." First of all, Durch notes, "A peacekeeping force derives its power from local consent, local perceptions of the impartiality and moral authority of its sponsoring organization, its ability to dispel dangerous misinformation, and active support of the great powers." Without these elements, he argues, peacekeeping will fail (1993a, 153).

Jarat Chopra has also written extensively on UN peacekeeping missions; one of his works (Chopra 1999) dedicates a whole chapter to MINURSO. Writing in 1994, Chopra argued, "The peace process [in the Western Sahara] is based and must continue to be based on the consent of both parties. There are two levels of consent: (i) to the initial UN-OAU Settlement Plan and (ii) to its subsequent interpretations and implementations" (3–5; see also Chopra 1997, 55).

Here it is worth noting the obvious theme running among Goulding, Durch, and Chopra's descriptions: the primacy of the consent of the parties involved. When MINURSO was created, consent was lacking, so most of the UN work was aimed at obtaining and maintaining consent from Morocco and Polisario. Of course, the Secretariat prioritized Morocco's consent over Polisario's. Polisario made all of the key concessions in the peace process (see this chapter and the next). The most dramatic concession came in 2003, when Polisario agreed to let Moroccans participate in the referendum, what Polisario had implicitly been fighting in the 1990s. Morocco's only major concession after 1981 was to say it wanted a referendum. This difference reflects not only the conflict's asymmetry, but also Morocco's importance to the West.

3. All UN documents indexed in this chapter by numbers starting with "S/" come from UN Secretary-General 1975–2007 unless otherwise cited.

4. There was then an effort to get the parties talking directly on these proposals at the technical level. On July 2, 1993, the secretary-general announced Morocco–Polisario negotiations in al-'Ayun, Western Sahara, set for mid-July. Rabat's delegation would be headed by its UN representative, Ahmed Snoussi, and backed by Basri's Sahara deputy, Mohammed Azmi, representing the Interior Ministry. Polisario's delegation would be led by founding members Bachir Mustapha Sayed and Mohammed Lamine Ould Ahmed. Once at

the table on July 17, however, Snoussi took a back seat to members of Morocco's CORCAS, led by Polisario defector Muhammad Shaykh Baydallah. This configuration was a clear signal to Polisario that Morocco was treating the issue as an internal matter rather than a foreign one. Following this initial affront and subsequent disputes over prominently displayed Moroccan flags and ubiquitous pictures of King Hassan, Polisario attempted to walk out but was coaxed back by a call from Washington. Then, at the July 19 meeting, the Moroccan delegation avoided all talk of the Settlement Plan. Snoussi read a patronizing statement from King Hassan that effectively ended the meeting. Despite the Moroccan behavior, Boutros-Ghali later said that the meetings were "marked by restraint and mutual respect" (quoted in *UN Chronicle,* Dec. 1993). In October, there was a push to stage another meeting, this time in more neutral New York, yet Polisario refused to participate when Rabat said it would send members of CORCAS plus Brahim Hakim and Omar Hadrami, two key Polisario defectors. In secret, on the secretary-general's behalf, members of MINURSO attempted to set up a high-level meeting between Polisario leader Abdelaziz and Hassan II in Geneva for January 1994. King Hassan, however, would send only Snoussi and a key confidant, General Abdelhak Khadiri. These two people fell well short of Abdelaziz's "head of state" level, so the talks failed to take place (Jensen 2005, 54–55).

5. According to two political observers from Polisario, Mohammed Lamine and Mohammed Rahal, who spoke with Jacob Mundy in Smara camp on the subject on September 10, 2003, Moroccan applicants often failed simple geographical tests posed by the shaykhs. For example, Moroccan-sponsored applicants who claimed they were from Dakhla often could not correctly locate the city's position relative to the ocean (i.e., when asked, "Is the ocean to the east or the west of the city?"). A group of several thousand Moroccan candidates similarly could not accurately describe the city they supposedly came from in Western Sahara, name any of its inhabitants, or provide its location relative to al-'Ayun, either north, south, east, or west.

6. John Damis notes that significant members of the Awlad Dulaym had settled near Sidi Kacem (1983, 20).

7. Article 9, paragraph 1, subsection 3 reads, "Candidates for identification who have appeared before the Identification Commission but who, in the latter's estimation, have not established their eligibility to vote according to the eligibility criteria referred to in article 5 of this document, where new circumstances or developments or any evidence of which the members of the Identification Commission who ruled on the case was [*sic*] not aware justify reconsideration of their case." See UN doc. S/1999/483, addendum 1.

8. A year later, in February 2001, the secretary-general released the final figures for appeals, totaling 131,038. Most of the appeals (115,645) claimed wrongful exclusion, justified on the grounds that each would present at least two witnesses—but no documentary evidence—to corroborate their Western Saharanness. A far smaller number of appeals (15,393) sought to argue against someone else's inclusion. Broken down by party, candidates waging appeals sponsored by the Moroccan government make up the lion's share at 95 percent. Applicants in the refugee camps and Mauritania accounted for the remainder of appeals, respectively 4 percent and 0.7 percent. By May 2001, MINURSO technically was ready to process appeals, although the Security Council and the Secretariat had long abandoned the referendum for a "third way."

9. Commenting on the resolution, Ian Williams, journalist and longtime observer of the UN, wrote, "It was a victory of sorts in the teeth of a failed French amendment [to the resolution] which had sought solutions other than the referendum. This was widely read by other delegates to mean that the Moroccans—and their French allies—realized in the end they would lose the referendum, so they should be ceded the territory by some other means" (*Middle East International,* Mar. 10, 2000, 19).

## 9. THE BAKER PLAN AND THE END OF THE PEACE PROCESS

1. The other obvious compromise approach to Western Sahara is a division of the territory. In its most basic form, such a division would allow for the creation of a smaller independent Western Saharan state and permit the

formal annexation of the remainder into Morocco. More ambitious land swaps have also been proposed, including trade-offs among Mauritania, Algeria, Western Sahara, and Morocco. In 1978, following the coup in Mauritania, the French government offered the Sahara Demain (or "Sade Plan"), proposing a small independent Saharan state federated with Mauritania and the rest ceded to Morocco. Mauritania would then give up some of its own territory to Morocco and Algeria (Damis 1983, 137). However, both Polisario and the Moroccan government have shunned almost all initiatives based on a division of the territory. Concerned Western powers and Polisario know that any division would compromise the viability of an independent Western Sahara, especially if the phosphates at Bukra' went to Morocco. Under autonomy, Morocco and Western Sahara would have a symbiotic, interconnected economic relationship. A miniature Saharan state based in the southern third or half of Western Sahara would be poor and cut off from Algeria. For Rabat, division requires a redrawing of maps that might be too difficult to swallow ideologically. Power sharing, in contrast, allows Morocco to continue its practice of claiming and depicting Western Sahara as "Moroccan." Any "severing" of the Sahara provinces would be as difficult for Morocco to sell domestically as a total loss of the territory. Algeria unilaterally proposed dividing Western Sahara in late 2001, claiming that it had Polisario support. The Security Council, however, refused to back this idea. African states, the most ardent supporters of self-determination, have been most opposed to establishing any precedent for dividing up colonially inherited boundaries. Although autonomy presents itself as a feasible solution to the Western Sahara issue, the politics behind this emerging consensus are not based in practicality.

2. In this chapter, all material from UN documents indexed by numbers starting with "S/" comes from UN Secretary-General 1975–2007.

3. In this chapter, all material from UN resolutions comes from UN Security Council 1975–2007.

4. In March 2003, retired Algerian general Khalid Nezzar, formerly one of the most powerful military hardliners in the regime, told a Moroccan newspaper, "At present, Algeria does not really need yet another country created at its borders. The creation of a Greater Morocco will help overcome this dead end" (quoted in *Beirut Daily Star,* Apr. 12, 2003). Nezzar's statements elicited condemnation within the Algerian government, quickly spurring a declaration from the Ministry of Communications and Culture that Algeria remained "attached to the principle of the Sahraoui people's self-determination" (Algérie Presse Service, Mar. 16, 2003). However, as journalist Toby Shelley (2003) noted, some domestic criticism focused on the fact that Nezzar made few demands on Morocco, not on the fact that he was willing to give up Western Sahara. Nezzar later told Polisario officials that the Moroccan press had taken him out of context.

5. Based on a comparison of the U.S. State Department's *Congressional Budget Justification for Foreign Operations* from fiscal year 2001 to fiscal year 2008.

6. A leading figure in the neoconservative movement, a strong supporter of the U.S. invasion of Iraq, Israeli unilateralism, and its 2006 invasion of Lebanon—not to mention a convicted criminal from the Reagan administration's Iran-Contra affair—Abrams saw continued Moroccan stability as key to U.S. policies in the Middle East in the war on terror. On Abrams, see *The New Yorker,* Oct. 31, 2005.

7. The independent Moroccan human rights group AMDH has accused both Benslimane and Laanigri of being directly involved in past state-orchestrated "disappearances." Past victims of human rights abuses in Morocco have identified Benslimane as one of the directors of the infamous detention centers Qal'at M'gouna and Agdez, where many Sahrawis were held. He has also been implicated in abuses in the Western Sahara. Laanigri, like Benslimane, is similarly linked to the Tazmamart death camp (Chicon and Bibas 2005). The limited mandate of Morocco's 2004 Instance Equité et Réconciliation (Equity and Reconciliation Commission), which was not allowed to "name names," guaranteed that these generals would escape direct accusations and would never have to sit accused in a court of law (see chapter 2). Laanigri's sudden dismissal from office in September 2006 following his failure to protect the Moroccan military from Islamist infiltration did little to change the culture of impunity in the Moroccan regime.

# References

NEWS SERVICES AND PERIODICALS

ABC, Spain
*Africa Confidential*
*Africa Research Bulletin*
*Africa Report*
*afrol News*
Agence France Presse
Algérie Presse Service
*Alhurra* (Springfield, Va.)
Association de soutien à un référendum libre et régulier au Sahara Occidental, *Weekly News* (at
    http://www.arso.org)
*Aujourd'hui le Maroc*
*Al-Bayane* (Morocco)
BBC Monitoring Service
*BBC News and World Service Online*
*Beirut Daily Star*
*Christian Science Monitor*
*The Economist* (London)
*Financial Times* (London) (FT)
*The Guardian* (Manchester)
*Inquiry* (Washington, D.C.)
*Le Journal Hebdomadaire* (Morocco)
*Los Angeles Times*
*Maghreb Arab Presse*
*The Middle East*
*Middle East International*
*Le Monde*
*Le Monde Diplomatique*
*Morocco Times*
*New African*
*New Internationalist*

*Newsday*

*The New Yorker*

*New York Times*

*NRC Handelsblad*

*Observer* (London)

*L'Opinion* (Morocco)

*El País* (Madrid)

*PESA News* (Petroleum Exploration Society of Australia)

Reuters

*Saharan Peoples' Support Committee Newsletter*

*Tel Quel* (Morocco)

*Time* magazine

*UN Chronicle*

*Washington Post*

*Washington Report on Middle East Affairs*


WORKS CITED


Ackerman, Peter, and Jack DuVall. 2001. *A Force More Powerful: A Century of Nonviolent Conflict.* New York: St. Martin's Press.

Ackerman, Peter, and Christopher Kruegler. 1994. *Strategic Nonviolent Conflict: The Dynamics of People Power in the Twentieth Century.* Westport, Conn.: Praeger.

Adebajo, Adekeye. 2002. *Selling Out the Sahara: The Tragic Tale of the UN Referendum.* Occasional Papers Series. Ithaca, N.Y.: Institute for African Development, Cornell Univ.

Aguirre, José Ramón Diego. 1988. *Historia del Sahara Español: La verdad de un traición.* Madrid: Kaydeda Ediciones.

Amnesty International (AI). 1977. *Amnesty International Briefing: Morocco.* Briefing Paper 13, AI Index PUB 78/00/77. New York: AI, Oct. 1977.

———. 1982. *Report of an Amnesty International Mission to the Kingdom of Morocco, 10–13 February 1981.* AI Index ASR 40/01/82. New York: AI, May.

———. 1990. *Morocco: "Disappearances" of People of Western Saharan Origin.* AI Index MDE 29/17/90. New York: AI, Nov.

———. 1991a. *Amnesty International Briefing: Morocco.* AI Index MDE 29/02/91. New York: AI, Mar.

———. 1991b. *Morocco: Political Imprisonment, "Disappearances," Torture.* AI Index MDE 29/01/91. New York: AI, Mar. 20.

———. 1994. *"Disappearances" and Political Killings: Human Rights Crisis of the 1990s, a Manual for Action.* AI Index ACT 33/01/94. Amsterdam: AI, Dutch Section.

———. 1996. *Human Rights Violations in the Western Sahara.* AI Index MDE 29/04/96. New York: AI, Apr. 18.

———. 1999. *"Turning the Page": Achievements and Obstacles.* AI Index MDE 29/01/99. New York: AI, June 1999.

———. 2002. "Morocco/Western Sahara: Free Prisoner of Conscience Ali-Salem Tamek." Press release, Oct. 23. AI Index MDE 29/004/2002.

———. 2003a. *Morocco/Western Sahara: Briefing to the Committee Against Torture.* AI Index MDE 29/011/2003. New York: AI, Nov.

———. 2003b. "Morocco/Western Sahara: Clampdown on Civil Society Activists." *The Wire* 33, no. 6 (July). Available at http://www.amnesty.org/en/library/info/NWS21/006/2003/en. Accessed Feb. 25, 2010.

———. 2004. *Morocco/Western Sahara: Torture and the "Anti-terrorism" Campaign—the Case of the Témara Detention Center.* AI Index MDE 29/004/2004. New York: AI, June.

Anderson, Benedict. 1991. *Imagined Communities: Reflections on the Origin and Spread of Nationalism.* New York: Verso.

Anderson, Lisa. 1997. "Prospects for Liberalism in North Africa: Identities and Interests in Preindustrial Welfare States." In *Islam, Democracy, and the State in North Africa,* edited by John Entelis, 127–40. Indianapolis: Indiana Univ. Press.

Annan, Kofi. 1997. Letter to James Baker, Mar. 5. Baker Institute, Rice Univ., Houston, Texas. Available at http://www.bakerinstitute.org/vrtour/jab30yr/baker37.html. Accessed Oct. 1, 2003.

Ashford, Douglas E. 1962. "The Irredentist Appeal in Morocco and Mauritania." *Western Political Quarterly* 15: 641–51.

Association marocaine des droits humains (AMDH). 2005. *Rapport de la commission d'enquête relatif aux événements qu'a connus la ville de Laâyoune à la fin du mois de mai.* Rabat: AMDH, Oct. 15.

Babbitt, Eileen F. 2006. "Mediating Rights-Based Conflicts: Making Self-Determination Negotiable." *International Negotiation* 11: 185–208.

Balta, Paul. 1986. "French Policy in North Africa." *Middle East Journal* 40: 238–51.

Barbier, Maurice. 1982. *Le conflit au Sahara Occidental.* Paris: L'Harmattan.

Beirouk, Khatry. 2006. *The Sahrawi Uprising: One Year On.* Grupo de Estudios Estratégicos, Colaboraciones 1033, June 20. Available at http://www.gees.org/articulos/2635. Accessed Feb. 15, 2010.

Belaala, Selma. 2004. "A New Kind of Fundamentalism." *Le Monde Diplomatique,* Nov. Available at http://mondediplo.com/2004/11/04moroccoislamists. Accessed Nov. 2007.

Bennoune, Mahfoud. 1977. "Mauritania: Formation of a Neo-colonial Society." *MERIP Reports* (Feb.): 3–26.

Bhatia, Michael. 2001. "The Western Sahara under Polisario Control." *Review of African Political Economy* 28: 291–301.

Bolton, John R. 1998. "Resolving the Western Sahara Conflict." Paper presented at the 1998 Congressional Defense and Foreign Policy Forum, Washington, D.C., Mar. 27. Available at http://www.arso.org/01-2-54.htm. Accessed Aug. 2006.

———. 2007. *Surrender Is Not an Option: Defending America at the United Nations.* New York: Threshold.

Bontems, Claude. 1987. "The Government of the Sahrawi Arab Democratic Republic." *Third World Quarterly* 9: 168–86.

Boulding, Elise. [1982] 2000. "Envisioning the Peaceable Kingdom." In *Peace Is the Way: Writings on Nonviolence from the Fellowship of Reconciliation,* edited by Walter Wink, 129–34. Maryknoll, N.Y.: Orbis.

Brett, Michael, and Elizabeth Fentress. 1996. *The Berbers.* Malden, Mass.: Blackwell.

Briggs, Lloyd Cabot. 1960. *Tribes of the Sahara.* Cambridge, Mass.: Harvard Univ. Press.

Bukhari, Ahmed. 1995. Letter from the Representative of the Frente POLISARIO to the United Nations, Dec. 7. On file with Stephen Zunes.

Bullard, Alice, and Bakary Tandia. 2003. "Images and Realities of Mauritania's Attempted Coup." *Middle East Report* (July 22). Available at http://merip.org/mero/mero072203.html. Accessed Aug. 30, 2004.

Bunch, Beth, Yogesh Chandrani, and Danielle Smith. 1992. *Peace for Western Sahara: Reality or Mirage? Field Report on the UN Peace Plan for Western Sahara and on the Conditions in the Refugee Camps.* Somerville, Mass.: Citizen's Committee for Western Sahara.

Bureau international pour le respect des droits de l'homme au Sahara Occidental. 2002. *El-Karama* 23 (Dec.) (entire issue).

———. 2004. *El-Karama* 27 (Mar.–Apr.) (entire issue).

Canadian Lawyers Association for International Human Rights (CLAIHR). 1997. *Western Sahara Initiative: Phase II Report: Fact Finding Mission to Morocco and Western Sahara.* Ottawa: CLAIHR.

Carapico, Sheila. 2001. "Euro-Med: European Ambitions in the Mediterranean." *Middle East Report,* no. 220 (autumn): 24–28.

Chaliand, Gerard. 1980. *The Struggle for Africa: Conflict of the Great Powers.* New York: St. Martin's Press.

Chatty, Dawn, and Gina Crivello. 2005. *Children and Adolescents in Sahrawi and Afghan Refugee Households: Living with the Effect of Prolonged Armed Conflict and Forced Migration.* Lessons Learned Report. Oxford, U.K.: Refugee Studies Centre, Univ. of Oxford, July.

Chichini, Malak. 1985. "Taming the Desert." *Refugees* (Feb.): 13–15.

Chicon, Emmanuel, and Benjamin Bibas. 2005. "IER, Between the Young and Old Guard." *International Justice Tribune,* Mar. 29. Retrieved via LexisNexis.

Chopra, Jarat. 1994. *United Nations Determination of the Western Saharan Self.* Oslo: Norwegian Institute for International Affairs.

———. 1997. "A Chance for Peace in Western Sahara." *Survival* 39: 51–65.

———. 1999. *Peace-Maintenance.* New York: Routledge.

Clark, Roger. 2007. "Western Sahara and the United Nations Norms on Self-Determination and Aggression." In *International Law and the Question of Western Sahara,* edited by Karin Arts and Pedro Pinto Leite, 45–58. Leiden: International Platform of Jurists for East Timor.

Cleaveland, Timothy. 1998. "Islam and the Construction of Social Identity in the Nineteenth-Century Sahara." *Journal of African History* 39: 365–88.

———. 2002. *Becoming Walata: A History of Saharan Social Formation and Transformation.* Portsmouth, N.H.: Heinemann.

Clément, Jean-François. 1986. "Morocco's Bourgeoisie: Monarchy, State, and Owning Class." *Middle East Report,* no. 142 (Sept.–Oct.): 13–17.

Copson, Raymond. 1994. *Africa's Wars and Prospects for Peace.* Armonk, N.Y.: M. E. Sharpe.

Crocker, Chester A., Fen Osler Hampson, and Pamela Aall. 2004. *Taming Intractable Conflicts: Mediation in the Hardest Cases.* Washington, D.C.: United States Institute of Peace.

———, eds. 2005. *Grasping the Nettle: Analyzing Cases of Intractable Conflict.* Washington, D.C.: United States Institute of Peace.

Crow, Ralph E., Philip Grant, and Saad E. Ibrahim, eds. 1990. *Arab Nonviolent Political Struggle in the Middle East.* Boulder, Colo.: Lynne Rienner.

Curtin, Philip D. 1971. "Jihad in West Africa: Early Phases and Inter-relations in Mauritania and Senegal." *Journal of African History* 12: 11–24.

Damis, John. 1983. *Conflict in Northwest Africa: The Western Sahara Dispute.* Stanford, Calif.: Hoover Institution.

———. 1984. "OAU and the Western Sahara." In *The OAU after Twenty Years,* edited by Yassin El-Ayouty and I. William Zartman, 273–96. New York: Praeger.

———. 1985. "The Western Sahara Dispute as a Source of Regional Conflict in North Africa." In *Contemporary North Africa: Issues of Development and Integration,* edited by Halim Barakat, 138–53. Washington, D.C.: Center for Contemporary Arab Studies, Georgetown Univ.

———. 1986. *U.S.–Arab Relations: The Moroccan Dimension.* Washington, D.C.: Council on U.S.-Arab Relations.

———. 1990. "Morocco and the Western Sahara." *Current History* 89: 165–68, 184–86.

———. 1993. "The United States and North Africa." In *Polity and Society in Contemporary North Africa,* edited by I. William Zartman and William Mark Habeeb, 221–40. Boulder, Colo.: Westview.

———. 1995. "Morocco's 1995 Fisheries Agreement with the European Union: A Crisis Resolved." *Mediterranean Politics* 3: 61–73.

———. 1998. "Morocco's 1995 Association Agreement with the European Union." *Journal of North African Studies* 3: 91–112.

———. 2000. "King Hassan and the Western Sahara." *Maghreb Review* 25: 13–30.

———. 2001. "Sahrawi Demonstrations." *Middle East Report,* no. 218 (spring): 38–41.

Daoud, Zakya, and Brahim Ouchelh. 1997. "Morocco Prepares for Change." *Le Monde Diplomatique* (June). Available at http://mondediplo.com/1997/06/maroc2. Accessed Nov. 2004.

Dean, David J. 1986. *The Air Force Role in Low-Intensity Conflict.* Maxwell Air Force Base, Ala.: Air Univ. Press.

De Froberville, Martine. 1992. "Sahara Occidental: Échec au plan de paix." *Le Monde Diplomatique* (Nov.): 13.

Demir, Mehmet. 1990. "Human Rights Briefing." *Middle East Report,* no. 163 (Mar.–Apr.): 38.

Disney, Nigel. 1976. "France Attacks Polisario." *MERIP Reports* (Feb.): 25.

Dryden, Douglas K. 1996. Address to United Nations Fourth Committee (Decolonization), Oct. 7. Available at http://www.arso.org/Dryden-96.htm. Accessed May 14, 2004.

Dunbar, Charles. 2000. "Saharan Stasis." *Middle East Journal* 54: 522–45.

Durch, William J. 1993a. "Building on Sand: UN Peacekeeping in the Western Sahara." *International Security* 17: 151–71.

———. 1993b. *The Evolution of UN Peacekeeping, Case Studies, and Comparative Analysis.* New York: St. Martin's Press.

Economist Intelligence Unit (EIU). 2002. *Country Profile 2002: Algeria.* London: EIU.

———. 2003. *Country Profile 2003: Morocco.* London: EIU.

———. 2005. *Country Profile 2005: Morocco.* London: EIU.

Entelis, John P. 1986. *Algeria: The Revolution Institutionalized.* Boulder, Colo.: Westview Press.

———. 2002. "Morocco: Democracy Denied." *Le Monde Diplomatique* (Oct.). Available at http://mondediplo.com/2002/10/13morocco. Accessed Nov. 2007.

Fiddian, Elena. 2002. "Promoting Sustainable Gender Roles during Exile: A Critical Analysis with Reference to the Sahrawi Refugee Camps." Master's thesis, School of Oriental and African Studies, London.

Finan, Khadja. 2006. "Western Sahara Impasse." *Le Monde Diplomatique* (Jan.). Available at http://mondediplo.com/2006/01/11impasse. Accessed June 2006.

Fisher, Roger, Andrea Kupfer Schneider, Elizabeth Bordwardt, and Brian Ganson. 1997. *Coping with International Conflict: A Systematic Approach to Influence in International Negotiation.* Upper Saddle River, N.J.: Prentice-Hall.

Foucault, Michel. 2003. *"Society Must Be Defended": Lectures at the Collège de France, 1975–76, Michel Foucault.* Translated by David Macey. New York: Picador.

Franck, Thomas. 1976. "The Stealing of the Sahara." *American Journal of International Law* 70: 694–721.

———. 1987. "Theory and Practice of Decolonization." In *War and Refugees: The Western Sahara Conflict,* edited by Richard Lawless and Laila Monahan, 9–15. New York: Pinter, 1987.

Freedom House. 2005. *How Freedom Is Won: From Civic Resistance to Durable Democracy.* New York: Freedom House.

Fukuyama, Francis. 1992. *The End of History and the Last Man.* New York: Free Press.

Gellner, Ernest. 1983. *Nations and Nationalism.* Ithaca, N.Y.: Cornell University Press.

Gobierno General del Sáhara. 1975. *Censo-74.* El-Aiún, Spanish Sahara: Editorial Gráficas Saharianas, 1975.

González, Ángel Pérez. 2002. *The Sahara Issue and the Stability of Morocco.* Madrid: Real Instituto Elcano de Estudios Internacionales y Estratégicos. Available at http://www.realinstitutoelcano.org/analisis/155.asp. Accessed Oct. 8, 2004.

Goulding, Marrack. 1993. "The Evolution of United Nations Peacekeeping." *International Affairs* 69: 451–64.

———. 2002. *Peacemonger.* London: John Murray.

Gretton, John. 1976a. "Saharan 'Realpolitik.'" *MERIP Reports,* no. 49 (July): 23.

———. 1976b. *Western Sahara: The Fight for Self-Determination.* London: Anti-slavery Society.

Grimmett, Richard. 2004. *Conventional Arms Transfers to Developing Nations, 1996–2003.* Washington, D.C.: Congressional Research Service.

Harrell-Bond, Barbara. 1981. *The Struggle for the Western Sahara.* Parts I–III. Hanover, N.H.: American Universities Field Staff Reports Service.

Hart, David. 1962. "The Social Structure of the Rgibat Bedouins of the Western Sahara." *Middle East Journal* 16: 515–27.

———. 1998. "The Rgaybat: Camel Nomads of the Western Sahara." *Journal of North African Studies* 3: 28–54.

———. 2000. *Tribe and Society in Rural Morocco*. Portland, Ore.: Frank Cass.

Hassan II. 1978. *The Challenge*. Translated by Anthony Rhodes. London: MacMillan.

Haut commissariat au plan. 2005. *Population légal du Maroc*. Rabat, Morocco: Haut commissariat au plan, Royame du Maroc.

Hodges, Tony. 1983a. "The Origins of Saharawi Nationalism." *Third World Quarterly* 5: 28–57.

———. 1983b. *Western Sahara: The Roots of a Desert War*. Westport, Conn.: Lawrence Hill.

———. 1985. "At Odds with Self-Determination." In *African Crisis Areas and United States Foreign Policy*, edited by G. J. Bender, J. S. Coleman, and R. L. Sklar, 257–76. Berkeley and Los Angeles: Univ. of California Press.

Hodges, Tony, and Anthony Pazzanita. 1994. *Historical Dictionary of the Western Sahara*. 2d ed. Metuchen, N.J.: Scarecrow.

Houser, George. 1980. "Blood on the Sahara." *The Progressive* (Dec.): 48–50.

———. 1989. *No One Can Stop the Rain*. New York: Pilgrim Press.

Hultman, Tami, and Patricia E. Larkin. 1985. "Sahrawi Arab Democratic Republic." In *Constitutions of Dependencies and Special Sovereignties*, edited by Albert P. Blaustein and Phyllis M. Blaustein, 1–67. Dobbs Ferry, N.Y.: Oceana.

Human Rights Watch (HRW). 1991. *Human Rights Watch World Report 1990*. New York: HRW/Middle East Watch.

———. 1992. "Morocco and Western Sahara." In *Human Rights Developments—1991*. New York: HRW/Middle East Watch. Available at http://www.hrw.org/reports/1992/WR92/MEW2-01.htm. Accessed Nov. 5, 2004.

———. 1995. *Human Rights in Morocco*. New York: HRW.

———. 2004. *Morocco: Human Rights at a Crossroads*. New York: HRW.

Huntington, Samuel. 1993. *The Clash of Civilizations and the Remaking of World Order*. New York: Free Press.

Husain, Mishal. 2004. "Sahara Marathon: Host Interview Transcript." Interview with James Baker. *Wide Angle*, Public Broadcasting System, Aug. 19. Available at http://www.pbs.org/wnet/wideangle/printable/transcript_sahara_print.html. Accessed Sept. 14, 2008.

Ibn 'Azuz Hakim, Muhammad. 1981. *Al-Siyadah al-Maghribiyyah fi al-Aqalim al-Sahrawiyyah min khilal al-Wath'iq al-Makhaziniyyah*. Casablanca, Morocco: Mu'assasatBansharah.

Institute for Advanced Strategic and Political Studies (IASPS). 2002. *African Oil: A Priority for US National Security and African Development*. Jerusalem: IASPS.

Instituto Europea de la Mediterránea (IEM). 2005. *Soluciones para El Sáhara: El Sáhara Occidental en la dinámica geopolítica del Maghrib*. Madrid: IEM, June 3–5.

International Committee of the Red Cross (ICRC). 2004. *Occupation and International Humanitarian Law: Questions and Answers*. Geneva: ICRC. Available at http://www.icrc.org/Web/Eng/siteeng0.nsf/html/634KFC. Accessed Feb. 25, 2010.

International Court of Justice (ICJ). 1975. *Western Sahara Advisory Opinion*. The Hague: ICJ Reports.

International Crisis Group (ICG). 2005a. *L'islamisme en Afrique du Nord IV: Contestation islamiste en Mauritanie: Menace ou bouc émissaire?* Middle East/North Africa Report no. 41 (May 11). Brussels: ICG.

———. 2005b. *Islamist Terrorism in the Sahel: Fact or Fiction?* Africa Report no. 92 (Mar. 31). Brussels: ICG.

———. 2006. *La transition politique en Mauritanie: Bilan et perspectives.* Middle East/North Africa Report no. 53 (Apr. 24). Brussels: ICG.

———. 2007. *Western Sahara: Out of the Impasse.* Middle East/North Africa Report no. 66 (June 11). Brussels: ICG.

International Human Rights Law Group. 1984. *Guidelines for International Election Observing.* Rome, Ga.: International Human Rights Law Group.

International Institute for Strategic Studies (IISS). 1976a. *The Military Balance, 1975/1976.* London: IISS.

———. 1976b. *Strategic Survey 1975.* London: IISS.

———. 1986. *The Military Balance, 1985–1986.* London: IISS.

———. 1988. *The Military Balance, 1987–1988.* London: IISS.

———. 1990. *The Military Balance, 1989–1990.* London: IISS.

———. 2002. *The Military Balance, 2001–2002.* London: IISS.

———. 2003. *The Military Balance, 2002–2003.* London: IISS.

Jamaï, Aboubakr. 2006. "Les survivants de Hassan II." *Le Journal Hebdomadaire* (Aug.). Formerly available at http://www.lejournal-hebdo.com/article.php3?id_article=8960, but no longer an active site. Accessed Jan. 27, 2008.

Jensen, Erik. 2005. *Western Sahara: Anatomy of a Stalemate.* Boulder, Colo.: Lynne Rienner.

Joffé, George. 1987. "Frontiers in North Africa." In *Boundaries and State Territory in the Middle East and North Africa,* edited by Gerald H. Blake and Richard N. Schofield. Wisbech, U.K.: Middle East and North African Studies, 1987. Available at http://arabworld.nitle.org/texts .php?module_id=4&reading_id=119. Accessed Sept. 2006.

Kamil, Leo. 1987. *Fueling the Fire: U.S. Policy and the Western Sahara Conflict.* Trenton, N.J.: Red Sea.

Kaplan, Robert D. 1994. "The Coming Anarchy." *Atlantic Monthly* (Feb.): 44–76.

———. 2001. *The Coming Anarchy: Shattering the Dreams of the Post Cold War.* New York: Vintage.

Karmous, Afifa, and Michèle Decaster. 2003. *Report: International Mission of Investigation in Western Sahara.* Paris: France Libertés.

Keck, Margaret E., and Kathryn Sikkink. 1998. *Activists beyond Borders: Advocacy Networks in International Politics.* Ithaca, N.Y.: Cornell Univ. Press.

Keenan, Jeremy. 2004. "Terror in the Sahara: The Implications of US Imperialism for North and West Africa." *Review of African Political Economy* 31: 475–96.

———. 2006. "Security and Insecurity in North Africa." *Review of African Political Economy* 33: 269–96.

Ketterer, James. 2001. "Networks of Discontent in Northern Morocco: Drugs, Opposition, and Urban Unrest." *Middle East Report,* no. 218 (spring): 30–33, 45.

Kilgore, Arthur. 1987. "The War in the Western Sahara: Unity and Dissension in the Maghreb." In *Africa in World Politics: Changing Perspectives,* edited by Stephen Wite and Janice N. Brownfoot, 155–80. Basingstoke, U.K.: Macmillan.

King, Mae. 1996. *Basic Currents of Nigerian Foreign Policy.* Washington, D.C.: Howard Univ. Press.

Klare, Michael, and Daniel Volman. 2006. "The African 'Oil Rush' and US National Security." *Third World Quarterly* 27: 609–28.

Klotz, Audie. 1994. *Norms in International Relations: The Struggle Against Apartheid.* Ithaca, N.Y.: Cornell Univ. Press.

Knight, Richard. 1979. *Report on a Visit to the Democratic Arab Saharawi Republic and Algeria.* Available at http://richardknight.homestead.com/visitws.html. Accessed May 2006.

Kriesberg, Louis. 1998. *Constructive Conflicts: From Escalation to Resolution.* New York: Rowman and Littlefield.

———. 2005. "Nature, Dynamics, and Phases of Intractability." In *Grasping the Nettle: Analyzing Cases of Intractable Conflicts,* edited by Chester A. Crocker, Fen Osler Hampson, and Pamela Aall, 65–97. Washington, D.C.: United States Institute of Peace.

———. 2009. "Waging Conflicts Constructively." In *Handbook of Conflict Analysis and Resolution,* edited by Dennis J. D. Sandole, Sean Byrne, Ingrid Sandole-Staroste, and Jessica Senehi, 157–69. New York: Routledge.

Kriesberg, Louis, Terrell A. Northrup, and Stuart J. Thorson, eds. 1989. *Intractable Conflicts and Their Transformation.* Syracuse, N.Y.: Syracuse Univ. Press.

Lalutte, Pauline. 1976. "Sahara: Notes toward an Analysis." *MERIP Reports* (Mar.): 7–12.

Lapidus, Ira. 1988. *A History of Islamic Societies.* New York: Cambridge Univ. Press.

Layachi, Azzedine. 1994. "The OAU and Western Sahara: A Case Study." In *OAU after 30 Years,* edited by Yassin El-Ayouty and I. William Zartman, 27–39. Westport, Conn.: Praeger.

———. 1998. *State, Society, and Democracy in Morocco: The Limits of Associative Life.* Washington, D.C.: Center for Contemporary Arab Studies, Georgetown Univ.

———. 2002. "Morocco: Will Tradition Protect the Monarchy?" In *The Middle East in 2015,* edited by Judith Share Yaphe, 43–57. Washington, D.C.: National Defense Univ. Press.

Lellouche, Pierre, and Dominique Moisi. 1979. "French Policy in Africa: A Lonely Battle Against Destabilization." *International Security* 3: 108–33.

Leveau, Rémy. 1997. "Morocco at the Crossroads." *Mediterranean Politics* 2: 95–113.

———. 1998. "A Democratic Transition in Morocco?" *Le Monde Diplomatique* (Dec.). Available at http://mondediplo.com/1998/12/06maroc. Accessed Nov. 2004.

Lewis, William H. 1985. "War in the Western Sahara." In *Lessons of Recent Wars in the Third World,* vol. 1: *Approaches and Case Studies,* edited by Robert E. Harkavy and Stephanie Newman, 117–37. Lexington, Mass.: D. C. Heath.

Lippert, Anne. 1991. "Western Sahara: Efforts Continue to Resolve the Conflict in Western Sahara." *Association of Concerned African Scholars Bulletin,* no. 32 (winter): 12–15.

———. 1992. "Sahrawi Women in the Liberation Struggle of the Sahrawi People." *Signs* 17: 636–51.

Lorcin, Patricia. 1999. *Imperial Identities.* London: I. B. Tauris.

Lydon, Ghislane. 2005. "Writing Trans-Saharan History." *Journal of North African Studies* 10: 293–324.

Madsen, Wayne. 2003. "Big Oil and James Baker Target the Western Sahara." *Counter Punch,* Jan. 8. Available at http://www.counterpunch.org/madsen01082003.html. Accessed Oct. 8, 2004.

Maghraoui, Abdeslam. 2001. "Political Authority in Crisis: Mohammed VI's Morocco." *Middle East Report,* no. 218 (spring): 12–17.

———. 2002. "Depoliticization in Morocco." *Journal of Democracy* 13: 24–32.

Mamdani, Mahmood. 2004. *Good Muslim, Bad Muslim: America, the Cold War, and the Roots of Terror.* New York: Pantheon, 2004.

Meltzoff, Sarah Keene, and Edward Lipuma. 1986. "The Troubled Seas of Spanish Fishermen: Marine Policy and the Economy of Change." *American Ethnologist* 13: 681–99.

Mercer, John. 1976a. "The Cycle of Invasion and Unification in the Western Sahara." *African Affairs* 75: 498–510.

———. 1976b. *Spanish Sahara.* London: Allen and Unwin.

Mortimer, Robert. 1982. "The Internationalization of the Conflict in Western Sahara." In *Middle East Annual: Issues and Events,* vol. 2: *1982,* edited by David H. Partington, 129–49. Boston: B & G Hall.

Moser-Puangsuwan, Yeshua, and Thomas Weber. 2000. *Nonviolent Intervention across Borders: A Recurrent Vision.* Manoa: Spark M. Matsunaga Institute for Peace, Univ. of Hawai'i.

Moynihan, Daniel Patrick, with Suzanne Weaver. 1978. *A Dangerous Place.* Boston: Atlantic–Little, Brown.

Mundy, Jacob. 2005. "Mixing Occupation and Oil in Western Sahara." *CorpWatch,* July 21. Available at http://www.corpwatch.org/article.php?id=12506. Accessed Sept. 2006.

———. 2006. "Neutrality or Complicity? The United States and the 1975 Moroccan Takeover of the Spanish Sahara." *Journal of North African Studies* 11: 275–306.

———. 2007a. "Colonial Formations in Western Saharan National Identity." In *North African Mosaic: A Cultural Reappraisal of Ethnic and Religious Minorities,* edited by Nabil Boudraa and Joseph Krause, 294–320. Newcastle-upon-Tyne, U.K.: Cambridge Scholars Press.

———. 2007b. "Performing the Nation, Prefiguring the State: The Western Saharan Refugees Thirty Years Later." *Journal of Modern African Studies* 45: 275–97.

Naylor, Philip Chiviges. 1987. "France and the Western Sahara: Colonial and Postcolonial Intentions and Interventions." In *Proceedings of the Annual Meeting of the French Colonial Historical Society,* 203–15. Medford, Mass.: French Colonial Historical Society.

———. 1993. "Spain, France, and the Western Sahara: A Historical Narrative and Study of National Transformation." In *International Dimensions of the Western Sahara Conflict,* edited by Yahia Zoubir and Daniel Volman, 17–51. Westport, Conn.: Praeger.

———. 2000. *France and Algeria: A History of Decolonization and Transformation.* Gainesville: Univ. of Florida Press.

Neuman, Stephanie G. 1986. *Military Assistance in Recent Wars: The Dominance of the Superpowers.* Washington Papers no. 14/122, Center for Strategic and International Studies. New York: Praeger.

———. 1988. "Arms, Aid, and the Superpowers." *Foreign Affairs* 66: 1044–66.

Norris, H. T. 1962. "Yemenis in the Western Sahara." *Journal of African History* 3: 317–22.

———. 1964. "The Wind of Change in the Western Sahara." *Geographical Journal* 130: 2–14.

———. 1986. *The Arab Conquest of the Western Sahara.* Beirut: Longman.

Nossiter, Bernard D. 1986. "Time to Settle the Saharan War." *The Nation* (Jan. 25): 79.

Organization of African Unity (OAU). 1983. *Resolution 104 (XIX).* June 6–12, 1983, AHG/Res.104 (XIX). Addis Ababa, Ethiopia: OAU.

Parker, Richard B. 1987. *North Africa: Regional Tensions and Strategic Concerns.* New York: Praeger.

Paul, Jim, and Susanne Paul. 1976. "With the POLISARIO Front of Sahara." *MERIP Reports,* no. 53 (Dec.): 16–21.

Pazzanita, Anthony. 1992. "Mauritania's Foreign Policy: The Search for Protection." *Journal of Modern African Studies* 30: 281–304.

———. 2006. *Historical Dictionary of Western Sahara.* 3rd ed. Lanham, Md.: Scarecrow.

Pérez de Cuéllar, Javier. 1997. *Pilgrimage for Peace: A Secretary-General's Memoir.* New York: St. Martin's Press.

Price, David Lynn. 1979. *Western Sahara.* Washington Papers no. 63, Center for Strategic and International Studies, Georgetown Univ. Beverly Hills, Calif.: Sage.

Putnam, Linda L., and Julia M. Wollondolleck. 2002. "Intractability: Definitions, Dimensions, and Distinctions." In *Making Sense of Intractable Conflicts,* edited by Roy J. Lewicki, Barbara L. Gray, and Michael Elliot, 35–59. Washington, D.C.: Island Press.

Quandt, William B. 2002. "US and Algeria: Just Flirting." *Le Monde Diplomatique* (July). Available at http://mondediplo.com/2002/07/08algeria. Accessed Oct. 8, 2004.

Ramonet, Ignacio. 1999. "Whither Morocco?" *Le Monde Diplomatique* (Aug.). Available at http://mondediplo.com/1999/08/01leader. Accessed Nov. 2004.

———. 2000. "Morocco: The Point of Change." *Le Monde Diplomatique* (July). Available at http://mondediplo.com/2000/07/01ramonet. Accessed Oct. 2004.

Ramsbotham, Oliver, Tom Woodhouse, and Hugh Miall. 2005. *Contemporary Conflict Resolution.* 2d ed. Cambridge, U.K.: Polity.

Ranger, Terence. 1983. "The Invention of Tradition in Colonial Africa." In *The Invention of Tradition,* edited by Eric Hobsbawm and Terence Ranger, 211–59. New York: Cambridge Univ. Press.

Refugee Studies Center (RSC). 2005. *The Transnationalisation of Care: Sahrawi Refugee Children in a Spanish Host Program.* Oxford, U.K.: RSC, Univ. of Oxford.

Reporters sans frontères. 2001. "Un journaliste arrêté et maltraité au Sahara Occidental." Press release, Nov. 23. Available at http://www.ifex.org/morocco/2001/11/23/journalist_arrested_and_mistreated/fr/. Accessed Feb. 25, 2010.

———. 2005. "Shock and Concern after Ali Lmrabet Banned from Practicing as a Journalist for 10 Years." Press release, Dec. 4. Available at http://www.rsf.org/Shock-and-concern-after-Ali.html. Accessed Feb. 25, 2010.

Reyner, Anthony. 1963. Morocco's International Boundaries: A Factual Background." *Journal of Modern African Studies* 1: 313–29.

Roberts, Hugh. 2003. *The Battlefield Algeria 1988–2002: Studies in a Broken Polity.* New York: Verso.

Rosemarin, Arno. 2004. "In a Fix: The Precarious Geopolitics of Phosphorous." *Geopolitics Down to Earth* (June 30): 27–34.

Ruddy, Frank. 1995a. *MINURSO: A Case Study on U.N. Peacekeeping Operations.* Falls Church, Va.: Defense Forum Foundation, Congressional Defense and Foreign Policy Forum, Apr. 25.

———. 1995b. Statement of Frank Ruddy before the Subcommittee on the Departments of Commerce, Justice, and State, the Judiciary, and Related Agencies. *Review of United Nations Operations and Peacekeeping.* Hearings. 104th Cong., 1st sess., Jan. 25. Available at http://www.arso.org/06-3-1.htm. Accessed Feb. 15, 2010.

Ruf, Werner. 1987. "The Role of World Powers: Colonialist Transformations and King Hassan's Rule." In *War and Refugees: The Western Sahara Conflict,* edited by Richard Lawless and Laila Monahan, 65–97. New York: Pinter.

Ruiz Miguel, Carlos. 2007. *The 2007 Moroccan Autonomy Plan for Western Sahara: Too Many Black Holes.* Grupo de Estudios Estratégicos, Analysis no. 196 (June 29). Available at http://eng.gees.org/articulo/214/. Accessed Jan. 27, 2008.

Sahrawi Red Crescent (SRC). 1983–84. *Fragmentation Bombs Against the Sahrawi People.* Algiers: SRC.

San Martin, Pablo. 2005. "Nationalism, Identity, and Citizenship in the Western Sahara." *Journal of North African Studies* 10: 565–92.

Sarkozy, Nicholas. 2007. "Speech by Mr. Nicolas Sarkozy, President of the Republic, before the Two Houses of the Moroccan Parliament." Rabat, Morocco, Oct. 23. Available at http://www.diplomatie.gouv.fr/en/article_imprim.php3?id_article=10200. Accessed Feb. 27, 2010.

Schock, Kurt. 2005. *Unarmed Insurrections: People Power Movements in Non-democracies.* Minneapolis: Univ. of Minnesota Press.

Seddon, David. 1984. "Winter of Discontent: Economic Crisis in Tunisia and Morocco." *MERIP Reports,* no. 127 (Oct.): 7–16.

———. 1989. "The Politics of 'Adjustment' in Morocco." In *Structural Adjustment in Africa,* edited by Bonnie K. Campbell and John Loxley, 234–65. New York: St. Martin's Press.

———. 1996. "Making Haste Slowly: Little Progress Towards the Referendum." *Review of African Political Economy* 23: 103–6.

———. 1999. "Western Sahara at the Turn of the Millennium." *Review of African Political Economy* 26, no. 82: 495–503.

———. 2000. "Western Sahara—Point of No Return?" *Review of African Political Economy* 27: 338–40.

Segal, Aaron. 1991. "Spain and the Middle East: A 15-Year Assessment." *Middle East Journal* 45: 250–64.

Sesay, Amadu, Olusola Ojo, and Orobola Fasehun. 1984. *The OAU after Twenty Years.* Boulder, Colo.: Westview.

Sharp, Gene. 2005. *Waging Nonviolent Struggle: 20th Century Practice and 21st Century Potential.* Boston: Porter Sargent.

Shelley, Toby. 2003. "Behind the Baker Plan for Western Sahara." *Middle East Report* (Aug.). Available at http://www.merip.org/mero/mero080103.html. Accessed Oct. 8, 2004.

———. 2004. *Endgame in the Western Sahara: What Future for Africa's Last Colony?* New York: Zed.

———. 2005. "Burden or Benefit? Morocco in the Western Sahara." Lecture given at the Middle East Studies Centre, Oxford Univ., Feb. 18.

———. 2006. "Natural Resources and the Western Sahara." In *The Western Sahara Conflict: The Role of Natural Resources in Decolonization,* edited by Claes Olsson, 17–21. Uppsala, Sweden: Nordiska Afrikainstitutet.

Slyomovics, Susan. 2001. "A Truth Commission for Morocco?" *Middle East Report,* no. 218 (spring): 18–21.

Smith, Jackie, Charles Chatfield, and Ron Pagnucco, eds. 1997. *Transnational Social Movements and Global Politics: Solidarity beyond the State.* Syracuse, N.Y.: Syracuse Univ. Press.

Smith, Teresa K. 1987. "Al-Mukhtufin: A Report on Disappearances." In *War and Refugees: The Western Sahara Conflict,* edited by Richard Lawless and Laila Monahan, 139–49. New York: Pinter.

Smith de Cherif, Teresa K. 1993. "Western Sahara: A Moroccan-Style Election?" *Review of African Political Economy* 20: 99–105.

Solarz, Stephen. 1979. "Arms for Morocco?" *Foreign Affairs* 58: 278–99.

Somerville, Keith. 1990. *Foreign Military Intervention in Africa.* New York: St. Martin's Press.

Soudan, François. 2006. "Le roi, les islamistes et le Sahara." *Jeune afrique,* July 2.

Stephen, Maria J., ed. 2009. *Civilian Jihad: Nonviolent Struggle, Democratization, and Governance in the Middle East.* New York: Palgrave Macmillan.

Stone, Martin. 1997. *The Agony of Algeria.* New York: Columbia Univ. Press.

Stork, Joe. 1990. "Europe's Other Frontier: North Africa Faces the 1990s." *Middle East Report,* no. 163 (Mar.–Apr.): 4–8, 44.

Stork, Joe, and Jim Paul. 1983. "Arms Sales and the Militarization of the Middle East." *MERIP Reports* (Feb.): 5–15.

Storm, Lise. 2008. "Testing Morocco: The Parliamentary Elections of September 2007." *Journal of North African Studies* 13: 37–54.

Sweet, Catherine. 2001. "Democratization Without Democracy: Political Openings and Closures in Modern Morocco." *Middle East Report,* no. 218 (spring): 22–25.

Swisher, Clayton E. 2007. "Elliot Abrams' Maghreb Plot." United Press International, Apr. 13. Available at http://www.upi.com/Business_News/Security-Industry/2007/04/13/Outside-View-Elliot-Abrams-Maghreb-plot/UPI-56961176498776/. Accessed Feb. 25, 2010.

Tessler, Mark. 1985. "The Uses and Limits of Populism: The Political Strategy of King Hassan II of Morocco." *Middle East Review* 17: 44–51.

Theofilopoulou, Anna. 2006. *The United Nations and Western Sahara: A Never-ending affair.* Special Report no. 166. Washington, D.C.: United States Institute for Peace.

———. 2007. *Western Sahara—How Not to Try to Resolve a Conflict.* Washington, D.C.: Center for Strategic and International Studies,Aug. 3. Available at http://forums.csis.org/africa/?p=45. Accessed Jan. 27, 2008.

Thobhani, Akbarali. 2002. *Western Sahara since 1975 under Moroccan Administration.* Lewiston, N.Y.: Edwin Mellen.

Transparency International. 2006. *Country Reports, 2005.* Berlin: Transparency International.

Trout, Frank E. 1969. *Morocco's Saharan Frontiers.* Geneva: Droz.

Tusa, Francis. 1988. "Responses to Low Intensity Conflict Warfare: Barrier Defense in the Middle East." *Royal United Services Institute for Defense Studies Journal* 133: 36–42.

United Nations (UN). 1945. *Charter of the United Nations.* Available at http://www.un.org/en/documents/charter/. Accessed Feb. 27, 2010.

———. 1967. "Ifni and Spanish Sahara." In *United Nations Yearbook 1965,* 584–85. New York: UN Office of Public Information.

———. 1969. "Ifni and Spanish Sahara." In *United Nations Yearbook 1967,* 676–80. New York: UN Office of Public Information.

———. 1975. "Spanish Sahara." In *United Nations Yearbook 1972,* 569–70, 579–80. New York: UN Office of Public information.

———. 1977. "Spanish Sahara." In *United Nations Yearbook 1974,* 794–96, 805–6. New York: UN Office of Public Information.

———. 1978. "The Question of Western Sahara." In *United Nations Yearbook 1975,* 175–90, 798–804. New York: UN Office of Public Information.

———. 1979. "Western Sahara." In *United Nations Yearbook 1976,* 737–57. New York: UN Office of Public information.

———. 1983. "Western Sahara." In *United Nations Yearbook 1980,* 1,087–89, 1,100. New York: UN Office of Public Information.

United Nations Development Fund for Women (UNIFEM). 2005. *Gender Profile of the Conflict in Western Sahara.* New York: UNIFEM.

United Nations Development Program (UNDP). 2000. *2000 Human Development Report.* New York: UNDP.

United Nations Environmental Program (UNEP). 2008. *Bou Craa, Western Sahara: Atlas of Our Changing Environment.* Available at http://na.unep.net/digital_atlas2/webatlas.php?id=369. Accessed Sept. 22, 2008.

United Nations General Assembly. 1977. *Report of the United Nations Visiting Mission to Spanish Sahara, 1975.* Official Records: 30th sess., suppl. 23, vol. 3, chap. XIII, A/10023/Add.5. New York: United Nations.

United Nations Secretary-General. 1975–2007. All reports of the secretary-general and letters to the Security Council on the situation concerning Western Sahara, 1975 to 2008. Referenced in the text by unique UN Security Council index numbers (e.g., S/21360, S/2000/131, and so on). Available at http://www.un.org/documents/repsc.htm.

United Nations Security Council. 1988–2008. All Security Council resolutions on the situation concerning Western Sahara, 1988 to 2008. Referenced in the text by unique UN Security Council index numbers (e.g., S/Res/1301). Available at http://www.un.org/documents/scres.htm.

———. 1995. *Report of the Security Council Mission to the Western Sahara from 3 to 9 June 1995.* S/1995/498. New York: UN, June 21.

United Nations Standing Committee on Nutrition. 2005. *Nutrition Information in Crisis Situations—Algeria.* Aug. Available at http://www.unsystem.org/scn/publications/RNIS/countries/algeria_all.htm. Accessed May 2006.

United States Agency in Development (USAID). 2002. *U.S. Overseas Loans and Grants, and Assistance from International Organizations, Obligations, and Loan Authorizations, July 1, 1945–September 30, 2001*. Washington, D.C.: USAID.

———. 2006. *U.S. Overseas Loans and Grants, Obligations, and Loan Authorizations*. Washington, D.C.: USAID. Available at http://qesdb.usaid.gov/gbk/. Accessed Sept. 2008.

U.S. Central Intelligence Agency (CIA). 1975. *Staff Notes: Middle East, Africa, South Asia*. June 12. Electronic document, CIA archive database, National Archives, College Park, Md.

———. 1988. "Morocco's Pilots—How Good Are They?" *Near East and South Asia Review* (May 20): 45–56. Redacted and released to the authors under the Freedom of Information Act.

U.S. Department of Defense. 1984. Defense Security Assistance Agency (DSAA). *Foreign Military Sales, Foreign Military Construction Sales, and Military Assistance Facts as of September 30, 1983*. Washington, D.C.: DSAA.

———. 1989. Defense Security Assistance Agency (DSAA). *Foreign Military Sales Facts, as of September 30, 1989*. Washington, D.C.: DSAA.

———. 1992. Defense Security Assistance Agency (DSAA). *Foreign Military Sales, Foreign Military Construction Sales, and Military Assistance Facts as of September 30, 1992*. Washington, D.C.: DSAA.

U.S. Department of Defense and U.S. Department of State. 1990. Defense Security Assistance Agency (DSAA). *Congressional Presentation for Security Assistance Programs, Fiscal Year 1991*. Washington, D.C.: DSAA and U.S. Department of State.

U.S. Department of State. 1975a. Telegram from Secretary of State to United States Embassy in Rabat, November 2. Folder "Morocco—State Department Telegrams from Secretary of State—NODIS," Box 4,Collection "NSA Presidential Country Files for Africa," Ford Library, Ann Arbor, Mich.

———. 1975b. Staff Meeting Minutes, November 5, 8:00 A.M. Series "Transcripts of Secretary of State Henry Kissinger's Staff Meetings, 1973–77," Record Group 59, National Archives, College Park, Md.

———. 1976. Telegram from Secretary of State to Secretary of Defense, the U.S. Central Intelligence Agency, and the U.S. Joint Chiefs of Staff, Feb. 27, 1976. Released to the authors from the Department of State under the Freedom of Information Act.

———. 1980. Arms Control and Disarmament Agency. *World Military Expenditures and Arms Transfers 1969–1978*. Washington, D.C.: U.S. Government Printing Office.

———. 1984. Arms Control and Disarmament Agency. *World Military Expenditures and Arms Transfers 1972–1982*. Washington, D.C.: U.S. Government Printing Office.

———. 1987. Arms Control and Disarmament Agency. *World Military Expenditures and Arms Transfers 1986*. Washington, D.C.: U.S. Government Printing Office.

———. 1989. Arms Control and Disarmament Agency. *World Military Expenditures and Arms Transfers 1988*. Washington, D.C.: U.S. Government Printing Office.

———. 1993. Arms Control and Disarmament Agency. *World Military Expenditures and Arms Transfers 1992*. Washington, D.C.: U.S. Government Printing Office.

———. 1994. Bureau of Democracy, Human Rights, and Labor. *Western Sahara: Country Reports on Human Rights Practices, 1993*. Washington, D.C.: U.S. Department of State.

———. 1995. Arms Control and Disarmament Agency. *World Military Expenditures and Arms Transfers 1993–1994.* Washington, D.C.: U.S. Government Printing Office.

———. 1996. Arms Control and Disarmament Agency. *World Military Expenditures and Arms Transfers 1995.* Washington, D.C.: U.S. Government Printing Office.

———. 1998. Arms Control and Disarmament Agency. *World Military Expenditures and Arms Transfers 1997.* Washington, D.C.: U.S. Government Printing Office.

———. 2000. Bureau of Democracy, Human Rights, and Labor. *Western Sahara: Country Reports on Human Rights Practices, 1999.* Washington, D.C.: U.S. Department of State. Available at http://www.state.gov/www/global/human_rights/1999_hrp_report/washara.html. Accessed Oct. 2004.

———. 2001a. Bureau of Democracy, Human Rights, and Labor. *Western Sahara: Country Reports on Human Rights Practices, 2000.* Washington, D.C.: U.S. Department of State. Available at http://www.state.gov/g/drl/rls/hrrpt/2000/nea/825.htm. Accessed Oct. 2004.

———. 2001b. Bureau of Verification and Compliance. *World Military Expenditures and Arms Transfers 1999–2000.* Washington, D.C.: U.S. Government Printing Office.

———. 2002. Bureau of Democracy, Human Rights, and Labor. *Western Sahara: Country Reports on Human Rights Practices, 2001.* Washington, D.C.: U.S. Department of State. Available at http://www.state.gov/g/drl/rls/hrrpt/2001/nea/8281.htm. Accessed Oct. 2004.

———. 2004. Bureau of Democracy, Human Rights, and Labor. *Western Sahara: Country Reports on Human Rights Practices, 2003.* Washington, D.C.: U.S. Department of State. Available at http://www.state.gov/g/drl/rls/hrrpt/2003/27941.htm. Accessed Nov. 5, 2004.

———. 2006. *2007 Congressional Budget Justification for Foreign Operations.* Washington, D.C.: U.S. Department of State.

U.S. Embassy Madrid, Spain. 1975. Telegram to U.S. Secretary of State, June 27. Record Group 84, Madrid Embassy files, National Archives, College Park, Md.

U.S. Embassy Paris, France. 1984. Telegram to U.S. Secretary of State, May 8. Heavily redacted and released to the authors by the U.S. Department of State under the Freedom of Information Act.

U.S. Embassy Rabat, Morocco. 1975a. Telegram to U.S. Joint Chiefs of Staff and Defense Intelligence Agency, Oct. 10, Record Group 84, Madrid Embassy files, National Archives, College Park, Md.

———. 1975b. Telegram to U.S. Secretary of State, Oct. 10. Folder "Morocco—State Department Telegrams to Secretary of State—EXDIS," Box 4, Collection "NSA Presidential Country Files for Africa," Gerald R. Ford Presidential Library, Ann Arbor, Mich.

———. 1975c. Telegram to U.S. Secretary of State, Dec. 24. Released to the authors by the U.S. Department of State under the Freedom of Information Act.

U.S. House of Representatives. 1977. Committee on International Relations, Subcommittee on Africa and on International Organizations. *Hearings on the Question of Self-Determination in Western Sahara.* 95th Cong., 1st sess., Oct. 12.

———. 1978. Committee on Appropriations, Subcommittee on Foreign Operations. *Hearings on Foreign Assistance and Related Agencies Appropriations for 1978.* 95th Cong., 1st sess., Mar.

———. 1979. Committee on International Relations, Subcommittee on International Organizations and the Subcommittee on Africa. *The Question of Self-Determination in Western Sahara.* 95th Cong., 1st sess., Oct. 13.

———. 1980a. Committee on Foreign Affairs, Subcommittees on Africa and on International Security and Scientific Affairs. *Hearings on Proposed Arms Sales to Morocco.* 96th Cong., 2d sess., June 24 and 29.

———. 1980b. Committee on Foreign Affairs. *Report on International Security and Development Cooperation Act of 1960.* 96th Cong., 2d sess., Apr. 16.

———. 1981. Committee on Foreign Affairs, Subcommittees on Africa and on International Security and Scientific Affairs. *Hearings on Arms Sales in North Africa and the Conflict in the Western Sahara: An Assessment of U.S. Policy.* 97th Cong., 1st sess., Mar. 25.

———. 1982. Committee on Foreign Affairs. *U.S. Policy toward the Conflict in the Western Sahara.* Report of a Staff Study Mission to Morocco, Algeria, the Western Sahara, and France. 97th Cong., 2d sess., Aug. 25 to Sept. 6.

———. 1983. Committee on Foreign Affairs, Subcommittee on International Security and Scientific Affairs and Subcommittee on Africa. *Review of U.S. Policy toward the Conflict in the Western Sahara.* Hearings. 98th Cong., 1st sess., Mar. 15.

———. 1992. Committee on Foreign Affairs, Subcommittee on Africa. *Status of the United Nations Peace Plan and Proposed Referendum for the Western Sahara.* Hearings. 102d Cong., 2d sess., Feb. 26, 1992.

———. 2000. Committee on International Relations, Subcommittee on Africa. *UN Referendum for Western Sahara: 9 Years and Counting.* Hearings. 106th Cong., 2d sess., Sept. 13.

———. 2005. Committee on International Relations, Subcommittee on Africa, Global Human Rights, and International Operations. *Getting to "Yes": Resolving the 30-Year Conflict over the Status of Western Sahara.* Hearings. 109th Cong., 1st sess., Nov. 17.

U.S. Senate. 1992a. Committee on Foreign Relations, Subcommittee on African Affairs. *U.N. Peacekeeping in Africa: The Western Sahara and Somalia.* Hearings. 102d Cong., 2d session, Oct. 1.

———. 1992b. Committee on Foreign Relations. *The Western Sahara: The Referendum Process in Danger.* Staff report. 102d Cong., 2d session, Jan. 1992.

Vilar, Juan Bautista. 1977. *El Sahara Español: Historia de una aventura colonial.* Madrid: Sedmay Ediciones.

Volman, Daniel. 1980. *A Continent Besieged: Foreign Military Activities in Africa since 1975.* Washington, D.C.: Institute for Policy Studies.

———. 1993. "The Role of Foreign Military Assistance in the Western Saharan War." In *International Dimensions of the Western Sahara Conflict,* edited by Yahia Zoubir and Daniel Volman, 151–68. Westport, Conn.: Praeger.

———. 1999. "Foreign Arms Sales and the Military Balance in the Maghreb." In *North Africa in Transition,* edited by Yahia Zoubir, 212–26. Gainesville: Univ. Press of Florida.

Waldheim, Kurt. 1986. *In the Eye of the Storm.* Bethesda, Md.: Alder and Alder.

Walters, Vernon A. 1978. *Silent Missions.* Garden City, N.Y.: Doubleday.

Weber, Max. 1949. *The Methodology of the Social Sciences*. Edited and translated by Edward Shills and Henry Finch. New York: Free Press.

Weexsteen, Raoul. 1976. "Fighters in the Desert." *MERIP Reports* (Mar.): 3–6.

Wehr, Paul, Heidi Burgess, and Guy Burgess, eds. 1994. *Justice Without Violence*. Boulder, Colo.: Lynne Rienner.

Weiner, Jerome. 1979. "The Green March in Historical Perspective." *Middle East Journal* 33: 20–33.

Welch, David. 2007. Remarks by Assistant Secretary of State for Near Eastern Affairs David Welch. In *Update on North Africa*. Hearing before the U.S. House of Representatives, Foreign Affairs Committee, 110th Cong., 1st sess. June 6. Available at http://internationalrelations.house .gov/110/wel060607.htm. Accessed Feb. 27, 2010.

Wenger, Martha. 1982. "Reagan Stakes Morocco in Sahara Struggle." *MERIP Reports* (May): 22–26.

Werenfels, Isabelle. 2007. *Managing Instability in Algeria: Elites and Political Change since 1995*. Abingdon, U.K.: Routledge.

White, C. G. 1976. "The Green March." *Army Quarterly and Defense Journal* 106: 351–58.

Whitfield, Teresa. 2007. *Friends Indeed? The United Nations, Groups of Friends, and the Resolution of Conflict*. Washington, D.C.: United States Institute of Peace.

Williams, Ian, and Stephen Zunes. 2003. "Self-Determination Struggle in the Western Sahara Continues to Challenge UN." *Foreign Policy in Focus* (Sept.). Available at http://www.fpif .org/papers/sahara2003.html. Accessed May 16, 2004.

Woodward, Bob. 1987. *Veil: The Secret Wars of the CIA*. New York: Simon and Schuster.

Woolbert, Robert. 1946. "Spain as an African Power." *Foreign Affairs* 24: 723–35.

Woolman, David. 1968. *Rebels in the Rif*. Stanford, Calif.: Stanford Univ. Press.

Wright, Claudia. 1984. "Journey to Marrakesh: U.S.–Moroccan Security Relations." *International Security* 7: 163–79.

Zartman, I. William. 1963. "The Sahara—Bridge or Barrier?" *International Conciliation*, no. 541 (Jan.): 1–62.

———. 1989. *Ripe for Resolution: Conflict and Intervention in Africa*. New York: Oxford Univ. Press.

Zartman, I. William, and Johannes Aurik. 1991. "Power Strategies in De-escalation." In *Timing the De-escalation of International Conflicts*, edited by Louis Kriesberg and Stuart J. Thorson, 152–81. Syracuse, N.Y.: Syracuse Univ. Press.

Ziai, Fatemeh. 1995. *Keeping It Secret: The United Nations Operations in the Western Sahara*. New York: Human Rights Watch.

Zindar, John. 1988. Testimony before the United Nations Special Committee on the Situation with Regard to the Implementation of the Declaration on the Granting of Independence to Colonial Countries and Peoples, Aug. 9. On file with Stephen Zunes.

Zoubir, Yahia. 1990a. "Western Sahara Conflict Impedes Maghrib Unity." *Middle East Report*, no. 163 (Mar.–Apr.): 28–29.

———. 1990b. "The Western Sahara Conflict: Regional and International Dimensions." *Journal of Modern African Studies* 28: 225–43.

———. 1993. "Moscow, the Maghreb, and the Conflict in the Western Sahara." In *International Dimensions of the Western Sahara Conflict,* edited by Yahia Zoubir and Daniel Volman, 103–25. Westport, Conn.: Praeger.

———. 1994. "Protracted Conflict and Failure to Achieve Prenegotiation in the Western Sahara Conflict." *Humboldt Journal of Social Relations* 20: 1–44.

———. 1996. "The Western Sahara Conflict: A Case Study in Failure of Prenegotiation and Prolongation of Conflict." *California Western International Law Journal* 26: 137–213.

———. 1997. "In Search of Hegemony: The Western Sahara in Algerian–Moroccan Relations." *Journal of Algerian Studies* 2: 43–61.

———. 2006. *American Policy in the Maghreb: The Conquest of a New Region?* Working Paper no. 13/2006. Madrid: Real Instituto Elcano.

Zoubir, Yahia, and Anthony Pazzanita. 1995. "The United Nations Failure in Resolving the Western Sahara Conflict." *Middle East Journal* 49: 614–28.

Zunes, Stephen, Sarah B. Asher, and Lester R. Kurtz, eds. 1999. *Nonviolent Social Movements: A Geographical Perspective.* Malden, Mass.: Wiley-Blackwell.

# Index

Aall, Pamela, 59

Abdallahi, Sidi Mohamed Ould Cheikh, 14

Abdelaziz, Mohammed, 24, 27, 84, 178; and Baker, 208, 223; elected Polisario secretary-general, 116–17, 121; leadership qualities of, 117; and Pérez de Cuéllar, 179, 182; saber rattling by, 122, 197

Abdelsalem, Omar, 145–46

Abkhazia, 85

Abrams, Elliot, 70, 243, 282n6

al-'Adl wa al-'Ihsan (Morocco), 47, 52

Afghanistan, 138, 276n4; Moroccans fighting in, 274–75n2; UN mission in, 193, 194

Africa: French troops in, 76; French-U.S. secret alliance in, 72–73; oil resources in, 227; rentier regimes in, 57; U.S. military command for, 227; Western Sahara as destabilizing factor, 259–60. *See also* Morocco; Spanish Sahara; Western Sahara

African National Congress (ANC), 125

African Oil Policy Initiative Group, 227

African Union, 27, 123, 178–79. *See also* Organization of African Unity (OAU)

Africa Occidental Española, 100

Africom, 227

Ahel es-Sahel, 276n1

Ait al-Hasan, 98, 269, 279n1

Akka, 16

'Alawi dynasty, xxii, 31, 71; historical origins of, 98–99

Albania, 124

Albright, Madeleine, 69

Algeria: and Baker, 221, 229; border war with Morocco, 5, 10, 31, 33; continuity of support to Polisario, xxix, 27, 34, 42–43, 49–50, 239, 249–50, 256, 258; direct involvement in Western Sahara war, 9; disappearances in, 145; dissent on Western Sahara, 274n1; economic conditions, 23–24, 32, 41–42, 43, 274n1; and Framework Agreement, 223, 224, 225; French colonialism in, 75, 94; and Mauritania, 11; military aid to Polisario, 9, 16, 17, 23–24; motivations for supporting Polisario, 34, 40–43; at Nouadhibou summit, 33, 171; in OAU debate, 177–78; overestimation of role of, xxiv, 30–31, 257; and Peace Plan, 229, 234–35, 239; political violence in, 43, 50, 56, 274n1; radical nationalist heritage of, 40–41, 257; refugee camps in, 128, 129, 130–31; relations with France, 75, 76, 79; relations with Morocco, 33–34, 36, 41, 49; relations with U.S., 66, 224, 234–35, 238; rumors concerning Polisario relations, 49, 120, 234, 249, 259, 282n4; as safe haven for Polisario, 9, 16, 258; Sahrawi solidarity organizations in, 162; and Soviet Union, 85; in UN debates, 170, 171; war of independence in, 21, 32–33, 75, 134

Allabouche, Benbrahim, 54

Amazigh (Berbers), 94, 162; under Peace Plan, 231, 232; and Western Sahara autonomy, 219–20

Amnesty International, 88, 145, 146, 149, 150

Anderson, Benedict, 92

Angola, 193

Annahj Addimocrati (Democratic Path, Morocco), 161, 274n1

Annan, Kofi, 27, 211, 213, 215, 221; appoints Baker, xxx, 142, 143, 206–7; background of, 206; and Framework Agreement, 221, 222, 225; issues "sobering assessment," 215, 216, 217; and Peace Plan, 229, 232, 233, 236, 237; warns Polisario, 228, 246

Arabic language, 96. *See also* Hassaniya dialect

Arab League, 10, 34, 49, 50, 87

Arab Maghrib Union. *See* Union du Maghreb arabe

Arab Steadfastness Front, 87

Arafat, Yasir, 125

Argentina, 145, 202, 215–16

Argoub, 24

Arias Navarro, Carlos, 80

Armitage, Richard, 239

Arms Export Control Act, 65

al-'Arusiyyn, 98, 269, 279n1

Ashford, Douglas, 36

Asociación de Familiares de Presos y Desaparecidos Saharauis (Association of Families of Sahrawi Prisoners and Disappeared), 145

Assa, 155

Association des familles des martyrs dans les commissariats de police marocains (Association of Families of Martyrs in Moroccan Police Stations, Western Sahara), 160

Association des originaires du Sahara anciennement sous domination espagnole (AOSARIO, Association of Natives of the Sahara Formerly under Spanish Domination), 104

Association des victimes de la torture de Smara (Association of Victims of Torture in Smara, Western Sahara), 160

Association marocaine des droits humains (AMDH, Moroccan Association for Human Rights), 161, 282n7

Association nationale des diplômés chômeurs au Maroc (National Association of Unemployed University Graduates in Morocco), 152

Association sahraouie des victimes des violations graves des droits de l'homme commises par l'état du Maroc (Sahrawi Association of Victims of Grave Human Rights Violations Committed by the Moroccan State), 160

Atherton, Alfred, 62–63

Aurik, Johannes, 26

autonomy, Western Saharan: and Amazigh, 219–20; conditions for, 245, 252; and Framework Agreement, 222–23; Morocco's unilateral declaration of, xxxi, 27, 220, 241–42, 243–45;

under Peace Plan, 229, 230; Pérez de Cuéllar on, 180; Polisario position on, 220; Rabat consideration of, 219, 222; Spain's plan for (1974), 33; U.S. stance toward, 71, 74, 243, 245, 248

Awlad Dulaym, 98, 269, 279n1

Awlad Hassan (Banu Ma'qil), 96

Awlad Tidrarin, 98, 269, 279n1

Awsard refugee camp, 127, 129, 130

Ayoub, Lahbib, 206

Ayt Mussa wa 'Ali, 99

al-'Ayun, xxix, 15, 113, 272; intifada in, xxxii, 151, 154; massacre of 1970 in, 103; under Spanish colonialism, 100, 101

al-'Ayun refugee camp, 127, 129, 130

Azmi, Mohammed, 54, 280n4

Aznar, José Maria, 83

Babbitt, Eileen, 263

Baker, James, 207–8, 256; Algeria and, 221, 229; appointed lead UN negotiator, xxx, 69–70, 142, 143, 206–7; and Framework Agreement, 221–25; and Houston Accords, 208–9; and Moroccan government, 196, 207, 210, 236–37; and Peace Plan, 229–31; and Polisario, 207, 208, 223, 249, 276n4; resigns as negotiator, 143, 238, 257

Ban Ki-moon, 243, 247

Basri, Driss, 51; dismissed from Moroccan government, 54, 142, 148, 216–17; and UN referendum in Western Sahara, 142, 187, 191, 210, 211

Bassiri, Mohammed Sidi Ibrahim, 103, 145

Bastagli, Francesco, 241

Baydallah, Muhammad Shaykh, 281n4

Beiba, Mahfoud Ali, 118, 120, 182, 206, 247

Belgium, 20, 171

Belkhir, Larbi, 250

Benaissa, Mohamed, 234, 235

Ben Ali, Zinedine, 199

Ben Barka, Mehdi, 37, 38, 39

Ben Bella, Ahmed, 33, 80

Bendjedid, Chadli, 42, 77, 83, 180, 181–82

Benmoussa, Chakib, 247

Bennani, Abdelaziz, 251

Bennou, Mohammed, 122

Bennouna, Mohammed, 236

Benslimane, Hosni, 251, 282n7

Berlin Conference (1884–85), 100

Bidan (Moors), 93, 270, 277n2

Bolton, John, 69; as ambassador to UN, 70–71, 242–43; as member of UN mission, 208–9, 221

Bosnia Herzegovina, 280n2

Bouabid, Abderrahim, 47

Boucetta, M'hamed, 175, 177

Boudiaf, Mohamed, 41

Boukhari, Ahmed, 247

Boulding, Elise, 113

Boumedienne, Houari, 76, 172; in negotiations over Western Sahara, 33, 34, 171; support for Polisario, 11, 41

Bouteflika, Abdelaziz, 229; as Algerian foreign minister, 33, 34; as Algerian president, 42, 43, 50, 79, 216, 249–50; pragmatic outlook of, 42, 224

Boutros-Ghali, Boutros, 125, 205, 281n4; declining influence of, 69, 206; pro-Moroccan background of, 197; on UN voter identification process, 198, 201–2

Brazil, 20, 126

Bukra' mine, xxix, 35, 102, 270

Bulgaria, 225

Burkina Faso, 125

Burns, Nicholas, 245

Burns, William, 236

Bush, George H. W., 66, 68; administration of, 64, 276n4

Bush, George W., 71, 74, 236, 248

Bush (George W.) administration, 84, 183, 224; and Baker, 228, 235, 238–39, 256–57; and continuity of U.S. policy, 64, 73; on Morocco as key ally, 56, 70, 238–39; and support for Moroccan autonomy proposal, 248

Cabral, Amílcar, 115

Cameroon, 225, 234

Camp David Accords, 73

Canada, 215–16

Canary Islands, 81–82, 98, 170

Canary Islands Independence Movement, 80

Cap Juby, 99

Carter, Jimmy, 17, 65; administration of, 17–18, 64–65, 67, 76

Casablanca, 53, 54, 77; 2003 terrorist attack, 55, 56, 70, 153, 233

Casey, William, 66

cell phones, 137, 161, 165, 277n1

census of 1974: list of tribal subfractions in, 199–200; Polisario position on, 191; statistics from, 191–92, 279n1; and voter identification process, 128, 184, 186, 191–92

Central America, 194

Central Intelligence Agency (CIA), 60–61, 72

Ceuta and Melilla, xxiii, 80, 100; history of Spanish rule in, 98; and Spain-Morocco relations, 4, 82, 83; Spanish population in, 81

Chad, 75, 87, 125

Chávez, Hugo, 126

Cheney, Dick, 227

Chile, 124, 145, 234

China, 138, 227, 235

Chirac, Jacques, 78, 79, 234, 239

Chopra, Jarat, 280n2

Cleaveland, Timothy, 94

Clinton, Bill, 240; administration of, 64, 69, 73, 207

Cold War: as motivation in U.S. policy, 72–73, 74, 164; and proxy wars, 71–72; significance of end to, xxv, 68, 138, 180–81, 194

Collectif des défenseurs sahraouis des droits de l'homme (Collective of Sahrawi Human Rights Defenders), 153–54, 160

Colombia, 225

colonial-settler societies, xxiv, 264. See also settlers, Moroccan

Comité d'action contre la torture (Committee of Action Against Torture, Western Sahara), 160

Comité des familles des disparus Sahraouis (Committee of Families of Disappeared Sahrawis), 160

Comité militaire de redressement nationale (Military Committee for National Recovery, Mauritania), 13

Comité national algérien de solidarité avec le peuple sahraoui (Algerian National Committee of Solidarity with the Sahrawi People), 162

Comité pour la défense du droit à l'autodétermination pour le peuple du Sahara Occidental (Committee for the Defense of the Right of Self-Determination for the People of Western Sahara), 159

Comité pour la protection des prisonniers politiques sahraouis à la Prison Noire (Committee for the Protection of Sahrawi Political Prisoners in the Black Prison), 160

Comité sahraoui pour la défense des droits de l'homme (Sahrawi Committee for the Defense of Human Rights), 160

Communist Party, Moroccan, 37, 40, 85

Comoros Islands, 75

Compagnies mobiles d'intervention (Mobile Intervention Companies, Morocco), 147

Compañía Comercial Hispano-Africana, 100

Confédération démocratique des travailleurs (CDT, Democratic Confederation of Workers, Morocco), 46, 48

Congo, 15, 193, 280n2. See also Zaire

Congress of Berlin (1884–85), 100

Conseil consultatif des droits de l'homme (CCDH, Human Rights Advisory Council, Morocco), 48, 150

Conseil royal consultative pour les affaires sahariennes (CORCAS, Royal Consultative Council for Saharan Affairs, Morocco), 157, 242, 281n4

Consejo del Mando de la Revolución (CMR, Council for the Command of the Revolution, Polisario), 116, 117, 120

Consultative Council of Shaykhs, 120

Corell, Hans, 226

corruption, 53, 158, 251

Cortina y Mauri, Pedro, 80

Costa Rica, 172

Crocker, Chester, 59, 208

Cuba, 115, 131, 137

Curtin, Philip, 94

Cyprus, 193

Daddach, Sidi Mohammed, 149–50, 159; released from prison, 153, 224, 263

Dakhla, 155; as fishing port, 228; under Spanish colonialism, 100, 101; during war, 13, 16, 21, 24

Dakhla refugee camp, 127, 129, 130

Darfur, 166

Declaration on the Granting of Independence to Colonial Countries and Peoples, 109, 170

de Gaulle, Charles, 56

Democratic Path. See Annahj Addimocrati

de Piniés, Jaime, 172

Derb Moulay Cherif prison, 146–47

De Soto, Alvaro, 239, 240

Diallo, Issa, 180, 184

Direction générale de la surveillance du territoire (General Directorate of Territorial Surveillance, Morocco), 147

Direction générale des études et de la documentation (General Office of Research and Documentation, Morocco), 147

"disappeared," 54, 187; as Moroccan practice, 52, 145, 146–49, 156–57, 282n7; Moroccan release of, 48, 148. See also prisoners, political

Djibouti, 75

Dlimi, Ahmed, 13, 47

Dra'a River, 31, 97, 272

Draper, Morris, 65–66, 67

drugs, illegal, 53, 81, 251

Dryden, Douglas K., 203

Duclos, Michel, 235

Dunbar, Charles, 201, 209, 210, 211, 240

Durch, William J., 280n2

Eagleton, William, 212, 221, 240

East Timor, 41; independence movement in, xxxv, 31, 257, 264; and international solidarity, 262; longtime UN inaction on, 64, 174; RASD's relations with, 126; UN referendum in, xxx, 142, 169, 186, 193, 217, 218, 252

Egypt, 20, 21, 73

Eisenhower, Dwight D., 71

Ejército de Liberación Popular Saharaui (ELPS, Saharan People's Liberation Army, Polisario), 3, 188; attacks on fishing ships, attacks in Mauritania, 11–12; 16, 82, 83; battle deaths of,

25; at beginning of war, xxviii–xxix; Boume-dienne Offensive of, 15; combat readiness, 28–29, 249, 273n4; in fight against Spanish colonialism, 104–5; military strategy, 7–9, 15, 22–23; military strength, 14–15; military victories, xxix, 3, 15; recruitment, 17; size, 28; surface-to-air missiles of, 16, 17, 28, 273n3; underestimation of, 6; weaponry, 9, 28. *See also* Western Sahara war

electrification, 52

El-Hiba, 99

El-Himma, Fouad Ali, 236, 247

Equatorial Guinea, 73

Eritrea, 31, 245; Polisario and, 124

Errachidia province, 38

*Esmeralda,* 108

Ethiopia, 73, 124, 245

Euro-Med Partnership, 50, 79, 86

European Coordination Conference of Support to the Sahrawi People, 87–88

European Union (EU), 51, 86; fishing agreement with Morocco, xxii, 82, 228

executions, 145–46

Fahd, King, 49

Fanon, Frantz, 115

Farsiyah, 24

al-Fasi, 'Allal, 36, 270

Fassi Fihri, Taieb, 247

Fatimid Caliphate, 96

Figuigi, Bashir (Edouard Moha), 103, 104

fisheries: in Morocco, 53, 82, 228; in Western Sahara, 35, 158, 226, 230, 251, 254

fishing waters: as battleground in war, 16, 81–82, 83; EU's agreement with Morocco on, xxii, 82, 86, 228; and Morocco's territorial limit, 82

FLU (Frente de Liberación y de la Unidad), 4, 103–4, 105

Forces armées royales (FAR, Royal Armed Forces, Morocco), 3, 27, 147; air force, 14, 15; battle casualties, 15, 25; command structure, 15; corruption within, 158, 251; failures, 15–16; size and strength, 14–15, 20, 27;

strategy and tactics, 9, 15–16. *See also* Western Sahara war

Ford, Gerald, 61, 62; administration of, 17, 64

Forum vérité et justice (Truth and Justice Forum). *See* Sahara Branch, Truth and Justice Forum

Fosfatos de Bu-Craa (Fosbucraa), 102

Framework Agreement (2001 draft Framework agreement on status of Western Sahara), xxi, 221–26; Algeria's criticisms of, 223, 224, 225; on autonomy, 222–23; French policy toward, 78–79, 225, 226; Moroccan enthusiasm with, 223; Polisario's criticisms of, 223, 225; on referendum, 223; Security Council debate on, 225–26

France: and Algerian war, 21, 75; and apartheid South Africa, 76–77; builds secret alliance in Africa, 72–73; colonial empire of, 31–33, 75, 94, 99, 100, 102; economic ties with Morocco, 77; and Franco-American consensus, xxv, 70, 84, 169, 170, 249, 256–59; military aid to Morocco, xxix, 12, 17, 44, 75–76, 78, 189; military inter-vention in Western Sahara war, 12, 76; Mitter-rand's election, 77; motivation for supporting Morocco, 59, 73–74; neutrality claim of, 60, 256; policy toward Maghrib region, 75–79; political support to Morocco, xxiv, xxxi, 25, 29, 84, 216, 239, 256, 258; relations with Algeria, 75, 76, 79; relations with Mauritania, 76; under Sarkozy, 245; in Security Council debates, 172, 202, 224, 225, 234; troops in Africa, 76; against Houston Accords, 216, 217–18, 221, 281n9

France Libertés, 276n5

Franck, Thomas, 169

Franco, Francisco, xviii, 4, 5, 36, 172

Frederick the Great, 15

French language, 130–31, 158

Frente de Liberación del Sahara bajo Dominación Española (Liberation Front of the Sahara Under Spanish Domination), 103

Frente de Libertação de Moçambique (FRELIMO), 115, 277n2

Frente Polisario. *See* Polisario Front

Front de libération nationale (FLN, National Lib-eration Front, Algeria), 33

Front pour la défense des institutions constitutio-
nelles (Front for the Defense of Constitutional
Institutions, Morocco), 38
Fukuyama, Francis, 137

Galbraith, Evan, 77
Galtah Zammur, 114; 1981 battle in, 17, 18, 24, 66,
177
Galtah Zammur declaration (1975), 110
Gendarmerie royale, 147
General Union of Palestinian Women, 277n4
Geneva Conventions, xxx, 114, 232, 262
Germany, 202, 234
Ghali, Ibrahim (Brahim), 118, 182, 206, 247
al-ghazi (raid), 9, 32, 270
Giap, Vo Nguyen, 115
Gibraltar, 71, 81, 86
Ginsberg, David, 275n3
Giscard d'Estaing, Valéry, 75, 76
globalization, xxv, 138
Golan Heights (Syria), 193; Moroccan contingent
in, 15, 73, 87
Gómez de Salazar, Federico, 80, 105
González, Felipe, 82
Goulding, Marrack, 182, 184, 196, 207, 280n2
Goulemine, 99
Great Britain. See United Kingdom
Greater Morocco, xxiv, 36, 103, 254, 271; and
Algeria, 33, 41; background of, 36–37; claims
on Ceuta and Melilla, 81; claims on Maurita-
nia, 10, 33; as justification for Western Sahara
seizure, xxiii, 31, 34–35, 40. See also Morocco
Greenland, 107
Green March (1975), xviii, 5–6; popular response
in Morocco, 5, 40; UN debate on, 63–64,
172–73, 260–61; U.S. stance on, 60–64, 172, 256
Green March (1991), 152, 195–96, 231
Gros Espiell, Héctor, 181
Groupe salafiste pour la Prédication et le Combat
(Salafi Group for Preaching and Combat,
GSPC, Algeria), 130
Guedira, Ahmed Reda, 48
Guinea, 225, 234
Guinea-Bissau, 177

Gulf of Guinea, 227
Gulf War. See Iraq war (1991)

Haba, Lina, 277n4
Haddi, Ahmed Mahmoud, 154
Hadrami, Omar, 118, 281n4
Haidar, Aminatou, 147, 155, 164, 248
Haig, Alexander, 18–19, 66
Haile Selassie, 33
Hakim, Ibrahim, 118, 120, 281n4
Hammad, H'med, 149–50
Hampson, Fen, 59
Hannum, Hurst, 229, 236
Hanoune, Louisa, 274n1
Harakat Tahrir Saqiyah al-Hamra' wa Wadi al-
Dhahab (Liberation Movement of the Saqiyah
al-Hamra' and Wadi al-Dhahab, Western
Sahara), 103
Hart, David, 93
Hartman, Arthur, 63
Hassan I, 99, 107, 108
Hassan II, 10, 23, 73, 77; on autonomy for Western
Sahara, 219; death of, xxx, 70, 142, 153, 193,
212; and Green Marches, 5–6, 63, 64, 172, 173,
195; irredentism of, 33, 34, 36; at Nouadhibou
summit, 33, 171; and OAU, 175, 176; political
control by, 38, 251; and Spain-Morocco tensions,
4, 5; in talks with Polisario, 182, 280–81n4; in
UN-sponsored negotiations, 187, 208
Hassan II mosque, 53
Hassaniya dialect, 96, 158, 270
Hawzah, 24
Hodges, Tony, 276n1
Houser, George, 112–13
Houston Accords (1997), 70, 208–9; abandoned by
Security Council, 215–16, 220, 221, 249; effort
to revive, 210–12
Human Rights Watch, 55, 88, 148; on "disap-
peared," 149, 150–51; on MINURSO, 69, 203–4
Huntington, Samuel, 137–38

Ibn Khaldun, 96
Ifni, xxiii, 100, 101, 103, 170

Ila al-'Amam (Forward, Morocco), 39, 40, 48, 273–74n1

immigrants and immigration: from Morocco, 54; Sahrawi, 131, 158, 164–65; in Spain, 81, 131, 158

India, 124

Indonesia, 41, 62, 169; and East Timor, xxx, 126, 169, 174, 186, 217, 252

Institute for Advanced Strategic and Political Studies, 227

International Committee of the Red Cross, 113–14, 194, 261–62, 276n5

International Court of Justice (ICJ), xxviii, 5, 106–10, 169, 171–72

International Federation for Human Rights, 88

International Federation for the Rights of Man, 114

International Federation of Human Rights Leagues, 145

International Human Rights Law Group, 279n2

International Monetary Fund (IMF), 46, 47, 51

international solidarity with Western Sahara, 162–63, 262–65; and Internet, 88; solidarity tourism to refugee camps, 136; in Spain, 83, 88; strategy for, 263–65; throughout Europe, 87–88

Internet, 88, 137, 161, 165, 377n1

intifada, Sahrawi, xxxii, 140, 249, 250; of 1999, 151–54; of 2005, 154–56; causes of, 154, 156–59; challenges of, 164–65; impact on Polisario, 122; repression of, 28, 140–41, 152, 155–56; role of Internet and cell phones in, 165; settler participation in, 159

Intifada al-Zamlah (1970), 103

Iran, 193; fall of shah in, 17, 65; under shah, 20; U.S. hostages in, 66

Iraq, 20, 193

Iraq war (1991), 184, 276n4; Moroccan demonstration against, 48; Moroccan troops and, 45, 87; UN and, 194

Iraq war (2003), 84, 262

Ireland, 224

irredentism. See Greater Morocco

Islam, 95

Islamism, 48, 50, 138; in Morocco, 47, 52, 55–56, 274–75n2; as threat to U.S. and France, 59, 70

Islas Chafarinas, 81

Isma'il, Mawlay, 98–99, 270

Israel, 21, 87; Morocco as ally of, 73, 275n3; RASD and, 124; U.S. support to, 19, 164

Istiqlal Party (Independence Party), 36, 37, 38, 47, 51, 270

Italy, 20, 21

Ivory Coast, 175

Izargiyyn, 98, 270, 279n1

Jama'a council, 95, 101–2, 116, 270

Jamai, Aboubakr, 162

Jamaica, 221, 224

Jaysh al-Tahrir (Army of Liberation, Morocco), 102, 270

Jdriya, 24

Jensen, Erik, 199, 206, 219, 250–51

Jettou, Driss, 55

Jeune afrique, 204, 275n2

Jews, 40, 275n3

Jordan, 20, 71, 87

Journal Hebdomadaire, Le, 162

Juan Carlos, King, 62, 82, 84

Kaplan, Robert, 138

Kashmir, 124, 193

Kasten, Robert, 67

Kawkaw, 98

Keiswetter, Allen, 70

Kennedy, Edward, 248

Kentaoui, Ali Habib, 115

Kenya, 126, 176

Kerr-McGee Company, 70, 226, 228

Khadad, Emhamed, 206, 247

Khadiri, Abdelhak, 251, 281n4

al-Khanga, 104

Khattabi, Abdelkarim, 54

Khatt al-Shahid (Line of the Martyr), 121–22, 250, 271

Khaya, Cheikh, 149–50, 153, 278n3

Kinloch, Robin, 210, 211

Kirkpatrick, Jeanne, 66

Kissinger, Henry, 60–63, 74, 275n2

Klotz, Audie, 262

Kodjo, Edem, 177

Kosovo, 85, 245, 264

Kriesberg, Louis, 26

Kutla Wataniyya, 38

Laanigri, Hamidou, 251, 282n7

Laghzal, Brahim, 153, 278n3

Lagwirah, 13, 100

Lalla Marnia Treaty (1845), 32

Lamari, Mohamed, 27, 250

Lamine Ould Ahmed, Mohammed, 104, 118, 146, 281n5

Law of the Sea Treaty, 82

Lebanon, 163, 193

Lebouirate, 15

Legal Status of Eastern Greenland, 107

Lembarki, Hamdi, 155

Lewin, André, 173

Lewis, William H., 15

Libération (Morocco), 47

Libya, 20, 21; relations with Morocco, 23, 73, 87; Sahrawi refugees in, 131; support to Polisario, 9, 16, 23, 34

Lippert, Ann, 114, 277n3

literacy rate: in Morocco, 52; Sahrawi, 130, 135

Lmrabet, Ali, 162, 277n1

Lugar, Richard, 240

Lula da Silva, Luiz Inácio, 126

Ma' al-'Aynayn, Shaykh, 99, 107–8, 271

Madagascar, 125

Madrid Agreement (1975), xxix, 6, 64, 113, 173

Madrid train bombings (2004), 275n2

Mahjoub, Salek, 122

al-mahr (bride-price), 136

Mali, 75, 221

Mandela, Nelson, 125, 205

Mansour, Abdalhay Muy, 273n4

Mansouri, Yassine, 247

Manz, Johannes, 183, 196

Marrakech Plan (1975), 75

Marrakech Treaty (1767), 108

Marxism, 115, 277n2

Massaoud, Laarbi, 153, 278n3

Mauritania, 11, 76, 170, 224, 227; becomes independent, 10, 75; claim on Western Sahara, 10–11; coups in, 12, 14; economic conditions, 10, 13; and Morocco, 10–12, 13, 103; at Nouadhibou summit, 33, 171; relations with Polisario, 13–14, 258; in war against Polisario and RASD, xxix, 9, 12–13; withdraws from Western Sahara, 3, 13

Mauritius, 224

Mbeki, Thabo, 125

Mediterranean Union, 79, 86

Medvedev, Dimitry, 85

Meknes Group, 278n2

Melilla. See Ceuta and Melilla

mercenaries, 12

Mercer, John, 277n3

Merebbi Rebbu, 99

Mesfioui, Benhamou, 102

Mexico, 138

milhafah, 136–37

Milosevic, Slobodan, 245

MINURSO (UN Mission for the Referendum in Western Sahara), 203–9; applicants vetted, 210; cost of, 185, 186; establishment of, xxx, 185; final voter tally of, 142, 192–93, 213–14; financial contributions to, 185, 240; functioning of, 200–201, 204; heads of, 239–40; and issue of consent, 280n2; Morocco's harassment and obstruction of, 68–69, 194, 203; Polisario criticisms of, 122; and refugee-exchange program, 112, 277n1; second round of identification process, 209–13; size of, 224; term extensions of, 212, 221, 224–25, 247; U.S. and, 69, 185, 243; human rights violations of witnesses, 149, 150. See also voter identification process

Mitterrand, Danielle, 276n5

Mitterrand, François, xxix, 77

Mobutu Sese Seko, 73

Mohammed V, 10, 36, 37

Mohammed VI Foundation, 55

Mohammed VI, 50, 83, 142; ascension to throne, 54, 70, 212, 216, 217; meets with Polisario, 206; personal wealth of, 55; releases political prisoners, 153, 154; stance in negotiations, xxx, 212,

223, 224, 241; U.S. and, 216, 238; uses fear of terrorism, 56, 74

Moi, Daniel arap, 176

Mokhtar, Brahim, 26

Mondlane, Eduardo, 115

Montevideo Convention on the Rights and Duties of States (1933), 124

Moratinos, Miguel Ángel, 84, 250

Moroccan American Committee for Policy, 112

Morocco (ECONOMY): austerity plan, 45–47, 48; costs of Western Sahara war, 23, 43–45, 46; fishing industry, 53, 82, 228; foreign debt, 46, 47, 52, 53; GDP, 52–53; phosphate industry, xxii, 34–35; as rentier state, xxii; trade deficit, 45, 48, 53

Morocco (GENERAL): 'Alawi dynasty in, xxii, 31, 71, 98–99; anticolonial insurgencies in, 100, 102; and apartheid South Africa, 20; becomes independent, 32, 75; border war with Algeria, 5, 10, 15, 31, 33; and Ceuta and Melilla, 4–6; constitutions in, 38–39, 50–51; corruption in, 53, 158, 251; coup attempts in, 39, 47; democratic opposition in, 153, 161; elections in, 38–39, 50–51, 55; EU fisheries accord with, xxii, 82, 228; French colonial rule in, 32–33, 94, 100; illegal drugs in, 53, 81; independent journalism in, 161–62; irredentism in, xxiii–xxiv, 10, 31, 33, 35–37, 40, 81, 103, 254, 271; Islamist opposition in, 47, 52, 55, 56, 274–75n2; Jewish community in, 40, 275n3; leftist opposition in, 37–38, 39–40, 161, 273–74n1; and Mauritania, 10–12, 103; and OAU, 177–79; political space in, 161–62; popular opinion on Western Sahara in, 40, 57–58; relations with Algeria, 33–34, 36–37, 41, 49–50; relations with Arab world, 87; relations with Libya, 23, 73, 87; relations with Soviet Union, 72, 85; relations with Spain, 20, 59, 80–82, 83, 237; religious establishment in, 40; repression within, 37–38, 39–40, 46–48, 55, 77; Saudi support to, xxix, 17, 18, 44–45, 189; sends troops to Congo/Zaire, 15, 73; sends troops to Equatorial Guinea, 73; sends troops to Golan Heights, 15, 73, 87; social backwardness and inequality, 39, 48, 52–53, 54; social unrest in, 38, 45–46, 47, 48; solidarity with Western Sahara in, 165–66;

stability of, xxix, 35–40, 56, 72, 74, 164, 254–55; support for Palestinians, 125; terrorist attacks in, 55–56, 274–75n2; unemployment in, 45–46, 47, 48, 51–52, 54; urbanization in, 54; uses terrorism threat, 56, 70, 233, 238, 278n4; and Zona del Draa, 100–101

Morocco (U.S./FRANCE RELATIONS): as ally in global war on terrorism, 70, 74–75, 257; economic ties, 71, 77; French military aid, xxix, 12, 17, 43, 75–76, 78, 189; Morocco's strategic importance, 71, 75, 235, 238, 280n2; U.S. intelligence support, 19–20; U.S. military aid, xxix, 17–18, 20, 44, 64–65, 66–67, 68, 71, 72, 78, 183, 275n2; U.S. military training, 19; U.S. relations after Baker plan, 207, 238, 256–57

Morocco (WESTERN SAHARA): Baker and, 196, 207, 210, 236–37; and domestic political control, 38, 40, 43; and Framework Agreement, 223; and Houston Accords, 209; and ICJ case, xxviii, 5, 106–10, 171–72; imposition of "autonomy" plan, xxxi, 27, 220, 241–42, 243–45; irredentism of, xxiii, 31, 34–35, 40; meetings with Polisario, 182, 206, 221, 222, 246–47, 280–81n4; motivation and aims of, 4, 26, 34–37, 39–40, 181, 254–55; at Nouadhibou summit, 33, 171; opposition within Morocco, 273–74n1; and Peace Plan, 121, 229, 232–33, 234–35, 265; refuses dialogue with Sahrawis, 156, 157; repression of Sahrawi protests, 122, 140, 144–51, 152, 154–55, 156–57, 249; and Sahrawi nationalism, 255–56; and Sahrawi self-determination, 59, 170, 171, 220, 244; and Settlement Plan, 180, 184, 186–87; unwillingness to compromise, 170, 250–51, 259; and voter identification process, 142, 191, 192, 193, 194, 195, 204, 212, 213, 215; war atrocities by, 113–14; and Western Sahara economic resources, 226–28. *See also* Western Sahara war

Moussaoui, Zacarias, 275n2

Mouvement du 21 août (August 21 Movement, Morocco), 103

Mouvement de Résistance "les Hommes Bleus" (Blue Men's Resistance Movement, Morocco), 103

Moynihan, Daniel Patrick, 63–64

*Al-Muharrir*, 47

al-Murabitun (Almoravids), 95–96, 271, 277n2

al-Muwahhidun (Almohads), 96, 271

Mzoudi, Abdelghani, 275n2

Namibia: in Security Council debates, 215, 221; UN mission in, 185, 186, 193, 194

napalm, 114

Nasser, Gamal Abdul, 33

Nassiri, Ahmed, 278n3

nationalism, Western Saharan, 139; Algerian support for, 40–43; as counter to Moroccan nationalism, xxiii–xxiv, 125, 254; and defense of culture, 158–59; galvanized by war, 25, 105, 255; and internationalization, 123, 141, 143, 159; and intifada, 135, 140, 154, 156–59, 250; origins of, 255–56; Polisario serves, 250, 259; and *Sahrawi* term, xxii, 95, 111, 278n1; strength of in refugee camps, 27, 28, 122–23, 137; as "tool of Algeria," 30–31; U.S. stance toward, 59, 72, 74, 143–44, 248

National Union of Sahrawi Women. *See* Uniòn Nacional de Mujeres Saharauis

Negroponte, John, 234, 235

neoliberalism, 138

Nepal, 163

New World Order, xxv, 68, 138

*New York Times*, 19, 176, 194, 262

Nezzar, Khalid, 120, 282n4

Nicaragua, 276n4

Niger, 75

Nixon (Guam) Doctrine, 72

Nonaligned Movement, 124

nongovernmental organizations (NGOs), 79, 276n5; and refugee camps, 128, 129, 136

nonviolence, 156; as strategy, 163–66, 263–64

Norris, H. T., 93, 96, 133

North American Free Trade Agreement, 138

Norway, 225, 228

Nouadhibou summit (1970), 33, 171

Nouakchott, Mauritania, 10, 11

Nouda, Abderrahmane, 48

Numeiri, Jaafar, 175

Nyere, Julius, 175

Obama, Barack, 248

Obasanjo, Olusegun, 175

Obiang Nugema Mbasogo, Teodoro, 73

oil, xxii, 227

Operation Ouragan (1958), 102

Organization of African Unity (OAU), 174–79; Charter of, 177, 179; Committee of Wisemen in, 175, 176, 178; Moroccan walkout and boycott, 177–79; RASD recognition by, 23, 123, 124, 174–75, 177–78; RASD role in, 125; and Western Sahara peace process, 77, 86, 169–70, 175–77, 181, 199, 279n1. *See also* African Union

Oslo Agreement (1993), 250

Ouarkaziz Mountains, 6, 16

Ouarkziz, 20

Oufkir, Mohammed, 39

Oujda Treaty (1984), 23

Ould Boucief, Ahmed, 13

Ould Daddah, Mokhtar, 10–11, 172–73; overthrown, 12, 76; in Western Sahara negotiations, 33, 34, 171

Ould Heydallah, Mohammed Khouna, 13, 14

Ould Lahbib, Ayoub, 118, 120, 206

Ould Nass, Ramdane, 118

Ould Rachid, Khalihenna, 105, 157, 242, 247

Ould Salek, Mohammed Salem, 104, 116

Ould Salek, Mustafa, 12, 13

Ould Sidati, Mohammed, 104

Ould Ziou, M'hammed, 116

Ouyahia, Ahmed, 224

Palestine, 164, 264

Palestine Liberation Organization (PLO), 77, 250, 277n4

pan-Arabism, 115

Pan-Sahel initiative, 74

Paris–Dakar Rally 2001, 26–27, 222

Parker, Richard, 61

Parti de la justice et du développement (PJD, Justice and Development Party, Morocco), 52

Parti de libération et socialisme (Liberation and Socialism Party, Morocco), 37

Parti démocratique et de l'indépendance (Democratic Independence Party, 37

Parti des travailleurs (Workers Party, Algeria), 274n1

Partido Africano da Independência da Guiné e Cabo Verde (PAIGC), 115, 277n2

Partido de la Unión Nacional Saharaui (PUNS, Party of Sahrawi National Unity, Spanish Sahara), 103

Partido Socialista Obrero Español (PSOE, Spanish Socialist Workers' Party), 82–83, 84

Parti du people mauritanien (Mauritanian Peoples' Party), 10

Parti du progrès et du socialisme (PPS, Party of Progress and Socialism, Morocco), 40, 51

Pazzanita, Anthony, 276n1

Peace Plan (2003 Peace Plan for the Self-Determination for the People of Western Sahara), xxxi, 229–33; autonomy under, 229, 230; debate over enforcement provisions, 233; final-status vote as linchpin of, 230; Moroccan opposition to, 121, 229, 232–33, 234–35, 265; Moroccan role under, 230; Polisario acceptance of, 121, 159, 234; Polisario objections to, 233; Security Council debate on, 234, 235; settlers under, 230, 231–32; on voter identification process, 229, 230–31

Pelissier, Rene, 171

Pelletreau, Robert H., 206

Peñón de Alhucemas, 81

Peñón de Vélez de la Gomera, 81

Percy, Charles, 66

Peres, Shimon, 73

Pérez de Cuéllar, Javier, 187, 188; approach to peace process by, 180, 181–82, 189–90; deceptiveness of, 184, 189–90, 196–97; visits region, 179, 183

phosphates: in Morocco, xxii, 34–35; in Western Sahara, 35, 102, 158, 226

Polisario Front: authoritarianism within, 116, 119, 121; on autonomy proposal, 220; and Baker, 207, 208, 223, 249, 276n4; on cease-fire preconditions, 176–77, 179; concessions during peace negotiations, 180n2, 187, 250, 280n2; constitution of, 117, 134; cooperation with UN peacekeepers, 195; defections from, 24, 118, 120, 157; democratic reforms in, 116, 119–20, 121–22; in direct talks with Morocco,

182, 206, 221, 222, 246–47, 280–81n4; on ethnic and tribal divisions, 118–19; Executive Committee of, 119, 120; first manifesto of (1973), 110; flag of, xxxii, 115; founding of, 104; and Framework Agreement, 221, 222, 223, 225; General National Program of, 125; and Houston Accords, 209, 221; and internal resistance movement, 159–60; Khatt al-Shahid faction within, 121–22, 250, 271; membership in, 159; morale problems in, 24; motivations of in peace process, 26, 181; name, xxi, 270, 273n1; National Secretariat, 120, 121, 160; and negotiation failures, 144, 239, 240, 247, 249; and Peace Plan, 121, 159, 233, 234; Political Bureau of, 116, 117, 120; political ideology of, 115; on problems of future transition period, 187, 251–52; and referendum, 141, 159, 187, 205, 256, 280n2; relations with Algeria, 9, 16, 17, 30–31, 40–43, 49–50, 116, 250; relations with Arab Steadfastness Front, 87; relations with Libya, 9, 16, 17, 87; relations with Mauritania, 13–14; relations with Soviet Union, 16, 72, 85; relations with Spain, 82, 83, 84; relations with U.S., 67, 68, 238, 248; and Sahrawi traditionalism, 134; and Settlement Plan, 180, 184, 186, 188; on settlers, 15, 232; support for in OAU, 175; support for in Sahrawi society, 160–61; threatens renewed hostilities, 26–28, 122, 164, 197, 222; unilateral cease-fire abandoned, 183; and voter identification process, 192, 197, 201, 202, 205, 210, 213, 215; war aims of, 4; work in refugee camps, 115. See also Ejército de Liberación Popular Saharaui (ELPS)

Polisario Front General Congresses: first (1973), 116; second (1974), 116; third (1976), 116–17; fifth (1982), 117–18; sixth (1985), 118; eighth (1991), 119–20; tenth (1999), 120; eleventh (2003), 121; twelfth (2007), 121, 122, 249

Portugal, 170, 171

Powell, Colin, 240

prisoners, political, 39–40, 69, 147, 158; extrajudicial killings of, 118; release of, 40, 148, 153–54, 224, 263; and secret prisons, 146–47; under Settlement Plan, 183, 185, 187; torture and abuse of, 146, 282n7. See also "disappeared" prisoners of war (POWs): held by Morocco, 146, 205; held by Polisario, 20, 205, 240, 276n5; Settlement Plan and, 183, 187

Putin, Vladimir, 85

Qadhdhafi, Mu'ammar, 23, 73, 87, 115

al-Qaida, 130, 275n2, 278n4

Rabat, 54

Rahal, Mohammed, 281n5

Ramos-Horta, Jose, 126

RASD (República Árabe Saharaui Democrática): in African Union peacekeeping missions, 178–79; constitution of, 21; derecognitions of, 86, 125; foreign relations of, 123–26; formation of, xxix, 116; Mauritania's recognition of, 14; name of, 110–11, 270; OAU recognition of, 23, 123, 124, 174–75, 177–78; oil contracts signed by, 227; Parliament of, 120; pursuit of recognition, 123–24; self-identification of, 123; and South Africa, 86–87, 124, 125–26, 164; and Soviet Union, 85; women in, 134–35

Reagan, Ronald, 18, 65, 66, 70: administration of, xxix, 18–19, 65–68, 78, 276n4

Reed, Joseph, 66

referendum, planned: doubts over, 142, 202–3; failure and abandonment of, 68, 70, 140, 193, 241; in Framework Agreement, 223; Hassan consent to, 176; Morocco's vote-stacking effort in, xxx, 142, 187, 191, 192, 195, 199, 210, 211, 259; OAU program for, 279n1; under Peace Plan, 159; Polisario and, 141, 159, 187, 205, 256, 280n2; Polisario confidence of victory in, 205, 256; postponements of, xxvii, 140, 172, 211; under Settlement Plan, xxx, 185, 187, 279n2; Spain announcement of in 1974, xxviii, 33, 171; winner-take-all character, xxx, 26, 170, 180, 217. See also voter identification process

refugee camps, 126–33; clandestine trade within, 130; and family visits, 240; financial aid to, 128; food supply, 131–32; formation of, 113–15; growing affluence in, 131–32, 135, 137; growing

militancy within, 27, 28, 122, 135, 137; housing in, 126, 136, 277n3; initial harshness of, 114; Moroccan charges about, 112, 277n1; Polisario work in, 115; political awareness at, 131; population of, 114, 127–28; response to Settlement Plan in, 187–88; role of remittances in, 136; romanticization about, 112–13; schools and hospitals in, 129, 130–31; as self-managed, 128, 129–30, 132–33; as social experiment, 114; solidarity tourism to, 136; structure of, 277n3; struggle against disease epidemics in, 130, 132; summer vacation programs in Spain, 83, 136, 162–63; transportation between, 130; women's role in, 9, 113, 114, 136–37

refugee-exchange program, 112, 277n1

refugee repatriation, xxx, 177, 185, 211, 215, 230; in Houston Accords, 209; in Peace Plan, 229, 230, 231; in Settlement Plan, 141, 183, 185; UNHCR census around, 128, 231

Renseignements généraux (General Intelligence, Morocco), 147

República Árabe Saharaui Democrática. See RASD

Rgaybat, 97, 118–19, 271

Rgaybat al-Sahil, 97, 279n1

Rgaybat al-Sharq, 92, 97, 279n1

Rhodesia, 187

Rice, Condoleezza, 71, 248

Río de Oro, xxviii, 100, 109, 171

Rockefeller, David, 66

Ross, Christopher, 71, 248

Roy, Armand, 195

Ruda, José Mara, 109

Ruddy, Frank, 69, 149, 203

Rupérez, Javier, 82

Russia, 84–85, 225, 235. See also Soviet Union

Rwanda, 124, 166

Sadat, Anwar, 87

Sa'di dynasty, 98

Safari Club, 72

Sahara Branch, Truth and Justice Forum, 149–50, 153, 160, 278n3

Sahel, Mostafa, 247

*Sahrawi,* xxiii, 271; conceptualization of term, 92–95, 110–11; as recent idea, 91, 93, 277n2; and "Western Saharan," xxi–xxii, 271n1

Sahrawi National Council, 116, 117

Sahrawi Red Crescent, 127, 128

Salek, Bazid, 278n3

Saqiyah al-Hamra', 6, 100, 109, 171

Sarkozy, Nicholas, 79, 86, 245

Saudi Arabia, 49, 87; financial support to Morocco, xxix, 17, 18, 44, 189

Sayed, Bachir Mustapha, 104, 117, 118; in talks with Morocco, 182, 206, 280n4

Sayed, El-Ouali Mustapha, 105, 115, 125; death of, 11, 116; and founding of Polisario, 104

Scowcroft, Brent, 61

Seddon, David, 44

self-determination, Western Saharan: Algeria's support for, 34, 40; Kofi Annan on, 232, 246; challenges of building movement for, 264–65; French rhetoric about, 78; ICJ endorsement of, xxviii, 106, 109; international consensus for, 59; Mauritania's support for, 10–11; Morocco's rejection of, 59, 220, 244; and resource exploitation, 226; Security Council abandonment of, 219, 241, 243, 245; settler support for, 152–53, 159, 264–65; Spain promises, 80; UN recognition of, 102, 109, 170–71, 174; U.S.-French opposition to, 59, 169, 171, 248

Senegal, 75, 178

Senniya, 134

Serbia, 163

Serfaty, Abraham, 48, 54, 161, 274n1

Settlement Plan (1991), 183–88; cease-fire under, 180, 183, 185, 186, 188; negotiations leading up to, 179–84; Polisario acceptance of, 188; Polisario criticisms of, 184, 186, 188; on political prisoners and POWs, 183, 187; on refugee repatriation, 141, 183, 185; response to in refugee camps, 187–88; Security Council debate on, 183–84; UN's abandonment of, 215; on voter identification process, 141, 180, 184, 185–86, 196; as war by other means, 189–90, 258; winner-take-all character of, 26, 170, 217

settlers, Moroccan, xxiv; and ethnic Sahrawis, 157–58; exploitation of Sahrawis by, 158; Peace Plan and, 230, 231–32; Polisario position on, 15, 232; and Rabat's vote-stacking efforts, xxx, 142, 187, 191, 192, 195, 199, 210, 211, 259; in Settlement Plan, 143; support for Western Sahara self-determination among, 152–53, 159, 264–65; and Western Sahara demographics, xxi, 264

Shaba Province, 73

al-Shabibah al-Islamiyyah (Islamic Youth, Morocco), 47

shaykhs, 120, 272; in voter identification process, 198–99, 201, 204

Shelley, Toby, 282n4

Shurbubba War, 96

Sidi Ahmad Rgaybi, 97

Sidi Ifni, 100

Sierra Leone, 176

Sinai, 193

Smara, xxix, 15, 113; protest demonstrations in, 155, 224; under Spanish colonialism, 99, 100, 101

Smara refugee camp, 127, 129

Snoussi, Ahmed, 280–81n1

socialism, 115, 138, 277n2

Socialist Party (France), 77

Société anonyme des mines de fer de Mauritanie (Corporation of Iron Mines of Mauritania), 10

Solarz, Stephen, 67, 275n3

Solís Ruíz, José, 80

Somalia, 69, 73, 280n2

Somerville, Keith, 12

Songhay kingdom, 98

South Africa (APARTHEID): antiapartheid struggle in, 163–64; arms embargo against, 76–77; comparisons of Morocco's occupation to, 203; international movement against, 262; opposition to RASD by, 124; sends arms to Morocco, 20; in UN debates on Western Sahara, 170, 171

South Africa (POSTAPARTHEID): interest in mediating Western Saharan conflict, 205; support for Polisario and RASD, 86–87, 125–26, 164

South Ossetia, 85

South West Africa People's Organization, 185

Soviet Union, 16, 72, 85. *See also* Russia

Spain: abandonment of Sahrawis by, 80, 105; African immigrants to, 81, 131, 158; announcement of Western Sahara referendum, xxviii, 33, 171; under Franco, 4–6; and Green March, 5, 62, 63, 172; Madrid terrorist bombings, 84; policy toward Western Sahara, 79–84; relations with Morocco, 20, 59, 80–82, 83, 237; relations with Polisario, 82, 83, 84; Sahrawi solidarity organizations in, 83, 88, 162–63; Socialist Party victory in, 82–83; tries to revive peace talks, 239; in UN debates, 83–84, 170–71, 172, 234, 235

Spanish language, 130, 158

Spanish Sahara, xxvii–xxviii, 101; al-'Ayun massacre in, 103; colonial conquest of, xxvii, 99–100, 255; and colonial treaties, 108–9; counterinsurgency campaign in, 102, 103–4; economic exploitation of, 102; European interest in, 98–99; manipulation of ethnic divisions in, 94–95; native insurgencies in, 100, 102, 103, 104–5; sedentarization of nomads in, 13, 103, 192, 276n1; Spain's decolonization plans, xxviii, 33, 171. *See also* Western Sahara

Srifi, Mohammed, 48

Stevens, Siaka Probyn, 176

Suárez, Adolfo, 82

Sunni 'Ali, 98

surrogate strategy, 72

Swing, William Lacy, 240

Syndicat national des lycéens (SNL), 39

Syria, 131. *See also* Golan Heights

Takfiris, 164, 274n2

Tamek, Ali-Salem, 278n1, 278n3

Tan Tan, 11, 15, 155

Tarfaya, xxiii, 16, 100

Tata, 16

Tazmamart prison, 147, 148, 282n7

*Tel Quel,* 162

terrorism: Casablanca bombings (2003), 55, 56, 70, 153, 233; Madrid bombings (2004), 84; Moroccan exploitation of threat, 56, 70, 233, 238, 278n4; and Moroccan Islamist groups,

55–56, 274–75n2; September 11, 2001, xxxi, 70, 138, 224; undid Union du Maghreb arabe, 50; U.S. global war on, xxv, xxxi, 56, 70, 74, 164, 220, 224, 257, 260

Tessler, Mark, 44

Tétouan, 100

Tétouan Treaty (1860), 108, 109

Theofilopoulou, Anna, 209

Tiknah confederation, 98, 99, 107, 272, 279n1

Timbuktu, 98

Tindouf, 4, 6, 32, 131; refugee camp in, 126–27

Tiris al-Gharbiyah, 13, 272

Tiznit, 99

Togo, 124

torture, 140, 146, 243, 249, 278n3

Trans-Saharan Counter Terrorism Initiative/Partnership, 74

Traoré, Moussa, 175

Treaty of Commerce and Navigation (1861), 108

Treaty of Peace and Amity (1960), 100

tribal and ethnic divisions, 93, 94, 138; Morocco's manipulation of, 244; within nationalist movement, 118–19; and voter identification process, 198–99, 200

Trinquet project, 32

Tropas Nómadas (Nomad Troops), 9, 104

Tunisia, 75

Tutwiler, Margaret, 228

23 Mars group, 39

Ukraine, 163

Um Draygah, 24, 114

unemployment: in Morocco, 45–46, 47, 48, 51–52, 54; in Western Sahara, 157

UN High Commission For Refugees (UNHCR): and family visits, 240; Moroccan harassment of, 194; and refugee camps, 127, 128–29; and refugee-exchange program, 112, 277n1

Union constitutionelle (Constitutional Union, Morocco), 47

Unión del Centro Democrático (Union of the Democratic Center, Spain), 82

Union du Maghreb arabe (UMA, Arab Maghrib Union), 49–50, 124–25, 181

Union marocaine de travail (Moroccan Labor Union), 37, 38

Unión Nacional de Mujeres Saharauis (UNMS, National Union of Sahrawi Women), 12, 124, 135.

Union nationale des étudiants marocains (UNEM, National Union of Moroccan Students), 39, 46

Union nationale des forces populaires (UNFP, National Union of Popular Forces, Morocco), 37–39

Union socialiste des forces populaires (USFP, Socialist Union of Popular Forces, Morocco), 46–47, 50–51

United Kingdom: British colonialism, 99, 108, 109; in UN debates, 170, 221, 224, 225, 234; and Western Saharan conflict, 85–86

United Nations: Charter, 106, 135, 233, 258, 260–61; and conflict resolution, 164–65, 166, 180, 193–94, 237, 280n2; East Timor referendum, xxx, 142, 186, 193, 217, 252; Fourth Committee of, 170, 173–74, 179, 203; mission of 1975 to Spanish Sahara, 105; Namibia referendum, 185, 186, 194; Republican Party criticisms of, 69; technical missions to Western Sahara, 179, 180, 184, 209

United Nations General Assembly: Resolution 31/45 (1976), 174; Resolution 32/22 (1977), 174; Resolution 33/31 (1978), 174; Resolution 34/37 (1979), 174, 261; Resolution 35/19 (1980), 179; Resolution 1514 (1960), 109, 170; Resolution 2072 (1965), 170; Resolution 2229 (1966), 102, 170–71; Resolution 2983 (1972), 102, 171; Resolution 3292 (1974), 106, 171–72; Resolution 3314 (1974), 261; Resolution 3458A (1975), 174; Resolution 3458B (1975), 174

United Nations peacekeepers, 193–95; arrival of, 140–41, 188; in Congo, 15, 193, 208n2; cost of, 185; Morocco's restrictions and surveillance of, 149, 194–95; number of, 188, 205; and peace enforcement, 279–80n2; Polisario cooperation with, 195; previous UN missions, 15, 193; in Western New Guinea, 62, 193

United Nations Security Council: abandons Houston Accords, 215–16, 220, 221, 249; abandons

self-determination, 219; as accessory to Moroccan occupation, 190; bad faith of, 246; and Framework Agreement, 83–84, 144, 225–26; on Green March, 260–61; Group of Friends for Western Sahara within, 69, 84, 204, 217, 226; on Houston Accords, 221–22; on independence as unrealistic, 247; on Moroccan resource exploitation, 226; neutrality questions about, 182, 236; and Peace Plan, 237, 241; secrecy and deceptiveness of, 182, 184, 189–90, 196–97, 237; and Settlement Plan, 179–84; Task Force for Western Sahara, 182, 185; unwillingness to pressure Morocco, 143, 217, 241, 252–53, 258–59; U.S. and French influence on, 78, 143, 258; and Western Sahara referendum, 24, 47–48, 55, 193

United Nations Security Council resolutions: Resolution 377 (1975), 172; Resolution 379 (1975), 173; Resolution 380 (1975), 63, 64, 173, 260–61; Resolution 658 (1990), 184; Resolution 690 (1991), 185; Resolution 809 (1993), 197–98; Resolution 1017 (1995), 202; Resolution 1291 (2000), 215–16; Resolution 1301 (2000), 221; Resolution 1359 (2001), 223–24; Resolution 1429 (2002), 226, 232; Resolution 1495 (2003), 235, 236; Resolution 1541 (2004), 237; Resolution 1754 (2007), 245

United Nations Working Group on Enforced and Involuntary Disappearances, 149

United States: Africa policy, 72–73, 227; and autonomy for Western Sahara, 71, 74, 243, 245, 248; and Cold War, 72–73, 74, 164; continuity of Western Sahara policy, xxiv, 25, 29, 64–65, 73, 74, 235; and failure of peace process, xxxi, 25, 57, 68–71, 217–18, 224, 240, 256, 258, 259; and global war on terrorism, xxv, xxxi, 56, 70, 74, 164, 220, 224, 257, 260; during Green March crisis, 60–64, 172, 256; and Houston Accords, 209, 221; influence on Security Council, 78, 143, 258; Islamist threat to, 59, 70; and Mohammed VI, 216, 238; Morocco as strategic ally of, 71, 75, 235, 238, 280n2; and Morocco-Polisario direct talks, 205–6, 280–81n4; and Morocco's stability, 72, 74, 164; neutrality claims of, 60, 68, 256; opposition to Western

United States (*cont.*)

Sahara self-determination, 59, 169, 171, 248; and Peace Plan, 234, 235, 238, 249; policy motivations of, 71–75; relations with Algeria, 234–35, 238; relations with Polisario Front, 67, 68, 238, 248; role of during Moroccan invasion, 60–64; and Settlement Plan, 207, 238, 256–57; support to Israel, 19, 164; and voter identification process, 69, 185, 202, 243; and Western Sahara nationalism, 59, 72, 74, 143–44, 248. *See also* Morocco (U.S./France relations); *individual presidential administrations*

United States Congress, 69; and Morocco, 65, 70, 228, 239

Uruguay, 126

U.S. Geological Survey of World Energy, 227

Vance, Cyrus, 65

Van Walsum, Peter, 241, 246, 247–48

Varnier, Maurice, 32

Veliotes, Nicholas, 65

Venezuela, 124, 126

Vietnam, 21, 194

Viguri y Gil, Luis Rodríguez de, 80

voter identification process: appeals, 212, 213, 215, 281n8; Baker compromise on, 208; Boutros-Ghali on, 198, 202; bribery in, 204; functioning of, 200–201; MINURSO final tally of, 142, 192–93, 213–14; Morocco's vote-stacking effort in, xxx, 142, 187, 191, 192, 195, 199, 210, 211, 259; under Peace Plan, 229, 230–31; Pérez de Cuéllar on, 196–97; Polisario and, 192, 197, 201, 202, 205, 210, 213, 215; round one of, 203–9; round two of, 209–13; and Settlement Plan, 180, 183–84, 185–86; settler lack of qualifications, 193, 281n5; and Spanish 1974 census, 128, 184, 186, 191–92; suspension of, 142, 201, 205; and "tribal subfractions," 198, 199–200. *See also* MINURSO; referendum, planned

Waldheim, Kurt, 172–73, 182

Al-Wali, Mohammed, 133

wall, defensive (berms): description of, 21; expansion of, 189; locations of, 7; military impact of, 3, 23, 189, 258, 273n2; Polisario strategy to counter, 22–23; U.S. and French support for, 3, 22, 273n2

Walters, Vernon, 18–19, 61, 197, 275n2

Weinberger, Caspar, 18, 66

Welch, David, 245

West, Francis, 18, 66

Western New Guinea, 62, 169, 193

Western Sahara: Arabization of, 95–98; changing demographics of, xxi, 264; colonial border of, 31–32; colonial conquest of, 99–100; colonial interest in, 98–99; colonial legacy of, 80; culture of, 158–59, 198; economic conditions, 157; economic exploitation of, 157–58, 226–28; economic resources: fisheries, 35, 158, 226, 230, 251, 254; economic resources: phosphates, 35, 102, 158, 226; emigration from, 131, 158, 164–65; failure of peace process, xxxi, 25–26, 27–28, 57, 68–71, 217–18, 224, 240, 256, 258, 259; as "forgotten conflict," 259; geography of, xxi, 6; human rights organizations in, 160; idea of division of, 224, 281–82n1; and international law: Morocco's violation of, 260–62; kinships in, 96; as last colony in Africa, xxi, 232; population of, xxi, 192–94, 279n1; stakes of Western Sahara in, 260; traditions of armed resistance in, 6–7; tribal and ethnic divisions in, 93, 94, 118–19, 138, 198–99, 200, 244. *See also* nationalism, Western Sahara; self-determination, Western Sahara; Spanish Sahara; Western Sahara war

Western Sahara Authority (WSA), 230

Western Sahara Resource Watch, 35

Western Sahara war: atrocities by Morocco, 113–14; attacks on fishing ships, 16, 81–82, 83; battle casualties, 15, 25; battles during, 15, 16, 17, 20, 24, 273n3; causes refugee exodus, xxix, 127–28; cease-fires in, 24, 68, 180, 183, 185, 186, 188; and departing Spanish troops, 9; economic costs for Morocco, 23, 43–45, 255; French military intervention in, 12, 76; in Mauritania, xxix, 9, 11–12; military stalemate in, xxix, 3–4, 20, 23, 24–25, 47, 189, 258; military strengths in, 14–15; Moroccan attacks of 1991, 188; Moroccan failures during, 15–16; Moroccan strategy in, 3, 15–16, 20–21; Polisario attacks of 1983, 23; Polisario attacks of 1989, 183; Polisario strategy during, 7–9; Polisario victories in, xxix, 3, 15; role of defensive wall in, xxix, 3, 20–24, 189, 258, 273n2; surface-to-air missiles in, 16, 17, 66, 273n3; tide turns against Polisario, xxix, 3, 17, 189, 258; Tiris al-Gharbiyah region in, 13–14

Wifaq (Concord, Morocco), 51

Wilayah Popular Assemblies, 131

Williams, Ian, 281n9

Williams, James, 66

women, 133–35; attitudes within PLO on, 277n4; literacy rates for, 52, 135; Polisario's efforts around, 133, 134; role of in refugee camps, 9, 113, 134, 136–37. *See also* National Union of Sahrawi Women

World Bank, 44–45, 47

World Trade Organization, 138

World War II, 71

Yacine, Shaykh 'Abdessalam, 52, 274n1

Yaqub-Khan, Sahabzda, 197

Yata, Ali, 125

Youssoufi, Abderrahmane, 50–51, 222

Yugoslavia, 69, 124, 138

Zag, 16, 24

Zaire, 73. *See also* Congo

Zammur Massif, 6

Zapanta, Albert, 68–69

Zapatero, José Luis Rodríguez, 84, 237

Zapatistas, 138

Zartman, William, 26

Zenagah Berbers, 96, 272

Zenagah dialect, 96

Zeroual, Liamine, 208

Zimbabwe, 187

Zona del Draa, 100

Zouerate, Mauritania, 11